THE COLLECTED WRITINGS OF EDWARD RUSHTON (1756–1814)

I0593036

LIVERPOOL ENGLISH TEXTS AND STUDIES 65

THE COLLECTED
WRITINGS
OF EDWARD RUSHTON
(1756–1814)

edited by
PAUL BAINES

LIVERPOOL UNIVERSITY PRESS

First published 2014 by
Liverpool University Press
4 Cambridge Street
Liverpool
L69 7ZU

This paperback edition first published 2021

British Library Cataloguing-in-Publication data

A British Library CIP record is available

ISBN 978-1-78138-136-6 cased
ISBN 978-1-80034-916-2 paperback

Typeset by Carnegie Book Production, Lancaster

Contents

Acknowledgements ix

Abbreviations and Short Titles xi

Introduction 1

Poems 25

An Irregular Ode (1781) 27

To the People of England (1782) 30

The Dismember'd Empire (1782) 33

West-Indian Eclogues (1787) 42

The Neglected Tars of Britain (1787) 62

Neglected Genius: or, Tributary Stanzas to the Memory
of the Unfortunate Chatterton (1787) 64

Poor Ben (1790) 74

A Song, Sung at the celebration of the anniversary of
The French Revolution, at Liverpool, July 14, 1791
(1791) 76

The Fire of Liberty (1792) 78

Human Debasement. A Fragment (1793) 80

Seamen's Nursery (1794) 83

Stanzas on the Anniversary of the American Revolution
(1794) 85

The Tender's Hold (1794) 87

Blue Eyed Mary (1796) 89

Elegy [To the Memory of Robert Burns] (c. 1796) 91

Sonnet [The Swallow] (c. 1796) 95

The Remedy [The Leviathan] (1797) 96

Song [Mary le More] (1798)   97

Written for the anniversary of the Liverpool Marine
    Society (1799)   99

Song. [From *Hymns, &c. for the Blind*] (c. 1799)   101

The Maniac (1800)   102

Lucy's Ghost. A Marine Ballad (1800)   104

Sonnet by a Poor Man. On the approach of the Gout
    (1801)   107

Will Clewline (1801)   108

Ode. Sung at St. John's Chapel, Lancaster, on Tuesday
    last, being the Anniversary of the Lancaster Marine
    Society (1801)   110

Ode, To France (1802)   112

Stanzas on Blindness (1805)   115

To a Redbreast in November, Written near one of the
    Docks of Liverpool (1806)   116

Solicitude (1806)   119

Toussaint to his Troops (1806)   120

On the Death of Hugh Mulligan (1806)   122

To a Bald-Headed Poetical Friend (1806)   124

The Ardent Lover (1806)   125

The Lass of Liverpool (1806)   126

Woman (1806)   127

Mary's Death (1806)   128

The Halcyon (1806)   130

The Shrike (1806)   131

Briton, and Negro Slave (1806)   132

Absence (1806)   134

On the Death of a Much Loved Relative (1806)   135

Entreaty (1806)   137

A Caution to my Friend J. M. (1806)   138

The Throstle (1806)   139

The Complaint (1806)   142

The Pier (1806)   144

CONTENTS

Mary (1806)   146

The Origin of Turtle and Punch (1806)   149

Parody of a Passage in Measure for Measure (1806)   151

The Farewell (1806)   152

The Return (1806)   154

To the Gout (1806)   156

On the Death of Miss E. Fletcher (1806)   157

The Chase (1806)   158

The Winter's Passage (1806)   159

Stanzas on the Recovery of Sight; Addressed to
    Mr. B. Gibson, Surgeon, of Manchester (1809)   161

Lines, to the Memory of William Cowdroy, Proprietor of
    the Manchester Gazette (1814)   164

The Fire of English Liberty (1816)   166

[Lines Addressed to Robt. Southey, Esq. Poet Laureat
    on the Publication of his "Carmen Triumphale"] (1817)   168

The Exile's Lament (1824)   171

The Coromantees (1824)   174

An Epitaph on John Taylor, (of Bolton le Moors) who
    died of the yellow fever, at New York, Sept. 11, 1805
    (1824)   177

To the Memory of Bartholomew Tilski, a Native of the
    North of Poland... (1824)   178

Jemmy Armstrong (1824)   180

Prose   183

Expostulatory Letter to George Washington, of Mount
    Vernon, in Virginia, on his continuing to be a
    Proprietor of Slaves (1797)   185

[Letter to Thomas Paine] (written c. 1800; published 1809)   191

[Monthly Retrospect of Politics] (1810)   194

[Extracts from Letters] (written 1805–1813; published 1814)   196

A Few Plain Facts relative to the Origin of the Liverpool
    Institute for the Blind (written 1804; published 1817)   200

An Attempt to prove that Climate, Food, and Manners, are not the Causes of the Dissimilarity of Colour in the Human Species (unknown date; published 1824)   205

[Letter to Samuel Ryley, 12 August 1814] (written 1814; published 1903)   216

Mr Rushton's Remarks on Slavery (unknown date; unpublished)   217

[Letter to Thomas Walker, 30 January 1806] (written 1806; unpublished)   220

Commentary   223

Glossary   224
Poems   225
Prose   309

Appendix I: Other poems possibly by Rushton   321

Appendix II: Poems to and about Rushton   325

Bibliography   327

Index   341

Acknowledgements

Much of the work for this edition has been carried out in the Sydney Jones Library of the University of Liverpool, particularly in Special Collections and Archives, and I am grateful to the staff there for their unfailing assistance and patience with my many requests. The National Library of Scotland efficiently provided scans of unique items associated with Rushton and in one case helped to decipher a cropped imprint. Liverpool Central Library and Liverpool Record Office provided me with every necessary assistance, as did the British Library in London. I am grateful to the librarians of the Athenaeum in Liverpool for their willingness to admit me to a private collection in the interests of research. I have benefited from conversations with Charles Forsdick, Eve Rosenhaft, Greg Lynall, Jill Rudd, Alex Robinson, Alex Broadhead, and particularly Franca Dellarosa, whose knowledge of Rushton's context and whose expertise in literary and theoretical approaches to his work has been hugely helpful to me; it is a particular pleasure to be publishing an edition of Rushton alongside her comprehensive study of his work. I am grateful to Anthony Cond and the staff of Liverpool University Press for practical help and advice (and for forbearance); thanks are also due to the Press's several academic readers for guidance, instruction and support. Many thanks also to Sue Barnes and the copy-editing team at Carnegie Book Production for their lively and eagle-eyed interest in the detail and design of this edition. My wife, Katy Hooper, 'to whose exertions we owe more than words can express' read the entire edition as it was being constructed, from the perspective of both rare books librarian and reader of poetry, and made invaluable comments on points of textual detail and annotation.

Acknowledgement

Abbreviations and Short Titles

ESTC: English Short Title Catalogue (http://estc.bl.uk/)
IGI: International Genealogical Index (https://familysearch.org/
         search/collection/igi)
OED: *Oxford English Dictionary* (http://www.oed.com/)
ODNB: *Oxford Dictionary of National Biography*, ed.
         H. C. G. Matthew and Brian Harrison (Oxford: Oxford
         University Press, 2004) (http://www.oxforddnb.com/)
SJ: Samuel Johnson, *A Dictionary of the English Language*, 2 vols
         (London: W. Strahan, J. and P. Knapton, and others, 1755)

1806:   Edward Rushton, *Poems, By Edward Rushton* (London:
          J. M'Creery for T. Ostell, 1806).
1824:   Edward Rushton, *Poems and other Writings by the late
          Edward Rushton; to which is added, A Sketch of the Life of the
          Author, by the Rev. William Shepherd* (London: Effingham
          Wilson, 1824).
Beilby and Bewick: Ralph Beilby and Thomas Bewick, *History
          of British Birds*, volume I, *Land Birds* (Newcastle: Beilby &
          Bewick; London: G. G. and J. Robinson, 1797).
Burke: *Eighteenth-Century English Labouring-Class Poets 1700–1800*,
          Volume 3, *1780–1800*, ed. by Tim Burke (London: Pickering
          and Chatto, 2003).
Cocker and Mabey: Mark Cocker and Richard Mabey, *Birds
          Britannica* (London: Chatto and Windus, 2005).
Dellarosa: Franca Dellarosa, *Talking Revolution: Edward Rushton's
          Rebellious Poetics, 1782–1814* (Liverpool: Liverpool University
          Press, 2014).
Gleanings: *Gleanings: Consisting of Extracts from the Writings of
          Edward Rushton, (The Blind Poet of Liverpool,) and various
          other Authors* (Nantucket: R. and G. S. Wood, 1829).

Harland and Wilkinson: John Harland, ed., *Ballads & Songs of Lancashire, Ancient and Modern*; second edition, corrected, revised and enlarged, by T. T. Wilkinson (London: Routledge, 1875).

Letters of a Templar: William Lowes Rushton, ed., *Letters of a Templar, 1820–50* (London: Simpkin, Marshall & Co.; Liverpool: Ed. Howell, 1903).

Richardson: Alan Richardson, ed., *Slavery, Abolition, and Emancipation: Writings in the British Romantic Period*, volume 4, *Literary Forms: Verse* (Brookfield, VT: Pickering and Chatto, 1999).

Williamson: Karina Williamson, ed., *Contrary Voices: Representations of West Indian Slavery, 1657–1834* (Kingston, Jamaica: University of West Indies Press, 2008).

Line references to some frequently-mentioned major writers are in accordance with the following editions:

John Milton: *The Major Works*, ed. Stephen Orgel and Jonathan Goldberg (Oxford: Oxford University Press, 2008)

Alexander Pope: *The Twickenham Edition of the Poems of Alexander Pope*, general editors John Butt and Maynard Mack, 11 vols (London: Methuen; New Haven, CT: Yale University Press, 1938–1968)

William Shakespeare: *The Complete Works of Shakespeare*, ed. David Bevington, seventh edition (London: Longman, 2012)

Introduction

Edward Rushton went to sea at the age of ten, a natural enough thing for a boy born in Liverpool in 1756, with limited alternative prospects for work. But the marine life was for him already in one sense a literary life: at the age of ten, he 'read Anson's voyage, resolved to be a sailor, and was bound as an apprentice to Watt and Gregson, and before he entered his eleventh year, he was a sea boy in the West Indies'.[1] 'Anson's voyage' was *A Voyage Round the World, in the Years MDCCXL, I, II, III, IV* (London, 1748), a long and well-illustrated record of the circumnavigation performed under the command of Commodore George Anson (1697–1762). Rushton was inspired to go to sea; others, such as the poet William Cowper, made more direct poetic capital out of Anson in poems such as 'The Castaway'. Nonetheless there is something significant in the fact that for Rushton the book came before the sea.

Rushton was born in John Street, Liverpool, on 13 November 1756.[2] William Shepherd, his friend and champion, was disposed to be rather disparaging about his father, Thomas, who 'had been originally brought up to the business of a hair dresser; in which, having saved a little money, he doubtless, in his own opinion, and in that of his neighbours, rose a degree in the order of society, by becoming a dealer in spirits'.[3] However, amongst other occupations, he ventured into poetry, though of a very different kind from that which his son would write. Shepherd asserts him to be the author of *Party Dissected: or, Plain Truth. A Poem. By a Plain Dealer* (London, 1770), a pro-government satirical poem. Perhaps Rushton's later adversarial voice is in part derived from his resistance to his father's high Tory loyalism. At any rate, Edward Rushton was taught to read at a local school and embarked on his naval career. The early biographies tell us that he was an excellent seaman, credited with saving his own ship near Liverpool harbour, at the age of 15, by taking control of the helm when 'the captain and crew were wandering about in despair', and that this act of bravery was noted on his indentures (*Sketch*, p. 474; *Life*, pp. xi–xii). He thereafter signed on as second mate. Rushton was nearly drowned when the boat he was in capsized, and was saved by the self-sacrificing act of an African called Quamina, whom he had taught to read. Rushton was evidently an effective narrator in conversation; his son recalled 'I can remember well his telling me this story with tears in his eyes. It made an impression on my mind, which no time can ever efface' (*Sketch*, pp. 474–75).[4] At the expiry of his apprenticeship, he signed on a slaving voyage, getting into trouble for protesting about the conditions 'with that boldness and integrity which characterized his every action'. His 'strong and pointed language', and contempt for authority, prefigure the verse (*Sketch*, p. 475).

During a stopover at Dominica, he caught an eye-infection then known as ophthalmia, now more commonly referred to as trachoma. In Shepherd's account (*Life*, p. xiv) this was the result of an attempt to help the infected slaves when others refused, though the son's account omits this detail. Both state that 'his left eye was totally destroyed; and that the right was entirely covered with an opacity of the cornea' (*Sketch*, p. 475); hence the eye patch that Rushton wears in the oil painting of him by Moses Haughton which hangs in the Royal School for the Blind, Liverpool. In 1776, his father took him to London to consult various eye-surgeons, without success (*Sketch*, p. 475; *Life*, p. xv). His father's affection could not however survive the opposition of Rushton's stepmother, a woman of 'violent temper'; in Shepherd's words: 'an interference on his part to prevent the ill treatment of one of his sisters, so strongly excited the indignation of his father, that, helpless as he was, he banished him from his house, and doomed him to subsist as he could, on the miserable allowance of four shillings a week' (*Life*, p. xv).[5] He lived with an aunt, and 'managed to pay a boy two-pence or three-pence a week, for reading to him an hour or two in the evenings' (*Sketch*, p. 475). Shepherd approves of Rushton's course of 'judicious reading': Joseph Addison, Richard Steele, Samuel Johnson, and 'the other celebrated English essayists'; voyages and travels, history. He read 'the best poets', though Shepherd does not say who these were, apart from Milton (whose politically radical prose he also read) and Shakespeare. We know from other sources that he read Pope, and there is evidence from the poems that he was reading Thomas Gray and William Cowper as well.

Shepherd says that 'He also occasionally amused himself with poetical composition, which, being handed about in manuscript, and now and then finding their way into a newspaper, gradually brought him into notice, and became the means of extending his acquaintance with men of cultivated minds' (*Life*, p. xiii). Rushton's poems 'found their way' into newspapers because that is where he sent them, though the earliest possible entry in the canon (late 1780) is problematic, since the scrap from which it is known in modern times no longer appears to be available to researchers (see the first item in Appendix I). A more definite entry, the first poem included in this edition, is 'An Irregular Ode', published in a London newspaper, *Lloyd's Evening Post*. This was followed by 'To the People of England', which appeared in the *Morning Post*. Both appeared over the signature 'Liverpool. Edward Rushton'. These were poems of conflicted patriotism during the last years of the American War of Independence (1775–1783), and were partly absorbed into Rushton's first independent publication, *The Dismember'd Empire* (1782), published anonymously in Liverpool and London and reviewed in national periodicals (see Commentary). Shepherd, writing in 1824, says that it 'contains some good poetry, and evinces much patriotic feeling', but he did not elect to reprint it (*Life*, p. xvi). It is a quarto pamphlet of some 28 pages, containing over 300 lines of heroic couplets in a tone of public exhortation; a high-end publication, it is not clear how its production was paid for. Politically, it follows the views of William Pitt, Earl of Chatham (1708–1778), the intellectual leader of the opposition in parliament, who had campaigned for some form of conciliation with the American colonies, against the government drive for outright victory. Rushton declares himself 'an advocate for liberty, tho' an enemy to rebellion', but the poem's wish that some version of the link between America and Britain could be sustained had already been largely defeated by events. None of these poems was included in later collections, no doubt in part because of the shift in Rushton's views towards a more critical sense of the British Empire.

Rushton's stay with his aunt lasted, according to the early sources, for seven years, and both his son and Shepherd consider this neglect a 'shameful' dereliction of duty on Thomas Rushton's part. At length, in about 1783, his father set up Rushton and one of his sisters in a tavern, apparently at 19 Crooked Lane, in Liverpool, where he lived 'for some years' (*Sketch*, p. 475). This sister was probably, though not certainly, 'Bessey', the sister whose death Rushton later mourned in 'On the Death of a Much Loved Relative'. During this period, both the sister and Rushton, the latter at the age of 29 (i.e. around 1785), married; Rushton's wife's name was Isabella Rain or Rains.[6] Rushton's son says that he gave up the tavern business because he 'found his pecuniary circumstances rather diminishing than increasing' (*Sketch*, p. 475); Shepherd intimates in addition (*Life*, p. xiv) that his anti-slavery views were not likely to win many customers in a slaving port like Liverpool.

After *The Dismember'd Empire*, Rushton was apparently silent for five years, though it is entirely likely that Rushton published verse in local papers that has not been found: the survival rate of the many newspapers known to have been published is not very high. The appearance of an early version of the poem later known as 'The Neglected Tar' in a London paper of October 1787, and subsequently in a Liverpool compilation of songs, suggests more of a continuation of activity rather than a new start. This poem also shows how Rushton's work escaped into the quasi-viral world of copyright-free ballad and newspaper publishing, with several slipsongs, broadsides and chapbooks printing the poem without any obvious connection to Rushton himself; what he wrote had a genuine popular edge, like a sort of authored folksong. The pattern would be repeated for several of Rushton's shorter poems, especially those with a campaigning quality.

Rushton was probably working for some time on the abolitionist *West-Indian Eclogues*, his longest single work and the piece for which he is probably best known; it was published in London, anonymously, as a quarto pamphlet late in 1787. In the years 1787–1788 there was a substantial knot of poets in Liverpool supporting the abolitionist cause, including the lawyer and businessman William Roscoe (1753–1831), whose poem *The Wrongs of Africa* appeared in 1787 before his prose work on the subject; the engraver and poet Hugh Mulligan, whose verse letter to Rushton appeared in his *Poems, Chiefly on Slavery and Oppression* (1788), and less eminent figures such as Peter Newby, whose poem *The Wrongs of Almoona* was published at Liverpool in 1788. These years were among the busiest for the first major campaign to abolish the slave trade, with the Dolben Act (which sought to improve conditions on the Middle Passage) passing the Commons in 1788, but William Wilberforce's bill to abolish the whole trade defeated in 1791. Abolitionists in Liverpool were mainly from Quaker, Unitarian and Methodist backgrounds, and the poets of Liverpool (as of Bristol) were strongly galvanised by anti-slavery sentiment.[7] The London-based abolitionist Thomas Clarkson (1760–1846) visited Liverpool on his fact-finding tour of 1787 and met several people he already knew, such as William Rathbone (1757–1809), one of the few local merchants to make a stand against the slave trade, Roscoe, and James Currie (1756–1805), a physician who also wrote against slavery; but there was also 'a fourth, upon whom I called, tho' I did not know him': this was Rushton. Passing through Chester, where he stayed with William Cowdroy, a friend of Rushton's, Clarkson had heard of Rushton's attempt, through the *West-Indian Eclogues*, to alert the public to 'the evils of the Slave-trade' and to excite 'their indignation against it'. As Shepherd later put it, 'Clarkson had many interviews with Rushton, and has given his name to a tributary stream 'in his fanciful chart of the abolition of the Slave trade'.[8]

It is possible that the prose fragment known as 'Mr Rushton's Remarks on Slavery', preserved among the Roscoe papers at Liverpool Record Office, was recorded at one of these meetings. At any rate, *West-Indian Eclogues* was widely, and relatively positively, reviewed, though not without considerable discomfort and some disbelief at the horrors it described; some of the commentary (and the advertising) preferred to concentrate on the poem's natural history descriptions, which Rushton supplied both in verse and in substantial prose notes. Shepherd (*Life*, p. xv) described the four pieces, loosely based on the neoclassical form of Alexander Pope's *Pastorals* of 1709, as 'among the most finished of Mr. Rushton's compositions … in incident and dramatic effect they are highly interesting'; but they were dropped from Rushton's 1806 collection and Shepherd restored the first three only in 1824, omitting the fourth Eclogue (in which an enraged slave takes bloody revenge).

Shortly afterwards, Rushton published another single-poem quarto pamphlet, *Neglected Genius: or Tributary Stanzas to the Memory of the Unfortunate Chatterton* (1787), again anonymously. This also had a substantial prose apparatus, detailing Rushton's sense of grievance on the failure of those in authority (patrons and scholars) to support the young Bristol poet Thomas Chatterton, who had died, apparently by suicide (though many now doubt this) in London. This poem was again reviewed in the London journals, and attracted at least one other notable reader in the form of Samuel Taylor Coleridge (see Commentary), who noted it as 'by far the best poem on the subject'. By the end of the 1780s therefore, Rushton had begun to establish himself as a radical poet of resistance and protest. His real theme is not slavery, or party politics: it is power, and specifically, its tendency to produce oppression. 'The Neglected Tars of Britain' may well have been sung in pubs as if it were John Gay's 'Black-Ey'd Susan' or Charles Dibdin's 'Tom Bowling' (each popular exemplars of the apolitical marine ballad); but the point of Rushton's song is the corrupt failure of people with money, authority, and power to support those without it.

Shepherd's 'men of cultivated minds', whose acquaintance Rushton made by virtue of his writings, would include the already-mentioned

Roscoe, Rathbone, and Currie, but also the historian William Smyth (1765–1849), and William Shepherd (1768–1847) himself: the so-called 'Roscoe Circle'.[9] Rushton was not of the same economic class as these men (though Roscoe himself was born in a pub, and Rathbone's merchant firm was still relatively new in the 1780s). The members of the group were predominantly Unitarian or Quaker, except for Smyth, who was, like Thomas Gray before him, a poet as well as Professor of Modern History at the University of Cambridge, and thus required to conform to the Anglican dispensation. Rushton does not seem to have had any particular denominational form of faith, but the writings suggest a Unitarian sense of a benign and just Creator, with little interest in a redemptive Christ.[10] Rushton would develop other networks beyond this group, which was itself somewhat depressed by surveillance in the anti-Jacobin panics of the 1790s. According to his 'A Few Plain Facts' he was, in 1790, a member of an 'association, consisting of ten or a dozen individuals, who assembled weekly for the purpose of literary discussion', and this was something different from the Roscoe circle. Liverpool in Rushton's period was expanding extremely rapidly, in terms of its economy (strongly focused on the docks, which in turn was strongly funded by the slave trade) but was also struggling to establish a wider cultural life in the literary and musical arts, theatre, libraries, and public debate; Roscoe was particularly tireless in this respect, though the lasting fruits of his endeavours would not be seen until the nineteenth century in the Liverpool Botanic Gardens (1802) and Royal Institution (1817).[11]

The slavery debates, vicious and fierce as they were in Liverpool, were exacerbated by the events of 1789–1794 in France, and the repressive responses of the British government under the younger William Pitt.[12] The radical Friends of Freedom group which met between 1789 and 1795, mostly in private homes, had close links with the Roscoe circle, and Rushton was certainly among the members.[13] Roscoe was the author of several songs celebrating the fall of the Bastille, and Rushton's work on the same theme was publicly sung at revolution celebrations in Liverpool: 'A Song, Sung at the celebration of the anniversary of The French Revolution, at Liverpool, July 14, 1791' was published in American newspapers, no doubt from a Liverpool source. The first version of his 'The Fire of Liberty' appeared in the *Manchester Herald* in 1792, before being collected in the innocent-sounding but actually politically radical *A Choice Collection of Civic Songs* (Sheffield, 1795). Meanwhile at least three poems definitely by Rushton, and more that could be by him, appeared in a curious pamphlet called *Liberty Scraps*, devoid of all identifying features except the imprint 'Printed in the Year 1794' (see Appendix I). Some lines from Shepherd's 1792 *Epistle to Edward Rushton* (see Appendix II) appear as the epigraph, but it has not been possible to establish the full extent of Rushton's connection with the little book. What is certain is that during a period of intense hostility towards free speech of the radical kind, during which several individuals were tried for seditious libel or treason, Rushton continued to publish campaigning verse as openly as he dared. He had experienced some direct pressure in his editorship of a newspaper, the *Liverpool and Lancashire Weekly Herald*, between about 1788 and 1790. Only one issue of this title is known to survive, from 27 March 1790; it contains the first known version of Rushton's ballad 'Poor Ben', submitted by 'Z. Z.'. Rushton's son says that he pursued this editorial endeavour 'with much pleasure, and little profit', but 'finding it impossible to express himself in that independent and liberal manner which his reason and his conscience dictated, he threw up his situation' (*Sketch*, p. 475). Shepherd (*Life*, pp. xvi-xvii) is more particular: Rushton is supposed to have written an editorial complaining about 'an act of atrocity, perpetrated in the port of Liverpool, by a Press Gang ... in the language of just indignation'. When the lieutenant of the gang demanded an apology, Rushton refused, but terminated his share because of the consternation of his business partner. According to a much later note by John M'Creery, the partner was Mulligan.[14] Impressment was subsequently the theme of at least one poem.

In about 1792, Rushton took over a bookshop, 'his habits and his pursuits' rendering this occupation 'more eligible than any other' (*Sketch*, p. 475; *Life*, p. xix). He had an initial capital of 30 guineas, and a very competent wife 'to whose exertions we owe more than words can express', according to his son, by then one of five children. We know little of Rushton's actual business, which is listed in Gore's *Liverpool Directory* of 1796 at 56 Paradise Street.[15] He was an agent for *A Chronological Account and Brief History of the Events of the French Revolution*, by J[ulie] Talma, 'now a dentist in Chester' (London, 1795; for Rushton see p. 243), among other works. His son says that he suffered during the early period, when 'politics ran very high in Liverpool', and that Rushton was not only harassed and shunned but actually shot at 'by some illiberal villain'. He and his friends were 'marked' by government loyalists in town. Rushton's shop was one of the publicised venues for the signing of a petition, sponsored by the Friends of Freedom (Liverpool, 28 November 1795) against the Seditious Practices Act.[16] Rushton was offered any financial assistance he might require by Roscoe and Rathbone, but declined it from a spirit of independence (*Sketch*, p. 476; *Life*, p. xxi). Shepherd says that Rushton admired the poet and politician Andrew Marvell (1621–1678), reduced to a garret but preserving his freedom (*Life*, p. xxvii). The business continued, however, to support Rushton and his family until his death, and he was able to use it to publish his own work.

In 1796 Rushton engaged with other Liverpool poets, including Roscoe, in a small volume of poems on the death of Robert Burns (1756–1796), collected from the *Liverpool Pheonix*. This was a charity venture on behalf of Burns's family, but for Rushton, Burns's death was also a matter of the failure of aristocratic patronage, as it had been for the young Chatterton. On his own footing he wrote a forceful prose letter to George Washington, commending his heroic struggle for liberty but pointing out that it was incompatible with the ownership of slaves; when the president of the newly-formed United States returned it unanswered, Rushton published it (1797).[17] The rising of the United Irishmen in 1798 provided Rushton with another model of the struggle of an oppressed people for self-determination in the wake of the American and French revolutions, and his ballad 'Mary le More' rapidly gained status as a campaign song amongst Irish nationalists themselves; indeed it was at one point regarded as the work of an Irish poet. 'Mary le More', widely disseminated in slipsong and broadside form, was deemed seditious by at least one local worthy in Nottingham, who sent it to the Home Secretary, and its contents were apparently still regarded as treasonous well into the nineteenth century (see Commentary). Many of Rushton's poems, especially those celebrating liberty, American-style, or those like 'Mary le More' which showed the British in a bad light, were taken up enthusiastically in American newspapers such as *The Time-Piece* (1797–1798), which did much to establish Rushton's surprisingly strong reputation for pathos and libertarian sentiment in America.

Another element in Rushton's success during this period was the emergence in Liverpool during 1792 of John M'Creery (1768–1832), an Irishman who had been apprenticed to a Liverpool printer and who opened his independent account with Thomas Hall's *Achmet to Selim, or, The Dying Negro*, an anti-slavery poem, in 1792.[18] Rushton was an agent for a pamphlet, *The Crime of Neglecting Inoculation*, which M'Creery printed in 1793, and by 1797 they were clearly close friends and colleagues. William Stanley Roscoe writes to his father, William Roscoe, on 1 September 1797, a letter of news, including this glimpse of Rushton's milieu:

My Mother & I last night supped with M^r McCreery & I met Dr Currie, Simms, Binns & Rushton & M^r W Clark; we had a very pleasant evening & Rushton gave us a song one of his own composition.[19]

At this point Rushton was writing several songs which M'Creery would print in broadside form. These were not the same as the cheaply-produced and largely anonymous slipsong versions of poems like 'Mary le More': M'Creery had high aspirations as a printer, which he expressed graphically in his *The Press. A Poem* (1803), which included praise of Rushton, Mulligan and other Liverpool poets. (A second part appeared in 1827, with a combined issue of 1828 giving further notes and information on these matters.) Rushton and he collaborated on separate printings of *Blue Eyed Mary* (1799); *Lucy's Ghost. A Marine Ballad* (1800); and *Will Clewline* (1801), Rushton's affecting ballad of victimisation by pressgang, illustrated with the kind of fine engraving not normally found on such populist work. M'Creery was also the printer of a sheet of *Hymns, &c.* of unknown date, produced on behalf of the institution, founded by Rushton and some friends in 1791, which would become the Royal School for the Blind, Liverpool; at least one of the hymns is probably Rushton's. (Rushton also wrote charity songs for the Liverpool Marine Society and the Lancaster version of the same thing.) M'Creery printed heavy-duty scholarly work for Roscoe, such as his *Life of Lorenzo de' Medici* (2 vols., 1796), and was the printer of Currie's four-volume edition of the *Works of Robert Burns* (1800), for which Rushton was a Liverpool agent; the same arrangement pertained to *The Vision for Coquettes: an Arabian Tale* (1804). In due course M'Creery would print Rushton's *Poems* of 1806.

Shepherd (*Life*, p. xxiii) describes the situation leading to Rushton's book:

> From time to time ... Mr. Rushton had composed a variety of fugitive pieces of poetry, some of which had been printed in newspapers and periodical publications, whilst others slept in his portfolio, or were communicated to his friends in manuscript. From these he was frequently advised by some individuals whose personal attachment to him was the only reason of his questioning their judgment as to the poetical merit of his compositions, to make a selection, which they assured him would furnish matter for a small volume. After some hesitation, he listened to their suggestions, and in the year 1806 published the volume...

Poems, by Edward Rushton was published as a small octavo volume in London by Thomas Ostell, Ave-Maria-Lane. It was printed by M'Creery (who had moved in 1805 to Black-Horse-Court, Fleet-Street). It was advertised at six shillings in the London paper, the *Morning Post*, on 31 March 1806. There is no preface, the poems being presented to speak for themselves. Altogether the volume contained 45 poems, of which at least 16 had appeared in some previous form. Rushton completely omitted all work before 1787. The poem on Chatterton was drastically remodelled and shortened. Most surprisingly, Rushton omitted *West-Indian Eclogues*, replacing the four poems with a shorter dramatic scene, 'Briton, And Negro Slave'; perhaps by 1806, with the full abolition bill about to go through, it was felt that the *Eclogues* had served their purpose, or perhaps it was felt advisable to say much less on the subject as the process unfolded. Rushton's stirring poem 'Toussaint to his Troops', on the slave rebellion in St Domingo, was newly printed, however. Alongside an extended portfolio of marine ballads and campaign songs were lighter pieces, on gout (from which Rushton suffered), baldness, and alcohol; a number of poems about birds, many of them oddly threatening; elegies, including one on the Liverpool anti-slavery poet Hugh Mulligan; and several love songs, often marked by anxiety about female fidelity or vulnerability.

The volume was reviewed at least eight times. The harshest critiques were confessedly motivated by political opposition: *The Anti-Jacobin Review* 23 (March 1806, p. 336) declared: 'Several of these poems display evident marks of genius, and exhibit undoubted proofs of a heart warmed with sensibility. Most of them have considerable merits'. But 'the bard's enthusiastic zeal for freedom ... carries him rather too far, when it leads him to sing the praises of rebellion', as in the poem by then called 'American Independency'. In a generally caustic account, *The British Critic* (28 November 1806, pp. 561–62), admitted that the poems 'are in general harmonious, and, in some instances, pathetic and interesting; but we cannot approve of the author's political principles, nor deem all of his poems of a beneficial, or even harmless tendency'.

> The tendency of the several dismal poems of this author on a Mary le More (whom we presume to be an imaginary personage), seems to be only to revive the animosity of parties in Ireland, and inflame the discontents (if any remain) which have desolated that kingdom. In every mention of the Americans, the poet eagerly embraces the opportunity of vilifying the conduct of Britain.

Rushton is chided for failing to 'cherish more rational and British feelings'. But he 'is certainly a pleasing versifier, though not a first rate poet'. 'The Swallow' is selected, for brevity, as a sample.

The Critical Review III.7 (April 1806, pp. 439–41), found that Rushton's 'poems of the light kind have considerable merit; where he attempts the ode, he fails'. It disliked the poem on Chatterton, but reprinted the whole of the verses on the death of Burns as 'uniformly good', and 'worthy of their subject'. There was sufficient material even in these antipathetic reviews for suitable quotations to be garnered for further advertising, as in the *Morning Chronicle*, 4 December 1806. Meanwhile *The Monthly Review* 50 (May 1806, pp. 95–96), warned:

> To the rigid exacters of correctness and elegance in poetical composition, we cannot promise any high gratification from a perusal of this little volume; since they will find the versification too often deficient in harmony, and the diction, in numerous instances, feeble, harsh, and inaccurate.—The less fastidious reader, however, will probably deem these imperfections in a great degree compensated by the frequent display of a strong and glowing imagination, pouring forth its manly conceptions in an animated manner, undisfigured by any affectation in sentiment or in language. In description, we think the author is peculiarly happy: he is a spirited delineator, as well as a faithful observer of nature; and scenes, which he probably witnessed in early life, have furnished him with a rich store of marine and tropical imagery. As a pathetic writer, also, Mr. R. manifests considerable powers: but his plaintive strains not unfrequently sink into a style somewhat gloomy and splenetic.

'Toussaint to his Troops', the elegy on Mulligan, and 'The Lass of Liverpool' were cited as good samples. The reviewer was unsure about the Mary le More poems, finding them guilty of 'gloomy complacency'; and it found fault with phrasing in 'The Neglected Tar', 'The Complaint', and the elegy on Chatterton, concluding, 'In a second edition of this interesting volume, or in the publication of a farther collection, we trust that similar blemishes will be avoided'.

The Literary Journal, 1 (May 1806, pp. 558–59), concentrated on the marine aspects of the volume, finding that 'if the poems are not to be placed in the first ranks in the scale of excellence, the greater part of them are such as will be read with considerable interest'. *The Poetical Register*, 6 (1806, p. 505), stated 'among the minor poets, Mr. Rushton is entitled to a respectable station. There is much ease, simplicity, and feeling, and occasionally vigour, in his poems. His naval songs are among the best of the kind'. *The New Annual Register*, 27 (1806, p. 370), perhaps slightly over-egged the sentimental pudding: 'they are the effusions of a poor, blind bard, labouring to support himself and family by this only mean [*sic*] that appears to remain to him, and ... they are tender, pathetic, and elegant'. An American journal, the *Monthly Register, Magazine, and Review* 2 (February 1807, p. 187), promised periodically to 'present the reader with a selection from Rushton, because, although he seldom, or ever pens a single stanza without discovering his want of a liberal education, and his imperfect acquaintance with the English language, yet his lays are poured so directly warm from the heart, and abound in such exquisite touches of nature and feeling, that he must, be, indeed, squeamishly fastidious, who cannot over-look the little inaccuracies of the untaught bard, for the sake of the beauties, which he so abundantly, and continually produces'.

The personal angle was a strong element of positive responses, as the political one was of negative. *The Annual Review*, 5 (1806, pp. 523–25), quoted 'Blindness' entire, not only as a 'touching little poem' but as evidence of Rushton's 'persevering energy of mind'.

> It was by his own strenuous exertions that he acquired, under the pressure of poverty, obscurity, and circumstances the most unfriendly, the high degree of moral and intellectual refinement manifested in the productions before us; it has been by his own industry that he has found means, in a state of almost total blindness, to support and educate a large family, in a creditable, though humble independency...
>
> The high spirit of freedom, the genuine sentiments of tenderness and humanity, which they breathe, must excite the sympathy of every honest heart; the expression of these sentiments is often strong, and sometimes elegant and poetical ... [his early profession] has furnished him with many novel images, conveyed with that graphical accuracy which personal observation alone can supply. An occasional want of polish will be felt, and an imperfection of taste is betrayed by the admission of several terms either too vulgar or too technical, or too abstract for the purposes of poetry. But defects like these, which originate neither in affectation, nor in a want of native talent, give little interruption to the strong tide of feeling, and are therefore among those which a true lover of the art will find it most easy to forgive.

Two further whole poems ('On the Death of a Much Loved Relative' and 'The Winter's Passage') were reprinted to assure 'the reader, whose sympathies with modest genius and suffering virtue may tempt him to become a purchaser, that it contains several pieces of equal merit'.

This review must have come from someone with quite close knowledge of Rushton's circumstances, since it mentions the sequence of eye operations he was undergoing at the time, including the fact that the process appeared not to be working. *The Annual Review* was run by Arthur Aikin (1773–1854), son of John Aikin (1747–1822) and nephew of Anna Letitia Barbauld (1743–1825); it was associated with the influential reformist movement of the dissenting establishment. A copy of the volume from John Aikin's library is in Liverpool University Library's special collections. Other owners include William Rathbone, to whom Rushton presented a copy inscribed with the words 'To Mr Willm Rathbone – the Friend of Liberty, and of Man, who when the path of rectitude lay thro the froth and venom of Persecution turned not aside. This little Volume is presented By the Author with his best wishes and respects'.[20] It is known that the poet and (at that point) radical Robert Southey (1774–1843), who visited Rushton in his shop, had a copy (see Commentary on 'Lines Addressed to Robt. Southey'). An Irish poet, James Gilland, wrote a poem of appreciation for the volume's libertarian spirit (see Appendix II).[21]

As the *Annual Review* mentions, Rushton was undergoing a series of operations in an effort to regain his sight. According to Rushton's son, he consulted the Manchester-based eye-surgeon Benjamin Gibson (1774–1812) from the autumn of 1805 to the summer of 1807, enduring without anaesthetic and without the conventional restraint, five operations, which partially restored the sight of one eye. His long poem of gratitude to Gibson was published in 1809, and the event was also celebrated in three poems by other authors: the Irish Quaker Mary Leadbeater (1758–1826), John M'Creery, and the radical activist and lecturer John Thelwall (1764–1834), another poet-friend (see Appendix II).[22] Shepherd (*Life*, xxiv–xxv) says that 'His sight, indeed, was somewhat misty; but it was so far restored, that he could accurately distinguish colours, and the lineaments of the human countenance. He could even discern and discriminate distant objects. He could walk the streets without a guide; and, by the aid of a glass, could read tolerably sized print'. Rushton's own private comments are recorded in a letter (see the Prose section) to John Hancock (1762–1823), co-editor of the *Belfast Monthly Magazine*, with whom Rushton had a close association outside his Liverpool circle, occasionally contributing to the magazine.[23] Perhaps the eye operations were a distraction from politics; at any rate, his poetical talent does not seem to have been exercised during the stream of political songwriting associated with Roscoe's surprise election to parliament in November 1806 (though 'Edward Rushton, Mariner' of Paradise Street did vote for him).[24] Rushton was not writing as much at this period, though his son cites 'Jemmy Armstrong' (another Irish-themed ballad) and 'The Fire of English Liberty' (actually a reworking of an earlier piece) as specimens of continued intellectual vigour and reformist principle. He was involved in the Liverpool Forum, or Original Debating Society, which met to discuss (without political or religious bias, at least in theory) questions such as the intellectual capabilities of women, in late 1807, and was identified as an agent for the proposed *Liverpool Herald: or Political and Literary Register*, at the same period.[25] He clearly had links not only with the *Belfast Monthly Magazine*, which later printed a selection of extracts from his letters, but with the *Manchester Herald*, run by William Cowdroy, whose death in 1814 Rushton lamented in an elegy, perhaps his final poem. He was an early member of the Liverpool Literary and Philosophical Society, founded in 1812, and of the republican pressure group The Concentric Society.[26] Through this he came to the attention of Thomas Noble (active 1808–1821), a Liverpool journalist and poet, one of the staff writers for the *Liverpool Mercury*, founded by Egerton Smith (1774–1841) in 1811 as an outlet for the radical side of political reporting. Rushton was an agent for the paper, and regularly advertised in it, allowing us to trace some of his later bookselling ventures: Shepherd was also a member of the Concentric Society, and his speech there in 1813 was published in Liverpool, sold by Rushton and advertised by him in the *Liverpool Mercury*, 21 January 1814. He also sold John Wright's *Right of Free Discussion Claimed and Exercised*, a talk given at the Independent Debating Society, another radical group (26 November 1813) by a local Unitarian minister. Like most booksellers, Rushton sold other things such as patent blacking and theatre tickets, as well as tickets for the Independent Debating Society. He was an agent for the sale of two counting houses, and advertised for an apprentice a year before he died.[27]

In 1807, Rushton's eldest daughter, named Isabella after her mother, married Richard Preston, a liquor merchant of Liverpool. Rushton's wife died in January 1811, after what his son calls 'a tedious illness'; and one of his daughters, Ann, died on 25 May 1811 (*Sketch*, p. 476; *Life*, p. xxviii). Rushton speaks feelingly about these events in letters to Hancock of 29 August 1807 and 25 February 1812. Rushton's own death, apparently from an ill-advised dose of Eau Medicinale, a proprietary gout remedy, occurred on 22 November 1814.[28] His last days are described in mournful detail by his son in the *Biographical Sketch* (pp. 477–78). The notice in the *Liverpool Mercury* was immediately reprinted in the *Belfast Monthly Magazine*, 13.76 (November 1814, pp. 439–40), alongside a letter of tribute from a Liverpool contact, as part of the 'monthly retrospect of politics'. Mr Casey, perhaps the contact, delivered an impassioned eulogy on Rushton's public and domestic virtues at the second anniversary of the Concentric Society, including the memorable image 'He stood like a rampart and spoke like an oracle'.[29] Rushton's son contributed his *Biographical Sketch* the next month (13.77, pp. 474–78), and the editors included further details (pp. 478–82), with quotations from private letters and notes of Rushton's prose writings, including mention of a letter to the radical hero Thomas Paine (1737–1809), which they had already published anonymously.

Rushton's death was noted in *The Gentleman's Magazine*, 84 (December 1814, p. 610). *The Monthly Repository of Theology and General Literature* reprinted the *Biographical Sketch* (10.110, February 1815, pp. 67–69). *The New Monthly Magazine*, 2 (January 1815, p. 573), noted his literary talents, and the pleasure he took, once able to see, in walking through Liverpool and looking at 'the prospect of many public buildings which had been erected during the long privation of light he had suffered'. *The Monthly Magazine*, 38 (January 1815, p. 576), singled out 'The Neglected Tar' as his best-known piece, but also testified:

> In his works we are irresistibly led to sympathise with the sorrows of the wretched Africans, or the impressed victim of our own wars. His sentiments were never better supported than by his own private conduct, and it was in his domestic circle and friendly relations that the sincerity of them was exemplified.

There was talk of an edition. Hancock had promised, among the December 1814 materials in the *Belfast Monthly Magazine*:

> as the family of E. Rushton will publish a new edition of his works, the poems mentioned as written within the last few years must at present be withheld from the public. When this new edition is published, the admirers of good poetry, and the lovers of freedom and the best interests of man, will experience much gratification in the perusal' (p. 477).

In the event it would take almost another decade for the new edition to appear. In the meantime, Rushton's son (1795–1857) carried on the bookselling business, merging it with the printing firm of Melling (he married Ann Melling, who was also a niece of Egerton Smith, in 1817), producing further works on freedom of speech by John Wright, amongst other material, and frequently finding himself at the centre of radical causes in Liverpool. Also in 1817, he was moved to send to the *Liverpool Mercury* his father's 'A Few Plain Facts Relative to the Origin of the Liverpool Institute for the Blind', in defence of the elder Rushton's role in founding that institution, and in the same year Rushton's poem of defiance to Robert Southey, by then poet laureate and widely regarded as a turncoat, was published, also in the *Liverpool Mercury* (and elsewhere).

In 1824, finally, Effingham Wilson of London published *Poems, and other Writings, by the late Edward Rushton. To which is added, a Sketch of the Life of the Author by the Rev. William Shepherd.* The Liverpool firm of 'Rushton and Melling' printed it. The volume included some 44 poems, though not the same ones as were included in the 1806 collection. The editors dropped twelve poems from the earlier volume, including some of the more humorous material, but also some ballads, and a couple of the 'bird' poems ('The Throstle', 'The Shrike'). 'Briton, and Negro Slave', was also cut, perhaps because the editors had restored the first three, but not the apocalyptic fourth, of the *West-Indian Eclogues.* Another song of African heroism and British perfidy, 'The Coromantees', also extended the anti-slavery content. Some of the other 'new' poems had been published in some form already, including the 'Epitaph on John Taylor', first 'published' on an actual gravestone in New York. The *Expostulatory Letter to George Washington* was included, as was an unpublished essay on race and skin colour which Shepherd says had been preserved 'by his family in manuscript'. Shepherd appears to associate this with the intellectual group Rushton was in *c.* 1790, but it was read posthumously at a meeting of the Liverpool Literary and Philosophical Society in 1815 (see Commentary). Variants in the 1824 text of poems originally published before Rushton's death may indicate authorial revision, but it is likely that Shepherd and Rushton's son did some cleaning up, to punctuation and occasionally to word choice: there are variants between the *Liverpool Mercury* text of 'The Fire of English Liberty', published in 1816, and that presented in the volume, which must derive from editorial intervention.

Shepherd contributed a sizeable *Life*, elegantly expanded from the son's *Biographical Sketch.* Shepherd was highly sympathetic to Rushton's republican principles and firmness of mind, though his acknowledgement that he could also be inflexible and politically maladroit (p. xxviii) saves the biography from being too hagiographic. Shepherd's *Epistle to Edward Rushton* was also included, as was a poem by Thomas Noble (see Appendix II). Rushton's son inscribed a presentation copy 'To W.ᵐ Rathbone Esqʳ from Edward Rushton with his best respects June 1. 1824'.[30] The book was quietly advertised in the *Liverpool Mercury* of 4 June 1824, with a larger account in the news section of the paper. It had previously been announced in *The Examiner* of 23 May 1824. The publication was noted briefly in at least six magazines (such as *The British Critic*, 21 May 1824, p. 557) but received fewer actual reviews, being regarded as a reprint. It was also, of course, ten years since Rushton's death, and much had changed (all the 'second generation' Romantics, such as Keats, Shelley, and Byron, had already died, the last as recently as April 1824). However, the *Monthly Review* 105 (November 1824, pp. 325–26), found much of interest attaching to Shepherd's biographical account and in the newly-attached prose writings.

> His language, though not very classical nor much adorned, is always free, nervous, and eloquent; and his arguments, delivered in so bold and impassioned a strain, can scarcely be too strongly recommended at the present moment, when the advocates of slavery employ every weapon of sophistry that self-interest can place at their command.

It referred to the review of the 1806 volume, for the poems themselves: 'We gave them credit for power, pathos, and descriptive merit, while we pointed out their want of polish and classical taste'. The reviewer was pleased to have the material again in this new form, and considered that the whole 'advocates so many excellent principles, and is throughout embued with so much good sense and good feeling, devoted to the cause of humanity and truth'. *The New Monthly Magazine and Literary Journal* 12.46 (October 1824, pp. 460–61), found the poems 'very creditable to the feelings and talents of its Author. They do not, indeed, display a rich and powerful imagination, nor are they distinguished by high poetical expression; but they exhibit the more substantial qualities of pure principle, of sound taste, of honourable and humane feeling'.

These later reviews show the influence of a changed literary climate. By the time that he died, Rushton had established a strong individual reputation, rooted in Liverpool politics and maritime concerns; he was known nationally for his ability to write powerfully both in genuinely proletarian and high-status genres, and celebrated (and occasionally reviled) in America for his strongly-worded poems on liberty. His splicing of the high diction of Pope and Gray with the populist lyric forms sung by actual sailors in pubs made him a kind of unconscious proto-Romantic. His cultural networks, linking London, Manchester, and Belfast with Liverpool, made him undoubtedly more widely known in 1814 than William Blake was, though the younger generation of Romantics, whom he missed completely, and the growing prominence of Wordsworth and Coleridge, whom he does not appear to have read, would completely eclipse him over the next fifty years. But as the commentary to the poems shows, Rushton's work, in part because of its appearance at several levels of print culture, continued to be cited and reprinted in various forms, with and without attribution, in sometimes surprising contexts, throughout the nineteenth century. His could be a poetry of broadsides, chapbooks, newspapers, and journals on both sides of the Atlantic, as well as anthologies and books. Rushton was the main named author in a strange collection published at Nantucket in 1829: *Gleanings: Consisting of Extracts from the Writings of Edward Rushton, (The Blind Poet of Liverpool,) and Various other Authors*. The 'other authors' include Wordsworth, Cowper and Southey, though these are not named. A fanciful frontispiece displays the blind Rushton dictating poems to a daughter in his study, or possibly bookshop. Four years later he was one of 14 poets featured in *Sketches of Obscure Poets, with Specimens of their Writings* (1833). Some of his songs were reproduced with music and fine engravings for the Victorian parlour piano, while *Ballads & Songs of Lancashire Ancient and Modern*, ed. John Harland and T. T. Wilkinson (1875), included 'The Ardent Lover' and six sea songs in a separate section, stating that they had found a 'local Dibdin in the benevolent and lamented Edward Rushton of Liverpool, a few of whose songs we have obtained permission from his descendants to copy' (p. 517). These were instances of a sentimental and depoliticised presence in the later period, which generally preferred its poets to be less obviously engaged in fomenting popular revolution. Rushton's response to the personal affliction of blindness received sympathetic attention in James Wilson's *Life of Thomas Blacklock* (1838, pp. 150–57), on the grounds of comparison with the blind poet Blacklock, and similarly in Thomas Lund's sermon for the Liverpool School for the Blind, *Blindness: Or, Some Thoughts for Sighted People* (1887). But his political importance was not in fact forgotten either: the societies in which Rushton had been involved continued to toast his memory at their anniversary dinners, and these events continued to be reported. He was the subject of newspaper sketches, as in the *Preston Guardian*, 30 December 1854, perhaps prompted by the eulogy of Rushton as an exemplary autodidact in Saxe Bannister's *The Worthies of the Working Classes and their Friends* (second edition, 1854, pp. 7–12). His unflinching political stance had indirect consequence through his son's tireless work for social causes, which also kept the father's memory alive. The younger Rushton started a newspaper, *The Liverpool Commercial Chronicle*, in 1825, trained (like Roscoe) as an attorney, was called to the bar in 1831 and after some disappointments on the national stage of politics was appointed stipendiary magistrate at Liverpool, where he worked on juvenile delinquency, capital punishment, catholic emancipation, and similar reformist causes. He was highly conscious of the legacy of his father, whom he idolised, and to whose careful education he paid tribute. (Though not himself much of a poet, the younger Rushton did write an epitaph on William Shepherd, who died in 1847, and he had some contact with Wordsworth, in 1832, as well as Thomas Campbell and other writers.)[31]

Rushton was much less remembered in the first half of the twentieth century, and the early cultural history of Liverpool, then a declining port, was also little studied. More recently however, there have been attempts to recapture something of Rushton's complex engagement with the tense history of Britain and the north west during the revolutionary era. His position as a local hero, in relation to the Liverpool School for the Blind, has been established in a short biography of him by Mary Gladys Thomas (1949) and by Michael Royden's history of the School (1991); his wider importance as a dissentient voice within a dominant Liverpool culture of slavery-based commerce has been fiercely celebrated by Bill Hunter (2002).[32] His critique of slavery has been an important feature of some revisionist anthologies; *West-Indian Eclogues* was included in Alan Richardson's edition of slavery-related verse in volume four of *Slavery, Abolition, and Emancipation: Writings in the British Romantic Period* (London: Pickering and Chatto, 1999), and several pieces are present in Karina Williamson's selection, *Contrary Voices: Representations of West Indian Slavery, 1657–1834* (Kingston, Jamaica: University of the West Indies Press, 2008).[33] Rushton appears only to have recognised only two classes, those with power, and those without it; but given his family background, he was a natural if atypical inclusion in the anthology *Eighteenth-Century English Labouring-Class Poets*, with a useful selection and commentary by Tim Burke (volume III: London: Pickering and Chatto, 2003). Rushton has a strong presence, based on his varied use of lyric verse forms rather than on his subject matter, on the Spenserians website, http://spenserians.cath.vt.edu/.

It has seemed timely to assemble a comprehensive collection to celebrate the radical (in every sense) achievement of this singular writer, whose unusual combination of personal fortitude and political outspokenness produced verse of such formal range and emotional appeal. 2014 marks the 200th anniversary of Rushton's death, an event commemorated in exhibitions, tours, and even a play in the city of Liverpool; this edition forms what I hope will be a welcome complement to these civic tributes, as well as a companion to Franca Dellarosa's groundbreaking and enthralling study, *Talking Revolution: Edward Rushton's Rebellious Poetics, 1782–1814* (Liverpool: Liverpool University Press, 2014), to which the commentary presented here is much indebted.

The Edition

The principle followed here is to use the earliest version of each poem as copytext. Texts are transcribed with as little alteration as possible from the earliest known and dated printing, with everything else, including authorial revisions from the *1806* volume, registered as a variant. This is done less out of literary commitment to first thoughts as against laboured revisions than out of a sense that this is the best way to retain some kind of faithful archaeological witness to the material traces of the kind of authorship Rushton practised. Evidently he had aspirations as an author, as shown by the early and substantial quarto printings, the M'Creery broadsides, and the 1806 volume; at the same time he was writing songs which were sung in pubs, in theatres and music halls, at meetings, and on the street, and these were being widely printed and circulated in slipsong form, in newspapers, and in other demotic, unauthorised (and non-copyright) forms. The edition seeks to reflect and indeed to celebrate something of the multifarious nature of Rushton's output, publication history, and readership; his ability to work simultaneously in both genuinely working-class forms and high-status literary genres is a strong feature of his remarkable career. Poems appearing for the first time in the 1806 volume are printed in the order in which they appear there, a procedure duplicated for the new poems of the 1824 volume.

There are some difficulties with the approach: in one case Rushton rewrote his poem so much that it has been necessary to print two versions rather than a set of variants of the type that the poem on Chatterton, for example, has generated. With some poems it has not proved possible to trace an ur-text: I have not located the gravestone on which Rushton's epitaph for John Taylor was originally 'published'. The textual history of 'Mary le More' is particularly complicated, in ways which help to illuminate the context in which Rushton was working, as it appeared in slipsongs and chapbooks which do not bear a location or date (in part to elude censorship). 'Stanzas on Blindness' is printed from the *Merrimack Magazine* of 21 December 1805, not because that is where Rushton sent it but because it is the first dated appearance of the poem I have found; it was clearly printed earlier in a Liverpool newspaper which I have not found. Many of Rushton's poems will have first appeared in local newspapers which do not survive or have not been accessible, and then reprinted in the 1806 volume. Further research will no doubt yield some earlier versions of poems than I have presented here, and possibly additions to the canon. Appendix I lists poems possibly by Rushton not included here, with such evidence relating to authorship as I have found.

The titles are as given in the first publication, slightly standardised; where a poem is better known from a later title, this is given inside square brackets. In the Commentary, the textual witnesses for each poem are listed, followed by significant variants where these have been found, keyed to the edition or text where they are found. Not all variants are listed; punctuation changes, except where possibly significant, have not been noted, though minor verbal changes (from a singular to plural noun, for instance) are given. Variants in texts which have no demonstrable connection to Rushton have in general not been noted, though the trail of reprints through various formats is given to the best of my knowledge in order to trace the dissemination of Rushton's work. A few emendations have been introduced either from later texts or, in a very few instances, as simple corrections; these are noted in textual commentary. Otherwise the poems have been transcribed as they first appeared without the imposition of modern spelling and punctuation, and without adopting a uniform modern format, except for lineation and for the conversion of the eighteenth-century 'long s' to the modern form. Rushton's own capacious notes to *West-Indian Eclogues* and *Neglected Genius*, and the much shorter authorial notes to other poems, have been included as part of the text. This is done to give weight to the original arrangement and appearance of the texts, and to avoid confusion between Rushton's annotation and mine, which follows in the separate sequence of commentary.

Notes

1 The main biographical sources for Rushton are the 'Biographical Sketch of Edward Rushton, Written by his Son', *Belfast Monthly Magazine* 13.77 (December 1814): 474–78; and William Shepherd's 'Life of Edward Rushton', prefixed to Rushton's *Poems, and other Writings* (1824). 'Sketch' and '*Life*' refer to these texts respectively. The pagination of *Life* is affected by duplication of page numbers xiii–xvi. Quotation from *Life*, p. xi.

2 International Genealogical Index (IGI) (https://familysearch.org/search/collection/igi) confirms the date of birth and records that he was christened at St. George's, Castle Street, 7 December 1756.

3 *Life*, p. x. Gore's *Liverpool Directory* for 1774 lists a Thomas Rushton as a peruke-maker in Pool Lane, with another of the same name running a shoe warehouse. The same *Directory* for 1781 lists 'Thomas Rushton, Brewer' in Dale Street, but also 'Rushton and Palmer, hairdressers' in the same street; another Rushton, John, was a sailmaker in Argyle Street. A handbill advertisement headed 'Liquors in Perfection', for Thomas Rushton's spirits business at 39 Pool Lane, is conjecturally dated '1788'

by the John Johnson Collection of Ephemera, Bodleian Library, Oxford. Gore's *Directory* for 1796 has Thomas Rushton as a hairdresser on the south side of Old Dock. The relationships between various Rushtons in Liverpool in the period have not so far been fully disentangled.

4 The story was retold, from the 1824 *Life*, in the *Aberdeen Journal*, 13 July 1825 and *Caledonian Mercury*, 22 August 1825; it appeared also as a 'Remarkable Instance of Attachment in a Negro' in American papers such as the *National Advocate*, 21 July 1825; *Portland Advertiser*, 29 July 1825, and at least three others that year. A poem by John Allen Walker, 'The Negro Friend' based on the incident, appeared in *The South Devon Monthly Museum* I.5 (1833), 184–88.

5 According to IGI, a marriage took place between Thomas Rushton and Margaret Blackmore at St. Peter's in Church Street, Liverpool, on 7 November 1771; this would be approximately the right date.

6 IGI lists the marriage of Edward Rushton to Isabella Rain at St Peter's, Church Street, on 12 October 1785. She may be the Isabell Rein whose birth on 31 January 1750 in Liverpool is also recorded. The marriage of Elizabeth Rushton to George Broadhurst, 27 July 1783, is recorded at St. Nicholas's, and this may be the sister; a birth record for Elizabeth Rushton, 7 July 1761, christened 13 June 1761, with a father named Thomas, is also in IGI.

7 For a subtle reading of the Liverpool literature, see Tim Burke, '"Humanity is now the pop'lar cry": laboring-class writers and the Liverpool slave trade, 1787–1789', *Eighteenth Century*, 42:3 (2001), 245–63. The local history is discussed in *Liverpool, The African Slave Trade, and Abolition*, eds. Roger Anstey and P. E. H. Hair (Liverpool: Historic Society of Lancashire and Cheshire, 1976) and *Liverpool and Transatlantic Slavery*, eds. David Richardson, Suzanne Schwarz and Anthony Tibbles (Liverpool: Liverpool University Press, 2007); see especially Brian Howman's discussion of Rushton at pp. 283–89.

8 *Life*, pp. xv–xvi; Thomas Clarkson, *The History of the Rise, Progress and Accomplishment of the Abolition of the African Slave-Trade by the British Parliament*, 2 vols (1808), I.370–73; Rushton's name is in the lower left corner of this 'chart', opposite I. 259). Clarkson is in error in stating that Rushton published the *Eclogues* with his name on them, but his authorship was clearly common knowledge, at least locally.

9 See Ian Sutton, 'The extended Roscoe Circle: art, medicine and the cultural politics of alienation in Liverpool, 1762–1836', *British Journal for Eighteenth Century Studies*, 30 (2007), 439–58, and Arline Wilson, *William Roscoe: Commerce and Culture* (Liverpool: Liverpool University Press, 2008). For Currie's estimate of Rushton's 'truly original genius', see William Wallace Currie, *Memoir of the Life, Writings, and Correspondence of James Currie*, M.D., 2 vols (London: Longman, Rees, Orme, Brown and Green, 1831), I. 266–67. Rushton was an agent for George Walker's funeral sermon for Currie; see *Liverpool Chronicle and Commercial Advertiser*, 1 January 1806.

10 While Rushton married (as was required) in an Anglican church, two of his children, his son Edward and a daughter, Elizabeth, born 22 September 1795 and 1 May 1797 respectively, appeared to have been christened at the Renshaw St Chapel (IGI).

11 A still useful introduction to the nuts and bolts of the history of Rushton's Liverpool is Richard Brooke, *Liverpool as it was During the Last Quarter of the Eighteenth Century, 1775 to 1800* (1853). Chapter 2, 'Civic Liverpool 1680–1800',

of *Liverpool 800: Culture, Character and History*, ed. John Belchem (Liverpool: Liverpool University Press, 2006), gives a useful overview of attempts to enhance the cultural life of the city; Wilson, *Roscoe*, chapters 1, 4, 5, and 6, details Roscoe's role.

12 See Kenneth Johnston, *Unusual Suspects: Pitt's Reign of Alarm and the Lost Generation of the 1790s* (Oxford: Oxford University Press, 2013). M'Creery's *The Press* (1803) was bitterly ironic about Pitt's measures.

13 See R. B. Rose, 'The Jacobins of Liverpool', *Liverpool Bulletin: Libraries, Museums and Arts Committee*, 9 (1960–61), 37–49.

14 M'Creery, *The Press: A Poem, in Two Parts*, second edition (1828), pp. 64–65.

15 The number is variously given (54, 66, 10, 13); see Michael Perkin, *The Book Trade in Liverpool to 1805* (Liverpool: Liverpool Bibliographical Society, 1981), p. 25. In 1837, Rushton's son paid a sentimental visit to the street; *Letters of a Templar*, p. 237.

16 University of Liverpool Library, Special Collections and Archives, Rathbone Papers, RPII. 4. 16, p. 57: Rathbone's Scrapbook 1790–1808.

17 Shepherd (*Life*, pp. xxii–xxiii) comments on the rhetorical force of the letter but admits it was 'more strong than courteous'.

18 See J. R. Barker, 'John McCreery: a radical printer, 1768–1832', *The Library*, 5th ser., 16 (1961), 81–103, and Peter Isaac, *John M'Creery: A Revised Checklist of His Printing* (Wylam: Allenholme Press, 1999).

19 Liverpool Record Office, 920 ROS/4016. 'Binns' could be either Jonathan Binns (1747–1812), a Liverpool physician and abolitionist, or John Binns, from the London Corresponding Society, who visited Rushton at the Paradise Street shop in May 1797 and attended a group dinner with him that month; Binns, John, *Recollections of the Life of John Binns*, (1854), pp. 72–73.

20 These copies are from Sydney Jones Library, University of Liverpool, Y80.3.708 and H91.18(1) respectively.

21 The Liverpool Library (later the Lyceum) had a copy of the 1806 volume; it also held *West-Indian Eclogues*, but without indication of authorship. The Athenaeum, founded in 1797, holds two copies of the 1806 volume, both by later donation. Both libraries later took the 1824 edition. Rushton was not a shareholder in the Liverpool Library and certainly not president, as Rathbone, Roscoe and Currie were or had been by 1801, though his son was a proprietor by 1830. Rushton's books do not appear in the sale catalogue of Roscoe's library 1816, but that was mainly a fundraising sale of luxury books.

22 Rushton was an agent for at least two of Thelwall's pamphlets, and his *Poems Chiefly Written in Retirement* (1801); see *Liverpool Chronicle and Commercial Advertiser*, 1 February and 28 March 1804.

23 For this periodical, which was strongly associated with the United Irishmen, see Jonathan Jeffrey Wright, *The 'Natural Leaders' and their World: Politics, Culture and Society in Belfast, c.1801–1832* (Liverpool: Liverpool University Press, 2012), pp. 57–96. M'Creery celebrated William Drennan, another of the editors, in *The Press* (1827).

24 *A Compendious and Impartial Account of the Election ... at Liverpool* (Liverpool: Wright and Cruikshank, 1806). The 1806 and 1807 elections produced a torrent of anonymous political verse, but the collections yield nothing that looks like Rushton, who did not vote in the latter election. He was however associated with Roscoe as a reformer; Thomas Parkes sends letter about a publication of his on

public order to Roscoe but also to Rushton, 18 November 1809; Liverpool Record Office, LRO, 920 ROS/2874.

25 For the latter see *Liverpool Chronicle and Commercial Advertiser*, 26 August, 5 and 16 September; and for the Liverpool Forum, see weekly advertisements in the same paper, 28 October to 23 December 1807.

26 See Barbara Whittingham-Jones, 'Liverpool Political clubs, 1812–1830', *Transactions of the Historical Society of Lancashire and Cheshire*, III (1959), 117–38.

27 *Liverpool Mercury*, 12 February and 3 December 1813, 14 January, 11 March, 6 May, and 28 October 1814. Advertisements for publications can be found on 22 November 1811, 11 September 1812, 19 February and 18 June 1813.

28 The Eau Medicinale d'Husson was advertised e.g. in the *Morning Chronicle*, 9 July 1810. For controversy about the treatment see William Henry Williams, *Observations proving that Dr. Wilson's Tincture for the Cure of Gout and Rheumatism is Similar in its Nature and Effects to that Deleterious Preparation the Eau Medicinale* (London: Callow, 1818).

29 Casey's speech appeared in the *Belfast Recorder*, 23 December 1814, and was reprinted in *The Shamrock*, 18 November 1815. See further the materials reprinted in *Letters of a Templar*, pp. 6–7, where Rushton's grandson recalls his mother's description of Rushton's imposing stature. Rushton's death was discussed in a letter from Robert Roscoe to William Roscoe, 24 November 1814; Liverpool Record Office, 920 ROS/3765.

30 Special Collections and Archives, Sydney Jones Library, University of Liverpool (H89.29).

31 See *Letters of a Templar*, 122, 169–70, 175–76, 206, 234, 275, 301. His son, also Edward (1820–1900), studied at Jesus College, Cambridge and qualified as a lawyer at the Inner Temple, being called to the Bar in 1849; he continued the poetic tradition of the family with *Lament for Caubul* (1845).

32 Thomas, *Edward Rushton* (National Institute for the Blind Biographies, I, London 1949); Hunter, *Forgotten Hero: The Life and Times of Edward Rushton, Liverpool's Blind Poet, Revolutionary Republican & Anti-Slavery Fighter* (Liverpool: Living History Library, 2002); Royden, *Pioneers and Perseverance: A History of the Royal School for the Blind, Liverpool, 1791–1991* (Liverpool: Countryvise Ltd, 1991). See also Mike Royden's local site, http://www.roydenhistory.co.uk/mrlhp/local/rushton/rushton.htm.

33 Given the praise for courage, range and joined-up radicalism awarded to Roscoe, Mulligan and Thelwall in Marcus Wood's *The Poetry of Slavery: An Anglo-American Anthology 1764–1865* (Oxford: Oxford University Press, 2003), it is surprising that Rushton is completely omitted.

POEMS

An Irregular ODE.

(1781)

As when the rugged blast spreads uproar wide,
  And the loud surge of each green mountain curls,
Then on some shatter'd vessel's crazy side,
  With all-destroying force its fury hurls:
    The staggering bark reels to and fro,   5
    Stunn'd with the dreadful thund'ring blow,
    Then instant hoists her tatter'd sail,
    And drives along before the gale;
    Away she flies, an isle appears,
    Into whose friendly port she steers,   10
    And free from every danger lies,
    While all around the giddy tempest flies:
So when fair Liberty was forc'd to fly
The gripe of ruthless tyranny,
The continent she left, and straight   15
In Britain's island found retreat;
Whose iron shores, and martial race,
She knew would shield her from disgrace,
And boldly dare to vindicate her reign
On the rough briny surge, or on th' embattl'd plain.   20
  Britannia on her sea-beat shore,
Receiv'd the Goddess with a gracious smile;
  Welcome, she cry'd, and evermore
May'st thou, oh Liberty! protect my Isle.
    Fear not (the stranger said) thy foes,   25
    Tho' all the warring world oppose;
Still, still undaunted on the foaming waves,
Thy daring Sons shall lord it over Slaves.
    Our Sires receiv'd the heavenly Guest,
      And vow'd to keep her free from stain;   30
    A Stewart fled at her request,
      And, oh! may Liberty preserve her reign!
Still may her liberal blessings wide extend
To every clime, in ample bounty given;
Free as the fostering vernal showers descend,   35
Free as the pure unbounded light of heaven.

The prowling tyger, when he once enjoys
    The blood of human kind, rejects his former fare;
  So he who once has tasted Freedom's joys,
    Rejects the yoke which servile wretches bear.   40
Wretches mean, whose abject souls
Dominion easily controuls;
Who tho' oppressed, scarce complain,
Nay, strange to tell, who hug the chain,
And tamely own their tyrants right,   45
As men born blind feel not the loss of sight.
  Time roll'd, and Liberty each Briton fir'd
    With strong attachment to the rights of man;
  And tho' across th' Atlantic some retir'd,
    They still adher'd to Freedom's sacred plan.   50
    Mourn, Britons, mourn the evil hour,
    When blinded by your thirst of power,
        You wish'd to tyrannize;
    And, oh! ye Colonies obey,
    Accept a Parent's gentle sway,   55
        Be loyal, and be wise.
No longer now Britannia aims t'oppose
Your long-contested rights—then prudent close
The scene of blood—the present moment seize,
And welcome Liberty ally'd to Peace.   60
  Oh quit your errors, join your Parent-state,
    A fractur'd limb, set by a skilful hand,
  Becomes more strong: So throw aside your hate,
    And the whole Empire shall more vig'rous stand.
Religion, language, customs, laws and blood,   65
  Should all conspire to link us close again;
For tho' at first our vengeance ye withstood,
  Rebellion now stalks thro' your wide domain.
    And oh! to your eternal shame,
    Join'd with our deadly foes, you aim   70
To pull Britannia from her tow'ring height;
    But tho' all Europe should combine,
    And aid the treacherous design,
Th' attempt must fail, would Britons all unite.
  For even now as some huge rock,   75
    Amid the war of angry waves,
  Unmov'd receives the tempest's shock,
    And all its awful thunder braves;
So Britain, spite of Bourbon, stands;
Despight of her rebellious bands;   80

And tho' the rugged Northern Powers combine,
Still o'er them all shall British glory shine.

To the PEOPLE of ENGLAND.

(1782)

I.

WHEN bellowing warfare lords it round,
And death and loud uproar abound,
When Gallia, wild ambitious foe,
Oh! Britain aims thy overthrow;
When proud Iberia drains each mine,   5
Big with the same accurst design;
When Belgia's bold rapacious knaves
Have basely join'd th' aspiring slaves,
And foul rebellion, with averted eyes,
Rejects the offer'd terms, and all thy pow'r defies,   10

II.

When thus with foes encircled round,
And not a friendly pow'r is found;
Is this a time, Oh Britons say,
On Pleasure's lap to die away?
Is this a time for long debate,   15
For narrow views, and factious heat?
Is this a time for calm repose,
When half the warring world are foes?
Oh! Britons rouse to patriotic deeds,
For oh! oppress'd with numbers, see your country bleeds.   20

III.

Where is that glowing ardent zeal,
That spirit Britons wont to feel?
Where are your bold exertions gone,
And where the public virtue flown?
Heavens! how alter'd, how supine,   25
How slow t'embrace each great design,
How worthless pride and coward fears,
Keep thin your corps of Volunteers;
But languish Britons, view to your disgrace,
What animation marks Hibernia's manly race.   30

IV.

When danger shew'd her frightful mien,
No impotent attempts were seen.
No frigid meeting stain'd their land,
They rose a bold, a patriot band:
No narrow views, no dastard fear,   35
No supercilious pride was there,
All ranks, all parties feel the flame,
And glow at Freedom's sacred name;
All, all self-arm'd and self-array'd appear,
And at the artist's side is seen the noble Peer.   40

V.

'Twas thus they rose, and thus they stand,
The guardians of a rising land,
Disdaining ease, respected, fear'd,
And with a nation's plaudits cheer'd;
Oh! that Britannia's sons would rise,   45
Like them intrepid, bold, and wise,
Like them deserve the patriot name,
And rise from apathy to flame—
Ambition soon wou'd give the contest o'er,
And soon wou'd meek-ey'd peace be wafted to our shore.   50

VI.

Tho' baleful anger spreads around,
Yet sparks of virtue still are found,
SUFFOLK, whose sons shall live in fame,
And thee, Oh! LOWTHER, thee, whose name
Can never die, whose noble mind   55
High-soaring, tow'rs above thy kind.
Oh! Britons, join this godlike man,
Swift, swift adopt his patriotic plan,
Your country then may raise her aweful form,
And with unequal fury hurl the warring storm.   60

VII.

Each envious state wou'd loath the sight,
And curse a flame so wond'rous bright;
Ambition, with desponding mien,
And nerveless arm would then be seen;
Despair wou'd sit on Treachery's face,   65
And Craft, dismay'd, wou'd point at Peace;
Ingratitude wou'd drop her crest,

And fold a parent to her breast;
And Albion then invincible wou'd stand,
Ride o'er the boist'rous surge, or wave the olive wand.　　　70

VIII.

Then Britons rouse, your strength combine,
And baffle every fell design:
Oh! emulate your sires of old,
Whom pride or danger ne'er controul'd,
Rouse, and defend this spot of earth,　　　75
This sea-girt isle that gave you birth,
Let every breast with vengeance glow,
And every arm prepare the blow;
Then, like a wounded lion robb'd of prey,
Wou'd Briton strike her foes with terror and dismay.　　　80

THE DISMEMBER'D EMPIRE.

(1782)

IF the hours which have been appropriated to the production of the following Poem, had not been thus employed, they would probably have been past in brooding over the greatest of all human calamities – in lamenting a sightless existence. – To divert the mind from her misfortunes, and engage her in any pleasing pursuit, is to the afflicted almost a cessation of pain; yet he who is possessed of any degree of Patriotism, cannot be supposed to have gained much, if after detaching his thoughts from his own misfortunes, he finds them immediately fixed on the distresses of his overpowered (tho' bravely struggling) country.

The boisterous element, which the author has been enur'd to from his infancy, is supposed by some, to blunt the finer feelings of the soul; such an opinion, however just, has not been powerful enough to deter him from making this hazardous attempt.

He is an advocate for liberty, tho' an enemy to rebellion; he has no poetical reputation to lose, and to attempt gaining one, he is afraid would be a task much too arduous for one of his limited acquirements.

LIVERPOOL,
November, 1782.

    SEVEN times the globe has made its annual round,
Sublimely rolling thro' the vast profound,
Since Britons first aspir'd to govern slaves,
And hurl'd destruction 'cross th' Atlantic waves;
Since freedom's boasted sons, elate with pride,   5
Deny'd to others what themselves enjoy'd;
Since they resolv'd to banish freedom's reign,
And bind three millions with oppression's chain,
Or raise aloft grim warfare's crimson'd head,
And strew their wide domain with mangled dead.   10
Such your resolves, O Britons! such your aim,
You wish'd to smother that exalted flame
Which first obtain'd, and still preserves your rights,
Despite of kings, or kingly parasites:
Perchance ye thought, the ocean cross'd, and then   15
Britons became another race of men,

A dastard herd, a low, contemptuous crew,
Whom the rude gripe of pow'r would soon subdue,
As if the plenteous soil possest a charm
Which could the soul of all its strength disarm.   20

   Oh! dire delusion! oh! ill fated hour!
When Britain, blinded by her love of power,
Unsheath'd the sword in foul oppression's cause,
And stain'd her annals, to enforce her laws.
But oh! how vain; at Freedom's earnest call   25
Thousands arose, in her defence to fall;
The clang of arms was heard in every wood,
And all the furry tenants trembling stood;
Slaughter, besmear'd with blood, with giant stride
And ruthless front, was seen on every side;   30
Yet animated with that sacred flame
Which prompts to deeds of everlasting fame,
All sects, all ranks, all parties, undismay'd,
Grasp'd the brown musket, and the shining blade,
Resolv'd to spurn the ignominious plan,   35
And dar'd to vindicate the rights of man.

   O Liberty! where e'er thou deign'st to smile,
On Afric's burning Coast, or Britain's Isle,
Or where the hardy Swiss disdains controul,
Or where Old Ocean's Western surges roll;   40
Thy manly sons with gen'rous ardor glow,
And, nerv'd by thee, repel each tyrant foe:
O may the lib'ral blessings wide extend,
In every clime may'st thou mankind befriend;
May'st thou, with amplest bounty still be given,   45
Free, as the pure, unbounded, light of heaven.

   Ambition long had been the parent's guide,
Who now, incens'd to find her claims deny'd,
Resolv'd by dint of prowess to subdue
A brave (though proudly term'd a rabble) crew: 50
As when, with hunger prest, in search of food
A meagre lion roams the mazy wood,
And meets a porcupine, his flashing eyes
Declare his joy, and with a bound he flies;
The humble brute, of nature's arms possest,   55
Roll'd in his quills, repels the kingly beast,
And lies secure, though every vengeful blow

Brings crimson torrents from the growling foe:
So Britain strove, but found her efforts vain,
Nature, great parent, fought for Freedom's reign,   60
And though the wily arts of war were try'd,
Though powerful aids were lavishly supply'd,
Yet, even this rabble ting'd their creeks with blood,
And all the skill of veteran hosts withstood.
Britons! 'twas thus your island rose to fame,   65
Your dearest rights from noble struggles came;
'Twas thus, when kings became their subjects foes,
Your bearded sires of old, indignant rose,
And, cas'd in armour, trod their martial plain,
Resolv'd, or Death or Freedom to obtain;   70
Each hardy breast the kindling fury own'd,
And on each front sat Liberty enthron'd,
Each nobly firm, despis'd the regal frown,
And their rough arms set limits to a crown;
Such were the manly souls a Lack-land found,   75
Such *Charles* withstood, and such a *William* crown'd;
And such, I trust, undaunted, firm and free,
Will Britain's sons continue still to be.

Now, o'er the pine-clad soil Contention spread,
Wisdom neglected, from our councils fled,   80
Commerce no longer swell'd the spacious tide,
And British hands with British blood were dy'd;
Oh! piteous sight! to see those kindred hands,
Once firmly link'd in friendship's social bands,
Uplifted now, to pierce each others breast,   85
While Bourbon, smiling, rear'd her haughty crest,
And aim'd the deadly blow she long had plan'd,
To curb the glory of a rival land.

Three long campains had thin'd each warring train,
And Devastation held her dreary reign,   90
When Britain, from her horrid frenzy woke,
And to her Offspring thus compunctive spoke:—
Oh! my lov'd sons, this deadly strife forego,
Great are your wrongs, but greater far my woe;
Claims of disputed power I now resign,   95
And in return, be filial duty mine;
O grant me this, the furious contest cease,
And welcome Liberty, ally'd with Peace.
Thus Britain spoke; oppression instant fled,

35

And white-rob'd justice, smiling, rais'd her head,   100
Then with uplifted balance try'd the cause,
And gave th' afflicted Parent just applause.
Not so, her Offspring; deaf to nature's call,
They heard the gen'rous terms, yet spurn'd them all;
Their rights regain'd, they soar'd on frantic wing,   105
And, freed from grievances, disown'd a king:
And, strange to tell! as Britain threw aside
Her haughty tone, and supercilious pride,
Her Offspring these assum'd, and now became
Revengeful, insolent, and void of shame.   110

    Ambition, active fiend, no sooner saw
The wise repeal of each oppressive law,
Than, in disgust, from councils she withdrew,
And eagle-wing'd, o'er ocean's surges flew;
There, taking Freedom's form, she whisper'd round   115
That Independence was the only ground
On which to build their happiness sincere;
And sons, she cry'd, be great! still persevere!
And should your spirits droop, O turn your eyes
On mighty Belgia's long-contested rise.   120
Thus curst Ambition, man's eternal foe,
Britain forsook, and sought to work her woe;
For what she spoke infatuated all,
And lo! the league was form'd with faithless Gaul.

    Thou, who with sacred friendship's silken bands,   125
Bind'st up the enmities of neighb'ring lands,
O lovely Peace! how gentle is thy reign,
With arts and commerce smiling in thy train;
Yet, meek-ey'd Power! when e'er th' insulting foe
With red'ning arm, prepares the deadly blow,   130
Be banish'd still, nor let thy gentler hand
Check the just vengeance of an injur'd land.

    Britannia on a western craig reclin'd,
Her sea-green locks disorder'd in the wind,
The laurel wreath which bound her brows, decay'd,   135
And frequent throbs her inward woe betray'd;
And oft her sorrowing eyes were anxious cast
Where deep-mouth'd ocean roar'd with every blast;
Yet, when the hateful tidings caught her ear,
Her aspect fir'd, she grasp'd the deadly spear,   140

And stalk'd indignant o'er the threaten'd land,
And bade each county, rouse its martial band.
In every port, To Arms! my sons, she cry'd,
To Arms! To Arms! her hardy sons reply'd;
And soon, with force impetuous, undismay'd,   145
Her warring thousands pour'd on Gallia's trade,
Swept o'er the deep, with India's wealth return'd,
And soon the wily enemy had mourn'd
Her treach'rous arts; when lo! Iberia rose,
And added millions to Britannia's foes;   150
Thus war's devouring flame, Ambition fed,
And rapid o'er the watry world it spread,
Europe soon felt the conflagrating foe,
And empire, after empire, own'd the woe.
Conspicuous long, amongst the warring train,   155
Whose bulky navies press the watry plain,
Unaw'd, unshaken, had Britannia stood,
The mightiest power that ever swell'd the flood;
Oft had insulting treachery seen her rise,
With awful vengeance darting from her eyes,   160
Long had her splendid glory fill'd each state
With envy, jealousy, and deadly hate:
And now, dismember'd, robb'd of half her pow'r,
To bring her prostrate, each believ'd the hour
Was near at hand; and Gallia first began   165
To put in force the foul, malignant plan;
Iberia next, with golden spear combin'd;
And in their schemes low-thoughted Holland join'd.
O race ungrateful! mean, designing knaves,
To craft, and yellow dirt, eternal slaves;   170
A time may come, nor distant far the date,
When the red vengeance of an injur'd state
May, wing'd with terror, blast your sordid train,
And prove she still maintains her watry reign,
Despite of annual multiplying foes,   175
Increasing vast, like Alpine rolling snows.

    The rest, whose navies cut the northern tide,
No less her foes, th' unequal strife enjoy'd,
And by their Arm'd Neutrality, display'd
The canker'd wound which envy long had made.   180

    Thus low'rs the warring world on Britain's reign,
While in her bosom faction's sland'rous train

Exultant rise, exaggerate her woes,
Distract her councils, and exalt her foes,
Spread fell despondence, damp her martial flame,   185
Mislead her sons, and blot her well-earn'd fame,
And ardent wish, the senate and the throne,
As mighty states, would foul rebellion own;
But, Britons! Offspring of a glorious race,
O never! never! yield to such disgrace;   190
For, Trade destroy'd, that source of all your might,
And Naval Glory instant takes its flight.
Oh! spite of foreign and domestic foes,
Indignant spurn a scheme so big with woes,
So full of ills, that Britain soon would feel   195
Her bosom bare to Bourbon's vengeful steel.
Her towering treasures in the torrid zone,
Would soon the rule of other masters own;
Her fam'd Antilles, whose extended plains,
And hilly risings, teem with mantling canes,   200
Whose cultur'd coasts, when sail'd along, display
Luxuriant prospects, nature ever gay;
The lofty mountains, clad with lively green,
On whose huge breasts the misty clouds are seen,
The bounded lawns, the gently swelling hills,   205
The planters' houses, and the busy mills,
The wide extended works, the cluster'd sheds
Where toiling negroes rest their weary'd heads;
The scatter'd trees, in all their bloom array'd,
Some spread their tops, and form the cooling shade,   210
Whilst others, more majestic, intervene,
Raise their tall heads, and beautify the scene.
These, these bright gems, no longer would remain,
Should proud rebellion Independence gain;
Nay, Orient India's trade would soon expire,   215
And Commerce soon to other shores retire,
And in her train, reluctant, would depart
Power, Industry, and ev'ry polish'd art:
No more, from rosy morn 'till evening gray,
Would busy Trade her chearful front display;   220
No more her Fleets would then, with active toil,
Give up the produce of each distant soil:
And like a swarm of bees, that hum around
Where e'er the balmy essences abound,
No more the Sons of Commerce would be seen,   225
With chearful aspect, bright'ning all the scene.

For, Oh! how different will the view be found,
If e'er rebellion with success is crown'd.
Depopulated streets will then relate,
In mournful terms, her lost commercial state;   230
The domes, assign'd for want and pale distress,
Will then o'erflow with human wretchedness;
The drooping tradesman, with dejected face,
Will then lament his country's sad disgrace,
Will view, with sorrow swelling at his heart,   235
The crowded once, but now forsaken mart:
The hollow warehouse, and the grass-grown quay,
The empty docks, swift crumbling to decay,
The mold'ring moles, and harbours chok'd with sand,
All, all will shew – a ruinated land!   240

Thus, my lov'd country, once the dread of slaves,
The scourge of tyrants, mistress of the waves,
The soul of commerce, patroness of arts,
The nurse of arms, and men of god-like parts;
Thus will thy glory set in endless night,   245
If e'er thou yield'st thy just, maternal right.

   But, O ye worthies! friends to Britain's weal,
Ye real patriots! here display your zeal,
Reject with warmth the proud, injurious claim,
And still, O still preserve your country's fame.   250
What Briton, who should see another stand,
And nobly keep at bay a ruffian band,
But, unimplor'd, would chear his drooping heart,
And all th' assistance in his power impart?
So, unassisted when his country stands,   255
And boldly braves the storms of vengeful lands,
Each British bosom should with ardor glow,
And every deed from patriot motives flow.

   When rugged tempests lift the surges high,
And on some struggling bark impell'd they fly,   260
The hardy seamen, through the dreary night,
Undaunted brave the elemental fight,
Assiduous, active all, intent to save
The shatter'd vessel from the ruthless wave:
So Britons now, should join with heart and hand,   265
To snatch from ruin's jaws a sinking land;
To punish craft, ingratitude, and pride,

And shew the world, that Albion, unally'd,
Like some tall craig, amid the watry swell,
Firm, and unmov'd, can every stroke repel.   270

   O Unanimity! assume thy reign,
Link every Briton in thy powerful chain,
One heart, one hand, will then direct the blow,
And hurl the death-wing'd vengeance on the foe;
Faction, that monster, with an hundred tongues,   275
Malignant eyes, and adamantine lungs,
Who views, with laughing front, his country's woes,
And sighs, desponding, at defeated foes,
Whose venom'd maw still belches slander forth,
And daubs a Shelburne, as he daub'd a North;   280
This deadly foe, would Britons once unite,
With fierie-ey'd Discord soon would take his flight.
Call forth then, Britons! all that active zeal,
That Public Spirit Britons wont to feel,
Let every breast with generous ardor glow,   285
Let every arm, uplifted, aim the blow;
Let Albion's Navy raise its head on high,
And never more from tow'ring Bourbon fly;
For, Oh! her glory soon will fade away,
If e'er the azure main disowns her sway.   290

   Her Seamen! heav'ns! how resolutely bold,
Or in the torrid heat, or frigid cold,
'Tis equal all, they brave the storm's career,
Laugh at all danger, and despise all fear;
And, when loud thunders shake the vaulted skies,   295
And the blue light'ning dances in their eyes,
When the fierce tempest roars in all its pride,
And dissolution yawns on every side,
When deep immers'd in sulph'rous smoke and fire,
And every ball is wing'd with vengeance dire,   300
When death, with weary'd arm, stalks o'er the deck,
And limbless, lifeless trunks, bestrew the wreck,
When horrid dying groans invade the ear,
Still, still untam'd, undaunted, all appear.

   Such are the men who former glories won,   305
And, with such men, what actions might be done!
If those who rule the war, direct her right,
And jarring parties in the fleet unite,

If in the Naval Scale her weight be thrown,
And on the foaming surge, and there alone,   310
Britannia tries her strength, ye mighty pow'rs!
How soon again may victory be ours.
As skims along the flying, finny brood,
When by the keen-ey'd dolphin swift pursu'd;
Or like the timid flocks, that bound before   315
The prowling lion's death-devouring roar;
How soon may Britain, with exultant joy,
Behold again the fleets of Bourbon fly.
But, Unanimity! without thy aid,
Her strength with glory ne'er will be display'd: 320
O banish Faction, and unite the land
In one connected, steady, loyal band;
Let every vigorous arm a musket grace,
Let every county Suffolk's plan embrace,
Let every British breast like Lowther's glow,   325
And vengeance soon would fasten on each foe;
Soon would Ambition, with desponding mein,
And nerveless, unavailing arm, be seen;
Soon would Despair be fix'd on Treach'ry's face,
And, justly punish'd Craft, would point at Peace;   330
Ingratitude would drop her tow'ring crest,
And gladly fold a Parent to her breast:
And, like her own huge rock, which nobly braves
The fleets and armies of besieging slaves,
Firm, and unshaken, would Britannia stand,   335
The envy, dread, and wonder of each land.

The END.

WEST-INDIAN ECLOGUES

(1787)

ADVERTISEMENT.

THE author of the following Eclogues has resided several years in the West-Indies. They, who have spent only a small portion of time there, must have been frequent witnesses (it is to be hoped, unwilling *ones also) of barbarities similar to those, which are here related.*

In delineating the following scenes, the author has painted from actual observation. He writes from the heart: for he feels what he describes. In striving to give simplicity of stile to the dialogue, he may have too much neglected those ornaments, of which Poetry ought never, perhaps, to be entirely destitute. But the praise, due to poetic excellence, has not been the author's chief hope. Humanity has been the first, the leading, motive of this undertaking. And if these Eclogues shall contribute, in their humble sphere, to prevent excessive punishments from being *unnecessarily* inflicted on that wretched race, to whom they relate,———the *author of them will receive the highest gratification, of which his mind is capable, in the pleasing consciousness, that*

> *"One moral, or a mere well-natur'd deed,*
> *"Doth all desert in sciences exceed."———*

TO THE

RIGHT REVEREND

B E I L B Y,

LORD BISHOP of CHESTER,

(IN GRATITUDE FOR HIS DISCOURSE ON THE

CIVILISATION, IMPROVEMENT, and CONVERSION,

OF THE NEGRO-SLAVES

IN THE BRITISH ISLANDS IN THE WEST-INDIES,

AND

FOR HIS CONTINUED PATRONAGE OF EVERY

SUBSEQUENT ENDEAVOUR TO ATTAIN THOSE SALUTARY
OBJECTS)

THE FOLLOWING ECLOGUES

ARE MOST HUMBLY

AND MOST RESPECTFULLY

DEDICATED,

BY

JULY, 1787.

THE AUTHOR.

ECLOGUE the FIRST.

SCENE—JAMAICA.—TIME—MORNING.

THE Eastern clouds declare the coming day,
The din of reptiles [a] slowly dies away.
The mountain-tops just glimmer on the eye,
And from their bulky sides the breezes [b] fly.
The Ocean's margin beats the varied strand,   5
It's hoarse, deep, murmurs reach the distant land.
The Sons of Mis'ry, Britain's foulest stain,
Arise from friendly sleep to pining pain;
Arise, perchance, from dreams of Afric's soil,
To Slav'ry, hunger, cruelty, and toil:—   10
When slowly moving to their tasks assign'd,
Two sable friends thus eas'd their lab'ring mind.
                    JUMBA.
Oh say, ADOMA, whence that heavy sigh?
Or is thy YARO sick—or droops thy Boy?
Or say what other woe—
                    ADOMA.
                          These wounds behold.—   15
                    JUMBA.
Alas! by them too plain thy griefs are told!
But whence, or why these stripes? my injur'd friend,
Declare how one so mild could thus offend.
                    ADOMA.
I'll tell thee, JUMBA.—'Twas but yesterday,
As in the field we toil'd our strength away,   20
My gentle YARO with her hoe was nigh,
And on her back she [c] bore my infant Boy.
The sultry heats had parch'd his little throat,
His head reclin'd I heard his wailing note.
The Mother, at his piteous cries distress'd,   25
Now paus'd from toil and gave the cheering breast.
But soon alas! the savage Driver [d] came,
And with his cow-skin cut her tender frame;
Loudly he tax'd her laziness,—and then
He curs'd my boy, and plied the lash again!   30
—JUMBA, I saw the deed,—I heard her grief!
Could I do less?—I flew to her relief;
I fell before him—sued, embrac'd his knee,
And bade his anger vent itself on me,

Spurn'd from his feet I dar'd to catch his hand,   35
Nor loos'd it, JUMBA, at his dread command:
For, blind with rage, at one indignant blow
I thought to lay the pale-fac'd villain low!
But sudden stopp'd;—for now the whites came round,
They seiz'd my arms,—my YARO saw me bound!   40
Need I relate what follow'd?
         JUMBA.
               Barb'rous deed!
Oh! for the pow'r to make these Tyrants bleed!
These, who in regions far remov'd from this,
Think, like ourselves, that liberty is bliss,
Yet in wing'd houses cross the dang'rous waves,   45
Led by base av'rice, to make others slaves:—
These, who extol the freedom they enjoy,
Yet would to others every good deny:—
These, who have torn us from our native shore
Which (dreadful thought!) we must behold no more:—   50
These, who insult us through the weary day,
With taunts our tears, with mocks our griefs, repay:
Oh! for the pow'r to bring these monsters low,
And bid them feel the biting tooth of woe!
         ADOMA.
JUMBA, my deep resolves are fix'd! my friend,   55
This life, this slavish journey, soon shall end.
These fest'ring gashes loudly bid me die,
And by our sacred Gods I will comply.
Yes JUMBA, by each great *Fetish* ᵉ I swear,
This, worse than death, I cannot, will not bear.   60
         JUMBA.
What! tamely perish? no, ADOMA, no—
Thy great revenge demands a glorious blow.
But dar'st thou bravely act in such a cause?
Friends may be found,—what say'st thou?—why this pause?
         ADOMA.
JUMBA, thou mov'st me much.—Thy looks are wild,   65
Thy gestures passionate—
         JUMBA.
              If to be mild
In such a cause were virtue,—on the ground
JUMBA would crawl, and court the causeless wound.
—How oft, my friend, since first we trod these plains
Have trivial faults call'd forth the bitt'rest pains!   70
How oft our Tyrants, at each dext'rous lash,

With joyous looks have view'd each bleeding gash;
How oft to these, with tortures still uncloy'd,
Have they the *Eben*'s prickly branch ᶠ applied!
And shall we still endure the keenest pain, 75
And pay our butchers only with disdain?
Shall we, unmov'd, still bear their coward blows?
—No:—vengeance soon shall fasten on our foes,
Lend but thy succour—
ADOMA.
Comfort to my soul
Thy words convey, and ev'ry fear controul. 80
Their last, base, cruel act so steels my heart,
That in thy bold resolves I'll bear a part.
JUMBA.
Enough:—Our glorious aims shall soon succeed,
And thou in turn shall see th' oppressors bleed.
Soon shall they fall, cut down like lofty Canes, 85
And (oh! the bliss) from us receive their pains.
Oh! 'twill be pleasant when we see them mourn,
See the fell cup to their own lip return,
View *their* pale faces prostrate on the ground,
Their meagre bodies gape with many a wound; 90
View with delight each agonizing grin,
When melted wax ᵍ is dropp'd upon *their* skin:—
Then bid them think—
ADOMA.
Hark! from yon plaintain trees
Methought a voice came floating on the breeze.
—Hark!—there again—
JUMBA.
'Tis so: our tyrants come.— 95
At eve we'll meet again:—mean time be dumb.

End of the first ECLOGUE.

ECLOGUE the SECOND.

TIME—EVENING.

THE twinkling Orbs which pierce the gloom of night
Now shine with more than European light.
Slow from the vap'ury mountains comes the breeze,
And on it's dewy wings sits pale disease.

Rising from distant reefs and rocky shores,   5
Where vex'd with recent gales old Ocean roars;
Now up the slopes where spiry canes appear,
A faint unvaried din assails the ear.
The lurking reptiles now begin their rounds,
And fill the air with shrill discordant sounds,   10
And now with varied hum in search of prey,
Unnumber'd insects wheel their airy way;
There glowing fire [h] seems borne upon the wing,
And here the keen Mosquito darts his sting.
The wearied Negroes to their sheds return,   15
Prepare their morsels, and their hardships mourn,
Talk o'er their former bliss, their present woes;
Then sink to earth, and seek a short repose.
—'Twas now the sable friends, in pensive mood,
In a lone path their doleful theme renew'd.   20

ADOMA.

JUMBA, those words sunk deep into my heart,
Which thou in friendship didst this morn impart.
Still at my toil my mind revolv'd them o'er,
But grew, the more I mus'd, dismay'd the more.
Oh! think on PEDRO, gibbetted alive! [i]   25
Think on his fate—six long days to survive!—
His frantic looks,—his agonizing pain,—
His tongue outstretch'd to catch the dropping rain;
His vain attempts to turn his head aside,
And gnaw the flesh which his own limbs supplied;   30
Think on his suff'rings, when th' inhuman crew,
T' increase his pangs, plac'd Plantains in his view,
And bade him eat—

JUMBA.

                        If thus thy promise ends,
If thus thy dastard heart would aid thy friends,
Away, mean wretch, and view thy YARO bleed,   35
And bow submissive to th' unmanly deed!—
Thou speak'st of PEDRO.—He possess'd a soul,
Which nobly burst the shackles of control.
He fell betray'd, but boldly met his death;
And curs'd his tyrants with his latest breath.   40
—But go, ADOMA, since to live is sweet,
Go, like a dog, and lick the white men's feet;
Tell them that hunger, slav'ry, toil, and pain,
Thou wilt endure, nor ever once complain:
Tell them, though JUMBA dares to plot their fall,   45

That thou art tame, and wilt submit to all.
Go poor submissive slave,—Go, meanly bend,
Court the pale butchers, and betray thy friend.
ADOMA.
How!—I betray my friend!—Oh, JUMBA, cease;
Nor stab ADOMA with such words as these.   50
Death frights me not; I wish revenge like thee;
But oh! I shudder at their cruelty.
I could undaunted, from the craggy steep
Plunge, and be swallow'd in the raging deep;
Fearless I could with Manchineel, or knife,   55
Or cord, or bullet, end this hated life.
But oh, my friend, like PEDRO to expire,
Or feel the pangs of slow-consuming fire,—
These are most terrible!—
JUMBA.
    A ling'ring pain
Thou fear'st, and yet canst bear thy servile chain! 60
Canst bear incessant toil, and want of food,
Canst bear the Driver's lash to drink thy blood!
Say, doom'd to these, what now does life supply
But ling'ring pain, which must at length destroy?
—Yet go, poor timid wretch, go fawn and grieve: 65
And as those gashes heal, still more receive:
Go, and submit, like oxen to the wain;—
But never say thou fear'st a ling'ring pain.
ADOMA.
Thy charge is just. But, friend, there still remain
Two ways to free us from this galling chain.   70
Sure we can bid our various sorrows cease
By quitting life, or how, or when we please:
Or we can quickly fly these cruel whites
By seeking shelter on the mountains' heights,
Where wild hogs dwell, where lofty Cocoas grow, 75
And boiling streams of purest waters flow.
There we might live; for thou with skilful hand
Canst form the bow, and jav'lin, of our land.
There we might freely roam, in search of food,
Up the steep crag, or through the friendly wood, 80
There we might find—
JUMBA.
    Alas! thou dost not know
The King of all those mountains is our foe; [k]
His subjects num'rous, and their chief employ

48

To hunt our race, when fled from slavery.
Lur'd by the hope of gain such arts are tried,   85
No rocks can cover us, no forests hide.
Against us evn' the chatt'ring Birds combine,
And aid those hunters in their curs'd design:
For oft, through them, [l] the fugitives are caught,
And, strongly pinion'd, to their tyrants brought.   90
O'er vale, or mountain, thus where'er we go,
The suff'ring Negro surely finds a foe.
     ADOMA.
Ah, JUMBA, worse, much worse our wretched state,
Thus vex'd, thus harass'd, than that fishes [m] fate,
Which frequent we beheld when wafted o'er   95
The great rough water from our native shore.
He, as the tyrants of the deep pursu'd,
Would quit the waves their swiftness to elude,
And skim in air:—when lo! a bird of prey
Bends his strong wing, and bears the wretch away! 100
No refuge, then, but death—
    JUMBA.
       What! tamely die!
No! vengeance first shall fall on tyranny!
We'll view these white men gasping in their gore;—
Then let me perish! JUMBA asks no more.—
     ADOMA.
Oh! peace,—think where thou art; thy voice is high: 105
Quick drop the dang'rous theme.—My shed is nigh;
There my poor YARO will our rice prepare;—
I pray thee come.—
    JUMBA.
     Away, and take thy fare,
For me, I cannot eat,—haste to thy shed.
Farewell, be cautious,—think on what I've said.   110

End of the second ECLOGUE.

ECLOGUE THE THIRD.
―――――――――――
TIME—NOON.
―――――――――――

Now downward darts the fierce meridian ray,
And nature pants amid'st the blaze of day,

Though pitying Ocean, to her suff'rings kind,
Fans her warm bosom with his eastern wind.
Now the huge mountains charm the roving eye,   5
Their verdant summits tow'ring to the sky.
The cultur'd hill, the vale, the spreading plain,
The distant sea-worn beach, the ruffled main,
The anchoring Bark o'erspread with awnings white,
All, now appear in robes of dazzling light.   10
The feather'd race their gaudy plumes display,
And sport, and flutter, 'midst the glowing day.
The long-bill'd, humming tribes ⁿ now hover round,
And shew their tints where blossoms most abound.
With eyes intent on earth, well pois'd in air,   15
Now useful Vultures seek their fated fare,
Where curls the wave, the Pelican on high,
With beak enormous, and with piercing eye,
If chance he sees a watry tenant rise,
Now headlong drops and bears away his prize.   20
Now variegated flies their pinions spread;
And speckled Lizards start at ev'ry tread.
Now oxen to the shore in pond'rous wains,
Drag the rich produce of the juicy canes.
Now wearied Negroes to their sheds repair,   25
Or spreading tree, to take their scanty fare:
Whose hour expir'd, the shell ° is heard to blow,
And the sad tribe resume their daily woe.
'Twas now, beneath a Tam'rind's cool retreat,
Two sable friends thus mourn'd their wretched fate.   30
                    CONGO.
Oh QUAMINA! how roll'd the Suns away,
When thus upon our native soil we lay;
When we repos'd beneath the friendly shade,
And quaff'd our palmy wine, and round survey'd
Our naked offspring sporting free as air,   35
Our num'rous wives the chearing feast prepare:
Saw plenty smile around our cane-built sheds,
Saw Yams shoot up, and Cocoas lift their heads.
—But now ah! said reverse! our groans arise,
Forlorn and hopeless, far from all we prize: 40
Timid we tremble at our tyrants' frown,
And one vast load of mis'ry bends us down.
                    QUAMINA.
Yes,—those were times which we in vain may mourn,
Times which, my CONGO, never will return!

Times, e'er the scourge's hated sound was known,   45
Or hunger, toil, and stripes, had caus'd a groan.
Times, when with arrows arm'd, and trusty bow,
We oft repell'd each rude, invading, foe.
Times, when we chac'd the fierce-ey'd beasts of prey
Through tangled woods, which scarcely know the day: 50
When oft we saw, in spite of all his care,
The bulky Elephant ᴾ within our snare.
            CONGO.
Twelve moons are past, for still I mark them down,
Since the fell trading race attack'd our town;
Since we were seiz'd by that inhuman band,   55
Forc'd from our wives, our friends, and native land.
Twelve long, long moons they've been; and since that day
Oft have we groan'd beneath a cruel sway.
Oft has the taper'd scourge, where knots and wire
Are both combin'd to raise the torture higher,   60
Brought bloody pieces from each quiv'ring part,
Whilst tyrant whites have sworn 'twas dext'rous art.
            QUAMINA.
Sharks seize them all! their love of torture grows,
And the whole Island echoes with our woes.
Didst thou know JUMBA?—Some close, list'ning ear,   65
Heard him last eve denounce in terms severe,
Deep vengeance on these whites. In vain he fled:
This morn I saw him number'd with the dead!
            CONGO.
A fate so sudden!—And yet why complain?
The white mans pleasure is the Negroes pain.   70
            QUAMINA.
Didst thou e'er see, when hither first we came,
An ancient Slave, ANGOLA was his name?
Whose vig'rous years upon these hills were spent,
In galling servitude, and discontent:
He late, too weak to bear the weighty toil,   75
Which all endure who till this hated soil,
Was sent, as one grown useless on th' estate,
Far to the town to watch his Master's gate,
Or to the house each morn the fuel bring,
Or bear cool water from the distant spring: 80
With many a toil, with many a labour more,
Although his aged head was silver'd oer,
Although his body like a bow was bent,
And old, and weak, he totter'd as he went.

CONGO.

I knew him not,

QUAMINA.

Often, each labour sped,   85
Has he with aching limbs attain'd his shed.
Attain'd the spot, dejected and forlorn,
Where he might rest his aged head 'till morn:
Where, wearied out, he op'd the friendly door,
And, entring, prostrate sunk upon the floor.   90
Feeble and faint some moons he toil'd away;
(For trifles toil become as men decay)
When late beneath the driver's lash he fell,
And scourg'd, and tortur'd, bade the world farewell.

CONGO.

But why the scourge? Wherefore such needless rage?   95
Is there no pity, then, for weak old age?

QUAMINA.

'Twas part of his employ, with empty pail,
To crawl for water to a neighb'ring vale:
And as he homeward bore the liquid load,
With trembling steps along the rugged road,   100
His wither'd limbs denied their wonted aid:
—The broken vessel his mishap betray'd.
This his offence:—for this, thrown on the ground,
His feeble limbs outstretch'd, and strongly bound,
His body bare, each nerve convuls'd with pain,   105
I saw and pitied him—but ah! in vain.
Quick fell the lash: his hoary head laid low,
His eyes confess'd unutterable woe.
He sued for mercy: the big tear apace,
Stole down the furrows of his aged face.   110
His direful groans (for such they were indeed!)
Mix'd with his words when e'er he strove to plead,
And form'd such moving eloquence, that none
But flinty-hearted Christians could go on.
At length releas'd, they bore him to his shed: 115
Much he complain'd, and the next morn was dead.

CONGO.

And was this all? was this th' atrocious deed?
Which doom'd this hoary sufferer to bleed?
May ev'ry curse attend this pallid race,
Of earth the bane, of manhood the disgrace.   120
May their dread Judge, who, they pretend to say,
Rules the whole world with undivided sway,

May he (if such he hath) display his pow'r,
Poison their days, appall their midnight hour,
Bid them to fear his wrathful, stern, controul,   125
Pour his whole cup of trembling on their soul,
'Till they, repentant, these foul deeds forego, q
And feel their hearts distress'd with others' woe!

End of the third ECLOGUE.

ECLOGUE THE FOURTH.

TIME—MIDNIGHT.

WITH dreadful darkness now the Isle is crown'd,
And the fierce northern r tempest howls around.
Loud roars the surf; the rocks return the roar,
And liquid fire seems bursting on the shore.
Swift darts the light'ning in fantastic guise,   5
And bellowing thunder rolls along the skies.
Convuls'd, the big black clouds drop sheets of rain,
And uproar lords it o'er the dark domain.
At this dread hour, deep in an orange grove,
The said LOANGO mourn'd his absent love.   10
    "Three nights in this appointed gloom I've past,
"No QUAMVA comes,—and this shall be my last.
"Hoarse thunder, cease thy roar:—perchance she stays,
"Appall'd by thee, thou light'nings fiery blaze:
"'Tis past the hour:—chill North, thy blasts restrain,   15
"And thou, black firmament, hold up thy rain:
"Let QUAMVA come, my wife, my sole delight,
"Torn from my arms by that accursed white; s
"That pale-fac'd villain,—he, who through the day
"O'erlooks our toils, and rules with bloody sway;   20
"By him, who proud of lordship o'er the field,
"By daily tortures made my QUAMVA yield;
"Him, who has stol'n my treasure from my arms,
"And now perhaps, now riots on her charms!
"Oh! 'tis too much:—Come dark revenge and death;   25
"He bravely falls, who stops a tyrant's breath.
    "Roar on, fierce tempests:—Spirits of the air
"Who rule the storms, oh! grant my ardent pray'r.
"Assemble all your winds, direct their flight,

"And hurl destruction on each cruel White:— 30
"Sweep canes, and Mills, and houses to the ground,
"And scatter ruin, pain, and death around:—
"Rouse all your blasting fires, that lurk on high,
"And, 'midst his pleasures, let the plund'rer die!
"But spare my QUAMVA, who, with smother'd sighs, 35
"The odious rape endures, but not enjoys,
"Wishing the Tyrant's senses drown'd in sleep,
"That she enraptur'd may her promise keep.
"Oh! 'tis too much:—Come dark revenge, and death;
"He bravely falls, who stops a tyrant's breath. 40
    "Yet let me pause. 'Tis said that woman's mind
"Still changes like the Hurricane's fierce wind, ᵗ
"Ranging from man to man, as shifts the Bee,
"Or long-bill'd Humming-bird, from tree to tree.
"How if she like the White, his gaudy cloaths, 45
"His downy bed for pleasure and repose;
"His shrivel'd frame, his sickly pallid face;
"And finds a transport in his weak embrace.
"It may be so.—Oh! vengeance on her head,
"It is, it is:—She likes the Driver's bed. 50
"For this she stays.—Ye hidden scorpions creep,
"And with your pois'nous bites invade their sleep;
"Ye keen CENTIPEDES, oh! crawl around,
"Ye sharp-tooth'd Snakes, inflict your deadly wound.
"Fool that I was to think her woman's soul, 55
"The love of beads, and fin'ry could controul:
"Or think that one so beauteous would endure,
"My lowly bed, a mat upon the floor;
"My Yam, or Plantain, water from the spring,
"And the small bliss LOANGO's love could bring. 60
—"No, 'tis too plain:—Come dark revenge, and death,
"And steel my soul to stop a wanton's breath.
    "The MANCHINEEL, how beauteous to the sight,
"But ᵘ ah! how deadly to the appetite!
"Such woman is, that loveliest of ills; 65
"If seen she charms, if more than seen she kills.
"When forc'd by savage Whites from *Afric's* soil,
"And doom'd by them to cruelty and toil;
"Death was my early wish: but QUAMVA found,
"All my past woes were in possession drown'd. 70
"Oft when I came at eve oppress'd with woe,
"Gloomy, and weary from the lab'ring hoe,
"Can I forget each soft, each soothing, art

"Which QUAMVA us'd to chear my drooping heart?
"Can I forget, 'though she my toil had shar'd,   75
"How soon the scanty viands were prepar'd?
"Oh! never:—but those blissful days are o'er;
"QUAMVA is false, and I am blest no more!
"QUAMVA is false:—Come dark revenge, and death,
"And steel my soul to stop a wanton's breath.   80
   "Glad through the herbage sport the reptile kind,
"To food and pleasure are their nights consign'd.
"Swift with his mate the bird unbounded flies,
"And on his native hills the bliss enjoys.
"Not so LOANGO:— he from peaceful plains   85
"Where plenty dwells, and no curs'd white restrains,
"Was dragg'd o'er wat'ry regions to this Isle,
"And doom'd to slavery, torture, want, and toil.
"Yet these I bore, while QUAMVA cheer'd my pains:—
"But QUAMVA's lost, and nought but death remains.   90
"Three long, long nights still absent! 'Tis too plain,
"The white man pleases, and my hopes are vain.
"Come then, revenge, and 'midst this horrid roar
"My thirsty knife shall drink their streaming gore.
"Come, swiftly come, and aid me to surprise   95
"These guilty lovers acting o'er their joys;
"Just then—great *Afric*'s Gods!—to strike the blow!
"Just then—what transports would the stroke bestow!
"Just then—my brain's on fire!—Come, pointed blade,
"And poor LOANGO's vengeance justly aid. ˣ   100
"Three, three must fall! for Oh! I'll not survive;
"I dread the white men's gibbeting alive,
"Their wiry tortures, and their ling'ring fires:—
"These he escapes, who by the knife expires.
"Come, then, revenge!—The deed will soon be o'er,   105
"And then LOANGO views his native shore;
"Rides on the fleeting clouds through airy roads,
"Nor stops 'till plac'd in *Afric's* bless'd abodes.
"Come pointed blade;—the Tyrant's house is nigh:—
"And now for vengeance, death, and liberty!—"   110

Then to the place, with frenzy fir'd, he fled,
And the next morn beheld the mangled dead!—

FINIS.

NOTES.

ECLOGUE I.

[a] Myriads of these reptiles nightly prowl through the woods, in search of prey; and, at the approach of morn, retire to their lurking places. Their out-cry is remarkbly shrill; but, when softened by distance, to some ears is not disagreeable.

[b] The wind blows gently from the land, in *Jamaica*, towards the sea in every direction, throughout the evening, and night; and continues to blow in the same manner until about the hour of nine in the morning. After that time the heat would soon become intolerable, were it not tempered by a brisk, refreshing, gale from the sea, which almost instantly succeeds the land-breeze. It is first seen to approach the shore in a fine, small, black curl, agitating the water; whilst that part of the sea, at which it hath not yet arrived, is calm and smooth. In the space of half an hour after it has reached the shore, it blows with some briskness, increases in strength until noon, and dies away by degrees about five in the afternoon; and it returns not until the following morning. This sea-breeze checks the fierce rays of the sun, chears the panting inhabitants, and renders this, and the neighbouring Islands, a supportable residence for Europeans.

[c] Three, and sometimes four, weeks are allowed for the recovery of the female slaves after child-bed. They are then sent into the field, and toil in common with their fellow-slaves; the infant being either carried on the back of it's mother, or placed on the ground near to the spot where she is directed to work.

[d] Though the Negro-drivers on this Island, are in general black-men, yet sometimes a subordinate European is stationed on the field, in order to superintend the whole. Wishing to ingratiate himself with his superiors, and to gain the reputation of being active and vigilant, he daily, under the mask of what is termed *necessary discipline*, inflicts the severest punishments, for the most trifling offences. The cow-skin, which is in common use, is a durable whip, composed of the tapered slips of cow or buffalo-hide, twisted to a point; to which is added, such a lash as the *tormentors* may think the best fitted for what they in a facetious tone have been heard to term, *cutting up the black-birds*.

[e] The *Fetish* or *Fetiche*, is a name given by the negroes to their deities: some of whom are supposed (in *Guinea*) to preside over whole provinces, and others, of an inferior rank, over single families only. These supposed divinities are sometimes trees, the head of an ape, or bird, or any other object of a wild fancy; but they are held by the negroes in the highest veneration.

[f] When the body of the unhappy sufferer is cut into furrows by the operation of the lash, it is frequently scourged a second time with a branch of the *Eben*,

strongly beset with sharp thorns. This greatly increases the torments of the sufferer; but it is said to let out the congealed blood, and to prevent a mortification. The last step of this process of cruelty, is to wash the mangled wretch with a kind of pickle; or to throw him headlong into the sea, the effect of the salt-water being supposed to be nearly equal to that of the pickle.

g WHEN the bodies of the negroes are covered with blood, and their flesh torn to pieces with the driver's whip, beaten pepper, and salt, are frequently thrown on the wounds, and a large stick of sealing-wax dropped down, in flames, leisurely upon them.

ECLOGUE II.

h THE *fire-fly* seems to be a species of the beetle. Under it's belly, and on each side of it's head, near the eyes, are certain prominent, circular, parts, which appear to be of a green colour in the day, but in the night-season emit a clear, strong, light. For some time after the death of this fly, it's body will still glow, and shine, in the dark; but not so powerfully as when alive. These flies live in rotten trees, and other places of concealment, in the day; but always come abroad in the night, and are sometimes so numerous as to illuminate the whole atmosphere.

i A PUNISHMENT not uncommon in the *West-Indies*. Some of the miserable sufferers have been known to exist a week in this most dreadful situation. (See a most affecting account of one instance of this kind, in the Rev. Mr. RAMSAY's Treatise.)

k WHEN this Island of *Jamaica* was surrendered to the *English*, in A. D. 1655, and the *Spaniards* themselves had retired to *Cuba*, the *Spanish* slaves were induced by magnificent promises, from their late masters, of speedy and effectual assistance, to retire to the strong fastnesses of the mountains, and to bid defiance to the *English* power. By the wise, and vigorous measures of Colonel D'OYLEY, the first Governor of *Jamaica*, (a cavalier, who had greatly distinguished himself by his courage, and conduct, in the civil wars) the power of these rebellious Negroes was soon so broken, as to be thought by many an object of small, or no concern. D'OYLEY, indeed, protested against this conclusion, and urged the necessity of improving the past successes of the *English* into a compleat, and decisive, subjugation of the revolters: but he was over-ruled. The consequence of this improvident conduct was,—that the small remnant of these revolted slaves, being gradually joined by others from the plantations below, soon made the mountains again terrible to the planters; whom they harrassed with continual, and frequently formidable, attacks for nearly a whole century. At length, in or about the year 1740, a peace was concluded with them by the Hon. EDWARD TRELAWNEY, then governor of the Island:—by the terms of which they were declared free. They were allowed to have a chief to govern them; but he was to be restrained from taking any important measure, without the consent of the governor of the Island. Several white-men were admitted, by the treaty, to live among the late revolters, to observe their actions. But the chief service expected from them, was, and still is,—to bring back to the planters those wretches, whom hunger, or cruelty, forces to the mountains for shelter. They are allowed a premium for every fugitive they restore, and are remarkably vigilant in their employment.

[l] CERTAIN birds, commonly called in *Jamaica* black-birds, frequent the inmost recesses of the woods; and at the sight of a human being, they begin a loud and continual clamour which is heard at a considerable distance. Their noise serves as a guide to the mountain-hunters, who immediately penetrate into that part of the wood, and seize the fugitives.

[m] THE *flying fish* (the *hirundo*, or *mugil alatus*, of some authors, and the *exocætus volitans* of the Phil. Trans. vol. 68, part 2d. page 791) has two long fins, which in some degree perform the office of wings. It is about the size of a herring, and of the same shape. When this Fish is pursued, in his native element, by the *Dolphin*, he springs out of the water, and skims above the surface to a considerable distance. Yet even here he is not safe. The *Albitrosses*, *Sea-gulls*, and other aquatic birds, are frequently seen to fall upon, and seize, him in his flight. Should he even escape these (which indeed he frequently does) as soon as his wings, or rather fins, become dry, he drops, and is instantly swallowed by his watry foe; who, during this aerial excursion, eyes him askance, keeping exactly under him: and, while thus pursuing, changes colour in so extraordinary a manner, as to form one of the most beautiful objects in nature. The *Bonetta*, or *Bonita*, is another enemy to this fish. It is a species of the *Tunny* or *Traclurus*: somewhat like a cod-fish, but much larger, and more beautiful.

ECLOGUE III.

[n] THE *humming-bird (Trochilus,* or *guainumbi)* is admirable for it's beauty, shape, smell, and for the whole of it's mode of existence. In flying it makes a noise exactly like the humming of a bee (from whence it takes it's name) and indeed is not much larger than the humble-bee. It is the least, and yet the most beautiful, of all birds. The colours of the feathers in it's neck, and wing, represent those of the rain-bow. Some of these birds have a vivid redness under their necks, which exceeds the finest carbuncle. The colour of the belly, and the under-part of the wings, is a bright yellow; the thighs are as green as an emerald; the feet, and beak, black as polished ebony, and the head of a fine sea-green colour. It makes a louder noise, in it's flight, than some of the largest birds. And it seems to delight in flying near the faces of travellers; whom it surprises in passing, like a little whirlwind. It's tongue is hollow like a reed,

but not larger than a small needle; which, as it can sustain itself a long time on the wing, it thrusts into the blossoms of the flowers, by the juice's of which it is fed, and supported. The only method of taking these beautiful creatures is to shoot at them with sand, which stuns them. But all die that are taken by this, or any other method; for no human art can supply them with their ordinary food.

[o] A LARGE *Conch* shell is used in some plantations to summon the slaves to their labour. On others the call is made by a bell.

[p] WHEN the Elephant's regular path to the neighbouring river is discovered, the Negroes in *Africa* dig a pit across it; in the center of which is fixed a sharp-pointed stake, of a large size. About an inch below the surface of the ground a platform is made, over this pit, of slips of cane, and small boughs of trees, upon which are placed the green sods of earth which had been before carefully taken up for that purpose. The huge animal, careless and inoffensive, comes slowly onward, cropping perhaps the pendent branches of the trees on each side of his path: when the first step that he takes on this deceitful covering, plunges him headlong into the pit, where if he be not transfixed by the pointed stake, the Negroes rush from their concealment, and with their javelins soon put an end to his existence.

[q] SOME few plantations on this island might be enumerated, where by kind and judicious treatment, the *Africans* have so far multiplied, as to render the purchase of new Negroes (as they are termed) altogether unnecessary. Might not this become general?—The same causes, if suffered to operate fully as they ought, would universally produce the same effects. Setting aside every motive of humanity, sound policy naturally dictates such proceedings as these. And a few, and those not expensive, encouragements held forth to this dejected race, would produce the desired effect: such as the allowance of more ease, and better food, to the Negroes; and a grant of particular privileges, nay even of freedom, to those mothers who have brought up a certain number of children. And the expence of such humane provisions, as well as the temporary abatement (if any should happen) in the exertions of any given number of slaves, would soon be amply repaid, even to the largest plantation, by the savings of the money usually expended in the annual purchase of fresh slaves, and by the great, and acknowledged, superiority of home-born Negroes to those imported from *Africa.* I am indebted for many of these observations to the 17th Sermon of that most excellent Prelate, to whom, although unknown to him, I have ventured to inscribe this little work: a discourse, in which the clearness of the understanding, is only to be surpassed by the goodness of the heart, of the Preacher; a discourse which abounds in philanthropy, and enforces humanity upon the most powerful motives, because it is dictated by the genuine principles of the Christian Religion.

ECLOGUE IV.

[r] IN our winter months the common trade-wind is frequently interrupted by heavy storms from the northward; which, on that side of the island, in particular, where the bays, and the plantations, are exposed to their violence, do immense damage. Thunder is not very frequent at *Jamaica*; but when it happens, it is astonishingly loud, and terrible.

[s] THIS cruel practice of the white master, or driver, in forcing the wives of the Negroes to a compliance, cannot be too severely reprobated. It has produced the most fatal consequences in every part of the *West-Indies*. One instance, which occurred in *Jamaica*, shall be particularly mentioned. In the first skirmishes which happened with the *Spaniards*, after the *English* obtained possession of the Island, those *Spanish* slaves, in general, who had deserted from their former masters, fought under the *English* banners with great courage. One slave, in particular, was observed, by Colonel D'OYLEY, the then *English* governor, to have exerted himself with uncommon intrepidity, and to have killed several *Spaniards* in close engagement. On inquiry it was found that this Negro had loved a young female slave to distraction; that he had been married to her for some years before the *English* invaded the Island; and that a short time before that invasion the tyrant, his master, had barbarously torn her from him, and compelled her to submit to his rapacious will. The injured husband implored, and remonstrated: and he was answered—by the whip. The disturbances, consequent upon the *English* invasion, afforded him an opportunity of an interview with his beloved wife. He told her, in a few words, that he still loved her with too sincere a passion, not to be sensible of what he had lost; but as their former days of love, and purity, could never return, he would not live to see her another's, when she could not be his own; for that, however innocent she might be in intention, he never could take an adulteress into his arms. "*Thus, therefore*" (says he) "*I now exert the rights of a husband.*"—and plung'd his poniard into her heart! He immediately fled to the *English*. And, in his first engagement with his former masters, having observed his cruel tyrant in the *Spanish* line, he flew to the place where he fought, and soon laid him, with several other *Spaniards*, at his feet. Colonel D'OYLEY declared him free, on the field of battle; and accompanied the grant of his freedom with the gift of a small plantation, upon which he lived ever afterwards in quiet, but with a thoughtfulness, and melancholy, which he could never overcome. He survived to a very advanced term of life, dying in the year 1708. His son behaved with the utmost gallantry against the *French*, in their invasion of *Jamaica* in A. D. 1695; and hazarded his life, on several occasions, against the mountain-Negroes, whilst they continued in rebellion.

[t] HURRICANES are so called from the *Indian* word *hurica*, which signifies the Devil. Immediately previous to this furious storm, the sea becomes calm on

a sudden; then the air instantly becomes darkened (even at noon-day) with thick, and pitchy clouds. Soon the sky seems on fire with horrible lightenings. Then follow dreadful claps of thunder; and the winds immediately succeed with such impetuous force, that they root up the strongest trees, overthrow the firmest houses; and destroy every thing within their vortex. They usually begin in the north; but within the compass of a very few hours, they traverse the whole round of the Heavens, and blow from every point of the compass.

ᵘ The *manchineel-tree (hippomane)* is very large; it's apple is beautiful to the eye, (being in appearance somewhat like a rich golden pippin) agreeable to the smell, and pleasant to the taste. But if eaten in large quantitites, it is certain death. The savages use the sap of this tree to poison their arms, the wounds of which are thereby rendered mortal. The drops of rain, which fall from it's leaves, raise blisters upon the human body in the most surprizing manner. These trees are in the vegetable, what Lions, and Tygers, are in the animal, kingdom. They make entire deserts in their neighbourhood. Even the shade of these trees is said to be fatal to those who sit long under them, unless their ill effects are timely prevented by proper applications. (Phil. Trans. vol. 50, p. 772.)

ˣ The desire of revenge is an impetuous, a ruling passion, in the minds of these *African* slaves. *"Being heathens not only in their hearts, but in their lives, and knowing no distinction between vice and virtue, they give themselves up freely to the grossest immoralities, without being even conscious they are doing wrong."* (Bishop of *Chester*'s Sermon, before quoted.) But were it necessary, many instances might be adduced to shew, that some Negroes are capable of kind, nay even of heroic, actions. The story of Quashi, related by Mr. Ramsay, is one signal proof of this assertion. Another can be given by the Author of these Eclogues; who was preserved from destruction by the humanity of a Negro slave. His deliverance, however, was purchased at a price which he must ever deplore. For, in saving his life, the brave, the generous, *African* lost his own!

F I N I S.

The NEGLECTED TARS *of* BRITAIN

(1787)

I SING the British seaman's praise;
   A theme renown'd in story;
It well deserves more polish'd lays,
   Oh! 'tis your boast and glory.
When mad-brain'd War spreads death around,   5
   By them you are protected;
But when in peace the nation's found,
   These bulwarks are neglected.
       Then, oh! protect the hardy tar,
         Be mindful of his merit,   10
       And when again you're plung'd in war,
         He'll shew his daring spirit.

When thickest darkness covers all,
   Far on the trackless ocean;
When lightnings dart; when thunders roll,   15
   And all is wild commotion;
When o'er the bark the white-topp'd waves,
   With boistrous sweep are rolling,
Yet coolly still the whole he braves,
   Untam'd amidst the howling.   20
       Then, oh! protect, &c.

When deep immers'd in sulphurous smoke,
   He feels a glowing pleasure;
He loads his gun—he cracks his joke,
   Elated beyond measure.   25
Though fore and aft the blood-stain'd deck:
   Should lifeless trunks appear;
Or should the vessel float a wreck,
   The sailor knows no fear.
       Then, oh! protect, &c.   30

When long becalm'd, on southern brine,
   Where scorching beams assail him:
When all the canvas hangs supine,

And food and water fail him;
Then oft he dreams of Britain's shore,   35
 Where plenty still is reigning,
They call the watch—his rapture's o'er,
 He sighs—but scorns complaining.
   Then, oh! protect, &c.

Or burning on that noxious coast   40
 Where death so oft befriends him;
Or pinch'd by hoary Greenland frost,
 True courage still attends him:
No clime can this eradicate;
 He glories in annoyance;   45
He fearless braves the storms of fate,
 And bids grim death defiance.
   Then, oh! protect, &c.

Why should the man who knows no fear
 In peace be then neglected?   50
Behold him move along the pier,
 Pale, meagre, and dejected!
Behold him begging for employ!
 Behold him disregarded!
Then view the anguish in his eye,   55
 And say, are tars rewarded?
   Then, oh! protect, &c.

To them your dearest rights you owe;
 In peace then would you starve them?
What say, ye Britain's sons?—Oh, no!   60
 Protect them and preserve them.
Shield them from poverty and pain,
 'Tis policy to do it;
Or when grim War shall come again,
 Oh, Britons, ye may rue it!   65
   Then, oh! protect, &c.

NEGLECTED GENIUS: OR, TRIBUTARY STANZAS TO THE MEMORY OF THE UNFORTUNATE CHATTERTON.

(1787)

INTRODUCTION.

HOWEVER *opposite the Opinions of the learned may have been, concerning the Poems attributed to* ROWLEY, *though some have strenuously contended, that they were written by a Monk in the Fifteenth Century; whilst others have clearly proved, that they are the extraordinary Productions of our own Times; yet, there is one Particular in which several of these rusty Champions have most cordially agreed, that is, to vilify the Memory of the unfortunate* CHATTERTON. *One celebrated Antiquarian has not scrupled to assert, that "all of the House of Forgery are Relations;" and "that though it be but just to* CHATTERTON's *Memory, to say, that his Poverty never made him claim Kindred with the most enriching Branches; yet, that he who could so ingeniously counterfeit Styles, and the Assertor, believes Hands, might easily have been led to the more facile Imitation of prose Promissory Notes, &c." How cruel must such an Insinuation appear, to those who are in the least acquainted with the Story of this wonderful Boy; particularly when we reflect, that this Honourable Gentleman was himself a literary Forger.*

Another, eminent for his historical Abilities, has informed us, that CHATTERTON *was a* PRODIGY OF GENIUS, *and that, in all Probability, he would have proved the First of English Poets; yet in the very same Sentence we are told, without the least Shadow of Truth, that he was an* UNPRINICPLED HIRELING. *A Third, who is a Preacher of that mild Religion which censures all Uncharitableness, has taken every Opportunity to stigmatise him, as an* ILLITERATE CHARITY BOY, DISSOLUTE, PROFLIGATE, *and* LICENTIOUS. — *Such are the Flowers, which these Men of Taste and Erudition have so profusely scattered over the Grave of this highly-gifted Genius; but their Malignities have proved ineffectual. A* CROFT, *a* HAYLEY, *and a* KNOX, *have moistened many an Eye upon this Subject; and a* TYRWHITT *has clearly proved that the Poems, which bear the Name of* ROWLEY, *are entirely the Inventions of this surprising Youth; yes, the Controversy is finished, and the Wreath is now placed upon the Brow of* CHATTERTON! *where it will continue to bloom, when the Works which contain those illiberal Expressions, and the learned Heads which fabricated them, are most deservedly forgotten.* CHATTERTON, *no* doubt, had Foibles; perhaps he had Faults; and which of his grave Accusers are without them? But he little merited those uncharitable Epithets which have been so liberally bestowed upon him. He was neither dissolute, unprincipled, profligate, nor licentious; but, on the contrary, according to the Testimony of his Mother and Sister, of Mr. LAMBERT, the Attorney, whom he was with at BRISTOL, and of his most intimate Acquaintance, we are informed, that he was dutiful, affectionate, honest, remarkably temperate, never absent from his Master's Office, during the Time allotted for Attendance, which was from Eight in the Morning, 'till the same Hour in the evening; nor was he ever known to stay out at Night after the appointed Hour, which was Ten o' Clock, except once, when he spent the Evening, with some Company, at his Mother's. Here then, ye sober Scholars, or rather ye formal Owls, who have thus fallen upon a poor dead Nightingale, and with the sharp Talons of Invective have endeavoured to mangle him in so cruel a Manner. Here then, let me ask you, Is this the Character of an unprincipled Profligate? No! It is the Character of the poor unfortunate CHATTERTON! given by those who knew him best; and Shame upon the Heads, however aged, or however eminent for Abilities, who have thus wantonly traduced One of the sweetest Bards, that ever appeared in this, or any other Country.

It would exceed the Limits of this little Performance, to give even a Sketch of CHATTERTON's Existence; suffice it to say, he was the Son of a Sexton, born at BRISTOL, NOVEMBER 20th, 1752, was remarkably dull at learning his Letters; in his Eighth Year, was admitted into a Charity School in that City; about the Age of Ten, a Love for Literature took Possession of his Soul; between Eleven and Twelve, he began to write Verses. In JULY, 1767, he was articled to an Attorney, with whom he continued 'till APRIL, 1770, when he left BRISTOL, for LONDON; where, on the 24th of AUGUST following, when he wanted Three Months of compleating his Eighteenth Year, he put an End to his Existence, by swallowing Arsenic in Water. It is not my Intention to justify this rash Act, but I will venture to say, with the celebrated Essayist Mr. KNOX, that he (CHATTERTON) "had all the tremulous Sensibility of Genius, all its Eccentricity, all its Pride, and all its Spirit; and that even his Death, unfortunate and wicked as it was, displayed a Magnitude of Soul, which induced him to spurn a World, where even his exalted Abilities could not vindicate him from Contempt, Indigence, and Contumely."

T' insult the Dead, is cruel and unjust.   —ODYSSEY

O THOU! who many a silent Hour
   Sat'st brooding o'er thy Plans profound;
O CHATTERTON! thou fairest Flower
   That ever grac'd poetic Ground:
'Twas thine, in Lyrics sweet and strong,   5
To bear th' enraptur'd Soul along;
'Twas thine, to touch domestic Woe,
And make the Drops of Pity flow;

'Twas thine, in HOMER's glowing Strain,
 To paint Contention's bloody Reign: 10
And Oh! 'twas thine, with unfledg'd Wings to soar
Upborne by native Fire, to Heights untry'd before.

 In lonely Paths, and Church Yards drear,
  When shrowded pale-ey'd Ghosts are seen,
 When many a wild Note strikes the Ear,   15
  From Fairies rev'ling on the Green:
 Then didst thou oft, with daring Fire,
 Sweep o'er the seeming Gothic Lyre;
a Then, whilst the broad Moon lent her Aid,
 To Times long past, thy Fancy stray'd;   20
 Then HASTINGS' Field was heap'd with dead,
 And BIRTHA mourn'd, and BALDWIN bled:
Yet what, alas! did all thy Pow'rs produce?
Why, when on Earth, Neglect! when in the Grave, Abuse!

 When all is hush'd, full oft to thee,   25
  Poor Child of Song, I sorrowing turn;
 Full oft bewail thy Misery,
  Full oft with Indignation burn:
 Gods! that a Genius such as thine,
 Equal to every vast Design;   30
 A Genius, form'd in SHAKESPEAR's Mould,
 Uncolleg'd, piercing, clear, and bold;
 Should find, in these enlighten'd Times,
 (When Bards are known from Men of Rhimes)
On BRITISH Ground, but cold Neglect and Woe, 35
And Envy's cankering Stings, when in the Grave below.

 But let Defamers rail their Fill,
  Throw weak Detraction on thy Name;
 Yet thou, who mock'd their learned Skill,
  Shall be for ever dear to Fame: 40
 Where Genius animates the Soul,
 Th' impetuous Fire disdains controul;
 No Want of Languages, or Rules,
 Nor all the pedant Pride of Schools;
 No Lack of Friends, nor Fortune's Frown,   45
 Can keep the mighty Magic down:
O wond'rous CHATTERTON! untimely lost,
Natures' unequal'd Work, and ENGLAND's Shame and Boast.

Compassion, o'er thy much-lov'd Clay,
    Shall duly drop the briny Tear;   50
Shall duly brush the Weeds away
    Which Pride and Envy scatter there:
Say, WALPOLE, Honourable Sage!
What Right hadst thou to brand the Page?
Why reprobate the great Design?   55
b Was not OTRANTO's forgery thine?
    But, tell me, What wouldst thou have thought,
    Had some rude Soul, with Venom fraught,
For that Offence attack'd thy Name, and cry'd
Beware the Felon's Fate, All Forgeries are ally'd.   60

When too, thou pierc'd the antique Cloak,
    And plainly trac'd the modern Hand;
Thou must have seen each beauteous Stroke,
    Each Charm that will for Ages stand:
And if thou didst, Why not enquire   65
Who thus could touch the sounding Lyre?
Why not, (if Excellence was plain,
If native Genius mark'd the Strain?)
Why not, from ROWLEY take the Praise,
And crown the minstrel Boy with Bays?   70
c Why not? 'twas Pride, thou saw'st his lowly State,
And Bards unborn, for this, thy Name shall execrate.

Lank Penury, thou chilling Sprite,
    Who fling'st Dejection o'er the Mind;
Who, with a Cloud of thickest Night,   75
    Veil'st many a Genius from Mankind;
Ah! little boots the Poet's Art,
That melts and animates the Heart;
If at his Side, with haggard Mein,
And palsied Step, thy Form is seen;   80
Genius, in tatter'd Garments deck'd,
Howe'er sublime, must feel Neglect:
But mark the World, let wealthy Witlings raise
The decorated Lyre, and all applaud the Lays.

Ye BRISTOL Patrons! but the Muse   85
    Disdains to brand a petty Train;
Disdains such Pigmies to accuse,
d   While Giant WHARTON claims the Strain:
    Yes, he whose learn'd historic Page,

Illumines many a darken'd Age;   90
He, who has crown'd with ardent Praise,
A CHATTERTON's unrivalled Lays;
E'en he has join'd th' invidious Cry,
And swell'd the Tide of Calumny:
Has rais'd, indeed, the Youth's poetic Fame,   95
But with a Charge unjust has damn'd his moral Name.

    Thou too, with antiquarian Eyes,
      Illiberal Critic, proudly mean;
    Thou Pattern for unjust Surmise,
e   Thou harsh, uncharitable Dean: 100
    Great Judge of Diction obsolete,
    Say, could'st not thou of ROWLEY treat,
    And lift his various Beauties high,
    Without traducing BRISTOL's Boy?
    Why fling thy sacerdotal Dirt   105
    On him who never did thee Hurt?
On him, who spurn'd a World where Scoffs abound,
Where Genius often droops, whilst Dulness lords it round.

    O CHATTERTON! ill fated Boy,
      In Poverty's low Mansion born;   110
    Nurs'd on the Lap of Charity,
      And sent to humble Pedants' Scorn:
    Such were the Friends thy Genius found,
    Where Science, Taste and Arts abound;
    Such fill'd thy scanty Days with Crimes,   115
    Because thou mimick'd monkish Rhymes;
f Yes, "Swotie Nyghte Larke," this was all
    Thou didst to merit ranc'rous Gall:
Gav'st to a barb'rous Age thy matchless Lays,
Haply to claim thine own, when crown'd with Learning's Praise.   120

    If this was Guilt, by yon bright Heaven,
      From whence thy tow'ring Genius came;
    To me had Powers like thine been given,
      Like thee would I have soar'd to Fame:
    For oh! by Intuition wise,   125
    'Twas thine to look through Man's Disguise;
    Thou saw'st with Penetration strong,
    That e'en thine own exalted Song,
g If giv'n as thine, (a Sexton's Son
    Who knew no Language but his own)   130

Would ne'er, through Prejudice, arrive at Fame,
'Twas therefore greatly judg'd to fix on ROWLEY's Name.

O Poesy! delusive Power!
 Thou Ignis Fatuus of the Soul;
Thou Syren of the solemn Hour,   135
 That 'lures full oft to Scenes of Dole;
Oh, how seducing are thy Smiles,
How powerful all thy 'witching Wiles;
Yet in the Foldings of thy Train
Lurk squalid Want, and mental Pain;   140
See, where thy wretched Victim lies,
 What frantic Wildness in his Eyes:
Hark! how he groans! see! see! he foams! he gasps!
And his convulsive Hand the pois'nous Phial grasps.

Stung by the World's Neglect and Scorn,   145
 While conscious Merit fir'd his Mind;
h Unfriended, foodless, and forlorn,
 With low'ring Eye the Bard reclin'd:
When lo! his Mantle cover'd o'er
With streaming and with clotted Gore;   150
The Offspring of Despair and Pride,
 Came stalking in, fell SUICIDE;
In wild Disorder o'er his Head,
 Full many a pois'nous Weed was spread:
And now his Purpose dire, his blood-stain'd Eyes, 155
And rugged Front, were veil'd in soft Compassion's Guise.

Rous'd from his Gloom, aghast and wild,
 "Ah! what art thou?" the Minstrel cried;
With wily Tongue, and Aspect mild,
 "Thy Guardian Power," the Shade replied,   160
"Sweet Bard, ah! why dost thou remain
"On this vile Orb, this Scene of Pain?
"Art thou not steep'd in black'st Woe?
"Hast thou a single Patron? No;
"Or can thy sweetly sounding Lyre   165
"Make stern Necessity retire?
"If not, be firm, these sordid Reptiles spurn,
"(Oh, Phœbus glowing Son) and to thy Sire return.'"

Stung to the Soul, the hapless Boy
 With greedy Ears the Sounds devour'd;   170

This the grim Phantom saw with Joy,
 And still the wordy Poison pour'd:
'Till slackening every selfish Spring
Which makes us to Existence cling;
"Would I a worthless World adorn,"   175
He cried, "that merits but thy Scorn?
"No, Misery's Son, this Cordial take,
"And Want, Neglect, and Pain forsake:"
With pale distracted Look, the Youth complied,
Tore many a beauteous Lay, and in wild Ravings died.   180

Unshelter'd, wither'd, scarcely blown,
 Thus like a blasted Flower he fell;
Thus pin'd, unnotic'd, or unknown,
 Thus bade a sorrowing Scene farewell:
Here gaze, ye gloomy querulous Train,   185
And ye immers'd in real Pain;
Here gaze, and combat with Distress,
All ye once known to Happiness;
Here gaze, ye glowing Sons of Song,
i Whom haply cold Neglect has stung;   190
And when Ideas black and sad arise,
Should Suicide appear, O spurn him, and be wise!

Thus headlong rush'd th' indignant Soul
 From Earth, where Tides of Rancour flow,
Where Folly's Sons in Affluence roll,   195
 And Merit droops, o'erwhelm'd with Woe:
Ye gen'rous Minds, if such there are,
Who make neglected Worth, your Care;
Where dwelt you, when he gaz'd around,
And not One Gleam of Comfort found?   200
Oh! what a Deed! what endless Fame
Had 'twin'd around that Mortal's Name,
Who, from Despair, had snatch'd this wond'rous Boy,
Foster'd his tow'ring Muse, and flush'd his Soul with Joy.

And One there was, yes, Fancy's Child,   205
 When thou the grisly Form obey'd;
k One Reverend Sage, humane and mild,
 Was then on Wing to give thee Aid:
And scarcely had the Parish Shell
Convey'd thee to the cold dank Cell;   210
When lo! he came! O piteous Tale!

But Pity! what wilt thou avail?
He came, by Love of Genius led,
Intent to raise thy drooping Head:
He came, he sigh'd, and down the Stream of Time,   215
For this, his Praise shall flow in many a splendid Rhyme.

Borne to the Grave, without a Friend,
l The Workhouse "Glebe" receiv'd thy Clay;
Thus did thy Scrap of Breathing end,
 But oh! thy Fame will ne'er decay: 220
E'en RADCLIFF, and her flowery Plains,
Where thou has ponder'd o'er thy Strains;
Thy natal Roof, and clay cold Bed,
With many a noisome Weed o'erspread;
When thy proud Scorners are no more,   225
And Moths have knaw'd their pedant Lore:
E'en these, the Sons of Fancy will revere,
Sigh o'er thy mournful Fate and drop the sorrowing Tear.

And now, where'er thy Spirit stalks,
 Great Framer of the antique Lay;   230
Whether thou haunts thy favourite Walks,
 Or hover'st o'er thy Bed of Clay:
Whether, with SAVAGE at thy Side,
Thou blam'st the World's Contempt and Pride;
Whether thou talk'st with OTWAY's Shade   235
Of all the Misery Life display'd;
Or glid'st in gloomy 'Guise along,
Aloof from all the ghastly Throng:
From One, inur'd to many a mental Pain,
O deign, immortal Youth! t' accept this heart-felt Strain.   240

a His Mother and Sister have heard him say, that he found he studied best towards the full of the Moon, and that he would often sit up all Night, and write *by Moonlight*.

b When the Castle of OTRANTO first made its Appearance, the Public were solemnly informed, that it was found in an ancient Catholic Family, in the North of ENGLAND, and, that it was printed in the black Letter, at NAPLES, 1529. Yet, in the Preface to the Second Edition, the real Author, this very Mr. WALPOLE, hopes he stands excused for having offered his Work to the World under the borrowed Title of a Translator. Where then is the mighty Difference betwixt this, and the Forgery of ROWLEY? The One, is said to be found in an ancient Family in the North of ENGLAND; the Other, in an ancient Chest, in RADCLIFF Church; the One, printed at NAPLES, above Two Hundred Years ago; the other, written by a Monk in the Fifteenth Century. From these Circumstances a common Observer would imagine, that both Writers were in the same Predicament; but mark the Influence of Wealth and Situation; whilst the One, is nothing more than the innocent Artifice of an honourable Author, the Other, is loudly reprobated as the vile Forgery of an obscure Charity Boy.

c When Mr. WALPOLE refus'd to return some of Chatterton's Pieces, which the latter had sent for Persual, and even went to FRANCE without complying with his Request, CHATTERTON, on his Return, told him in a Letter, that "He would not have dar'd to treat him so ill, had he not been acquainted with the Narrowness of his Circumstances." This, tho' manly and spirited, Mr. WALPOLE was pleased to call *singularly impertinent.*

d In his History of English Poetry, this eminent literary Character has loudly extolled the Genius of CHATTERTON; yet, with an unaccountable Prejudice, and without offering one single Proof in Support of his Charge, he has been pleased to brand him with the Epithet—*unprincipled.*

e This Extoller of ROWLEY, and most inveterate Enemy of CHATTERTON, when speaking of the Ballad of *Charitie,* has an Observation to the following Effect:

"This Poem (says he) was written by ROWLEY, in the Character of a moral Satyrist, censuring the Pride and Want of Generosity in the wealthy Ecclesiastics of *those* Times."

Now, tho' I revere the Clergy, and think them in general Men of great Abilities and Humanity, yet, I fear, a Character not very unlike the Abbot of St. *Goodwin*'s Convent, as described by CHATTERTON, might be found among the wealthy Ecclesiastics, even of *these* Times.

f See Battle of Hastings, Part 2d, Page 581.

g In one of Chatterton's Letters there is the following Passage:—"A Gentleman, who knows me at the Chapter, as an Author, would have introduced me as a Companion to the young Duke of *Northumberland*:— but, alas! I speak no Tongue but my own."

h Mrs Angel, the Person with whom CHATTERTON lodged, at the Time he put an End to his Existence, knowing that he had not eaten any Thing for Two or Three Days, asked him, on the fatal 24th of *August,* to take some Dinner with her; but CHATTERTON was offended at her Invitation (which seemed to insinuate that he was in Want) and told her, he was not hungry.

i "They who are in a Condition to patronize Merit (says Mr. CROFT) and they who feel a consciousness of Merit which is not patronized, may form their own Resolutions from CHATTERTON's Tale: Those, to lose no Opportunity of befriending Genius; these, to seize every Opportunity of befriending themselves, and, upon no Account, to harbour the most distant Idea of quitting the World, however it may be unworthy of them, lest Despondency should at last deceive them into so unpardonable a step."

k The late Dr FRY, Head of St. *John's* College, *Oxford*, went to *Bristol*, on Purpose to enquire into the Particulars of ROWLEY's Poems, and to patronize CHATTERTON, should he prove the Author, or to deserve Encouragement; but, alas! he was too late! All he could learn of this astonishing Boy, was, that within a few Days he had poisoned himself in *London*.

l CHATTERTON, in his Ballad of *Charitie*, calls the Grave the *Church Glebe-house.*— He was interr'd in the Burial Ground of *Shoe-Lane* Work-House.

POOR BEN.

[*A Ballad founded on fact.*]

(1790)

I HAD a mess-mate once who lov'd,
  (A braver soul ne'er faced the wind)
    But ah! a faithless maiden prov'd
  The rock which wreck'd his peace of mind;
A fairer wench girl the sun ne'er shone upon,   5
But she was false, and Ben, poor Ben, is gone!

    I saw her on the crowded pier,
  As setting sail awhile we lay;
    And when they cry'd, *cast off*, a tear
  She wip'd, or seem'd to wipe away;   10
This Ben beheld, and wav'd his hat, and sigh'd,
But ah! he little knew what would betide.

    The eastern blast blew keen and strong,
  And soon we near'd the sultry line;
    And nightly as we roll'd along,   15
  Whilst round us roar'd the fiery brine,
Poor Ben, and I have told our wand'rings o'er,
And talk'd of love, and all we left on shore.

    And now Jamaica's Isle was seen,
  Where British warriors oft hath griev'd,   20
    But here a month we had not been
  Ere the sad tidings were received,
The my poor mess-mate's love her cheeks had dry'd,
And just become a rich old landman's bride.

    Soon as the fatal lines were read,   25
  His sun-burn'd face declar'd his pain,
    His lips grew pale, he droop'd his head,
  He sigh'd, but never smil'd again:
And from that time when all retired to rest,
He walkd' the silent deck, by gloom oppress'd.   30

And now, poor soul, the can he sought,
  In hopes that grog would ease his woe;
    But grog the yellow-fever brought,
  And this, alas! soon laid him low:
Spring-Path* received him 'mong it's num'rous dead,   35
And round his grave a few kind drops were shed.

  Where many a reptile nightly plies,
    Far distant from his native shore,
    Beneath a Tam'rind-Tree he lies,
  His turf with weeds all cover'd o'er;   40
And oh! ye seamen his sad fate beware,
For maidens may be false, tho' very fair.

*A Burial-place in the nieghbourhood of Kingston.

A SONG,

Sung at the celebration of the ANNIVERSARY *of*
The FRENCH REVOLUTION, *at Liverpool, July* 14, 1791.

(1791)

GALLIA burst her vile shackles on this glorious day,
    And we dare to applaud the great deed;
We dare to exult in a tyrant's lost sway,
    And rejoice that a nation is freed:
For this we assemble, regardless of those   5
    Who wish to enslave the free mind:
Our foes we are conscious are liberty's foes,
    And our friends are the friends of mankind.
Oppression's dark vapours had shrowded the land,
    And the image of God was defac'd;   10
Man trembled and crouch'd at his lordling's command,
    And the foot, which had spurn'd him, embrac'd;
But at length, the horizon, by learning's bright rays,
    And Columbia's strong tempest was clear'd;
Light pour'd o'er the nation in one brilliant blaze—   15
    Man SAW—and his chains disappear'd.
If angel's e'er learn from the mansions above,
    Th' affairs of our planet to scan,
They could not this wonderful event but approve,
    As the noblest exertions of man;   20
An exertion which bids servile nations arise,
    And enjoy, what the deity gave.
To be free, is a duty man owes the allwise,
    And he sins, who is tamely a slave.
Where millions of bayonets shield her from harm,   25
    'Mong our neighbors, now liberty dwells;
She smiles, unappall'd, at each foreign alarm,
    And her smiles, all that's gloomy dispells.
On the rock of man's rights she a fortress has plann'd,
    Which, thro' many a bright age shall endure,   30
Like a craig, 'midst the waves, undisturb'd shall it stand,
    And preserve Heaven's blessing secure.
With electrical force, through the nations around,

Her fire may dear liberty dart;
'Mong the sons of the north may its glow soon be found;   35
   May it warm each Iberian heart;
'Cross the huge snowy alps, to a region once dear,
   May the soul-lifting influence be hurl'd;
May its radiance the whole human family cheer,
   And may tyrants be banish'd the world.   40

THE FIRE OF LIBERTY.

(1792)

WHEN o'er this sea encircled ground
  The Norman Conqu'ror grimly frown'd
    And quench'd the Nation's fires,
Th' oppressor could not all destroy
For thine, O heaven-born Liberty,   5
    Then glimmer'd 'mong our Sires.—

From reign to reign, it moulder'd on
Scarce warming; till dark-visag'd John
    Beheld the bursting flame—
He saw—and, by it, sign'd that deed   10
Which makes thy sward, O! Runnimede,
    For ever dear to Fame.

This sacred fire, through many an age
Of mental gloom and civil rage,
    A varied heat bestow'd—   15
But when at length 'twas sprinkl'd o'er
With some few drops of regal gore,
    An awful flame it shew'd.

'Twas this which lighted William o'er
This scar'd a bigot from our shore   20
    And shew'd an abject world
With how much ease those dreaded things,
Those scourges, call'd despotic Kings,
    May from their thrones be hurl'd.

Chear'd by the soul enlivening blaze,   25
Our Sires did much to merit praise,
    Tho' much was left undone—
Then be it ours to feel the flame
And nobly act, till but the name
    Of tyrant laws be known.   30

With awful charge from Sire to Son
O! may this fire be handed down,
   And watch'd with holy zeal.
O! may its heat expand the soul
And teach us, while we spurn controul,   35
   For others wrongs to feel.

Whate'er their tongue, their hue, their state,
Whate'er the God they supplicate,
   Or clime which gave them birth,
O! Liberty, may'st thou be given,   40
As bounteous as the light of heaven,
   To all the Sons of Earth.

HUMAN DEBASEMENT.

A FRAGMENT.

(1793)

              In early days,
If kings were made by men, and that they were,
The light of nature clearly shows,
How comes it then, that earth is fill'd with slaves?
How comes it then; that man, this reasoning thing,   5
This being with such faculties endow'd,
This being form'd to trace the great first cause,
Through many a wond'rous path; how comes it then
That he in every clime, should cringe, should crouch,
Should bend th' imploring eye, and trembling knee,   10
To mere self-raised oppressors—Heav'ns! to think
That not a tithe of all the sons of men
E'er kiss'd thy sacred cup, O liberty!
To find where'er imagination roves,
Millions on millions prostrate in the dust,   15
Whilst o'er their necks, with proud contemptuous mein,
Kings, emperors, sultans, sophies, what you will,
With all their pamper'd minions sorely press,
Grinding god's creatures to the very bone.
Yet man submits to all! he tamely licks   20
The foot uprais'd to trample on his right:
He shakes his chains, and in their horrid clank
Finds melody; else why not throw 'em off?
Seven hundred millions of the human kind
Are held in base subjection, and by whom?   25
Why, strange to tell, and what futurity,
As children at the tale of witch or spirit
Will bless themselves to hear, by a small troop
Of weak capricious despots, fiends accurs'd,
Who drench the earth with tides of human gore,   30
And call the havock, GLORY! Britons, yes!
Seven hundred millions of your fellow men,
All form'd like you the blessing to enjoy,
Now drag the servile chain. Oh! fie upon 't!

'Twere better far within the clay-cold cell   35
To waste away than be at such a price!
Poor whip-gall'd slaves. Oh! 'tis debasement all!
'Tis filthy cowardice, and shews that man
Merits too oft by his degenerate deeds
The yoke that bends him down. Power's limpid stream   40
Must have its source within a people's heart:
What flows not thence is turbid tyrannny;
Rank are the despot weeds which now o'er-run
This ample world, and choke each goodly growth;
But, that supine loud vaunting thing, call'd man,   45
Might soon eradicate so foul a pest,
Would he exert those powers which god has given
To be the means of good: and what more good,
More rational, nay, more approaching Heav'n,
Than the strong joys which flow from freedom's fount?   50
Yon radiant orb, vast emblem of the pow'r
Who form'd him, beams alike on all mankind;
The air, which like a mantle girts the world,
Is too a common good; and even so,
With amplest bounty liberty is given   55
To man whate'er his tint; swart, brown, or fair;
Whate'er his clime, hot, cold, or temperate;
Whate'er his mode of faith, whate'er his state,
Or rich, or poor, great nature cries — BE FREE.
How comes it then, that man neglects the call?   60
Nay like the callous felon, chuckles loud
Amidst corroding chains? Can that great cause
Who made man free, both mind and body free,
And gave him reason as a sentinel
To guard the glorious gift, can he be pleas'd   65
To see his rich donation cast away,
Or pass'd with inattention, as not worth
Th' acceptance, of his creatures? NO! my friends:
Whate'er God gives, he gives, to be enjoy'd
But not abus'd, and the mean wretch who 'neath   70
A tyrant's feet this precious jewel throws
Spurns the vast Power who plac'd it in his hands.
How comes it then, that minds are thus abased,
That man, though Nature loudly calls, BE FREE,
Has clos'd his ears against her, and become   75
A mean, a grov'lling wretch! Why, thus it is,
O Superstition! thou who point'st to man,
And call'st the fragile piece a demi-god;

Yes, thou who wand'rest o'er the world, array'd
In pure Religion's mantle; thou whose breath   80
Conveys those potent opiates to the brain
Which bring on reason's sleep; O dark-brow'd fiend,
All, all these works are thine! — —

SEAMEN's NURSERY.

(1794)

Haste, Oh! ye rulers of the nation,
    And Afric's trade destroy,
A trade that scatters devastation,
    And blasts each social joy;
A trade accurst, whose every feature   5
    A horrid wildness wears,
And which adown the cheek of Nature,
    Should draw incessant tears.

Lur'd by the promise of promotion,
    And hopes of speedy store,   10
Poor Jem, who oft had brav'd the ocean,
    Resolv'd for Afric's shore.
In vain each relative dissuaded,
    E'en Nancy sigh'd in vain;
He felt—but all they urged evaded,   15
    He smil'd, and sought the main.

Now on the coast his constitution
    Soon felt the baneful soil,
Yet still he faced with resolution,
    Each pestilential toil.   20
The smokes commenc'd, his vigour fail'd him,
    Home every thought possess'd,
The deadly nausea soon assail'd him,
    Ah!—need I speak the rest.

That Jem from this sad world was parted,   25
    The half-mast ensign told,
A braver youth, or more kind-hearted
    Ne'er on the salt wave roll'd.
The sun burnt crew with grief convey'd him,
    To where poor seamen lie,   30
And while they in the white-beach laid him,
    Tears flow'd from many an eye.

Thus far from every dear connexion,
    In sorrow doubly dear,
No tongue to whisper kind affection,   35
    Nor soothe each boding fear,
Uncheer'd, unnurs'd, nay unattended,
    'Midst noise and putrid air,
Thus the lov'd youth his being ended,
    And seamen, Oh! beware.   40

STANZAS

ON THE

ANNIVERSARY

OF THE AMERICAN REVOLUTION

(1794)

Ye men of Columbia, Oh! hail the great day,
    Which burst your tyrannical chain,
Which taught the oppress'd how to spurn lawless sway,
    And establish'd equality's reign;
Yes hail the bless'd moment, when awfully grand,   5
    Your congress pronounc'd the decree,
Which told the wide world that your pine-cover'd land,
    Spite of British coercion was free.

Those worthies who fell in your soul-cheering cause,
    To the true sons of freedom are dear,   10
Their deeds the unborn shall rehearse with applause,
    And bedew their cold turf with a tear.
Oh! cherish their names—let their daring exploits,
    And their virtues be spread far and wide,
And if fierce-eye'd Ambition e'er trench on your rights,   15
    Again shall her schemes be destroy'd.

As he tills your rich glebe, the old peasant shall tell,
    While his bosom with gratitude glows,
How your WARREN expir'd—how MONTGOMERY fell,
    And how WASHINGTON baffled your foes.   20
With transport his offspring shall catch the glad sound,
    And as freedom takes root in each breast,
Their country's defenders with praise shall be crown'd,
    While her *plunderers* they learn to detest.

In your groves ye Columbians, those friends of mankind,   25
    Who courts and court minions despise;

In your groves unmolested, those spirits shall find,
   Ev'ry blessing proud Britain denies,
Then who would continue a poor drudging thing?
   For tythe-men and tax-men to squeeze?   30
When the winds that would bear him from *church*, *peers*, and *king*,
   Would waft him to freedom and ease.

By those fields that were ravag'd—those towns that were fir'd,
   By those wrongs which your females endur'd,
By those blood-sprinkled plains where your warriors expir'd,   35
   Oh! preserve what your prowess procur'd,
And reflect—that *your* rights are the rights of mankind,
   That to *all* they were bounteously given,
And that he who in chains would his fellow-man bind,
   Uplifts his proud arm against heaven.   40

How can you who have felt the oppressor's hard hand,
   Who for freedom all perils would brave,
How can you enjoy peace while one foot of your land,
   Is disgrac'd by the toil of a *slave!*
Oh! rouse then in spite of a merciless few,   45
   And pronounce this immortal decree—
"Whate'er be man's *tenets*, his *fortune*, his *hue*,
   "*He is man*—and shall therefore be *free.*"

THE TENDER's HOLD.

(1794)

WHILE landmen wander uncontrol'd,
    And boast the rights of freemen,
O! view the Tender's loathsome hold,
    Where droop your injur'd seamen;
Dragg'd by oppression's savage grasp,   5
    From every dear connexion,
'Midst putrid air, O! hear them gasp,
    And mark their deep dejection.
        CHORUS.
Blush then, ye mean, ye pensioned host,
    Who wallow in profusion,   10
For yon foul cell proves all your boast
    To be but mere delusion.

If freedom be our birthright, say
    Why are not all protected?
Why is the hand of ruffian sway   15
    'Gainst seamen thus directed.
Is this your proof of British rights?
    Is this rewarding bravery?
O shame! to boast your tars' exploits,
    Yet doom those tars to slavery.   20
        CHORUS.
Blush then, &c.

O! that ambition's callous train,
    Who wish to shine in story,
Who tinge with blood the earth and main,
    And call their havoc glory,   25
O! that these scourges of the world,
    Who smile at man's undoing,
Might from their lordly seats be hurl'd,
    And taste the cup of ruin.
        CHORUS.
Blush then, &c.   30

Are Britons free?—ye vaunting crew,
   Who damn all reformation,
Deep in the Tender's Hold, O! view,
   The guardians of your nation:
Yes view them thus in durance laid,   35
   Though void of all transgression,
Then say, could Russia's bloody jade
   Display more foul oppression?
        CHORUS.
  Blush then, &c.

But just return'd from noxious skies,   40
   And winter's raging ocean,
To land the sun-burnt seaman flies,
   Impell'd by strong emotion,
His much loved Kate, his Children dear,
   Around him cling delighted,   45
When lo! the impressing fiends appear,
   And every joy is blighted.
        CHORUS.
  Blush then, &c.

Thus from each soft endearment torn,
   Here view your seaman languish,   50
His wife, his children, left forlorn,
   The prey of bitter anguish;
'Reft of those arms whose vigorous strength
   Their shed from want defended,
They droop, and all their woes at length,   55
   Are in a workhouse ended.
        CHORUS.
  Blush then, &c.

Mark then, ye minions of a court,
   Who prate of freedom's blessing,
Yet every hell-born war support,   60
   And vindicate impressing,
A time will come, when things like you,
   Mere baubles of creation,
No more shall make mankind pursue,
   The work of devastation.   65
        CHORUS.
  Blush then, ye mean, ye pensioned host,
    Who wallow in profusion,
  For yon foul cell proves all your boast,
    To be but mere delusion.

BLUE EYED MARY.

(1796)

In a cottage, embosom'd within a deep shade,
Like a rose in a desert, oh! view the meek maid;
Her aspect all sweetness, all plaintive her eye,
And a bosom for which e'en a monarch might sigh:
Then in neat Sunday gown, see her met by the 'Squire,　　　5
All attraction her countenance, his all desire;
He accosts her, she blushes; he flatters, she smiles;
And soon blue-ey'd Mary's seduc'd by his wiles.

Now with drops of contrition her pillow's wet o'er,
But the fleece when once stain'd can know whiteness no more;　　10
The aged folks whisper, the maidens look shy,
To town the 'Squire presses,—how can she deny?
There, behold her in lodgings, she dresses in style,
Public places frequents, sighs no more, but reads Hoyle;
Learns to squander; they quarrel; his love turns to hate;　　15
And soon blue-ey'd Mary is left to her fate.

Still of beauty possess'd, and not yet void of shame,
With a heart that recoils at a Prostitute's name,
She tries for a service; her character's gone,
And for skill at her needle, alas! 'tis unknown:　　20
Pale want now approaches; the pawnbroker's near;
And her trinkets and cloaths, one by one disappear;
'Till, at length, sorely pinch'd and quite desperate grown,
The poor blue-eyed Mary is forc'd on the town.

In a brothel next see her, trick'd out to allure,　　25
And all ages, all humours compell'd to endure;
Compell'd, tho' disgusted, to wheedle and feign,
With an aspect all smiles, and a bosom all pain:
Now caress'd, now insulted, now flatter'd, now scorn'd,
And by ruffians and drunkards oft wantonly spurn'd;　　30
This worst of all mis'ry she's doomed to endure,
For the poor blue-ey'd Mary is now an impure.

Next, to banish all thought, and stifle remorse,
To the bottle she flies! oh fatal resource!
Grows stupid and bloated, and lost to all shame,   35
Whilst a dreadful disease is pervading her frame:
Now with eyes dim and languid, the once blooming maid,
In a garret, on straw, faint and helpless is laid;
Oh! mark her pale cheek, see! she scarce takes her breath,
And lo, her blue-eyes are now seal'd up in death!   40

ELEGY.

[To the Memory of Robert Burns]

(c. 1796)

Poor, wildly-sweet uncultur'd flow'r,
Thou lowliest of the Muse's bow'r,
"Stern ruin's ploughshare, 'mang the stowre,
      "Has crush'd thy stem,"
And sorrowing verse shall mark the hour,   5
      "Thou bonnie gem."

'Neath the green turf, dear nature's child,
Sublime, pathetic, artless, wild,
Of all thy quips and cranks despoil'd,
      Cold dost thou lie;   10
And many a youth and maiden mild
      Shall o'er thee sigh.

Those pow'rs that eagle-wing'd could soar,
That heart which ne'er was cold before,
That tongue which caus'd the table's roar,   15
      Are now laid low,
And Scotia's sons shall hear no more
      Thy rapt'rous flow.

Warm'd with "a spark o' nature's fire,"
From the rough plough thou didst aspire   20
To make a sordid world admire:
      And few like thee,
Oh! Burns, have swept the minstrel's lyre
      With ecstasy.

Ere winter's icy vapours fail,   25
The violet, in th' uncultur'd dale,
So sweetly scents the passing gale,
      That shepherd boys,
Led by the fragrance they inhale,
      Soon find their prize.   30

So when to life's chill glen confin'd,
Thy rich, tho' rough, untutor'd mind,
Pour'd on the sense of each rude hind
        Such sonsy lays,
That to thy brow was soon assign'd   35
        The wreath of praise.

Anon, with nobler daring blest,
The wild notes throbbing at thy breast,
Of friends, wealth, learning, unpossess'd,
        Thy fervid mind   40
Tow'rds fame's proud turrets boldly press'd,
        And pleas'd mankind.

But what avail'd thy pow'rs to please,
When want approach'd, and pale disease;
Could these thy infant brood appease   45
        That wail'd for bread?
Or could they, for a moment, ease
        Thy woe-worn head?

Applause, poor child of minstrelsey,
Was all the world e'er gave to thee;   50
Unmov'd, by pinching penury
        They saw thee torn,
And now, kind souls! with sympathy
        Thy loss they mourn.

Oh! how I loath the bloated train,   55
Who oft had heard thy dulcet strain;
Yet, when thy frame was rack'd with pain
        Could keep aloof,
And eye, with opulent disdain,
        Thy lowly roof.   60

Yes, proud Dumfries—oh! would to Heav'n,
Thou hadst from that cold spot been driven,
Thou might'st have found some shelt'ring haven
        On this side Tweed:—
Yet ah! e'en here poor bards have striven,   65
        And died in need.

True genius scorns to flatter knaves,
Or crouch amidst a race of slaves;

His soul, while fierce the tempest raves,
       No terror knows,   70
And with unshaken nerve he braves
       Life's pelting woes.

No wonder, then, that thou shou'dst find
Th' averted glance of half mankind;
Shouldst see the sly, slow, supple mind   75
       To wealth aspire,
While scorn, neglect, and want combin'd
       To quench thy fire.

While wintry winds pipe loud and strong,
The high perch'd storm-cock pours his song;   80
So thy Æolian lyre was strung
       'Midst chilling times;
Yet clearly didst thou roll along
       Thy "routh of rhymes."

And ah! that routh of rhymes shall raise   85
For thee a lasting pile of praise.
Haply some wing in these our days,
       Has loftier soar'd;
But from the heart more melting lays
       Were never pour'd.   90

Where Ganges rolls his yellow tide,
Where blest Columbus' waters glide,
Old Scotia's sons, spread far and wide,
       Shall oft rehearse,
With sorrow some, but all with pride,   95
       Thy witching verse.

In early spring, thy earthy bed,
Shall be with many a wild flow'r spread;
The violet there her sweets shall shed,
       In humble guise,   100
And there the mountain daisy's head
       Shall duly rise.

While darkness reigns, should bigotry,
With boiling blood and bended knee,
Scatter the weeds of infamy   105
       O'er thy cold clay,

Those weeds, at light's first blush, shall be
      Soon swept away.

And when thy scorners are no more,
The lonely glens, and sea-beat shore,   110
Where thou has croon'd thy fancies o'er,
      With soul elate,
Oft shall the bard at eve explore,
      And mourn thy fate.

SONNET.

[The Swallow]

(c. 1796)

Go place the swallow on yon turfy bed,
Much will he struggle, but can never rise:
   Go raise him even with the daisy's head,
And the poor twitt'rer like an arrow flies.

   So oft thro' life the man of pow'rs and worth,   5
Haply the caterer for an infant train,
   Like BURNS, must struggle on the bare-worn earth,
While all his efforts to arise are vain.

   Yet should the hand of relative or friend,
Just from the surface, lift the suff'ring wight,   10
   Soon would the wings of industry extend,
Soon would he rise from anguish to delight.
Go then, ye affluent, go, your hands outstretch,
And from despair's dark verge, oh! raise the woe-worn wretch.

THE REMEDY
[THE LEVIATHAN.]

(1797)

As when the huge Leviathan is seen
Torpid and slumb'ring midst his native seas,
The seamen ply the oar with anxious mien
Quick every eye, and noiseless every voice—
And now the keen harpoon its entrance makes,   5
At first unfelt; till deeper grows the wound,
When lo! the enormous animal awakes,
And his broad tail spreads death and terror round—
So when a nation, cold and sluggish, lies,
Silent and slow th' oppressor drives his steel;   10
At first the wound's unfelt; again he tries,
Deep sinks the shaft, and now the people feel—
Pierc'd to the quick, the tail soon mounts on high,
And kings, peers, bishops, all in one proud ruin lie.

SONG.

[MARY LE MORE]

(1798)

Ah! soldiers of Britain, your merciless doings
Long, long must the children of Erin deplore;
All sad is my soul, when I view the black ruins
Where once stood the cabin of Mary Le More—
Her father, God rest him, loved Ireland most dearly,   5
All our wrongs, all our sufferings he felt most severely,
And with Freedom's firm sons he united sincerely;
But—gone is the father of Mary Le More—

One cold winter's eve, as poor Dermot sat musing,
Hoarse curses alarm'd him—and crash went the door;   10
The fierce soldiers enter'd, and straight 'gan abusing
The brave, yet mild, father of Mary Le More—
To their scoffs he replied not, with blows they assail'd him,
He felt all indignant, his caution now fail'd him,
He returned their vile blows, and all Munster bewail'd him,   15
For—stabb'd was the father of Mary Le More—

The children's wild screams and the mother's distraction,
While the father, the husband, lay stretch'd in his gore,
Ah! who can relate, and not curse the foul faction
That blasted that rose-bud, sweet Mary Le More?   20
"Oh! my father, my father," she cried, wildly throwing
Her arms round his neck, whilst his life's blood was flowing;
She kiss'd his cold lips—but poor Dermot was going;
He groan'd,—and left fatherless Mary Le More—

With destruction uncloy'd, this infernal banditti,   25
Tho' the rain fell in sheets, and the wind it blew sore,
These friends of the castle, these foes to all pity,
Set fire to the cabin of Mary Le More—
The mother and children, half naked and shrieking,
Escap'd from the flames where poor Dermot lay reeking,   30

And, while the sad victims for shelter were seeking,
Ah! mark what befel the poor Mary le More—

From her father's pale cheek, which her lap had supported,
To an out-house these ruffians the lovely girl bore;
With her tears, her entreaties, her sorrows they sported,   35
And by force they deflower'd the poor Mary Le More—
And now, a poor maniac, she roams the wide common,
'Gainst the soldiers of Britain she warns every woman;
And she sings of her father in strains more than human,
Till tears often fall for poor Mary Le More—   40

Oh! daughters of Ireland, your country's salvation,
Whilst the waves of old Ocean shall beat round your shore,
Remember the wrongs of your long shackled nation,
Remember the woes of poor Mary Le More—
And while your hearts swell, oh! with spirits all fire,   45
Your lovers, your brothers, your husbands inspire,
'Till the UNION shall make all oppressors retire,
From the soil where now wanders poor Mary Le More—

WRITTEN FOR THE ANNIVERSARY OF

THE LIVERPOOL

MARINE SOCIETY.

(1799)

WHAT is life but an ocean, precarious, as those
    Which surround this terraqueous ball?
What is man but a bark, often laden with woes,
    What is death but the harbour of all?
On our passage, to-day may be mild and serene,   5
    And our loftiest canvass be shewn,
While to-morrow, fierce tempests may blacken the scene,
    And our masts by the board may be gone.

On life's rosy morn, with a prosperous breeze,
    We all our light sails may display,   10
With a cloudless horizon may sweep at our ease,
    And of sorrow ne'er feel the salt spray;
But, ere we have reach'd our meridian, the gale
    From the point of ill-fortune may blow,
And the sun of our being, all cheerless and pale,   15
    May set in the wild waves of woe.

Experience, when bound o'er the turbulent waves,
    Remembers that ills may arise,
And with sedulous care, ere the danger he braves,
    His bark with spare tackle supplies: 20
So you, on life's ocean, with provident minds,
    Have here a spare anchor secur'd,
With which, in despite of Adversity's winds,
    The helpless will one day be moor'd.

When the strong arm of winter uplifts the blue main,   25
    And snow-storms and ship-wrecks abound,
When hollow-cheek'd Famine inflicts her fell pain,
    And the swamp flings destruction around,

When the folly of rulers embroils human kind,
    And myriads are robb'd of their breath,   30
This wise Institution may come o'er the mind,
    And may soften the pillow of death.

The poor widow'd mourner, the sweet prattling throng,
    And the veteran whose powers are no more,
Shall here find an arm to defend them from wrong,   35
    And to chace meagre WANT from their door:
This, is temp'ring the wind to the lamb newly shorn,
    This, is following the ant's prudent ways,
And, O blest Institution! the child yet unborn
    With rapture shall lisp forth thy praise.   40

SONG.

[From *Hymns, &c. for the Blind*]

(c. 1799)

WE have heard of the beauties which nature displays,
We have heard of your landscapes, your sun's brilliant rays,
But to us all creation is mantled in clouds,
And our nearest connexions thick darkness enshrouds.

Oh! how cheerless is blindness, tho' fortune be join'd,　　　　　5
But how dreadful the pressure when want is combin'd,
And alas! on life's journey oft shunn'd with disdain—
Such, such was the burthen we had to sustain.

Females.
As droops the pale flowret by tempests o'erturn'd,
So unshelter'd we droop'd and humanity mourn'd;　　　　　10
She mourn'd, she uprais'd us, she soften'd our pains,
And this much lov'd ASYLUM her blest arms sustains.

Males.
We were poor shatter'd barks 'midst the wild waves of woe,
When the kind hearted hail'd us, and took us in tow;
They saw the keen suff'rings we long had endur'd,　　　　　15
And in this peaceful harbour by them we were moor'd.

Both.
Yes, yes, we were bruis'd by adversity's hand,
And you found us, ye Worthies, a destitute band:
All helpless, by you we were aided to rise,
And you wip'd the big drops from our poor sightless eyes.　　　　　20

Receive then, ye friends of the blind, oh! receive,
Pure gratitude's breathings, 'tis all we can give;
We have felt, long have felt your compassionate care,
And our overcharg'd bosoms the rest will declare.

THE MANIAC.

(1800)

As I stray'd o'er a common on Cork's rugged border,
　　While the dew-drops of morn the sweet primrose array'd,
I saw a poor female, whose mental disorder
　　Her quick glancing eye and wild aspect betray'd;
On the sward she reclin'd, by the green fern surrounded,　　　　5
At her side speckled daisies and crow-flowers abounded;
To its inmost recess her poor heart had been wounded,
　　Her sighs were unceasing, 'twas Mary le More.

Her charms by the keen blasts of sorrow were faded;
　　Yet the soft tinge of beauty still play'd on her cheek;　　　10
Her tresses a wreath of pale primroses braided,
　　And strings of fresh daisies hung loose on her neck;
While with pity I gaz'd, she exclaim'd, "Oh! my mother!
"See the blood on that lash, 'tis the blood of my brother;
"They have torn his poor flesh, and they now strip another;　　15
　　" 'Tis Connor, the friend of poor Mary le More!"

"Tho' his locks are as white as the foam of the ocean,
　　"Those soldiers shall find that my father is brave;
"My father!" she cry'd with the wildest emotion,
　　"Ah! no, my poor father now sleeps in the grave;　　　　20
"They have toll'd his death-bell, they've laid the turf o'er him;
"His white locks were bloody, no aid can restore him,
"He is gone! He is gone! and the good will deplore him,
　　"When the blue wave of Erin hides Mary le More."

A lark, from the gold-blossom'd furze that grew near her,　　25
　　Now rose, and with energy caroll'd his lay:
"Hush! hush!" she continued, "the trumpet sounds clearer;
　　"The horsemen approach, Erin's daughters, away!"
Ah! Britons, 'twas foul, while the cabin was burning,
And o'er her pale father a wretch had been mourning!　　　　30
Go hide with the sea-mew, ye maids, and take warning,
　　Those ruffians have ruin'd poor Mary le More.

"Away! bring the ointment! Oh! God! see those gashes!
   "Alas! my poor brother, come dry the big tear;
"Anon we'll have vengeance for those dreadful lashes,   35
   "Already the screech-owls and ravens appear;
"By day the green grave, that lies under the willow,
"With wild flow'rs I'll strew, and by night make my pillow,
"Till the ooze and dark sea-weed, beneath the curl'd billow,
   "Shall furnish a death-bed for Mary le More."   40

Thus rav'd the poor Maniac in tones more heart-rending
   Than Sanity's voice ever pour'd on my ear,
When, lo! on the waste, and their march to'ards her bending,
   A troop of fierce cavalry chanc'd to appear.
"Oh! the fiends!" she exclaim'd, and with wild horror started,   45
Then thro' the tall fern, loudly screaming, she darted;
With an overcharg'd bosom, I slowly departed,
   And sigh'd for the wrongs of poor Mary le More.

LUCY's GHOST.

A MARINE BALLAD.

(1800)

KEEN blew the wind abaft the beam,
  The moon was wrapt in sable clouds,
The reefs were in, and many a spray
  High mounting wash'd the weather shrouds.
The middle watch was nearly closed,   5
  Hoarse thundering peals remote were heard,
When slowly moving o'er the deck,
  A shadowy female form appear'd.

Her cheek was whiter than the foam
  That caps the huge Atlantic wave,   10
Her lip was like the welkin's hue,
  Ere the dark storm begins to rave;
Her form a winding-sheet conceal'd.
  She paus'd—and awful shook her head,
Then with a hollow thrilling voice   15
  Thus to the fear-struck mate she said:

Well mayst thou tremble, faithless wretch,
  Thy clammy brow, that stifled groan,
Those glaring eye-balls, all confess
  That injured LUCY still is known;   20
Yes, EDWARD, here behold the shade
  Of her thy falshoods triumph'd o'er,
Of her who all thy vows believ'd,
  Of her who fell to rise no more.

Didst thou not say my cheek display'd   25
  The Tropic morn's delicious bloom?
Didst thou not say my breath excell'd
  The ripe Anana's* rich perfume?
Didst thou not say my azure eyes
  Surpass'd the cloudless Indian sky?   30

And yet to gain a wealthy bride,
　　Say, didst not thou from LUCY fly?

With pale and agonizing look,
　　My mother heard the tale of woe,
And tho' she tried to sooth my pangs,　　　　　　35
　　Yet silent throbs soon laid her low.
To the cold grave I saw her borne!
　　Ah EDWARD! what a scene was there!
A mother prostrate in the dust!
　　A daughter doom'd to dark despair!　　　　　　40

Abandon'd by the man I loved,
　　Cast on the world o'erwhelm'd with shame,
I droop'd like some poor blasted flower,
　　And soon I bore a mother's name;
My boy, my sweet one, breathed and died,　　　　　45
　　No tears of mine his turf bedew'd,
For withering grief had touch'd my brain,
　　And now I wander'd wild and rude.

Oft have I roam'd the flowery heath,
　　That skirts the ever-dashing wave,　　　　　　50
And there have pluck'd the primrose pale,
　　To deck a mother's grassy grave;
And when the wintry tempest howl'd,
　　With naked head and bosom bare,
Oft have I swept the frozen snows,　　　　　　55
　　And laugh'd to scorn the troubled air.

Pale as the snow-drop on the waste,
　　Now wildly chaunting would I rove,
Now venting curses on thy head,
　　And now all softness, breathing love.　　　　　60
Where sea-fowls lodge, last night of all,
　　As on the breezy steep I stood,
Methought I heard thy well-known voice,
　　I scream'd, and headlong reach'd the flood.

And now, all on a bed of weeds,　　　　　　65
　　Full many a fathom deep, is laid
That form thy wily tongue has prais'd,
　　That form thy faithless heart betray'd;
But mark, Oh EDWARD! mark thy doom,

Thou never more must peace enjoy,   70
By day remorse shall gnaw thy breast,
   By night my shade shall still be nigh.

When livid lightnings flash around,
   High on the yard I'll pierce thine ear;
In calms with thee I'll walk the deck,   75
   And cross thee midst the storm's career;
At sea I'll haunt thy hammock's side,
   And draw thy curtains when on shore!
Thy flesh shall waste, and soon or late
   The dark dark surge shall whelm thee o'er.   80

And mark—she paus'd, for now the east
   Display'd the first faint streaks of day,
The phantom quick dissolv'd in air,
   And the pale seaman died away;
The watch now bore him from the deck,   85
   He lived a while, oppress'd by gloom,
And Lucy nightly kept her word,
   Till Edward found a watery tomb.

THE END.

*Pine Apple.

SONNET BY A POOR MAN.

ON THE APPROACH OF THE GOUT.

(1801)

'Tis strange that thou shoudst leave thy downy bed,
 The Turkey carpet, and the soft settee;
Shouldst leave the board with choicest dainties spread,
 To fix thy odious residence with me.
'Tis strange that thou, attach'd to plenteous ease,   5
 Shouldst leave those dwellings for a roof like mine,
Where plainest meals keen appetite appease,
 And where thou wilt not find—one drop of wine.
'Tis passing strange;—yet shouldst thou persevere,
 And rack these bones with agonizing pangs,   10
Firm as a rock thy tortures will I bear,
 And teach the affluent how to blunt thy fangs;
Yes—shouldst thou visit me, capricious Gout;
Hard fare shall be thy lot;—by Jove—I'll starve thee out.

WILL CLEWLINE.

(1801)

FROM Jamaica's hot clime, and her pestilent dews,
    From the toil of a sugar-stowed bark,
From those perilous boatings that oft thin the crews,
    And fill the wide maw of the shark;
From fever, storm, famine, and all the sad store   5
    Of hardships, by seamen endured,
Behold poor Will Clewline escaped! and once more
    With his wife and children safe moor'd!

View the rapture that beams in his sun-embrowned face
    While he folds his lov'd Kate to his breast,   10
While his little ones trooping to share his embrace,
    Contend who shall first be caress'd;
View them climb his lov'd knee while each tiny heart swells,
    As he presses the soft rosy lip,
And of cocoa-nuts, sugar, and tamarinds tells,   15
    That are soon to arrive from the ship.

Then see him reclined in his favourite chair,
    With his arm round the neck of his love;
Who tells how his friends and his relatives fare,
    And how their dear younglings improve: 20
The ev'ning approaches—and round the snug fire,
    Their little ones sport on the floor,
When lo! while each accent, each glance is desire,
    Loud thund'rings are heard at the door.

And now like a tempest that sweeps through the sky,   25
    And kills the first buds of the year,
Oh view, 'midst this region of innocent joy,
    A gang of fierce ruffians appear:
They seize on their prey, all relentless as fate,
    He struggles—is instantly bound,   30
Wild scream the poor children, and lo! his lov'd Kate
    Sinks pale and convulsed to the ground!

To the hold of a tender, deep, crouded, and foul,
    Now view the brave seaman confined;
And on the bare planks, all indignant of soul,   35
    All unfriended behold him reclined;
The children's wild screamings still ring in his ear,
    He broods on his Kate's poignant pain;
He hears the cat hauling—his pangs are severe;
    He feels—but he scorns to complain.   40

Arriv'd now at Plymouth, the poor enslav'd tar
    Is to combat for freedom and laws;
Is to brave the rough surge in a vessel of war:
    He sails, and soon dies in the cause.
Kate hears the sad tidings, and never smiles more,   45
    She falls a meek martyr to grief,
The children, kind friends and relations deplore,
    But the parish alone gives relief.

Ye statesmen who manage this cold-blooded land,
    And who boast of your seamen's exploits,   50
Ah! think how your death-dealing bulwarks are mann'd,
    And learn to respect human rights:
Like felons no more, let the sons of the main
    Be sever'd from all that is dear;
If their sufferings and wrongs be a national stain,   55
    Let those sufferings and wrongs disappear.

ODE. Sung at St. John's Chapel, Lancaster, on Tuesday last, being the Anniversary of the LANCASTER MARINE SOCIETY.

Written by a Gentleman of Liverpool, excepting the Chorus, which is from the pen of Mr. Waller, of Lancaster.

(Set to music by Mr. Langshaw, Organist at St. Mary's Church.)

(1801)

WHEN the broad arch of heaven is blue and serene,
 And Ocean reflects the bright day,
When, unswell'd by the breeze, the bleach'd canvas is seen,
 And the bows are unwash'd by the spray;
When the morn is thus smiling, each mariner knows,   5
 Who the perilous tempest oft braves,
That the loftiest bark, ere the day's dreadful close,
 May float a mere wreck on the waves.

So on life's changeful ocean, with souls all elate,
 And with prospects all placid and clear,   10
While Fortune's soft gales on our efforts await,
 For Wealth's flattering harbour we steer;
When lo! Disappointment's dark vapours arise,
 And the winds of Adversity roar,
And Hope's tow'ring canvas in tatters soon flies,   15
 And Sorrow's wild waves whelm us o'er.

Since Life's brightest azure may thus be o'ercast,
 And soon threat'ning clouds may appear,
O! 'twas wise to prepare for the soul-piercing blast,
 Ere you feel its destructive career;   20
Yes, men of old Lune, to the surge long inur'd,
 O! 'twas wise this fair harbour to form,
Where your dearest connexions may one day be moor'd,
 Unexpos'd to the pitiless storm.

At eve, when the little ones climb your lov'd knee,   25
   And the mother looks on with a smile,
When they prattle around you, all frolic and glee,
   And soften the day's rugged toil;
When you view the lov'd group with affection's strong glow,
   When you feel Sensibility's tear,   30
O! reflect, men of Lune, that should Death lay you low,
   Protectors and *Guardians* are here.

And oft when the Petrel his dark wings displays,
   In the trough of the mountainous wave,
When the craggy lee-shore is perceiv'd through the haze,   35
   And the breakers all dreadfully rave;
'Neath the vertical sun, when contagions arise,
   Or when battle the atmosphere rends,
O! with comfort reflect, that your soul's dearest ties,
   Shall here find *Protectors* and *Friends*.   40

CHORUS.

To HIM, who is King over earth, sea, and sky,
   Creator and Parent of all,
Without whose concern and whose provident eye,
   Not even a sparrow can fall:
To HIM, who with kind and compassionate love,   45
   Each bountiful effort surveys,
In unison with the bright seraphs above,
   Be glory, thanksgiving, and praise.

Ode, To France.

(1802)

Canst thou, who burst with proud disdain
Each high-wrought link in Slav'ry's Chain;
Canst thou, who cleans'd with noble rage
The Augean Filth of many an age;
Canst thou, whose mighty vengeance hurl'd   5
Destruction on thy foes—the World,
Yet bade th' infuriate slaughter cease
When vanquish'd Despots whin'd for Peace;
Canst thou, O FRANCE, from heights like these descend,
And, with each nerve unbrac'd, to BONAPARTE bend!   10

Was it for this thy Warriors rose,
And paralys'd vast hordes of Foes;
For this, all prodigal of life,
They rush'd amid the bellowing strife,
And, like the Desart's burning breath,   15
Where'er they rush'd they scatter'd Death;
For this, with many a gaping wound,
Thy daring Sons have strew'd the ground,
And, girt with smoking gore and hills of slain,
Have gloried in their CAUSE, and spurn'd th' Oppressor's Chain!   20

When BRITAIN join'd th' unjust array,
And her proud Navy plough'd the sea,
Was it for this beneath the wave
Thy Seamen found a watry grave?
For this, when all around was wreck,   25
And mingled horrors stain'd the deck,
When slowly settling towards their fate,
While the broad banners waved elate—
Was it for this they "*Vive la Nation!*" cried,
Scorn'd the submissive act, and felt th' o'erwhelming tide!   30

Was it for this the sorrowing Sire
Has seen his bleeding Boy expire;
For this the Matron sad and pale

Has told her Son's disastrous tale;
For this the Widow oft has prest   35
With tears the Nursling to her breast;
Was it to lift th' ambitious Soul
Of ONE, above the Law's controul
That thus dire War left millions to deplore,
And the broad Earth and Seas were ting'd with Human Gore!   40

No:—Fearless FRANCE shall ne'er be found
Like the huge Brute on India's ground,
That thro' the ranks impetuous sweeps
And loads the field with mangled heaps,
But yet, each scene of carnage o'er,   45
Obeys THAT Goad he felt before!
  No:—Fearless FRANCE shall still maintain
  Those Rights that millions died to gain;
And soon, tho' Laurel Wreaths her Chains adorn,
Shall shew a grov'ling World that Chains ARE STILL HER SCORN!   50

Oh, FRANCE, thine energetic Soul
Will never brook UNJUST controul,
Will never crouch to Slav'ry's load
Nor bear th' Oppressor's iron goad!
No:—FRANCE, who bade her Monarch fall,   55
Will ne'er before this Idol crawl;
Will ne'er receive with abject awe
A MARTIAL DESPOT'S WILL as LAW!
No:—Banish fear, ye Friends of Human Kind—
FRANCE to a Giant's Arm unites a tow'ring Mind!   60

He who o'erwhelms his Country's Foe,
Yet lays his Country's Freedom low,
Must fear, tho' girt with Guards and State,
From each bold arm THE STROKE OF FATE;
And Thou, usurping Warrior—Thou   65
To whom the weak, the timid bow—
Thou SPLENDID CURSE, whose actions prove
That States may be undone by LOVE;
Thou Foe to Man, upheld by Martial breath,
Thy march is on a Mine, thy ev'ry dream is Death.   70

And, when this Meteor's baleful rays
Are lost in Freedom's ardent blaze—
Yes:—when indignant FRANCE shall rise,

Her form all nerve, all fire her eyes,
And scorning e'en the Bayonet's sway,   75
Shall sweep this impious scourge away,
Then with degraded mien no more
Shall Man his Fellow-man adore;
Then o'er his powers shall PRINCIPLE preside,
And the bright star of Truth shall prove his polar guide!   80

STANZAS ON BLINDNESS.

(1805)

AH, think, if June's delicious rays
 The eye of sorrow can illume,
Or wild December's beamless days
 Can fling o'er all a transient gloom.
Ah, think, if skies, obscure or bright,   5
 Can thus depress, or cheer the mind,
Ah, think, mid clouds of utter night,
 What mournful moments wait *the blind*!

And who can tell his cause for woe?
 To love the wife he ne'er must see,   10
To be a Sire, yet not to know
 The silent babe that climbs his knee,
To have his feelings daily torn,
 With pain the passing meal to find,
To live distress'd, and die forlorn,   15
 Are ills that oft await *the blind*!

If to the breezy uplands led,
 At noon, or blushing eve, or morn,
He hears the red-breast o'er his head,
 While round him breathes the scented thorn.   20
But ah! instead of Nature's face,
 Hills, dales, & woods, & streams combin'd,
Instead of tints, and forms, and grace,
 Night's blackest mantle shrouds *the blind*!

If rosy youth bereft of sight   25
 Midst countless thousands pines unblest,
As the gay flower withdrawn from light
 Bows to that earth where all must rest,
Ah, think! when life's declining hours
 To chilling Pen'ry are consign'd,   30
And pain has palsied all his powers,
 Ah, think! what woes await *the blind*!

TO A REDBREAST

IN NOVEMBER,

Written near one of the Docks of Liverpool.

(1806)

THOU, on whose breast in early days,
With pleasure-beaming eye we gaze,
Remembering how, in times of yore,
The babes with leaves were covered o'er;
Poor bird, 'tis strange that thou shouldst roam   5
So far from thy sequester'd home,
Shouldst leave the pure, the silent shade,
For all this filth, this crash of trade,
And, while dark-visag'd winter holds his reign,
Shouldst hither come, sweet fool, to waste thy warbling strain.   10

The Lark may reach the rosy cloud,
And strike his epic lyre aloud;
The high perch'd Throstle, clear and strong
May roll his nervous ode along;
The Blackbird from the briery bower   15
His deep ton'd elegy may pour;
Yet these could never soothe my ear
Like thee, delightful sonneteer;
Like thee, who thro' the raw and gusty day
Chaunt'st from yon lofty pile, thy brief, thy pensive lay.   20

Thus, richer than the dew-wash'd rose,
On some lone bank the violet blows,
And ere the frowns of winter fail,
Like thee, with sweetness freights the gale;
And thus, full oft, in shades obscure,   25
Th' unbending minstrel, proud and poor,
All shivering in misfortune's storm,
While half nutrition wastes his form,
From fancy's heights beholds the crowd below,
And spite of varied ills, uncheck'd his raptures flow.   30

Sweet are thy notes, yet minds intent
On life's prime object – cent. per cent.
Heed not thy soft delicious strain,
Nor any notes, save notes of gain;
Oh Ruddock, couldst thou name some shore   35
By Britain's trade uncurs'd before,
Where Afric's injur'd race would come
In crowds, for half the present sum,
Or couldst thou aid the speculating throng,
The great commercial few would pause, and praise thy song.   40

Sweet are thy notes, and yet I fear
Thou hast a dull and tasteless ear,
Else why forsake the lonely glen
For this dire deaf'ning din of men;
The rattling cart, the driver's bawl,   45
The mallet's stroke, the hawker's call,
The child's shrill scream, the windlass-song,
As slow the vessel moves along,
All these commix'd, with many a harsh sound more,
Rise to thy bleak abode in one discordant roar.   50

Sweet is thy song, and yet its flow
Comes o'er me like a tale of woe;
And ah! I fear, poor friendless thing,
That thou hast cause to droop thy wing;
If tempests whirl, and hailstones fly,   55
Thou hast no nest, no shelter nigh;
If famine pinch thee to the bone,
Thou canst not feed on slates and stone,
And tho' the corn-room near thy station lies,
Yet men have callous hearts, and cats have piercing eyes.   60

Poor Robin, yes, when howling blasts
Are heard among the neighbouring masts,
When dark clouds drive, and rain and sleet
Against the window fiercely beat,
It grieves me sore that thou, whose strains   65
Have sooth'd full oft my mental pains,
Shouldst feel within thy tiny craw
The bane of song, fell hunger's gnaw,
And oft I wish that thou wouldst hither come,
And make, in these hard times, my shelter'd box thy home.   70

What tho' I have an unfledg'd brood,
That daily chirp and gape for food,
There's not a nestling but with glee,
Would spare a crumb or two for thee;
Come then sweet bird, and thou shalt find   75
Protection from the nipping wind,
Shalt have thy orange doublet stor'd,
With the best fare our means afford,
And ere the snowdrop shews its spotless head,
Free as the mountain winds thy pinions may be spread.   80

SOLICITUDE.

(1806)

Oft when the tempest lords it wide,
   I skirt the roaring sea, Mary,
Or thro' the rocking forest glide,
   And mope and brood on thee, Mary;
Now dark despair my mind enshrouds,   5
   Now hope displays her light, Mary,
Like the wan moon 'midst driving clouds,
   Now muffled, and now bright, Mary.

If in the social circle press'd,
   While all around is glee, Mary,   10
Unmoved I sit, a silent guest,
   And think on love and thee, Mary;
I see thee girt with splendid beaux,
   Yet these no tortures bring, Mary,
The butterfly plays round the rose,   15
   But has no power to sting, Mary.

The gorgeous fool, who vaunts his wealth,
   Creates no anxious thought, Mary,
Like mental peace and rosy health,
   Thy love can ne'er be bought, Mary;   20
But oh! perchance some polish'd youth,
   Well skill'd in guile and art, Mary,
With witching tongue may vow his truth,
   And steal into thy heart, Mary.

Yet even then, refus'd, depress'd,   25
   Nay steep'd in blackest woe, Mary,
Yes, even then, if thou wert bless'd,
   No more my plaints should flow, Mary;
But oh! my heart declares the lie,
   Declares! it then would burst, Mary,   30
Indeed thou must each suit deny,
   Or oh! I shall be curst, Mary.

TOUSSAINT
TO HIS TROOPS.

(1806)

WHETHER forc'd from burning shores,
Where the tawny lion roars,
Whether doom'd with stripes and chains,
Here to dress your native plains;
Men of noble daring, say,   5
Shall we crouch to Gallia's sway;
Shall we wield again the hoe,
Taste again the cup of woe,
Or shall we rouse, and with the lightening's force
Blast the relentless foe, and desolate his course?   10

When the world's eternal sire
Placed on high yon glorious fire,
Were the splendid beams design'd,
For a part of human kind?
No! ye sable warriors, no!   15
All that live partake the glow;
Thus on man th' impartial God
Light, and winds, and rains bestow'd,
And widely thus were pour'd his dearest rights,
And he who slights the gift—th' Almighty donor slights.   20

Now with canvas white as foam,
See the vaunted legions come,
Nerv'd by freedom once they rose
And o'erwhelm'd a world of foes.
Now by freedom nerv'd no more,   25
Lo! the miscreants seek our shore;
Yes, the French who waste their breath,
Chaunting liberty or death,
Sweep the blue waves at usurpation's word,
And bring, oh fiends accurs'd! oppression or the sword.   30

Men whose famish'd sides have felt,
Strokes by dastard drivers dealt,
Men whose sorrowing souls have borne,
Wrong and outrage, toil and scorn,
Men whose wives the pallid brood,   35
Have by torturing arts subdu'd,
Friends of Toussaint! warriors brave!
Call to mind the mangled slave!
And Oh! remember, should your foes succeed,
That not yourselves alone, but all you love must bleed.   40

Fathers—shall the tiny race,
Objects of your fond embrace,
They who 'neath the tamarind tree,
Oft have gaily climb'd your knee;
Fathers, shall those prattlers share,   45
Pangs that slaves are doom'd to bear?
Shall their mirth and lisping tones,
Be exchanged for shrieks and groans?
And shall those arms that round your necks have twin'd,
Be to the twisted thong, and endless toil consign'd!   50

Towering spirits! ye who broke,
Slavery's agonizing yoke;
Ye, who like the whirlwind rush'd,
And your foes to atoms crush'd;
Ye, who from Domingo's strand,   55
Swept the daring British band;
Ye, oh warriors! ye who know,
Freedom's bliss, and slavery's woe,
Say! shall we bow to Buonaparte's train,
Or with unshaken nerves yon murderous whites disdain?   60

From those eyes that round me roll,
Wildly flash th' indignant soul;
On those rugged brows I see,
Stern unyielding liberty.
Yes! your daring aspects show,   65
France shall soon repent the blow;
Soon shall famish'd sharks be fed;
Vultures soon shall tear the dead;
Oh glorious hour! now, now, yon fiends defy,
Assert great nature's cause, live free, or bravely die.   70

ON

THE DEATH

OF

HUGH MULLIGAN.

(1806)

A Bard from the Mersey is gone,
　　Whose carols with energy flow'd;
Whose harp had a wildness of tone,
　　And a sweetness but rarely bestow'd.
Then say—ye dispensers of fame,　　　　　　　　　　5
　　Of wreathes that for ages will bloom,
Ah! say, shall poor Mulligan's name,
　　Go silently down to the tomb?

When the lordly are call'd from their state,
　　The marble their virtue imparts,　　　　　　　　　10
Yet the marble, ye insolent great,
　　Is often less cold than your hearts.
When the life of the warrior is o'er,
　　His deeds every tongue shall rehearse,
And now a pale Bard is no more,　　　　　　　　　　15
　　Ah! would you deny him a verse!

The thrush from the icicl'd bough,
　　Gives his song to the winterly gale,
And the violet, 'midst half melted snow,
　　Diffuses its sweets thro' the vale.　　　　　　　　20
And thus, while the minstrel I mourn,
　　'Mid the blasts of adversity pin'd,
While he droop'd all obscure and forlorn,
　　He pour'd his wild sweets on the wind.

Tho' the clouds that had sadden'd his days,　　　　　25
　　Were scatter'd and ting'd near the close;
Tho' he saw a few comforting rays,
　　Twas too late, and he sunk to repose.

122

So the bark, that fierce winds has endur'd,
  And the shocks of the pityless wave,   30
Finds a harbour, yet scarcely is moor'd,
  When she sinks to the dark oozy grave.

To the turf where poor MULLIGAN lies,
  The lover of genius shall stray,
And there should a rank weed arise,   35
  He shall pluck the intruder away.
But lowly, and simple, and sweet,
  Ah! should the wild violet appear,
He will sigh o'er an emblem so meet,
  And will water its cup with a tear.   40

TO A BALD-HEADED

POETICAL FRIEND.

(1806)

WHENE'ER a mount rich ore contains,
    Of trees, and shrubs, tis ever bare;
So where we find poetic brains,
    We seldom see luxuriant hair.
Perhaps the heat which minerals yield,   5
    The vegetative power destroys,
So where poetic fire's conceal'd,
    The surface oft uncover'd lies.
The mount is too an emblem meet,
    Of his reward who strikes the lyre,   10
For in these days howe'er replete,
    The bard may be, with innate fire,
Yet will his covering, spite of all his care,
Prove but too often like the mountain's—bare.

THE
ARDENT LOVER.

(1806)

Ah Mary! by that feeling mind,
Improved by thought, by taste refin'd,
And by those blue bewitching eyes,
And by those soul-seducing sighs,
And by that cheek's delicious bloom,   5
And by those lips that breathe perfume,
Here do I bow, at beauty's shrine,
And pledge this glowing heart of mine.

The tame, the impotent of soul,
A haughty mandate may control,   10
May make him slight a Helen's charms,
And take a dowdy to his arms;
But when did dark maternal schemes,
Or the stern father's towering dreams,
Or when did power, or affluence move   15
The heart, sublim'd by real love?

The cold slow thing that tamely woos,
Just as his worldly friends may chuse,
Is but a snail on beauty's rose,
That crawls and soils where'er he goes.   20
Not so the youth, whose mantling veins,
Are fill'd with love's ecstatic pains,
He heeds nor gold, nor craft, nor pride,
But strains, all nerve, his blushing bride.

Come then, oh come! and let me find   25
A pleader in thy feeling mind,
And let the beams from those blue eyes
Disperse the clouds that round me rise;
And let those lips, that breathe perfume,
With speed pronounce my blissful doom,   30
With speed before the sacred shrine,
Pledge thy dear self for ever mine.

THE
LASS OF LIVERPOOL.

(1806)

WHERE cocoas lift their tufted heads,
 And orange blossoms scent the breeze,
Her charms the mild Mulatto spreads,
 And moves with soft and wanton ease;
And I have seen her witching wiles,   5
 And I have kept my bosom cool,
For how could I forget thy smiles,
 O! lovely lass of Liverpool.

The softest tints the conch displays,
 The cheek of her I love outvies,   10
And the sea breeze 'midst burning rays,
 Is not more cheering than her eyes;
Dark as the pettrel is her hair,
 And Sam, who calls me love-sick fool,
Ne'er saw a tropic bird more fair   15
 Than my sweet lass of Liverpool.

Tho' doom'd from early life to brave
 The feverish swamp, and furious blast,
Tho' doom'd to face the foam-capt wave,
 And mount the yard and quivering mast;   20
Tho' doom'd to brave each noxious soil,
 And train'd in stern misfortune's school,
Yet still, O! 'twould be bliss to toil
 For thee, sweet lass of Liverpool.

And when we reach the crowded pier,   25
 And the broad yards are quickly mann'd,
O! should my lovely girl be near,
 And sweetly smile, and wave her hand,
With ardent soul, I'd spring to shore,
 And scorning dull decorum's rule,   30
To my fond bosom o'er and o'er
 Would press the lass of Liverpool.

126

WOMAN.

(1806)

LET the hawk shew his wing and each warbler shall cease,
   Let the north keenly rage and each flow'ret shall close,
Yet woman, sweet woman, more simple than these,
   Oft looks for protection to merciless foes.
O! may she when lovers with fervency plead,   5
   All their glances, their sighs, and their vows, disbelieve,
And if whinings and oaths to their flattery succeed,
   O! may she reflect that e'en these may deceive.

The dolphin pursuing his swift-flying prey,
   Shews a thousand rich tints which before were unseen,   10
So in love's glowing chase woman's foes oft display
   New ardors of mind, and new graces of mien;
Yet ah! when new ardors, new graces arise,
   New arts are contrived to allure and enslave,
And passion a pathway of roses supplies,   15
   O'er which the poor female oft trips to the grave.

The man who in dealing with man is correct,
   In dealing with woman, a traitor shall prove,
Shall attempt to seduce where he ought to protect,
   And blight with his sighs the sweet blossoms of love;   20
Then be firm, Oh ye maids! and the bold still repel,
   And with keen circumspection the artful disarm,
For man is a rattle-snake, wily and fell,
   And you the poor birds oft destroy'd by his charm.

MARY'S DEATH.

(1806)

To the cliffs, while below the huge surges are foaming,
    No more with wan cheek shall poor Mary retire,
'Mong the dark waving fern shall no more be seen roaming,
    Nor chaunting wild strains, o'er the grave of her sire.
Ah no! the straw shed in which Dermot delighted,   5
And Dermot whose vows to poor Erin were plighted,
And Dermot's sweet rose-bud so shamefully blighted,
    Like the blue mists of morn are all melted away.

Yes Erin's fair daughters, the love-beaming Mary,
    Whose bosom had nothing of snow but its hue,   10
Who was once like yourselves all attractive and airy,
    Has bow'd her sweet head, and bade outrage adieu.
No more the unfeeling despoiler shall harm her,
Nor the blood-sprinkled scythe of oppression alarm her,
Nor can all the soft joys of the cabin now charm her,   15
    For the winds deeply moan as they sweep o'er her grave.

Tho' her cheek grew more wan, and more languid each motion,
    Yet still to her haunts she would daily withdraw;
Would climb to the verge of the blue rolling ocean,
    Or roam the wide heath with her basket of straw.   20
And still from those scenes, with the day star descending,
A few whispering children her footsteps attending,
She would hie to the willow, and mournfully bending,
    Would scatter fresh flowers o'er the grave of her sire.

Like the pale frosted flow'ret, to earth slow returning,   25
    Thus the sufferer declined whilst her relatives mourn'd,
Yet still the hoarse rage of the elements scorning,
    To the grave of her father she duly return'd.
When lo! at the close of a day dark and dreary,
From the sea fowl's bleak craigs, came the once beauteous Mary;   30
All drench'd were her cloathes and her steps faint and weary,
    Yet in tones wildly sweet thus she sung o'er her sire.

"Ah! view the long grass, see it waves as in sadness,
    "It sighs in the blast and its green head is low;
"When, when, shall I wing to the regions of gladness,   35
    "Dear mother come strip me this 'kerchief of snow.
"I saw the red arm, saw the steel's dreadful gleaming,
"Oh! how cold were his lips, while the life's blood was streaming,
"On the verge of yon cloud, see his bright form is beaming,
    "He beckons, and hark, oh! 'tis Mary he calls.   40

And now the poor soul, while the bleak winds swept o'er her,
    On her father's cold grave sigh'd her being away,
And long shall thy daughters, oh Erin! deplore her,
    And deck the green turf that now mantles her clay,
And at eve, when the spoiler's dark doings are stated,   45
The fate of poor Dermot shall oft be related,
And the cabin's brave tenants, with fire unabated,
    Shall brand thy destroyers, sweet Mary le More.

THE HALCYON.

(1806)

When the keen Halcyon o'er the watery plain,
   Spreads his gay plumage in the blaze of day,
Lured by the splendid tints the finny train,
   Leave the dark ooze, and near the surface play.
Side-long they glide, now flounce above the stream,   5
   Charm'd is their eye, their fears no more abound;
And now the plunderer, with his lynx-like beam,
   Unerring darts, and scatters ruin round.
So the coy maiden, from the peaceful groves,
   Is lured by man's gay garb and winning wiles;   10
Pleas'd she beholds the pest—anon she loves,
   And the soft passion every care beguiles;
When lo! the ever-watchful spoiler springs,
And to the poor charm'd wretch, o'erwhelming ruin brings.

THE SHRIKE.

(1806)

Perch'd on yon moss-grown bough, keen-eyed and strong,
   Behold the dingy shrike! his treacherous throat
Now imitates the throstle's ardent song,
   And now the blackbird's wild mellifluous note:
These witching strains, that wounds and death precede,   5
   From the the thick brake the feather'd folks decoy;
And now the ruffian, with the lightning's speed
   Wild screaming darts, and now the victims die:
So, on the unsuspecting virgin's ear,
   The soft seducer pours his flattering strain,   10
Sounds so delicious calm each rising fear,
   Her steps impel, and thrill thro' every vein,
Charm'd, she advances—softer strains arise,
When lo! the foul fiend darts, and reputation dies!

BRITON, AND NEGRO SLAVE.

(1806)

SCENE.— *A Plantation in Jamaica.*

BRITON.

AWAY, rebellious dog—or by this arm—

NEGRO.

E'en use me as you list—rail, threaten, torture,
All, all I will endure, so my lov'd Zuna,
My wife, my comfort, be not ravish'd from me.
    B. I tell thee once for all she is thine no longer,   5
And now, one other word—
    N.   What do I hear!
Not mine! O white-man think on what you're doing,
For by our sacred—
    B.   Villain dost thou threaten,
Here's what shall make thee humble.   *(beats him.)*
    N.   Ever thus,
Unjust and cruel we poor negroes find you;   10
But mark, by Obi! and our Gods I swear!
Never to rest till she whom you have forced,
Is to my hut restored.
    B.   What, threaten still!
What, brave me to my face; then will I try
Which first shall tire, this arm or thy base tongue!   15
                          (beats him again.)
    N. Your lash may drink my blood, but cannot change me,
No, were I burning by your ling'ring fires,
Or gibbeted alive, and to resign her
Would bring me life, nay, with it even freedom,
I'd spurn them both, and welcome my destruction.   20
    B. Is this the tractable, the patient Egbo,
This the meek slave so much extoll'd by white-men,
Why, thou hast mutiny in every glance,
But soon thy master shall be undeceived,
And that fierce threat'ning soul of thine be humbled.   25
    N. O give me Zuna back, and not a steer

That drags your produce to the distant beach,
Shall bear the yoke more meekly than myself;
But if she be denied me, not a shark
That prowls your bays, shall more delight in blood; 30
Look to't I say, for by my father's ghost
You shall not tamely wrong me.
    B.   Sable villain,
Is this a language fitting for thy station,
Fit for a white-man's ear.
    N.   I have a wife,
And who would force her from me does me wrong, 35
Whatever be his colour.
    B.   Thou'rt a wretch,
A dog, a slave, and shou'dst have learnt submission.
    N. Long have I borne oppression, long have felt
All the hard pangs that slavery is heir to,
But Zuna softens all, O! she's the prop 40
Which makes me bear this load, pluck her away,
Down, down, the poor distracted Egbo comes,
But in his fall may pluck destruction round him.
    B. Oft the musquito's bite brings on his ruin
Although he cannot hurt; be cautious then, 45
Or thro' these threat'nings thou too may'st be crush'd;
As to thy Zuna, as thou call'st her, mark me,
She is at present mine, and shall remain so,
Till like a boy that feeds on ripe Bananas
I'm surfeited with sweets—then if thou wilt, 50
Thou may'st again embrace her.
    N.   Oh! cursed white-men.
    B. Now by the rolling of those eyes I see
How much thou art delighted.
    N.   Damn'd oppressors!
    B. Aye swear a little, slave 'twill do thee good,
I'll to thy master now and tell him all 55
The gentle things thou'st said, and ere the shell
Has call'd thee thrice to labour, I perchance
May find some way to cool these fiery humours.

ABSENCE.

(1806)

WHEN thro' the wild unfathom'd deep,
Wet with the briny spray we sweep,
To Kate, to lovely Kate, and home,
My anxious thoughts unceasing roam.
Again I see her on the pier, 5
Again behold the falling tear,
Again I view her bosom swell,
And hear the sorrowing word farewell.

When all is calm, and the bleach'd sails
Are furl'd, or hanging in the brayls, 10
The wide expanse of glassy sea,
And sky from cloudy vapours free,
While thoughtless o'er the side I lean,
Bring to my mind the placid mien,
Of that dear girl whom I adore, 15
And left in tears on Albion's shore.

Or when the fierce tornadoes howl,
And nerve the fearless seaman's soul,
The towering surges as they break
Display the whiteness of her neck, 20
The pettrels too that seem to tread,
The foamy brine with wings outspread,
Oft bring the ebon locks to mind,
Of that dear girl I left behind.

When on my watch the dawn full oft, 25
Has shewn those tints so mild and soft,
That mark the lip and cheek of her,
Whom I 'bove all her sex prefer;
And thus where'er the seaman goes,
'Midst torrid heat or polar snows, 30
Some image still recalls to mind,
The 'witching charms he leaves behind.

ON THE DEATH

OF

A MUCH LOVED RELATIVE.

(1806)

SHALT thou, oh my sister! my friend!
  Go down to the sorrowful cell,
And shall I, the sad pageant attend,
  And not bid thee a solemn farewell?
Yes, yes, the farewell shall be thine   5
  In a strain thou wert wont to approve,
And oh! while remembrance is mine,
  I will mournfully cherish thy love.

From the world when mere kindred retire,
  The wounds of the bosom soon heal,   10
But when those we delight in expire,
  To the heart's deep recesses we feel.
Ah! Bessey, thro' life's chequer'd way,
  Thou wert never unmindful of me,
Nor do I remember the day,   15
  When I felt not affection for thee.

Now memory recalls the sweet hours,
  When in childhood we gaily have stroll'd,
Have gather'd the dew-spangled flowers,
  Or adown the lov'd brow we have roll'd;   20
And perchance when with exercise warm'd,
  As we sat on the earth's verdant lap,
For thee the bark-pipe I have form'd,
  Or with rushes have made thee a cap.

When a sea-boy just 'scaped from on board,   25
  Just 'scaped from a pestilent sky,
Thy rapture remembrance has stor'd,
  And the beams of thy dark-laughing eye;

And oh! when of vision bereft,
    And when science pronounc'd the decree,   30
To my agonized soul there was left,
    An affectionate soother in thee.

'Twas thus oh! my sister! my friend!
    With our beings our fondness increas'd,
Wert thou wrong'd, I was proud to defend,   35
    If I sorrow'd thy gaiety ceas'd.
And when other duties were known,
    When our cares with our little ones grew,
The sun of our kindness still shone,
    And no dark chilling mists ever knew.   40

As droops the wild rose on the spray,
    When the clouds not a rain-drop bestow,
So wert thou slowly wither'd away,
    By the hectic's infuriate glow.
And now deeply worn, yet serene,   45
    And more softly than falls the light leaf,
Thou hast glided from life's flowery scene,
    And o'erwhelm'd thy connexions with grief.

Ah! couldst thou thy partner descry,
    As he hangs o'er those pledges so dear,   50
Couldst thou witness the deep-heaving sigh,
    While his cheek is bedew'd with a tear;
Couldst thou pierce the deep folds of the heart
    And thy relatives see undisguis'd,
Ah! Bessey, the view would impart,   55
    How worth and how sweetness are priz'd.

And now while my tremulous woes,
    To these poor beamless eyeballs upswell,
Oh! let the warm tear as it flows,
    Be my silent, my solemn farewell.   60
Thou art gone—dearest friend of my heart,
    Thou art gone to the awful unknown,
And, hereafter, wherever thou art,
    Oh! may I, on that region be thrown.

ENTREATY.

(1806)

Ah Mary! when I'm far away,
  And landmen spread their wily snares,
Ah! heed not what those flatterers say,
  But think on one whom ocean bears.
On one, who when the furious blast,   5
  Tears up, and whitens o'er the sea,
High on the yard or quivering mast,
  Oft heaves a sigh, and thinks on thee.

When gay trimm'd sparks about thee swarm,
  Like humming-birds round some sweet flower,   10
And praise with pertness every charm,
  And oft confess thy 'witching power;
Say Mary wilt thou then forget,
  That youth who scorns all flattery,
That youth who broils 'midst torrid heat,   15
  And spite of perils, sighs for thee?

Should form, and art, and wealth unite,
  In one of these—Ah! Mary, say,
Couldst thou his soft advances slight,
  For sake of one so far away?   20
Couldst thou forego an affluent state,
  And all the pomp of high degree,
To share perhaps the lowly fate,
  Of one who brings but love for thee?

If so, ah! tell me, tell me why,   25
  Should we the rapturous hours delay,
Be mine, and all my doubts will fly,
  Like fogs before the rising day.
Yes, dearest girl, while yet on shore,
  Oh! let me taste of ecstacy,   30
Give, give thy hand, I ask no more,
  For 'twill be bliss to toil for thee.

A CAUTION
TO MY FRIEND J. M.

(1806)

ROUND her precious productions wise nature oft flings
   Her dull cheerless colourings and rugged array;
In a rust-coloured doublet the Nightingale sings,
   And the russet-clad Lark hails the first blush of day.
Mark the crust of the diamond, when first 'tis descried,   5
   View the coat of the cocoa, how homely and rough,
See the luscious anana, Pomona's chief pride,
   Conceal'd in a garb of inelegant stuff;
Now 'tis thus with the form in which genius is shrin'd,
   Ever plain is the mantle, the hues ever deep,   10
Nay fate has oft shrouded this essence of mind,
   In the pauper's grim cloak, and the hide of a sweep;
Then of splendor, thou son of the muse, Oh beware!
For the true mark of talent, is dingy and bare.

THE THROSTLE.

(1806)

ERE the dark driving tempest was pass'd,
　Or daisies had dizen'd the spring,
A throstle, despising the blast,
　In the garden of Gripus would sing;
And Gripus, who heard with delight　　　　　　　5
　The music which flow'd without pay,
Bade William beware, and not fright
　The high-sounding minstrel away.

In the morning, ere Gripus arose,
　The throstle was pouring his song,　　　　　　10
Or at noon, if a ramble he chose,
　The notes were mellifluous and strong.
Oh how rich, the old merchant would cry,
　Is the music thus bounteously given,
With that cadence what mortal can vie,　　　　15
　And those trills were all furnish'd by heaven.

Now spring shew'd her changeable face,
　Her tresses with primroses bound,
And scatter'd, with exquisite grace,
　Her blooms and wild flow'rets around.　　　　20
And the minstrel, his partner to cheer,
　As she sat on their embryo brood,
Now pour'd the wild song on her ear,
　And now brought her the choicest of food.

In a cherry-tree's fork the fond pair　　　　　25
　Had fashion'd their clay-lined abode,
And round them their favourite fare
　In clusters deliciously glow'd:
In a region thus plenteously stored,
　With joy they expected their young,　　　　　30
They were feasted at nature's broad board,
　And all was wild rapture and song.

But ah! as the sun's brightest ray,
    To the darkest of clouds may give birth,
As the lily, all stately today,   35
    May to-morrow be trampled to earth:
So, now the poor throstle, whose flow
    Could the ear of a Gripus enchant,
Beheld all his joy turn to woe,
    And all his abundance to want.   40

Old Gripus, who saw in his rounds,
    That his fruit was diminish'd and peck'd,
Resolved from his garden and grounds,
    The poor feather'd folks to eject;
And calling for William, he swore,   45
    That the nest should be taken away,
That his precious *white-hearts* should no more
    Be left to those plunderers a prey.

Now William, with feelings distress'd,
    Up-mounting the tree, soon declared,   50
That an unfeather'd brood fill'd the nest,
    And begg'd the poor souls might be spared.
No! No! cried the merchant, with ire,
    Not a chirper shall 'scape from my gripe,
Thou may'st praise the sweet powers of their sire,   55
    But scoundrel! my cherries are ripe.

Oh! 'twas piteous to see the old pair,
    As they flutter'd with anguish around,
And to hear the sharp notes of despair,
    When the nestlings were thrown to the ground.   60
Oh! 'twas piteous, but Gripus, whose soul
    Nor flutterings nor wailings could sway,
Made William up-raise the long pole,
    And chase the meek mourners away.

As the patron who favours a bard,   65
    While the bard rich effusions can give,
Yet kindly withdraws his regard,
    When he finds the poor warbler must live;
So the wretch who applauded the song,
    While his garden display'd not a leaf,   70
Now cherries around him were hung,
    Devoted the minstrel to grief.

And for this may the throstle no more
    Change his notes for old Gripus's fruit,
From his grounds may the Lark never soar,   75
    On his boughs may the Ruddock be mute;
And, for this may his bloom be the prey
    Of the keen-gnawing worm and the blight
And may rooks prove his syrens by day,
    And owls and dark ravens by night.   80

THE COMPLAINT.

(1806)

THE bulfinch no music can boast,
   While wandering the gardens among,
But nature, when freedom is lost,
   Endows the poor captive with song.
So, I, ere my heart could approve,   5
   Regarded not melody's page,
But now I am fetter'd by love,
   And with sounds I my anguish assuage.

When I caroll'd of war and of wine,
   In hopes to abandon my pain,   10
Discordance has mark'd every line,
   And I've found all my efforts were vain.
'Tis the plaintive alone which can please,
   'Tis the plaintive which soothes my fond soul,
Yet often those cordials that ease,   15
   Raise a malady 'bove all control.

The notes of the Lark give me pain,
   His music too cheerfully flows,
But the Robin's soft querulous strain
   Is in unison still with my woes.   20
I have heard of the Nightingale's lay,
   But his song to the north is unknown,
Ah! would he but travel this way,
   I would listen all night to his moan.

The joyous I cautiously shun,   25
   Their mirth is disgusting to me;
Nay I loathe e'en the glare of the sun,
   For it acts on my feelings like glee.
When the mole leaves his darksome retreat,
   When the urchin is seeking for prey,   30
When the poor harass'd hare quits her seat,
   O'er the moorlands by moonlight I stray.

When I dream of my love, and awake,
   Tho' disdain had appear'd in her eye,
Chagrin'd, every method I take   35
   The delusion again to enjoy.
Oh Lucy! attend to the strain
   Of one who but feebly can sue,
Oh Lucy! reject not a swain
   Who loves with a passion so true.   40

THE PIER.

(1806)

THE distant signal kiss'd the gale,
  Th' expecting soul was cheer'd,
And soon with bleach'd expanded sail,
  The wish'd-for bark appear'd;
When blue-ey'd Kate of rosy hue,   5
To meet her fearless seaman flew.

The breeze her well-turn'd ankle shew'd,
  One hand her cloak fast held,
Her colour'd ribbons gaily flow'd,
  Her heart tumultuous swell'd;   10
With eager step she reach'd the pier,
And found the towering vessel near.

And now with agitated mien,
  The sun-burnt crew she eyed,
No Ben, alas! could there be seen,   15
  "Ah! where's my love?" she cried;
At length his well-known voice she heard,
High mounted on the pendant yard.

Now sparkling joy and trembling fear,
  In Kate's blue eyes were found,   20
While Ben survey'd the crouded pier,
  And pass'd his gasket round;
Their eyes soon met—they smiling gazed,
And each th' expressive hand uprais'd.

The canvas furl'd, with ardor strong,   25
  Swift to his love he press'd,
And there, amidst a tittering throng,
  He strain'd her to his breast;
"And do I fold thee, Kate," he cried,
"And oh my Ben," she faint reply'd.   30

And now behold, with heart as light
   As is the salt sea foam,
And eyes with rapture beaming bright
   The tar safe moor'd at home;
And here tho' whirling storms arise,   35
In Kate's fond arms secure he lies.

MARY.

(1806)

GRIM was the night, the winds were up,
　　And round the mansion fiercely howl'd,
In forky gleams the lightning flew,
　　And quick the awful thunders roll'd;
When lo! a flash to Mary's eyes,　　　　　　　　　　　5
　　A wan and shadowy form display'd,
That close beside her curtain stood,
　　All in a seaman's garb array'd.

Again the livid lightning flash'd,
　　Again she heard the driving storm,　　　　　　　　10
And while her veins with horror thrill'd,
　　Again she saw the shadowy form;
His dark dim eyes on her's were fixed,
　　In speechless agony she lay,
And now she saw his pale lips move,　　　　　　　　15
　　And wildly mournful heard him say.

"From that far shore, where rest my bones,
　　"Beneath the cooling tamarind's shade,
"Permitted o'er the waves I come,
　　"To shew the havoc thou hast made,　　　　　　　20
"Thou know'st, oh Mary! how I lov'd,
　　"My ardent soul was full of thee,
"And thou remember'st passing well,
　　"The solemn vows thou mad'st to me.

"When on the pier, our sails all loose,　　　　　　　25
　　"I warmly press'd thee to my heart,
"And saw the tear bedew thy cheek,
　　"I found 'twas almost death to part;
"Yet scarcely was our canvas spread,
　　"When lured by gold and splendid shew,　　　　　30
"Thou gav'st that palsied thing thy hand,
　　"And laid thy faithful lover low.

"Deep in the foldings of thy heart,
    "To these sad eyes exposed and bare,
"I view my image strongly traced,   35
    "But see no love of husband there.
"No! no, thou loath'st his very touch,
    "The gall of bitterness is thine,
"Oh! fatal act that curst thy days,
    "And bade dark sorrow finish mine.   40

"Now what avails thy rich attire,
    "The costly room, the downy bed;
"Or what avails thy husband's gold,
    "Since peace is from thy bosom fled.
"At this dread hour, (the bell toll'd one)   45
    "To thee my visits must be paid,
"Nor can they cease, 'till thy fair form,
    "With many a writhing worm is laid.

"Poor trembler yes, where'er thou art,
    "Or at the cheering festive board,   50
"Or mingling in the joyous dance,
    "Or here beside thy ancient lord,
"Where'er thou art at this dread hour,
    "My form shall agitate thy breast,
"And when I leave thee, those false lips,   55
    "Shall be, oh Mary! thus imprest."

And now she felt his icy touch,
    And now she heard the dull farewell,
Convulsed she scream'd, her husband slept,
    But Mary's feelings who can tell?   60
Time roll'd along, and still she found,
    The spectre kept th' appointed hour,
Time roll'd along and Mary droop'd,
    And all bemoan'd the fading flower.

And now with wan and hollow cheek,   65
    And maniac wildness in her eye,
She told her pitying friends her tale,
    And own'd her love, and wish'd to die;
And she would sit in gloomy guise,
    And she would mope the live-long day,   70
And she would start with woe-touch'd brain,
    And thus would pour the sorrowing lay.

"An ensign was my true love's pall,
  "The ship-bell toll'd him to the shore,
"They lodged him 'neath the tamarind's tree,   75
  "The sun-burnt crew lamenting sore.
"By day he haunts the rosy clouds,
  "By night his visits never fail,
"See where he glides—I come my life!
  "But prithee do not look so pale.   80

"I love him not—but hush—no more,
  "He's kind, and how can I despise,
"The raven's wing is not so black,
  "As were my fearless seaman's eyes.
"His jacket was of crimson fine,   85
  "His trowsers like the drifted snow,
"The morn's fresh tint was on his cheek,
  "Oh shame on her who laid him low!

Thus Mary raved, till one gray morn,
  When beating wild her throbbing breast,   90
"See where he waits on yon dark cloud,
  "I come!" she cried, and sunk to rest,
And now, with pompous solemn rites,
  They bore her to her earthy bed,
A proof that glare and gold are trash,   95
  If from the bosom peace be fled.

THE ORIGIN

OF

TURTLE AND PUNCH.

(1806)

As round their ambrosia, the Gods once were met,
   And goblets of nectar went rapidly round,
What pity, cried Bacchus, that no such a treat,
   For my followers on yon rolling orb can be found;
          Well, well, exclaimed Jove,   5
          Now thy hint we approve,
And to show thee that mortals have much of our love,
We will—that no deity venture to rise,
Till some choice dish is named which terrestrials may prize.

A fig for mankind and their paltry affairs,   10
   Cried termagant Juno, and turned up her nose;
Jove frown'd, and said, madam, no more of those airs,
   And now ocean's God let us hear thee propose,
          Old Neptune roar'd fish!
          That's an excellent dish!   15
Lisp'd amorous Venus, but Pallas cried pish!
To mortals more dear is the sirloin's rich roast,
Than all the scaled dainties thy ocean can boast.

Give them fowl, wild and tame, cried the God of the strings,
   And to relish the feast add a ham nicely cured,   20
Momus swore that beef rashers were excellent things,
   But Hermes cried pshaw! they will ne'er be endured.
          Thus their clamours increase,
          When old Jove thunders, peace!
We will this contention do instantly cease,   25
Upon fish, flesh, or fowl, you will never agree,
So a creature I'll form shall include all the three.

At this, loud applause, thro' the Deities ran,
   All said 'twas a thought worthy wisdom so hoar,

When sparkling-eyed Bacchus, still friendly to man,   30
   Thank'd his sire, but declared he had one request more.
        Let us hear it my boy!
        Cried the king of the sky,
  Why father said Bacchus, and look'd rather sly,
Since you to those mortals such viands have given,   35
Let the whole be wash'd down with a draught worthy heaven.

Right, right, quoth old thunder, and seemed in high glee,
   Thou know'st to man's comfort I nothing will grudge,
But I leave mortals nectar entirely to thee,
   For in things of this nature, who like thee can judge.   40
        For mercy's sake Jove!
        Exclaim'd Wisdom and Love,
  Let its strength be no more than what we shall approve,
For my part, quoth Jove, your weak stuff I detest,
But I leave it to Bacchus, for he should know best.   45

For thy trust, and for thus disregarding their spite,
   I thank thee, great Jove! cried the God of the vine,
And since fish, flesh, and fowl, in their feast will unite,
   So shall sour, sweet, and strong, in their beverage combine.
        Thus Bacchus, the friend   50
        Of poor mortals obtained,
  From the sire of the Gods, what should ne'er be disdain'd,
No, since turtle and punch were thus bounteously given,
To enjoy them must surely be pleasing to heaven.

PARODY

OF A PASSAGE IN MEASURE FOR MEASURE.

Aye, but to die, &c.

(1806)

Aye, but to love, and not be lov'd again,
To nurse a hopeless passion, and to pine,
This body strong and healthy to become
A walking mummy—and the once cheerful mind
To feel keen torturing doubts, or to despair   5
And moping sit in melancholy mood,
To feel the gusts of love and wild desire,
And know friends, fortune, person, all combine
To blast our hopes—or to feel tortures keener still,
To see a rival snatch away the prize;   10
Heavens! 'tis too horrible—the keenest pangs
That e'er the body felt, stone or rheumatic,
Amputated limb, nay, even gout itself,
Is perfect ease compared with hopeless love.

THE FAREWELL.

(1806)

THE shivering topsails home are sheeted,
   And cheerly goes the windlass round,
Heave, heave, my hearts, is oft repeated,
   And Mary sighs at every sound.
The yellow fever scattering ruin,   5
   The shipwreck'd veteran's dying cries,
And war, the decks with carnage strewing,
   All, all, before her fancy rise.

As bends the primrose meek and lowly,
   All bruis'd by April's pelting hail,   10
So, while the anchor rises slowly,
   Poor Mary droops, distress'd and pale.
And oft, while at his handspike toiling,
   Full many a glance her seaman steals,
And oft he tries by gaily smiling   15
   To hide the parting pang he feels.

Now thro' the blocks the wind is howling,
   The pilot to the helmsman cries,
And now the bulky ship is rolling,
   And now aloft the sea-boy flies.   20
The whiten'd canvas swift is spreading,
   Around the bows the surges foam,
And many a female tear is shedding,
   And thoughts prevail for love and home.

Her tar among the sun-burnt faces,   25
   Now Mary views with fond regard,
Now o'er the deck his form she traces,
   Now trembling sees him on the yard.
Where'er he moves, alert and glowing,
   Her beauteous azure eyes pursue,   30
Those eyes that shew, with grief o'erflowing,
   Like violets wet with morning dew.

Unmoved, midst regions wild and dreary,
    Poor WILL had pass'd thro' woes severe,
Yet now from far he views his Mary,   35
    And turns to hide a falling tear.
The biting winds blow strong and stronger,
    And the broad waves more wildly swell,
WILL hears the boat can wait no longer,
    And springs abaft to bid farewell.   40

Oh my sweet girl! with strong emotion,
    The tar exclaims, now, now adieu!
I go to brave the changeful ocean,
    Yet thou shalt find me ever true.
With quivering lip and deep dejection,   45
    Heaven shield my WILL, she cries, from harms,
His look bespeaks extreme affection,
    And now he locks her in his arms.

Again the boatmen, hoarsely bawling,
    Declare they cannot, will not stay,   50
And tho' the crew the cat are hawling,
    Yet WILL must see his love away.
Now at the side expression ceases,
    She gains the skiff, she makes for land,
And 'twixt them as the brine increases,   55
    They gaze, they sigh, they wave the hand.

THE RETURN.

(1806)

HOARSE swept the gale o'er Cambrian snows,
　　And capt old Mersey's brine with foam,
Hoarse swept the gale, in dark clouds clad,
　　When Mary sighing left her home.
The bark that bore her love, 'twas fear'd,　　　　　　　　5
　　Had founder'd midst th' Atlantic roar,
And e'en those friends that talk'd of hope,
　　Believ'd she ne'er would see him more.

Full many a wild and fearful night
　　Had Mary listen'd to the storm,　　　　　　　　　　10
And cankering grief had now assail'd
　　Her rosy cheek and lovely form.
Heaven's brightest azure tinged her eye,
　　Profuse her auburn ringlets flow'd,
And tho' to pursy pomp unknown,　　　　　　　　　　15
　　Her heart was virtue's pure abode.

O'er the rough beach the mourner stray'd,
　　Sad brooding thoughts had nerv'd her mind,
Unmoved she heard the wild waves beat,
　　Unmoved she braved the piercing wind.　　　　　　20
And now beyond the sable point,
　　With snow-white sails and crippled mast,
Rock'd by the surge a bark appear'd,
　　And soon the ponderous anchor cast.

Awhile with hope the wanderer gaz'd,　　　　　　　　25
　　But now in tones to nature true,
"A three-mast ship is mine," she cried,
　　"And yon, alas! has only two."
The sea-mew scream'd, the night approached,
　　The tempest swept with wilder roar,　　　　　　　　30
And tho' her cheeks were cold as death,
　　Yet still she press'd along the shore.

And now the whirling blast increas'd,
 She paus'd—she eyed the raging flood,
When lo! a skiff with rapid wing,   35
 Made for the rocks on which she stood.
The well-arm'd crew soon reach'd the shore,
 'Twas frolic all, and gibe, and joke,
When one with manly port drew near,
 And thus to trembling Mary spoke—   40

"But just return'd to Britain's strand,
 "To all that seamen hold most dear,
"We dread the press, and you my love,
"Can say if we have ought to fear."
 "Oh God! that voice," poor Mary cried,   45
"Oh 'tis my WILL! my joy! my life!"
 Expression ceas'd, and quick as thought,
WILL sprung and caught his falling wife.

"Oh heavens! 'tis she, the tar exclaim'd,
 And strain'd her to his glowing heart,   50
"Oh! 'tis my love, and would to heav'n,
 "We never, never, more might part."
And now the sun-burnt crew advance,
 And now thro' secret paths they roam,
And noiseless soon all reach the town,   56
 And taste the dear delights of home.

TO THE GOUT.

(1806)

LORD of the trembling nerve and sleepless eye,
   Full sixteen winters now have roll'd away,
   Since first I felt thy lacerating sway,
And bow'd before thee with a sullen sigh.
Yes, sixteen years, and 'mid th' inclement blast,   5
   Still to my cozie hearth, and elbow chair,
   In flannels wrapt, would'st thou, oh gout! repair,
Making each visit longer than the last.
Oh! how I loathe thy presence, yet as true
   As is the swallow to the April flower,   10
   Still wouldst thou come with renovated power,
And more than all my former pangs renew.
But now — oh! thanks to Zoonomia's page
Pure element I quaff, and scorn thy bloated rage.

THE DEATH

OF

MISS E. FLETCHER.

(1806)

As late the king of terrors stalk'd around,
  The radiant form of virtue he descry'd,
Then with malignant look, and hollow sound,
  Mankind's preserver, "whither now?" he cried—

Unaw'd at this salute, the form replies,   5
  "I go, grim power, to mend the human heart,
"To teach the young thy terrors to despise,
  "The old by temperance to avoid thy dart."

"Indeed," with horrid grin, return'd the king,
  "Then mark me, virtue, ere the sun appears,   10
"With this unerring hand, this bow, and string,
  "I'll do a deed shall drown thine eyes in tears.

"One of thy choicest favourites now shall fall,
  "Whose beauty few can equal, none excel,
"Scarce nineteen summers ripe, belov'd by all,   15
  "Yet even she shall bid the world farewell."

He drew a shaft from his unerring bow,
  Virtue o'erwhelm'd with terror heard the sound,
But oh! ye mortals, what must be her woe,
  When FLETCHER, lovely FLETCHER, felt the wound.   20

THE CHASE.

(1806)

FROM the coarse clumsy clown, to his high polish'd grace,
From mere rags to brocade, all mankind are in chase,
All, all, mount their hobbies, and thro' life's short day,
After fame, wealth, or pleasure, cry hark! hark away!
Hark away is the word, passion sounds her sweet horn, 5
And mortals too often leave reason forlorn.

From virtue's fair heights, to the deep glens of shame,
View the wily seducer pursuing his game,
She doubles, she pauses, and then 'tis all o'er,
For the maid who once pauses must live to deplore. 10
Hark away, &c.

Mock patriots while thundering aloud in debate,
In fancy are chasing some office of state,
And courtiers who grin at such paltry grimace,
Oft hunt for expedients to keep their dear place. 15
Hark away, &c.

The rough son of Neptune hunts wealth on the seas,
In hopes to come to, in the harbour of ease,
And when crimson war makes the nations all mourn,
Why, he hunts Britain's foes—or is chas'd in his turn. 20
Hark away, &c.

Behold how the miser keeps interest in view,
Nor till thrown in the dirt, will he cease to pursue,
View the trader hunt orders, tho' oft, tis well known,
He must mount the dun horse in pursuit of his own. 25
Hark away, &c.

Thus the world's a wide forest, abounding with game,
Where we dash with wild hope, after wealth, pleasure, fame,
For as children chase rainbows, so day after day,
Tho' we find all delusion, we cry, hark away! 30
Hark away, &c.

THE
WINTER'S PASSAGE.

(1806)

In labouring home from noxious skies,
   While winter holds his furious reign,
Severest hardships oft arise,
   To Britain's rugged sea-beat train.
Then list to what these fearless souls,   5
   Are doom'd alas to undergo,
While you enjoy convivial bowls,
   And all that friendly hearths bestow.

When for Hibernia's craggy shore,
   The seaman looks with anxious gaze,   10
And thinks his sufferings nearly o'er,
   And talks of future joyous days;
Oft clad in ice, and hail, and snow,
   The baleful eastern blasts will come,
Inflicting many a bitter woe,   15
   And baffling all attempts for home.

Impetuous now the tempest raves,
   The bark no longer cleaves the deep,
But lies exposed to hideous waves,
   That with o'erwhelming fury sweep;   20
While with the surges still in view,
   And holding fast, whene'er they break,
The patient tar drench'd thro' and thro',
   All shivering walks the slippery deck.

The sleet descends in cutting showers,   25
   And now the blasts grow more severe,
The pumps require unusual powers,
   The boats one block of ice appear;
Each cord is glazed, and now the frost,
   Fills the poor seaboy's limbs with pain,   30
Yet all with firmness keep their post,
   All feel, but know not to complain.

Still fiercely howls the adverse storm,
   And now their putrid fare grows scant,
Yet all their perilous tasks perform,   35
   Unmurmuring at the pangs of want;
Yes, tho' innur'd to scorching soils,
   Tho' now of food and lodging bare,
With hollow cheek each veteran toils,
   Yet scorns the meanness of despair.   40

Soon as the dreary watch expires,
   He seeks that balm which sleep affords,
And now he dreams of glowing fires,
   Of cheering bowls, and plenteous boards.—
All hands are call'd, he wakes, he sighs,   45
   Throws on his cold and dripping clothes,
Then mounts the deck, and there descries
   That change which softens all his woes.

The wind's at west, the frost is o'er,
   With glee they loose each long-furl'd sail,   50
And now the vessel makes for shore,
   And none but soothing thoughts prevail;
The dark-plum'd divers now appear,
   And soon is seen the snow-clad land,
Swift past the rocky coast they steer,   55
   And view at length old Mersey's strand.

STANZAS ON THE RECOVERY OF SIGHT; ADDRESSED TO MR. B. GIBSON, SURGEON OF MANCHESTER.

(1809)

OH! Gibson, ere those orbs of thine
Received the sun's resplendent light,
In far-off regions these of mine,
With many a pang, were clos'd in night:
And in this soul-subduing plight,   5
Forlorn I reach'd my native shore,
Where some, extoll'd for talent bright,
Believed my days of vision o'er.

From men of skill on Mersey's Strand,
Whose fam'd solution nought avail'd,   10
To men of skill throughout the land,
I pass'd; but every effort fail'd.
Time paced along, and now assail'd
By ills that oft on blindness wait,
I felt, yet neither crouch'd nor wail'd,   15
But with firm silence bore my fate.

When first Creation's forms withdrew,
The tones of Hope were sweet and clear,
But soon they faint, and fainter grew,
Then gently died upon my ear.   20
And thus in rosy youth's career
Was I of light and hope bereft,
Thus doom'd to penury severe,
Thus to the world's hard buffets left.

Now more than thirty times the Globe,   25
Had round the Sun her progress made,
Since Nature in a dark grey robe,
To these sad eyes had been array'd;
When lo! by rigorous duty sway'd,
To thee, oh Gibson! I applied,   30

And soon by thy transcendent aid,
The new-form'd opening light supplied.

Oh! what a contrast!—thus to rise,
From dungeon darkness into day!
To view again yon azure skies, 35
And all the blooming flush of May;
Through busy streets to wind my way,
And many a long lost form to mark,
Oh! what a Heaven do these display,
Compar'd with ever-during dark! 40

To me the Seasons roll'd all gloom,
But now the vast Creation glows,
With bliss the hawthorn's silvery bloom,
I view, and Summer's blushing rose.
With bliss when withering Autumn blows 45
The leaves slow falling I descry;
And mark, amidst the Wintry snows,
The flakes in whirling eddies fly.

Before thy powers to me were known,
My steps some friendly arm would guide, 50
But now midst piping winds alone,
I range the country far and wide;
And oft while towering vessels glide,
And skiffs athwart the white waves steer,
I mark them, as I skirt the tide, 55
And fearless walk the crowded pier.

What though the light bestow'd by thee
Is not the light of former days?
Though mists envelope all I see,
Yet take, oh! take my heart-felt praise; 60
For was not I from Heaven's blest rays
Shut out through many a rolling year,
And oft remembering this I gaze,
Till feeling pours the grateful tear.

Oh! thou hast wrought a wond'rous change, 65
Hast usher'd me to light once more,
Hast given the mighty power to range
Through mental paths unknown before,
Hast placed within my grasp the lore

Of ancient and of modern days,   70
And while I thus delighted pore,
Shall I forget a Gibson's praise?

When the lov'd partner of my woe,
And all our young ones I survey,
Can I forget to whom I owe   75
Those joys that through my bosom play?
No! Gibson! every passing day
Declares the debt I owe to thee;
Declares, whatever Spleen may say,
The wonders thou hast done for me.   80

She who has long her Seaman mourn'd
As laid beneath the waves at rest,
Yet now beholds the bark return'd
And once more folds him to her breast;
Oh! she who thus has been distress'd,   85
And thus the highest bliss has known,
Oh! she *my* woes can fancy best,
And judge *my* transports by her own.

LINES,

To the Memory of William Cowdroy,
Proprietor of the Manchester Gazette.

(1814)

Ye lovers of social delights,
Whose bosoms are mild and humane,
Ah! pause—from your perilous rites,
And mark for a moment my strain.
Poor Cowdroy, by nature endowed 5
With talents to please and illume,
To nature's dread fiat has bowed,
And silently sunk to the Tomb.

There are who remember his powers,
Ere his nerves by decay were unstrung, 10
Who remember how Night's witching hours
By his fancies were speeded along;
Who remember his eloquent eye,
And those lips where benevolence played;
And these, with true feeling, shall sigh 15
O'er the turf where their fav'rite is laid.

I know there are minds who disdain
The verse that extols the obscure,
But if fortunes were measured by brain,
What numbers of those would be poor! 20
The treasures poor Cowdroy possess'd
Were funds of wit, humour, and whim,
And thousands with PLUMS may be blest
For one that is favoured like him.

As the Elephant's trunk can upraise 25
The lords of the forest or straws,
So Cowdroy could pun on a phrase,
Or could advocate Freedom's great cause.

If hate ever rankled his breast,
'Twas against the dark foes of Mankind,   30
And each chain that corrodes the oppress'd
'Twas the wish of his soul to unbind.

His heart was the nest of the dove,
There gentleness found an abode;
And, like the bright day-star, his love   35
For the whole human family glowed.
But that Bosom with feeling once fraught,
And that Tongue the diffuser of mirth,
And those Eyes ever beaming with thought,
All, all are descended to earth!   40
                    A FRIEND.

THE FIRE OF ENGLISH LIBERTY.

(1816)

When o'er this sea-encircled ground
The Norman conqueror grimly frown'd,
   And bade his curfew ring;
With sullen brow the Saxon hind
To the straw couch his limbs consigned,   5
   And curst his tyrant king.

And long beneath th' oppressor's sway,
With scowling eye, poor England lay,
   And quench'd were all her fires;
Yet thy small spark, Oh! Liberty,   10
E'en then surviv'd each dark decree,
   And glimmer'd 'mongst our sires.

From reign to reign it smoulder'd on,
Scarce warming, till dark-visaged John
   Beheld the rising flame;   15
He saw, and by it signed that deed,
Which makes thy sward, Oh! Runnimede,
   For ever dear to fame!

This sacred fire thro' many an age
Of mental gloom and civil rage   20
   A varied heat bestow'd;
But when th' intrepid Hampden bled,
And Charles was number'd with the dead,
   An awful flame it shew'd!

This lighted Belgic William o'er;   25
This scared a Stuart from our shore;
   And shew'd an abject world,
With how much ease *despotic* Kings,
Those foul, inflated, plund'ring things,
   May from their thrones be hurl'd!   30

Unaw'd by man's infuriate foes,
'Twas thus our sturdy fathers rose
   And guarded freedom's fire;
Which we, a mean, degenerate race,
Corrupt, luxurious, sordid, base,   35
   Are suffering to expire.

Go then, ye reprobated few,
With souls to freedom ever true,
   Whom tyrants ne'er shall tame;
Go, spread the cheerless embers round,   40
And should a few faint sparks be found,
   Oh! fan them into flame!

Soon may that fire again appear,
Again a prostrate people cheer,
   Again be watched with zeal;   45
Soon may its light illume each land,
Its heat—the human heart expand,
   'Till the vast world shall feel.

Whate'er the tongue, whate'er the hue,
Whate'er the good they may pursue,   50
   Or clime which gave them birth;
Oh! Liberty, may'st thou be given,
As bounteous as the light of heav'n,
   To all the sons of earth!

[LINES ADDRESSED TO ROBT. SOUTHEY, ESQ. POET LAUREAT ON THE PUBLICATION OF HIS "CARMEN TRIUMPHALE"]

(1817)

When man's great curse, despotic sway,
Sweeps myriads from the realms of day;
When wide o'er all the Christian world
Destruction's banner's are unfurl'd;
When Europe with exhaustion reels,   5
Yet nor remorse nor pity feels;
At this dread period SOUTHEY stands,
The wild harp trembling in his hands;—
And whilst fanatic furor fires his mind,
"Glory to God," he cries, *"deliverance for mankind!"*   10

Ah, Southey, if thy boyish brood
Were prone to shed each other's blood,
Thou couldst not, with unruffled mein
Behold the agonizing scene:
Why then suppose the Sire of All   15
Is pleased to see his creatures fall;
Why then, if carnage strew the ground,
And groans, and shrieks, and yells abound;
Why then, if ruthless havock lord it wide,
Should bigot rage exult, and God be glorified?   20

I grieve when earth is drench'd with gore,
And realms with woe are covered o'er;
I grieve, and reprobate the plan
Of thanking God for slaughter'd man:
Nor can I hope that lawless sway,   25
Fierce as a tiger o'er his prey,
Will ever uncompelled resign
That power the priest proclaims divine:
No, Southey, no! oppressors ne'er unbind;
'Tis man—high-minded man must liberate mankind.   30

Appall'd by superstitious cares,
Despots of yore have crown'd their heirs,
But when, oh, Southey! tell me when
Have despots raised their slaves to men?
Vot'ries of Power, to this they bend,   35
For this eternally contend;
Whilst man, let despots rise or fall,
Poor abject man submits to all;
And should his wrongs beyond endurance swell,
Here glares the State's red arm, and there an endless hell.   40

Whether of home or foreign growth,
All despots from my soul I loath;
And as to rights—I should as soon
Expect a message from the moon,
As hope to see a courtly train   45
Combin'd, to cherish Freedom's reign—
Combin'd, to humanise the heart,
And bid the nurse's dreams depart:
No, Southey, no! these scourges, when combin'd,
May desolate a world, but never free mankind.   50

If proof be wanting, France may show,
In man's great cause how Monarchs glow:
Thou know'st, when one immortal stroke
Her lacerating shackles broke;
Thou know'st how Europe's savage swarms   55
Flew, like infuriate fiends, to arms;
And how the vaunting legions came,
To quench a never-dying flame;
And well thou know'st how France sublimely rose,
Bared her resistless arm, and crush'd th' aggressing foes.   60

If proof be wanting, turn thine eyes
Where poor partition'd Poland lies;
By many a barbarous band assail'd;
In Freedom's cause she fought, she fail'd;
She saw her children bite the dust,   65
O'erwhelm'd by rapine, murder, lust;
She saw her cities blaze, and all
That 'scaped the flames by ruffians fall;
Transfix'd by groves of pikes, she heard them groan,
Then back into the flames saw writhing thousands thrown.   70

Poor prostrate Poland! here we find
How despots liberate mankind;
And here, unblushing Bard, we see
The savage hordes extoll'd by thee:
But whether minstrels change with times,   75
And scatter flowers o'er courtly crimes;
Or Truth's firm sons imprison'd lie,
Or priests the reasoning powers decry;
Soon, like those brutes that shun the nightly fire
From Freedom's holy flame shall man's fierce foes retire.   80

THE EXILE'S LAMENT

(1824)

WHEN Ireland's sons arose,
    And Nature's rights defended,
I felt my country's woes,
    And in her ranks contended;
We fought,—we cannons braved   5
    And many a famed commander,
Yet still our isle's enslaved,
    And we are doom'd to wander.

My father fell at Ross,
    My brother fell at Gorey,   10
My mother mourns their loss,
    And tears her locks so hoary;
Whilst I, her only stay,
    Am now compell'd to leave her,
And soon in sad array   15
    The cold earth must receive her.

I, too, could wish a grave,
    With tear-drops to deplore me,
And Erin's grass to wave
    In mournful silence o'er me.   20
Yet, ah! where wild waves beat,
    With never-ceasing motion,
Perchance my winding sheet
    May prove the foam of ocean.

For thee, oh Erin dear!   25
    I left each calm enjoyment;
For thee, with brow severe,
    Made war my sole employment.
And now without a home,
    And girt with many a danger,   30
A foreign shore I roam
    A poor suspected stranger.

And oft, while thus forlorn
   I wander earth and ocean,
To thy green lap I turn   35
   With fervent fond devotion:
And if, amidst my woes,
   That love I cease to cherish,
Or e'er forget thy foes,
   Oh Erin! may I perish.   40

Yes, let misfortunes howl,
   Let every clime be cheerless,
In thy great cause my soul
   Shall still be firm and fearless.
The wretch whose arm maintains   45
   Oppression is the traitor;
But he who spurns his chains
   Obeys the great Creator.

Erin, my native land,
   Thy social manners warm me,   50
I love thy clime so bland,
   Thy glens and mountains charm me.
And oh! if thou wert free,
   No spot of heaven's creation
Would I prefer to thee,   55
   Thou dear delightful nation.

Though here the zephyrs blow,
   And Flora ne'er reposes,
Though winter's placid brow
  Is deck'd with budding roses;   60
Yet, what are genial skies,
   And realms howe'er enchanting,
Or wealth's all dazzling prize,
   If Liberty be wanting?

Through shadiest dells I rove,   65
   Or where the vines are glowing,
Or seek the orange grove
   While odorous gales are blowing;
Yet these, and bookish lore,
   Are all to me uncheering,   70
To me, whose feet no more
   Must press the turf of Erin.

No more! and why no more—
   Has heaven forsook our nation;
And must she writhe in gore,   75
   Or crouch in base prostration?
Oh no! she loathes the yoke,
   She feels undaunted bravery,
And soon by one grand stroke
   May burst her bonds of slavery.   80

And then, oh grant it, God!
   When every wrong has vanish'd,
When justice rules unawed,
   And man's proud foes are banish'd;
Let dead and living worth   85
   Be then embalm'd in story,
And soon the ample earth
   Shall sound with Ireland's glory.

THE COROMANTEES.

(1824)

ON the wing for Barbadoes, and sweeping along
    Before a brisk easterly gale,
An African trader with wretchedness stored,
With his crew half destroy'd and contagion on board,
    Beheld on his quarter a sail.   5

It was war, and the tri-colour'd flag soon appear'd,
    And a row of nine-pounders were shewn;
And now the poor slaves under hatches were placed,
And the British oppressors beheld themselves chased
    By a force far exceeding their own.   10

Now all their light sails to the turbulent wind
    The tars with despondency gave,
While around the keen dolphin, more brilliantly dress'd
Than the tropical morn or the humming-bird's breast,
    Made the flying-fish skim o'er the wave.   15

The master who saw that his flight was in vain,
    That the powers of his seamen were broke,
Now ordered each resolute negro with speed,
From his loathsome abode and his chains to be freed,
    And thus to the sufferers he spoke:—   20

"Yon bark, oh! ye warriors, belongs to a race
    "Who laugh at the gods you adore,
"Who will torture your frames, and enjoy your deep groans,
"Who will roast you, and boil you, and pick all your bones,
    "And your names shall be heard of no more.   25

"Then say, oh! ye negroes, ye Coromantees,
    "Whose prowess green Africa knows,
"Say, will you submit to this cannibal band,
"And be swallowed up quick—or, with musket in hand,
    "Say, will you these miscreants oppose?"   30

"Give us arms," cried a slave who had once been a chief,
    And whose scars shew'd acquaintance with blood,
"Give us arms, and those sharks that infest the blue main,
"Those vultures that feast on the flesh of the slain,
    "Shall pay, dearly pay for their food." 35

"Yes, yes, give us arms," the stern negroes exclaimed,
    And their eye-balls ferociously glared.
And now fore and aft, like the seamen array'd,
Undaunted the fast sailing French they survey'd,
    And stood for the conflict prepared. 40

The foe now approaches, the battle begins,
    And the bravest are stunn'd by the roar;
Deep immersed in thick smoke, every sinew is strain'd,
And they tug, and they shout, and the strife is maintain'd
    Amidst crashings, and groanings, and gore. 45

Now the French try to board, but their daring design
    The slaves like fierce tigers oppose;
Where danger appears like a torrent they sweep,
And the fearless assailants now plunge in the deep,
    Or expire on the decks of their foes. 50

With their sails all in tatters, exhausted, repell'd,
    Lo! the Frenchmen sheer off in despair;
While the English, all joyous, behold them retire,
Shake the hands of the negroes, their courage admire,
    And both with wild shouts rend the air. 55

Though the master exults, yet the conquering slaves
    Fill his soul with a thousand alarms;
Now he whispers the mates, and the brandy appears,
The dance is proposed, and received with three cheers,
    And the Africans lay down their arms. 60

As the sharks, all voracious, in Congo's broad stream,
    Quickly dart human flesh to devour,
So the mates and the master soon seize on their prey,
And soon to the arm-chest those weapons convey
    Which bend groaning millions to power. 65

And now the bashaws give their fears to the gale,
    And resume their imperious tone;

And now the poor negroes again are confined,
Again are their limbs to the deck-chains consign'd,
    And again in their fetters they groan.   70

Oh Britons! behold in these Coromantees
    The fate of an agonized world,
Where, in peace, a few lordlings hold millions in chains,
Where, in war, for those lordlings men open their veins,
    And again to their dungeons are hurl'd!   75

But the period approaches when poor prostrate man
    Shall enjoy what the Deity gave;
When the oculist Reason shall touch his dim eyes,
With a soul all abhorrence the sufferer shall rise,
    And undauntedly throw off the slave.   80

AN EPITAPH

ON JOHN TAYLOR, (OF BOLTON LE MOORS)

WHO DIED OF THE YELLOW FEVER,

AT NEW YORK, SEPT. *11*, 1805.

(1824)

FAR from his kindred, friends and native skies,
Here, mouldering in the dust, poor Taylor lies;
Firm was his mind, and fraught with various lore,
And his kind heart was never cold before.
He loved his country—loved that spot of earth 5
Which gave a Hampden, Milton, Bradshaw, birth;
But when that country, dead to all but gain,
Bow'd her base head and hugg'd the oppressor's chain,
Loathing the abject scene, he droop'd, he sigh'd,
Cross'd the wild waves, and here untimely died. 10
Stranger, what'er thy country, creed, or hue,
Go, and like him the moral path pursue;
Go, and for freedom every peril brave,
And nobly scorn to hold, or be a slave.

TO THE

MEMORY OF BARTHOLOMEW TILSKI,

A NATIVE OF THE NORTH OF POLAND,

Who, in attempting to free his country from the merciless grasp of foreigners, was taken prisoner, and, in the vigour of his days, publicly executed. Oh! men of *Poland*, remember Tilski, and never, never forget, that he who is tamely a slave offends his God, and proves a traitor to the human race. The heroic fortitude with which he met his fate, the exalted qualities of his head and heart, shall all embalm his memory, and send it down sweet and pleasant to myriads yet unborn.

(1824)

WHEN haughty Russia's bloody train,
  The scourge of half a groaning world,
Shall sleep beneath our green domain,
  Or from our craggy coasts be hurl'd,
Then, Tilski, o'er thy lowly grave   5
  Poland's warm sons shall sorrowing bend,
Shall say—Here rests the truly brave,
  The tyrant's foe, the people's friend!

When Poland's flag shall proudly fly
  In spite of Russia's stern command,   10
When injured millions shout for joy,
  And awful justice rules the land,
Then oft at eve, with dewy eyes,
  Full many a melting maid shall come,
And whilst they heave the softest sighs,   15
  Shall strew with flowers thy early tomb.

When the foul vampires of the state
  Shall fall, or flit in other skies;
When man, with equal laws elate,
  Shall feel the flood of mind arise,   20
Then to thy name the new-born land
  Shall many an ardent tribute pay,

And time, with soft and soothing hand,
   Shall wipe thy kindred's tears away.

Then, too, the hoary sire shall tell,   25
   Whilst round his sons indignant glow,
How the intrepid Tilski fell,
   Unmoved amid severest woe.—
Shall tell how torture stalk'd abroad,
   While smoking ruins mask'd his way,   30
How murder flesh'd his sword unawed,
   And ruffian rape e'en prowl'd by day;

Shall tell how these terrific woes
   The generous soul of Bartle fired,
And how he join'd the oppressors' foes—   35
   How in great Nature's cause expir'd!
Yes, Tilski! while yon Dwina rolls,
   His foaming torrents to the sea,
Dear, dauntless youth! true Polish souls
   Shall ne'er forget their wrongs nor thee.   40

JEMMY ARMSTRONG.

(1824)

ON a neat little farm in the north of green Erin,
    Lived poor Jemmy Armstrong, a stranger to woe,
Uninjured, his manners were mild and endearing,
    But the dark-brow'd oppressor soon found him a foe.
The rose had twice bloom'd since with soul all delighted,   5
To a love-beaming maiden his vows had been plighted,
And now those fine feelings of man were excited,
    Which none but the husband, the father can know.

When the wrongs of the female were daily increasing,
    And men were half murder'd to make them confess;   10
When the deeds of the fire-brand and lash were unceasing,
    And the castle's meek inmates refused all redress;
When Erin thus groan'd in the deepest prostration,
Brave Armstrong arose, and with keen indignation,
Resolved to unite for his country's salvation,   15
    And sweep off those ruffians who came to oppress.

Can resistance be wrong? did the all-wise creator
    Mistake when he form'd us for freedom inclined?
No! he who surrenders his rights is the traitor;
    Not he whose bold deeds would unshackle mankind.   20
The union that Irishmen then were pursuing,
May one day involve their oppressors in ruin,
But uniting, alas! was poor Armstrong's undoing;
    He was sworn to, arraign'd, and to death soon consign'd.

In a dank loathsome dungeon, with none to befriend him,   25
    Behold this state culprit hemm'd round by his foes,
Whilst with keenness the priest and the justice attend him,
    Disclosure or death—instant death, to propose.
"Oh! never," exclaim'd the brave Armstrong, "oh! never:
"All the ties that attach me to life you may sever;   30
"But Erin's warm friends shall be dear to me ever;
    "I can die, but their names I can never disclose."

Then view his pale partner, with aspect all sadness,
   His child in her arms, and despair in her eye:—
"Oh Armstrong!" she cried, "do not drive me to madness;   35
   "On my knees I entreat you, for Christ's sake comply.
"A widow, an orphan, oh! let me conjure you,
"Divulge, and a pardon these worthies ensure you;
"Let me—let your child, to existence allure you,
   "And reflect, if you suffer, for want we may die."   40

"Divulge! Oh my love! and would you too degrade me?"
   Poor Armstrong replied, in a heart-moving tone,
"Would you, for an odious existence, persuade me
   "The great cause of Erin and God to disown?
"You talk of the widow and orphan contending   45
"With life's thorny woes, till my heart-strings are rending;
"But reflect, should my fortitude prove not unbending,
   "What widows must weep, and what orphans must mourn!"

"And will you, Oh Armstrong! to shield them from anguish,
   "Will you leave this fond bosom, this baby, to mourn?   50
"Without your exertions, ah! how must we languish,
   "Exposed, all unfriended, to insult and scorn!
"When foodless, and tatter'd, and steep'd in dejection,
"Will the comrades you die for afford us protection?
"For their wives and children you shew warm affection,   55
   "Yet cold as the snow-blast you leave us forlorn."

"Then hear me," he cried,—"By the Great Power of Heaven,
   "Though the strong cords of nature are twined round my heart,
"By me not the name of a friend shall be given,
   "Nor one trace of their plans will I ever impart!"   60
He ceased, and the ear with wild sorrow was wounded,
The priest and the justice were stunn'd and confounded,
While the name of brave Armstrong through Ireland was sounded,
   Who died, and from virtue disdain'd to depart.

PROSE

Expostulatory Letter to George Washington, of Mount Vernon, in Virginia, on his continuing to be a Proprietor of Slaves.

(1797)

Oh reflect—that your rights are the rights of mankind,
  That to all they were bounteously given,
And that he who in chains would his fellow-man bind,
  Uplifts his proud arm against Heaven.

IN July last the following letter was transmitted to the person to whom it is addressed, and a few weeks ago it was returned under cover, without a syllable in reply. As children that are crammed with confectionary, have no relish for plain and wholesome food; so men in power, who are seldom addressed but in the sweet tones of adulation, are apt to be disgusted with the plain and salutary language of truth. To offend was not the intention of the writer; yet the president has evidently been irritated; this however is not a bad symptom, for irritation causelessly excited, will frequently subside into shame, and to use the language of the moralist, "Where there is yet shame, there may in time be virtue.—"

Liverpool, February 20th, 1797.

IT will be generally be admitted, Sir, and perhaps with justice, that the great family of mankind were never more benefited by the military abilities of any individual, than by those which you displayed during the memorable American contest. Your country was injured, your services were called for, you immediately arose, and after performing the most consipcuous part in that blood-stained tragedy, you again became a private citizen, and unambitiously retired to your farm. There was more of true greatness in this procedure than the modern world at least had ever beheld; and while public virtue is venerated by your countrymen, a conduct so exalted will not be forgotten. The effects which your revolution will have upon the world are incalculable. By the flame which you have kindled, every oppressed nation will be enabled to perceive its fetters; and when man once knows that he is enslaved, the business of emancipation is half performed.—France has already burst her shackles, neighbouring nations will in time prepare, and another half century may behold the present besotted Europe without a peer, without a hierarchy, and without a despot. If men were enlightened, revolution would be bloodless; but how are men to be enlightened, when it is the interest of governors to keep the governed in ignorance? "To enlighten men," says your old correspondent Arthur Young, "is to make them bad subjects." Hurricanes spread devastation; yet hurricanes are not only transient, but give salubrity to the torrid regions, and are quickly followed by azure skies and calm sunshine. Revolutions too, for a time, may produce turbulence; yet revolutions clear the political atmosphere and contribute greatly to the comfort and happiness of the human race. What you yourself have lived to witness in the united states is sufficient to elucidate my position. In your rides along the banks of your favourite Potowmack, in your frequent excursions through your own extensive grounds, how gratifying must be your sensations on beholding the animated scenery around you, and how pleasurable must be your feelings, on reflecting that your country is now an asylum for mankind; that her commerce, her agriculture, and her population, are greater than at any former period; and that this prosperity is the natural result of those rights which you defended against an abandoned cabinet, with all that ability which men who unsheathe the sword in the cause of human nature will, I trust, ever display. Where liberty is, there man walks erect and puts forth all his powers; while slavery, like a torpedo, benumbs the finest energies of his soul.

But it is not to the commander in chief of the American forces, nor to the president of the united states, that I have aught to address, my business is with George Washington, of Mount Vernon, in Virginia, a man who, notwithstanding his hatred of oppression and his ardent love of liberty, holds at this moment hundreds of his fellow beings in a state of abject bondage.— Yes! you, who conquered under the banners of freedom—you, who are now the first magistrate of a free people, are, (strange to relate) a slave-holder. That a Liverpool merchant should endeavour to enrich himself by such a business is not a matter of surprise, but that you, an enlightened character, strongly enamoured of your own freedom, you who, if the British forces had succeeded in the eastern states, would have retired with a few congenial spirits to the rude fastnesses of the western wilderness, there to have enjoyed that blessing, without which a paradise would be disgusting, and with which the most savage region is not without its charms; that you, I say, should continue to be a slave-holder, a proprietor of human flesh and blood, creates in many of your British friends both astonishment and regret. You are a republican, an advocate for the dissemination of knowledge and for universal justice—where then are the arguments by which this shameless dereliction of principle can be supported? Your friend Jefferson* has endeavoured to shew that the negroes are an inferior order of being, but surely you will not have recourse to such a subterfuge. Your slaves, it may be urged, are well treated—That I deny—man never can be well treated who is deprived of his rights. They are well cloathed, well fed, well lodged, &c. Feed me with ambrosia, and wash it down with nectar, yet, what are these, if liberty be wanting? You took arms in defence of the rights of man—Your negroes are men—Where then are the rights of your negroes? They have been inured to slavery, and are not fit for freedom. Thus it was said of the French; but where is the man of unbiassed common sense who will assert that the French republicans of the present day are not fit for freedom? It has been said too by your apologists, that your feelings are inimical to slavery, and that you are induced to acquiesce in it at present merely from motives of policy; the only true policy is justice, and he who regards the consequences of an act, rather than the justice of it, gives no very exalted proof of the greatness of his character. But if your feelings be actually repugnant to slavery, then are you more culpable than the callous-hearted planter, who laughs at what he calls the pityful whining of the abolitionists, because he believes slavery to be justifiable; while you persevere in a system which your conscience tells you to be wrong. If we call the man obdurate who cannot perceive the atrociousness of slavery, what epithets does he deserve who, while he does perceive its atrociousness, continues to be a proprietor of slaves. Nor is it likely that your own unfortunate negroes are the only sufferers by your adhering to this nefarious business; consider the force of an example like yours, consider how many of the sable race may now be pining in bondage, merely forsooth, because the president of the united states, who has the character of a wise and good man, does not see cause to discontinue the long established practice. Of all the slave-holders under heaven those of the united states appear to me the most reprehensible; for man never is so truly odious as when he inflicts upon others that which he himself abominates. When the cup of slavery was presented to your countrymen, they rejected it with disdain, and appealed to the world in justification of their conduct; yet such is the inconsistency of man, that thousands upon thousands of those very people, with yourself amongst the number, are now sedulously employed in holding the self-same bitter draught to the lips of their sable brethren. From men who are strongly attached to their own rights, and who have suffered much in their defence, one might have expected a scrupulous attention to the rights of others; did not experience shew, that when we ourselves are oppressed, we perceive it with a lynx's eye; but when we become the oppressors, no noon-tide bats are blinder. Prosperity perhaps may make nations as well as individuals forget the distresses of other times; yet surely the citizens of America cannot so soon have forgotten the variety and extent of their own sufferings. When your country lay bruised by the iron hand of despotism, and you were compelled to retreat through the Jerseys with a handful of half naked followers, when the bayonet of the mercenary glistened at your back, and liberty seemed about to expire, when your farms were laid waste, your towns reduced to ashes, and your plains and woods were strewed with the mangled bodies of your brave defenders; when these events were taking place, every breast could feel, and every tongue could execrate the sanguinary proceedings of Britain; yet what the British were at that period, you are in a great degree at this—you are boastful of your own rights—you are violators of the rights of others, and you are stimulated by an insatiable rapacity, to a cruel and relentless oppression. If the wrongs which you now inflict be not so severe as those which were inflicted upon you, it is not because you are less inhuman than the British, but because the unhappy objects of your tyranny have not the power of resistance. In defending your own liberties you undoubtedly suffered much; yet if your negroes, emulating the spirited example of their masters, were to throw off the galling yoke, and, retiring peaceably to some uninhabited part of the western region, were to resolve on liberty or death, what would be the conduct of the southern planters on such an occasion? Nay, what would be your conduct? You who were "born in a land of liberty, who "early learned its value," you, who "engaged in a perilous conflict to defend it," you who, "in a word, devoted the best years of your life "to secure its permanent establishment in your own country, and whose anxious "recollection, whose sympathetic feelings, and whose best wishes are irresistibly excited, "whensoever in any country you see an oppressed nation unfurl the banners of freedom,"** possessed of these energetic sentiments, what would be your conduct? Would you have the virtue to applaud so just and animating a movement as a revolt of your southern negroes? No! I fear both you and your countrymen would rather imitate the cold blooded British cabinet, and, to gratify your own sordid views, would scatter among an unoffending people, terror, desolation, and death. Harsh as this conclusion may appear, yet it is warranted by your present practice; for the man who can boast of his own rights, yet hold two or three hundred of his fellow beings in slavery, would not hesitate, in case of a revolt, to employ the most sanguinary means in his power, rather than forego that which the *truly* republican laws of his country are *pleased* to call, his property. Shame! Shame! That man should be deemed the property of man, or that the name of Washington should be found among the list of such proprietors.

Should these strictures be deemed severe or unmerited on your part, how comes it, that while in the northern and middle states, the exertions of the virtuous quakers, and other philanthropists, have produced such regulations as must speedily eradicate every trace of slavery in that quarter; how comes it, that from you these humane efforts have never received the least countenance? If your mind have not sufficient firmness to do away that which is wrong the moment you perceive it to be such, one might have expected, that a plan for ameliorating the evil would have met with your warmest support; but no such thing. The just example of a majority of the states has had no visible effect upon you; and as to the men of Maryland, of Virginia, of the two Carolinas, of Georgia, and of Kentucky, they smile contemptuously at the idea of negro emancipation, and, with the state constitutions in one hand, and the cow-skin in the other, exhibit to the world such a spectacle, as every real friend to liberty must from his soul abominate.

"Then what is man, and what man seeing this,
"And having human feelings, does not blush
"And hang his head to think himself a man."

The hypocritical bawd who preaches chastity, yet lives by the violation of it, is not more truly disgusting, than one of your slave-holding gentry bellowing in favor of democracy. Man does not readily perceive defects in what he has been accustomed to venerate; hence it is that you have escaped those animad-versions which your slave proprietorship has so long merited. For seven years you bravely fought the battles of your country, and contributed greatly to the establishment of her liberties; yet you are a slave-holder! You have been raised by your fellow-citizens to one of the most exalted situations upon earth, the first magistrate of a free people; yet you are a slave-holder! A majority of your countrymen have recently discovered that slavery is injustice, and are gradually abolishing the wrong, yet you continue to be a slave-holder! You are a firm believer too, and your letters and speeches are replete with pious reflections on the divine being, providence, &c. yet you are a slave-holder! Oh! Washington, "Ages to come will read with astonishment" that the man who was foremost to wrench the rights of America from the tyrannical grasp of Britain, was among the last to relinquish his own oppressive hold of poor and unoffending negroes.

In the name of justice, what can induce you thus to tarnish your own well earned celebrity, and to impair the fair features of American liberty, with so foul and indelible a blot? Avarice is said to be the vice of the age. Your slaves, old and young, male and female, father, mother, and child, might, in the estimation of a Virginian planter, be worth from fifteen to twenty thousand pounds. Now, Sir, are you sure that the unwillingness which you have shewn to liberate your negroes, does not proceed from some lurking pecuniary consid-erations? If this be the case, and there are those who firmly believe it is, then there is no flesh left in your heart; and present reputation, future fame, and all that is estimable among the virtuous, are, for a few thousand pieces of paltry yellow dirt, irremediably renounced.

EDWARD RUSHTON.

[Rushton's notes]

*Besides those of colour, figure, and hair, there are other physical distinctions proving a difference of race. They have less hair on the face and body. They secrete less by the kidnies, and more by the glands of the skin, which gives them a very strong and disagreeable odour. This greater degree of transpiration renders them more tolerant of heat, and less so of cold, than the whites. Perhaps too a difference of structure in the pulmonary apparatus, which a late ingenious experimentalist[§] has discovered to be the principal regulator of animal heat, may have disabled them from extricating, in the act of inspiration, so much of that fluid from the outer air, or obliged them in expiration, to part with more of it. They seem to require less sleep. A black, after hard labour through the day, will be induced by the slightest amusements to sit up till midnight, or later, though knowing he must be out by the first dawn of the morning. They are at least as brave, and more adventuresome. But this perhaps may proceed from a want of forethought, which prevents their seeing a danger till it be present. When present, they do not go through it with more coolness or steadiness than the whites. They are more ardent after their females: but love seems with them to be more an eager desire, than a tender delicate mixture of sentiment and sensation. Their griefs are transient. Those numberless afflictions, which render it doubtful whether heaven has given life to us in mercy or in wrath, are less felt, and sooner forgotten with them. In general, their existence appears to participate more of sensation than reflection. To this must be ascribed their disposition to sleep when abstracted from their diversions, and unemployed in labour. An animal whose body is at rest, and who does not reflect, must be disposed to sleep of course. Comparing them by their faculties of memory, reason, and imagination, it appears to me, that in memory they are equal to the whites; in reason much inferior, as I think one could scarcely be found capable of tracing and comprehending the investigations of Euclid; and that in imagination they are dull, tasteless, and anomalous. See *Jefferson's notes on Virginia, page* 230. Stockdale, London. [§]Crawford

**See the answer of the president of the united states to the address of the minister plenipotentiary of the French republic, on his presenting the colours of France to the united states.

[Letter to Thomas Paine]
(written c. 1800; published 1809)

[*To the Proprietors of the Belfast Magazine.*
Will you venture to publish the following letter of just remonstrance, written to Thomas Paine, some years before his death, by a worthy friend of mine in England? For justness of sentiment and energy of expression, I can recommend it to the true friends of philanthropy.]

"*Dear Sir,*

In retiring from the revolutionary scenes of Europe, you will not, I trust, retire from those labours which are now strongly agitating the human intellect, and making oppressors tremble. While enormity is the growth of every soil, and while crimes, sanctioned by law, are suffered to blur the fairest institutions of mankind, powers such as you possess can never want employment. Pregnant with the purest political wisdom, you contributed in no small degree to emancipate the people of America from the proud domination of Britain, and you are now called upon the name of suffering humanity, to aim at rescuing one part of that very American people, from the abominable grasp of the other. With tyranny, in whatever garb he may appear, you have waged perpetual war; and surely there cannot be a tyranny more truly execrable, than that of the republican planter lording it over his toil worn, lacerated slaves. Turn your attention then, to the southern states of the American union, and there among a people who have fought, and who have bled in defence of their own liberty, you may delineate the dark, and melancholy features of Negro slavery. Who, that is not familiar with wrong, could behold one of these pigmy despots, in the midst of his rice or tobacco plantation, without reprobating the government that can authorize such a system? Who that is not inured to outrage, could witness the incessant toil, the frequent exercise of the twisted thong, the Osnaburgh frock stained with human blood, and the sable countenance marked with inutterable anguish, without detesting the wretch, who tremblingly alive with respect to his own rights, can yet become the cruel violater of the rights of others? Who that is not an habitual hypocrite, could follow the democratic slave holder to the legislature of his country, and hear him declaim on the rights of American citizens, on violated constitutions, &c. without the strongest sensations of loathing and disgust? Or in short, who, that has the feelings of a man, could behold this complicated villainy, without adopting your own indignant assertion, "that tyranny and martyrdom, like taxation and representation, ought to go hand in hand?" To ameliorate the situation of man is evidently the object of your writings; and whilst your favourite America can exhibit such atrocities, it is impossible, I again repeat it, that powers such as you possess can ever want employment. The man who is truly a philanthropist, will ever be consistent; he cannot possess one class of feelings for white men, and another for negroes; no! his arms embrace the universe and all mankind are his brethren. From the head of the Chesapeak to the borders of Florida, and from the shores of the Atlantic to the banks of the Mississippi, is a widely extended region, in which you may have many admirers, who would no doubt take it in dudgeon, were you to appear inimical to their miscalled interest; yet notwithstanding this, I firmly believe that you will not inhabit a country, in which man is allowed to be the property of man, without becoming the enemy of the oppressor, and the fearless advocate of the oppressed. As the clear and energetic champion for broad and general liberty, you have not a superior in the annals of mankind, yet through the whole of your writings, I do not recollect a single passage that is particularly pointed against the slavery of the negroes—it is a subject that calls for intellect, gigantic as your own: it is an Augean stable, fit only for such an Hercules. Let me entreat you then, in the name of that liberty which you prize above all price, once more, to vindicate the rights of injured nature, and to show, that no laws, no affluence, no authority, can shelter the proprietor of human sinews, from the scorn and contempt of a regenerating world. Against you there is not an epithet in the vocabulary of baseness which will not be employed; yet in advocating the cause of negro wretchedness, your powers must prove irresistable."

[In communicating a copy of this letter to me, my friend thus wrote in the year 1807.]

"I congratulate you on the abolition of the slave trade, and have inclosed you a letter, which some time ago I addressed to Thomas Paine, on the subject of Negro Slavery in the United States. Since his receipt of this, he has frequently sent me his verbal respects, but will not commit himself to paper on the subject. In 1791 Thomas Paine, conversing with a gentleman on the subject of the slave trade, wondered that God Almighty did not send a thunderbolt to blast the d—d town of Liverpool; yet Thomas Paine now resides in the State of New York, surrounded by Negro slaves without either writing, or uttering a syllable against Negro slavery, though he may daily read such advertisements, as the following: "For sale, a well looking Negro woman, about 23, with or without her child of four years old; apply to the proprietor". I wish politicians and philosphers would learn to be consistent. Jefferson, the president of the United States, the freest country in the world, holds hundreds of his fellow creatures in a state of bondage. Horne Tooke, the celebrated English patriot, is an enemy to the abolition of the slave trade, and Cobbett, the redoubted Cobbett, has been the uniform advocate of Negro slavery!!!"

[Such sentiments, do honour to the head and heart of the writer, and tend to communicate a spark to electrify and energize congenial minds.

K.]

[Monthly Retrospect of Politics]
(1810)

[... Thus, in the present instance, the person who, for this time holds the pen, gladly avails himself for an introduction to this month's retrospect of the following energetic and just sentiments, conveyed to him in a letter, from a correspondent in England, who, for a spirit of lofty independence and just political opinions, is second to no man. The propriety of the reasoning, and the true delineation of the hardship in cases of supposed libels will recommend the extract to the true lovers of freedom, and tend it is hoped to revive the almost expiring embers of the once highly cherished but now almost apparently extinguished flame of liberty.]

"The severe sentence on Cobbett will have a tendency for a while to lower the tone of the press and to damp the extertions of the timid. But there are men who are not thus to be dismayed, whose spirit like the waves of the ocean, are known to rise in proportion to the storm.

"In this country justice between man and man may be fairly administered, but between man and the government, this, in my opinion, is not the case. Let us state, for instance, the proprietor of a newspaper. Sedition and libel cannot be defined. The attorney general fastens upon this, or that particular paragraph, and the clerk of the crown nominates a number of individuals, from whom a jury is to be selected, and though the accused person may have a right of challenge, yet if the vacancies in the jury are to be filled up from the number appointed by the officer of the crown, the situation of the individual is by no means improved. He is tried by a prejudiced and of course by a partial, jury, and nine times out of ten the decisions are in favour of government. I say prejudiced and partial and I think without exaggeration, for the clerk of the crown will ever be the creature of the crown, and will take care to nominate men whose political sentiments are in unison with his own. And thus the stream of justice becomes feculent at its very source and the liberty and property of man are decided upon by despotism in the disguise of free forms, which in my opinion, is the worst of all species of slavery. *From a nation that is enslaved and knows it, we can expect every thing; but a nation that is enslaved and imagines itself free, is in a perilous state indeed.*

"On the other hand, let us suppose the proprietor of a newspaper to have been prosecuted and acquitted, what is his situation? He has incurred the expense of two or three hundred pounds. The minds of himself and family have been greatly distressed; and he has not the least redress. Nay, in the course of a few weeks or months, the attorney general may pounce upon him again; and thus harrassed, he must either be ruined or lower his tone. The paper becomes flat and insipid, his customers fall off, the property is offered for sale, and purchased by some government agent, and thus oppression is triumphant. This is not an ideal picture, the proprietor of the Liverpool Chronicle was prosecuted by the attorney general, was convicted, and confined in Lancaster castle; his affairs went to ruin, and he is now a journeyman printer."

[Extracts from Letters]
(written 1805–1813; published 1814)

"With these men I have little or no intercourse. Religion and politics keep them aloof, and Edward Rushton has too much respect for himself, to think of soliciting any favour from the narrow, the bigoted, or the persecuting.
Nov. 23, 1805."

"I have ever valued the esteem of the worthy, particularly those who are the friends of liberty, and of man; while on the other hand, there are numbers in the world whose approbation I should deem the severest censure; and hence one of my favourite sentiments is, may we never be popular in bad times.
Aug. 29, 1807."

"We live in awful times, but while the great rough riders of the world will allow us domestic comforts, and while we possess conscious rectitude, we shall be enabled to weather the hurricane.
Jan. 10, 1810."

"I have just been informed, that in consequence of your opposition to the Orange faction, you have received several threatening letters, and have had your windows broken. If I have formed a just estimate of your character, you will not be greatly disturbed by these petty malignities. I know by experience, however, that such gad-flies are troublesome, and that their buzzings may injure the peace of a family; but he who will attempt to do good in bad times, will be sure to encounter violence. For many years I was inured to threatening letters, insults, and even outrages, but I have outlived them all, and now and then have found my political opponents converted into friends. A few weeks ago I was at a friend's house, where the conversation turning upon prejudice, a person told me before the whole company, that there was a time when he thought I deserved to be hung on the first lamp post, on account of my political opinions. He is now a well-informed, liberal character, and very much my friend. I mention this to shew you that those who are now your most bigoted enemies, may, in a few years, become your warmest advocates. Shall we have a peace? I trust we shall. War has done nothing for the cause of human nature. Despot worries despot, and mankind are swept from existence. What a world is this we live in! After twenty years of slaughter, of laceration of feeling, of debasement of heart, Europe is in a much worse situation than when the war commenced. If this be the finger of Providence, it resembles a nose of wax, and may be twisted to any shape.

Dec. 31, 1813."

"You would, no doubt, be pleased to hear of Mr. Roscoe's election. There is certainly the semblance of political virtue in the Liverpool voters returning an avowed advocate of the abolition of the slave trade, yet when we consider that from ten to twelve thousand pounds have been expended by the friends of Mr. Roscoe in this contest, every thing like political virtue melts into thin air. I have a poor opinion of my countrymen in general, and my townsmen in particular, and am confident without such an expenditure, the worth and talents even of a Roscoe would have been wholly disregarded. After all, then, what has been obtained by this contest? Why a cluster of petty despots, who call themselves a corporation, have been baffled, and their weakness completely exposed, but so long as 160 borough mongers can send a majority to the British commons, every contested election must, in the eye of reason, have the apperance of a mockery.

"I grant that a house of Commons composed of Roscoes, might do much, but a few virtuous men placed in the midst of corruption, are not only prevented from being useful, but there is a chance that they themselves, by coming familiar with political profligacy, may in time become more or less contaminated. He who should endeavour to purify a tub of soap-lees, by throwing into the putrid mass a few spoonfuls of essence of violets, would find himself wofully disappointed; yet such in my opinion is the state of the Imperial parliament.

Nov. 20, 1806."

"You wish me to take a trip to Ireland. I thank you for the invitation, and should I ever again set foot on your shore, it would give me no small pleasure to pass a few hours under your peaceful roof. This however is not likely to take place, I am now more confined than ever; my poor wife, from a rheumatic affliction, has not been able to walk for twelve months past, and whether she will ever enjoy that pleasure again, it is hard to say. If I have any partiality for the men of Ireland, and you think I have, it is not merely because I have a little Irish blood in my veins, but because they have been long an oppressed people; and if I do not esteem my own countrymen, it is because they are the oppressors of mankind. I know it will be said it is wrong to censure a people merely for the acts of their government, but as the great mass of the British people are the advocates and supporters of their government, they of course partake of the guilt, and should share the censure. If patriotism is to supersede justice; if the wealth and power of one nation cannot be supported without the pillage and slavery of others, then the names of patriot and plunderer ought to be synonymous.

"I think I perceive a strain of melancholy running through your last letter, but it is the melancholy of a benevolent mind brooding over the narrowness and miseries of the times. War, I am sure, has never found you amongst its advocates: whatever may be the result of the struggle, we may console ourselves with having been the uniform friends of peace, and this consolation is not without its value. I have long been of opinion that things must be worse before they are better, and therefor the darkness of the political horizon does not make me very uneasy. If troubles are to be encountered, let them be encountered rather by ourselves than by our children. The present generation of the British have been culpable, and deserve to feel, but their offspring being innocent ought not to suffer.

Nov. 8, 1810."

"Liverpool is in a most wretched state; some weeks ago your friend Mr. H—— told me that 25,000 of its inhabitants were ready to receive charitable relief. The shop keepers and tradesmen are gradually going to destruction; they resemble a vessel involved in the current of Maelstrom, on the coast of Norway; they see their danger, they look round for assistance; there is no relief, the vortex is gaping to receive them, and they are soon ingulphed. Or they may be compared to a poor wretch who plunges up to the knees in a quicksand; he endeavours to extricate himself, but his efforts sink him the deeper, the sandy fluid now circles his waist, now his shoulders; despair is in his eye, and he disappears never to rise again.

"Fearful of being thus overwhelmed, like many of my neighbours, I am looking out for a cottage, whilst I can answer every demand, and have a modicum left for the necessaries of life; there with few wants, and confined wishes, after struggling more than twenty years with persecution, and even personal outrage, I may at length enjoy something like peace and comfort. These, however, are the pleasing suggestions of hope, which often resemble the stuff of which dreams are made.

"The —— conduct will in all probability accelerate the political burst. When will human nature breech itself into manhood? Alas, that the welfare of so many millions of beings should depend upon such a ——. But I have done, let the hurricane come when it may, that you and yours may be preserved from its pitiless sweep, is the sincere wish of yours, truly.

Feb. 25, 1812."

"As to my sight, it is much the same as when you left Liverpool. I shall return to Manchester in a month or two, in order that Mr. Gibson may examine the present state of the eye, and should he think a fifth operation would be attended with the least prospect of success, I will most cheerfully acquiesce; and if not, I must make the best of my gloomy situation, having long ago discovered that the greatest misery of all, is not to be able to bear misery.

Sept. 11, 1806."

"You kindly inquire after the state of my sight; early in May I submitted to a fifth operation, it was neither so long nor so acute as some of the former, yet it was attended with considerable inflammation. In a few days the inflammation subsided, and gave me a glimpse of that world from which I have been excluded for more than thirty years. I can now wander in the country for half a dozen miles by myself; I can visit the docks and pier, and perceive the moving scenery around me; nay, with the assistance of a glass, I can read thirty or forty pages in a folio edition of Pope, and what is still more interesting to my feelings, I can distinguish the features of my family. The pleasure arising from all these, particularly the latter, you will more readily imagine than I can describe. It must be understood, however, that every thing I see is through a muddy medium, which time and medicine may perhaps remove. Whether or not I have gained much, I am, I assure you, perfectly satisfied. A person coming from perfect vision to my situation, would be much depressed, but coming from darkness to my situation, forms such a pleasurable contrast, as no power of mine will ever be able justly to delineate.

"*Aug.* 29, 1807."

"You mentioned the marriage of my daughter, and observe that few things contribute more to smooth the rugged descent of life, than the comfortable settlement of our children. The remark is just, yet after all, man is but a bundle of habits, and when those habits are abruptly broken in upon, a sort of mental laceration takes place. My daughter has been my close companion for years, and I feel her loss most sensibly, but the parent, who from motives of mere conveniency, would obstruct, or even retard, the happiness of his child, must, in my opinion, be selfish, and contemptible in the extreme.

Aug. 29. 1807."

"It is now more than a twelve-month since I wrote you, and during that period I have suffered much. In the space of four months, an exemplary wife, and an affectionate daughter, in her twentieth year, were taken from me; but you yourself have been a sufferer, and know how to feel. In amputating a limb, the tourniquet of the surgeon may mitigate the pain, but where is the tourniquet for the mind? The religionist will say it is here; 'the Lord giveth, and the Lord taketh away, and blessed be the name of the Lord.' The philosopher too will put in his claim with, 'every evil is necessary;' 'whatever is, is right;' 'the greatest misery of all, is not to be able to bear misery,' &c. But after all, when the mind has been deeply lacerated, it often happens that both religion and philosophy are for the most part powerless. Time, I am persuaded, is the only remedy, and time would be much more efficacious if it were not for memory, busy memory, which by calling up the tender images and comforts that are past, keeps the wounded mind in a state of irritation, and makes the healing process often tardy, and sometimes impracticable.

Feb. 25, 1812."

A FEW PLAIN FACTS
RELATIVE TO THE ORIGIN OF THE LIVERPOOL
INSTITUTE FOR THE BLIND.
(written 1804; published 1817)

Early in the year 1790 I regularly attended an association, consisting of ten or a dozen individuals, who assembled weekly for the purpose of literary discussion; and one evening, the conversation having turned on the recently established Marine Society, it was observed by a member of that body, Capt. W. Ward, that the committee for the management of the marine fund had declined the acceptance of any small donations. It immediately occurred to me, that if an institution could be formed, in Liverpool, for the relief of its numerous and indigent blind, the small donations, thus declined by the marine committee, might be brought to flow in a channel, not less benevolent, and prove of essential service in the establishment of a fund for the benefit of that unfortunate description of the community.

Forcibly impressed with this idea, I mentioned my design on the moment, and soon after produced two letters on the loss of sight, from the first of which the following is extracted:—"Among the various calamities by which poor human nature is buffeted, perhaps there is not one which, upon a close investigation, would be found more truly deplorable than that of the loss of sight. He who is in the full possession of this cheering sense, can have but a very inadequate idea of the state of mind which is generally produced by its total privation. The rays of light may, indeed, for a time be voluntarily excluded, and thus the gloominess of the blind be, in some degree felt; but the mind, conscious that such an exclusion depends upon the will, cannot, on this account, be very materially interested.—A human being, by the command of a Despot, might be immured in a dungeon dark as the eyeless socket yet, even here, the consciousness of still possessing sight, and the hopes of being one day or other enabled to enjoy it, would lift him far above the dreary sensations of irrecoverable blindness; sensations, which those who are blest with vision cannot imagine, nor those who are bereft of it justly describe. The long night of the poor Greenlander is, undoubtedly, gloomy, but during that period, the aurora borealis, the moon, and the stars are so extremely luminous as to afford, in some degree, a compensation for his loss; besides, he is constantly cheered with a certainty of the return of the great lamp. Not so the sightless being!—His loss has no compensation, his long, long night no brightness; nor can his mind be cheered with the expectations of returning light, for that he knows to be impossible, so that even Hope, the wretch's kindest friend, is to him, in this instance, utterly denied. How piteous then is blindness! The face of the country, with all its various beauties; the town, with its docks, piers, and stately edifices; the aspects of his friends, of his dearest relatives, of his partner, and his prattling offspring, are all to him a blank—are all involved in a mass of thick black clouds, which no summer's heat can dissolve, nor wint'ry storms disperse. How deplorable then is such an existence! even with a competence, how cheerless! but with indigence, how dreadful!"

The second of these letters contained the outline of an institution, by which it was hoped that the pecuniary distresses, and consequently the gloom of the sightless might, in some degree, be alleviated. My plan was briefly this:— that an association should be formed, consisting entirely of blind persons; that the names of females, as well as males, should be registered, and that each individual should contribute a small matter weekly, or monthly, with which, and the benefactions of the humane, such a fund might speedily be established, as would afford to each a weekly allowance in cases of sickness, superannuation, etc. This attempt I knew to be singular, and that I had no personal influence to recommend it; yet, as the sufferings of the indigent blind were great, and as good might be the result, I was resolved to persevere. There was also another stimulus: The Liverpool Marine Society had originated in a conversation between two individuals at the close of a convivial meeting, and the effects of this society were likely to prove highly beneficial; nor had I forgotten the invigorating remark of Shakespeare, "Our doubts are traitors, and make us lose the good we oft might gain, by fearing to attempt." Encouraged by these reflections, my letters on the blind were submitted to the opinion of our little community, in which, some months before, had originated the Liverpool Marine Society, and the idea of mitigating the misery of those hitherto neglected unfortunates, was unanimously approved. It was deemed advisable, however, not to insert the letters in the Liverpool papers, 'till the sanction or patronage of certain leading characters could be procured, and, with this advice, I thought it expedient to acquiesce.

Among the members of our small, but interesting society, was a respectable musician of the name of Lowe, who was himself in a sightless state; pleased with the plan, and having intercourse in the way of his profession with several affluent families, Mr. Lowe requested that he might be furnished with copies of the letters, in order to leave them in the hands of a few wealthy individuals, among whom, he was confident, he could soon procure patrons for so novel, yet so benevolent, an undertaking. The copies were accordingly made out, and Mr. Lowe had them in his possession for several months, during which time they were shewn to many respectable characters, and at length, about the middle of October, they were presented by Mr. Lowe to the Rev. Henry D[a]nnett.— This gentleman expressed himself warmly in favour of the design, enquired after the author of the letters, and sent a message by Mr. Lowe, requesting my company to breakfast on the following morning. But before I proceed, it will be necessary to mention a circumstance, which may prove of considerable importance in ascertaining the origin of the Liverpool Institution of the Blind. Some years previously to this period, a fellowship, in misfortune, had brought me acquainted with Mr. John Christie, musician, and this acquaintance, his modest worth and ingenuity, had ripened into friendship. To him therefore I communicated my design soon after it was formed, and by him that design was not only warmly approved, but he endeavoured to promote it, by shewing the copies of my letters wherever he thought they could be communicated with any prospect of success. Some months, however, had passed away, and little had been done towards furthering my plan of a beneficial institution. Mr. Lowe, indeed, had obtained some splendid promises, but not one particle of real support; when about the beginning of September, my friend, John Christie, mentioned to me, for the first time, the happy idea of having a place appropriated for the use of the blind, wherein, by gratuitous musical instruction, they might soon be enabled to provide for themselves, which to a well disposed mind must ever prove a source of the highest satisfaction. This judicious and humane idea, which I firmly believe to have originated with John Christie, was afterwards, at his request, expanded in the following letter, addressed to his benevolent friend, Mr. Edward Alanson, surgeon, of Liverpool. ...

[Quotes a letter from John Christie, 22 September 1790]

In the course of a few days after the above date, several manuscript copies of this letter were made, and on the advice of Mr. Alanson, put into circulation.—One was left with Mr. Gore, and another with Mr. Billinge, in order to be laid on their respective counters; and before I went to breakfast with Mr. Dannett, in consequence of the invitation brought by Mr. Lowe, I called upon J. Christie, procured a copy of the letter to Mr. Alanson, took it with me, and actually presented it to Mr. Dannett myself. This I mention the more emphatically, because it has been said, nay, even sworn by Mr. Dannett, that he never saw the letter of John Christie, nor any other document relative to the institution, previously to its being established. Nor is this the only particular in which Mr. Dannett has deviated from truth. He has stated, "that Christie, and, perhaps, Rushton, made application to him, as being a likely person, &c. &c."—Now Christie and Rushton being entirely unacquainted with Mr. D. never did apply, nor had they ever the least idea of applying to him; on the contrary, the application was made by Mr. Dannett to me, in consequence of the letters which had fallen into his hands, as before related. Mr. Dannett has also deposed that, in originating the Liverpool Institution for the Blind, he had no assistance from any being upon earth.—Now, if this statement be not the result of mental imbecility, I will venture to say, that it is one of the most singular, and shameless, that was ever made; but as the cause of truth can never be promoted by a warfare of positive assertions, I shall fearlessly proceed with my little narrative. After a lapse of fourteen years, passed amid the rancorous turmoil of a noisy world, it cannot be expected that I should particularise the conversation which took place during the first interview with Mr. Dannett; I shall only say in general, that I was received with every mark of attention; that my letters and that of J. Christie had his decided approbation; that he expressed himself pleased with the prospect of something being done for the indigent blind; talked of procuring subscriptions, and of preaching a sermon on the occasion, by which he hoped to obtain a collection of at least forty pounds, which would serve as a fund to commence with; and he appeared particularly anxious to have a meeting of a few individuals, friendly to the cause, some of whose names were then mentioned, in order to discuss the plan, and frame a few regulations for the government of the future institution. After staying about two hours, conversing chiefly on the subject which brought us together, I withdrew, leaving the three letters in the possession of Mr. Dannett, and believing if a meeting were to take place, that the benevolent business would speedily be carried into execution.—On my way home, I called to inform John Christie that I had left a copy of his letter with Mr. Dannett, and to give him the particulars of what had passed with which he was highly gratified. A week or ten days after this, I was invited to dine with Mr. Dannett. There were present, exclusive of Mr. D.[,] Mr. Roscoe, Rev. J. Smyth, Mr. Carson, Mr. Lowe, Mr. Christie and myself; Mr. Alanson, and Mr. Sutton were also invited, but the former was particularly engaged, and Mr. S. as I understood afterwards, not being acquainted with Mr. Dannett, supposed there must be some mistake, and therefore did not attend. Immediately after dinner, Mr. Dannett commenced the business by reading my two letters, and that of J. Christie's, no other manuscript or document whatever being produced. A sheltering establishment for the indigent blind appeared the ardent wish of all. There was, indeed, some difference of opinion as to the scale on which it should commence, and as to the employments which would prove the most suitable, but not a syllable was uttered against the thing itself. The ideas contained in John Christie's letter were discussed by the name of Christie's plan, and the beneficial scheme, as mine; and here it may be observed, that, by this meeting, the beneficial fund was incorporated with the design, and actually forms a part of the just printed documents, though it has never yet been carried into execution. With the suggestions of John Christie, as a ground-work, several rules and regulations committed to writing during the afternoon, and to these Mr. Roscoe appeared particularly attentive. It was late in the evening before the company separated, and in order that the infant scheme might benefit by the observations which had been made during the discussion, it was agreed that the second meeting should not be held till after the interval of a week. Accordingly on the following Monday, another meeting was held at the house of Mr. Dannett; the regulations made at the first meeting were deliberately read, and after some little alterations and emendations, of little moment, the documents were left in the hands of Mr. Dannett, in order that they might be committed to the press. Thus, in a brief unvarnished way, have I given the origin of the Liverpool Institution for the Blind. If I have stated falsehoods, those falsehoods may readily be refuted by an appeal to living testimony; if I have adhered to truth, the deposition recently made by the Rev. H. Dannett, whether proceeding from forgetfulness or design, must necessarily be erroneous.

EDWARD RUSHTON.

AN ATTEMPT

TO PROVE THAT CLIMATE, FOOD, AND MANNERS,

ARE NOT THE

Causes of the Dissimilarity of Colour

IN THE HUMAN SPECIES.

(unknown date; published 1824)

"When a rich man speaketh, every man holdeth his tongue; and lo! what he says is extolled to the clouds: but if a poor man speak, they say, What fellow is this?"

WHEN an important subject has been discussed by men eminent for abilities in the most polished nations of Europe, and the result has in general been uniform, it must have the appearance of great presumption in any one (particularly in an individual so humbly situated as myself) to endeavour to prove by arguments drawn from nature, that the hypothesis which they have founded is not quite so invulnerable as the learned fabricators may have fondly imagined. Yet, notwithstanding this, like the poor Greenlander, I here launch my little skiff to encounter a huge leviathan; and should I be so fortunate as to give him but a single wound, it may encourage some one, more expert and weighty than myself, to advance and transfix him in such a manner that he may be dragged from his profound depths, and deprived of that enormous strength which had been so long accumulating.

To account for that variety of colour which is found among the human species has employed the penetration of many celebrated writers. Climate with them is the primary, though not the only, cause of this remarkable difference;—food and manners have their influence. It is a part of their hypothesis, that the sable natives of Africa, were they brought into the temperate climates of France, or of England, would, in a series of generations, become white; and that their hair, instead of its present woolly appearance, would in time become like that of the Europeans. Again, that the fairest natives of our temperate zone, were they removed to the parching climates of Benin or Calabar, would, by conforming to the manners and food of the natives, in the like manner become black, and possess every peculiarity which now marks the negro inhabitants of that torrid situation.

But to elucidate this, continue they, and to shew the influence of climate in the strongest point of view, let us for a moment turn our attention to the various nations who occupy the intermediate space between the scorching climates of Negroland and ourselves, we shall then find the cause and the effect in uniform proportion.

At, and contiguous to, the equator, where the glowing sun exerts its utmost force, we find the human species entirely black. To the northward of this burning region, on the southern shores of Barbary, we meet with another race, not so black as those we have left, nor so fair as the Africans who border on the Mediterranean. To the northward of this tract, the Spaniards and Portuguese present themselves, not indeed so brown as the Moors, but many shades deeper than the inhabitants of France, or more northern situations. Thus (cry the advocates of climate) we have a regular gradation of shade from the jetty colour of the African to the roseate whiteness of the Briton: and as the hottest climates are found to produce the blackest, and the most temperate the whitest, of mankind, we have every reason to conclude that the sun's influence is the principal cause of that amazing dissimilarity which is found among the various tenants of the universe.

Such are the reasonings of Buffon and Clarkson on this curious and important subject; men, whose abilities I revere, and whose benevolent warmth in behalf of the poor oppressed Africans does infinite credit to humanity. I have read their generous productions, and also those of the humane Ramsey; and as I have resided a considerable time in Jamaica, and am not unacquainted with the Antilles in general, it is with some degree of confidence I can affirm, that the accounts which those gentlemen have given the world are not in the least overcharged: nay, that in many cases, the sufferings of the wretched negroes have either been concealed from an ill-timed respect to a particular description of men, or have never come to the knowledge of those able and manly contenders for the rights of human nature.

But to return to our subject.—Though it may appear arrogant in me to aim at refuting such eminent authorities; yet, with the utmost deference, I venture to maintain an opposite opinion. It is not my intention to assign any other cause for the various colours of the human race; the great Author of Nature can produce effects of every kind: I shall only attempt to prove, that climate, food, and manners, however combined, are not sufficient of themselves to produce this extraordinary phenomenon.

And first,—as to that regular gradation of shade, which is supposed to prevail from the equatorial regions of Africa to the northern extremities of the temperate zone, however plausible it may appear, I trust the following observations will, in some degree, evince the fallacy of such a mode of reasoning.

On the southern banks of the Senegal, which is nearly one thousand miles from the equator, we find men as black as any in the universe; consequently climate throughout this vast extent produces not the difference of a single shade. But mark the consistency of the hypothesis.—What climate could not effect in the space of one thousand miles is immediately brought about by the Senegal, the greatest breadth of which scarcely exceeds a thousand yards; for on the northern banks of this river, we immediately meet with another family of mankind, as many shades fairer than the Negroes on the opposite side as they themselves are darker than the Europeans on the banks of the Seine or the Thames.

Can this be termed a regular gradation? No: it is an abrupt transition from the sable colour of the Negro to the brown complexion of the Moor; and, in my opinion, it is utterly impossible that climate, in the space of a few hundred yards, should have the power of producing this remarkable dissimilarity.

But it is urged, that the Negroes on the southern banks are stationary, while the Moors on the northern, who possess flocks and herds, are a wandering race, pitching their tents wherever they find the richest pastures, and quitting them in quest of others when they will no longer afford subsistence for their cattle. Allowing this to be the case,—what then?—The Moors, in their peregrinations, being more exposed to the scorching rays of the sun, and to the parching effects of the east wind blowing over a vast continent, ought not, according to their mode of reasoning, to be a fairer people than the stationary negroes, who are remarkably indolent, and spend the hottest part of the day either reclining beneath their cane-built sheds or lolling under the umbrageous shelter of their spreading trees. But it may be urged that these Moors, being wanderers, may sometimes penetrate to the northward, and of course into more temperate climates. And why not to the eastward, along the fertile banks of the Senegal?—the periodical inundations of which, like those of the Nile, (both rivers having their rise in the same range of mountains) render it one of the most fruitful regions of the world, and consequently the best adapted to their patriarchal mode of life.

But, to finish this matter, the children of those Moors who skirt the Senegal, if not stained by a mixture with their sable neighbours, are as fair as the children of those who inhabit the countries of Barbary bordering on the Mediterranean. This sufficiently proves them to be of one family, and shews, that throughout this extensive territory, which occupies nearly twenty degrees of latitude, there is no other difference of colour than what is caused by the action of the sun on those parts of the body more exposed to its influence; which it would be as impossible to transmit to their offspring as the Indians of Tongataboo, who have a custom of lopping off the first joint of their little finger, to have children who at their birth shall be found deficient in that particular part.

Leaving the natives of Barbary, we next come to the Spaniards and Portuguese: and here, it may be asked, if climate be not the cause of colour, why are the inhabitants of this peninsula so many shades deeper than those who possess a more northerly situation? To this I answer, that the natives of these kingdoms are not so brown as they are generally represented; nay, that the difference between them and the whitest people in Europe is so trifling, that amongst the higher and middle ranks it is scarcely perceptible; and even were it greater it might justly be ascribed to a mixture of moorish blood in their veins rather than to climate: for as those Moors overran and possessed this country for many centuries, they of course mingled with the conquered, and by this means contaminated that whiteness which distinguishes the European from the rest of the world.

But these are only the minutiæ of the subject: let us now take a more extensive view of mankind;—let us trace them through the remotest regions;—and, in particular, let us avoid those misrepresentations which may be found even in eminent writers, when strenuously supporting a favourite opinion.

And here it may be remarked, that though I object to the learned hypothesis, yet I cannot suppose that mankind are either exalted by their whiteness, or degraded by their receding from this supposed favourite colour of nature. He who streaked the tiger, who spotted the leopard, and who gave the lion his tawny hue, could most certainly mark the externals of the rational animal with whatever tints he pleased. But to imagine that the wise Framer of the Universe is partial to this or that particular colour; or that he created a race of beings with sable complexions and woolly hair to be servile drudges to the rest, is, in my opinion, to degrade Omnipotence. Away then with this fancied superiority which the Europeans have vainly arrogated to themselves. Nature knows it not. However different in appearance, we are all the production of the same wonderful hand; and I shall now endeavour to prove that neither situation, food, nor manners, have the power to produce this striking—this incomprehensible variety in the colour of the human species.

While the eastern side of the Atlantic, from the Cape of Good Hope in the south to the islands of Orkney in the north, presents us with three distinct families of mankind, the black, the brown, and the white; on the opposite side of the same ocean, from the southern extremity of America to the banks of the river St. Lawrence, through all the various climates of the former, we find the human form of one invariable hue. Where then is that regular gradation of shade so strongly contended for?

If man varies his colour according to his remoteness from, or proximity to, the equator, then the inhabitants of Kamschatka, of Nootka Sound, of Labrador, and of England, situated at an equal distance from the supposed cause, ought, in this particular, to resemble each other: the Canadian should be as white as the European, and the natives of Brazil as black and as woolly headed as those of Mozambique or Angola.

In America are all the various climates of the habitable globe; yet America, when first discovered, had neither white nor black inhabitants. What reason can be assigned for this? If the influence of the sun produce that variety in the old world, ought it not also to produce similar effects in the new? Yet throughout this vast extent we do not find a single variation in the colour of the human frame. The children of Canada; of the nations to the east and west of the Mississippi; of Mexico, Peru, Chili; the Magellanic coast; nay, of Terra del Fuego, of Paraguay, Brazil, amongst the remnants of the Caribbs; and, in short, from the north to the south of this vast continent, for the space of six thousand miles, the children of the Aborigines are one uniform reddish brown, or copper colour; nor is there any variety among the adults but what is caused by the different paint and unctuous substances with which they discolour their bodies, partly by way of ornament, and partly to defend themselves from the inclemency of the weather.

A celebrated naturalist* has indeed asserted that the inhabitants of Quito, from their vicinity to the snowy Andes, are nearly white; but if boisterous regions, if frost or snow, can produce an effect of this kind, then the inhabitants of Canada, and the dreary Terra del Fuego, whose winters are remarkably long and severe, ought to be fairer than even those of Quito; yet the former are known to be as brown as any Indians on the continent.

This writer, however elegant and spirited, is not exempt from error; in his treatise on the varieties of mankind he observes, that the natives of Japan are browner than those of China, because they are situated farther to the south, and consequently exposed to the rays of a warmer sun.

Now the Japanese, though browner than the Chinese, are not situated farther to the south, but rather to the north-east of the latter; therefore in a more temperate climate, and ought not, according to his mode of reasoning, to be a browner race, but the reverse.

Instances like these should teach us to make use of that portion of intellect which the great Fountain of Wisdom has thought fit to pour upon us, and not servilely to conform to the opinions of any individuals, however eminent for wealth, titles, or understanding. It is not the uniform complexions of the Americans alone which bid defiance to the sun's influence: the discoveries of the present reign furnish additional proofs equally strong and convincing.

That vast ocean which lies between the Indian Archipelago and the western shores of South America is studded over with innumerable islands, for the most part inhabited. Some of them lift their rugged heads in the heart of the southern hemisphere; while others display their gay luxuriance on the verge of the northern tropic. The language, the manners, and the customs of most of these Indians, particularly of the New Zealanders, and the natives of the Friendly[,] Society and Sandwich islands are so remarkably similar, that every intelligent observer pronounces them only the wide extended branches of one huge family tree, the root of which is probably among the Malays in the East Indies. But whether they spread themselves from this quarter over the Pacific islands, in an opposite direction to the trade winds, which constantly prevail between the tropics; whether they come before the winds and waves from the western shores of South America; or whether these numerous islands are only the fragments of a once extensive and well peopled southern continent, which by some extraordinary convulsion of nature in the early ages, might have been overwhelmed, and nothing left above the surface of the ocean but its most elevated parts, which may now afford sustenance to the posterity of those who were so fortunate as to escape the dreadful wreck. Whether any one of these conjectures has probability for its foundation is no part of the present inquiry: to a Pennant, a Barrington, or a Forster, I leave the discussion of this curious question, and shall content myself with asserting that the inhabitants of the above-mentioned islands are only the spreading branches of one parent stock; and I think the truth of this observation will be admitted by all who have perused with attention the accounts of our late circumnavigators.

Here then we have another family of the human species, inhabiting the numerous islands that are scattered over this vast ocean; and whether they pant in the torrid zone, or shiver in the southern temperate; whether they traverse the fruitful plains and gently sloping hills of Otaheite, or wander among the rugged precipices and snow-clad mountains of New Zealand, the complexion of their children (which in a disquisition of this kind is the best criterion) is nearly, if not invariably, the same. Hence it appears, that among the Pacific Islanders, as among the Americans, climate, or the influence of the sun, has no effect; since in this extent of seventy degrees of latitude we find none of those varieties of shade which are supposed to prevail in the old world. According to the temperature of particular situations, New Zealand and France, though in opposite hemispheres, are equally remote from the equator; yet the New Zealander is copper-coloured, and the Frenchman white. The island of Otaheite is as near to the equator as the Senegal; yet the Negroes on the southern banks of that river are entirely black, while the natives of Otaheite, instead of the dark complexion one would expect from their situation, are, according to Captain King, a fairer race than even the New Zealanders, though the latter are situated in the heart of the temperate zone. What can the advocates of climate say to this undoubted fact? That the inhabitants of a temperate situation should be found browner than those of a torrid one, who are twice a year exposed to the scorching rays of a vertical sun, is, in my opinion, a flat contradiction to their hypothesis, and strongly proves the fallacy of those arguments to which the writers on this side the question have frequently had recourse.

In vain will sophistry exert her utmost powers to controvert the foregoing assertions. Facts are stubborn things, and will not easily yield to fanciful speculations, however bold, elegant, or ingenious. As this is not a regular disserta-tion, but rather a sketch of something that might be done on this subject, I shall not enter minutely into every particular. Much has been said of the white Indians on the isthmus of Darien, of a similar race of Negroes in the interior parts of Africa, and of that difference of complexion which is sometimes found among the inhabitants of the same island; as Ceylon, Madagascar, &c. Now, allowing these accounts to be authentic, and that this dissimilarity proceeds not from cutaneous disorders, it most assuredly makes against the advocates of climate, though the celebrated Buffon has dwelt largely upon it for a contrary purpose: for if climate, food, and manners can produce the various colours of mankind, it is evident that all human beings, who are exposed to the same degree of heat, and whose food and manners are the same, ought to possess a uniform similarity of complexion; and if so, whence the white Negroes, white Indians, &c.?

We have already seen how climate operates upon the copper-coloured Americans, and some of the South Sea Islanders: let us now turn our attention to New Holland and New South Wales, and we may thence probably draw other arguments in corroboration of what has been already asserted.

That vast mass of land which is situated in the southern hemisphere, and occupies above two thousand miles of latitude, is inhabited by a race of people as black and as woolly-headed as those of Guinea. Naked and rude as imagination can conceive, they wander the free tenants of a country, the extremities of which are as remote from each other as the river Thames from the Senegal; yet the natives of Adventure Bay in the south, and of Endeavour River in the north, are in complexion and texture of the hair exactly the same.

From the Senegal to the Thames, or from the Senegal to the southern shores of Europe, which is scarcely twelve hundred miles, we find three of the most marking varieties in the colour of mankind; the blackness of the Negro, the brownness of the Moor, and the whiteness of the European. Now, if the sun's influence on the eastern side of the North Atlantic is so active and powerful as to produce these striking distinctions in the space of twelve hundred miles, how comes it that in the southern hemisphere, through an extent of latitude nearly twice as great as the above, the same sun does not produce a single deviation of colour among the savages of this wild and enormous fragment of the earth? Nature, that universal parent who rolls round the various seasons, and who alternately elevates and depresses the vast body of waters, cannot produce, from the same cause, effects so remarkably dissimilar.

The European complexion is no where to be found among the Aborigines of the southern hemisphere; yet the southern hemisphere has all the various climates of the northern one: hence we are led to this natural conclusion, that climate is not the cause of human colour. In the latitude of forty-three degrees north, the Frenchman is white; in the latitude of forty-three degrees south, the native of Van Dieman's Land is black; both are equally remote from the equator, and yet scarcely any thing can be more different than their external appearance.

Should any one assert that fire can act upon the particles of water, in such a manner as to form them into a body of ice, our judgments would recoil, because we know that natural causes can produce only natural effects; yet it would be just as easy for fire to perform this, as for the sun, in situations equally remote from the equator, to produce, by the power of his rays, two complexions so diametrically opposite as black and white.

From this remote situation, then, this sea-girt continent, we are furnished with other arguments; we find that the inhabitants of this extensive region vary not their colour according to their remoteness from, or proximity to, the equator; and we find also that torrid heat is not the cause of blackness, for at Adventure Bay, in the heart of the temperate zone, mankind are of a uniformly sable complexion.

Buffon has asserted that black men are only to be found within the tropics, and that the Africans who border on the Cape of Good Hope are not black, but tawny, as they are more remote from the equator. Unsupported assertions, however bold, must quickly vanish before truth, like mists of the morning before the sun. Captain Cook, in his last voyage, found the inhabitants of Van Dieman's Land, in the latitude of forty-three degrees south, as black as any of the human species; this fact is incontrovertible, and, in my opinion, sufficient of itself to overturn all that has been advanced by the advocates of climate. Arguments drawn from such authorities are arguments drawn from nature, and will maintain their ground against all the assaults of wily sophistry of elegant declamation.

After taking this cursory view of the most striking varieties of colour, it may be necessary to remark another peculiarity in their externals, which seems to divide the human species into separate families, and shews that all are but distinct parts of one amazing whole; I mean the texture of the hair, in which particular the inhabitants of the earth differ as much from each other as in the colour of their bodies.

It has been said that the woolly appearance of the Negroes' hair is entirely owing to their being situated in a torrid climate; but this is fallacious. The Moors, according to Mons. Adanson, differ not more from the Negroes in complexion than in the covering of their heads, which is long and bushy; yet both are exposed to the same degree of heat, being separated only by the narrow river Senegal.

We have just seen that torrid heat is not the cause of blackness, and the same fact will shew us that this crispness of the hair is not confined to the Negroes; for the natives of Adventure Bay possess these peculiarities in as great a degree as the African who pants beneath the scorching rays of an equatorial sun. Nor is it the sable race alone who are thus particularly distinguished. The Americans, and most of the South Sea Islanders, are as strongly marked from the rest of mankind by their coarse, lank, and, in general, black hair, as by their uniform reddish brown or copper-coloured complexions; both of which are transmitted from sire to son: nor is it in the power of climate to make the least alteration in either. This may be elucidated by the native American; for whether he erect his wigwam on the borders of the lake Ontario, or cultivate his little plantation among the mountains of St. Vincent; whether he wander on the banks of the river Amazon, or launch his canoe on the Magellanic Straits, it is immaterial; both are equally permanent; both seem to be strongly imprinted upon him by the hand of nature; and, in my opinion, both would remain invariably the same to the latest period of time, were it not for the admixture with the other families of mankind.

Here, then, to avoid the imputation of prolixity, I shall close my observations on this supposed primary cause of complexion with a few remarks on its collateral assistants, food and manners.

That the various colours of mankind should be ascribed to the heat of the sun is not surprising, since the effects of his vertical rays upon the European externals are evident to every one; but that food should be deemed an auxiliary in the grand work is to me somewhat extraordinary: however the following plain facts will enable us to determine more precisely what degree of credit ought to be given to this opinion.

The food of the interior African is principally vegetable; the yam, the plantain, the banana, rice, pepper, palm oil, &c., compose his choicest viands; while the native of Adventure Bay, similar in complexion and texture of the hair, possesses none of these: shell-fish from the surrounding rocks, with sometimes a kangaroo, or a wild fowl, when he has skill to obtain them, form the whole of his humble fare.

The Sandwich Islander and the native of New Zealand are in externals exactly similar; yet the former has his bread fruit, his plantains, his yeddoes, his hogs, &c.; while the latter, unacquainted with these, and possessed of few vegetables, is supplied from his rocky shores and coves with plenty of fish; to these he adds the flesh of dogs fatted for the purpose, and not unfrequently a horrid repast from the body of some slaughtered enemy.

The Canadian traverses his vast forest of oak and pine in pursuit of the moose, the bear, &c., on which he principally subsists; the Brazilian on the other hand uses little animal food. Situated in a luxuriant country, where nature pours forth her vegetable stores in the greatest abundance, his food nearly resembles that of the interior African; while the wanderer of the bleak and inhospitable Terra del Fuego in his food differs materially from both, having neither the flesh of brutes nor the productions of the earth; to the ocean only, which thunders on his dreary coast, he looks for subsistence. With pleasure he devours the raw blubber from the back of the seal, or patiently broils his finny tribe, or roasts the lympit, welk, &c., at his little fire. Scarcely any thing can be more different than the aliment of these widely separated people; yet in complexion and texture of the hair they are exactly the same.

Where, then, is the influence of food, and where the influence of climate? If they have any, except in the imagination of speculative writers, why does it not operate on all mankind? Why have the natives of America one uniform complexion, though scattered through all the various climates of the habitable globe, and with every possible variety of food, while the inhabitants of the old world are supposed to vary their appearances according to their torrid or temperate situations? Why are the natives of the Owhyhee and New Zealand so exactly alike, though with seventy degrees of latitude between them, and with food so materially different; whilst the New Zealander and the native of Van Dieman's Land, situated at no great distance from each other, in exactly the same climate, and with food not very different, are yet in externals so remarkably dissimilar? Or why is there so strong a resemblance between the Negro on the banks of the Gambia and the native of Adventure Bay, though separated by nearly half the circumference of the globe, and though in different hemispheres, different zones, and with food so totally different; while the Africans on each side the Senegal, the greatest breadth of which is scarcely a single mile, are yet, in complexion and texture of the hair, so strongly distinguished from each other?

To these interrogatories what answer can be made? That climate and food are not the causes, is, in my opinion, sufficiently evident; but as manners, the other collateral assistant, yet remains, let us examine how far it is probable that the human frame can be affected by this supposed auxiliary. Manners, so far as they relate to human colour, can only mean that one man, or nation, from particular habits, may be more exposed to the influence of climate, or, from particular customs, more discoloured by unctuous substances than another. But whatever shade the European may acquire, whose complexion is perhaps the only one that can be materially altered; however brown the English seaman may become by being long exposed to the glowing rays and parching coasts of Africa; and however this tawny hue may tinge the whole surface of his body, yet, with all due submission, I would ask these celebrated advocates of climate whether this can be deemed the seaman's natural complexion? Or whether the innate principles of colour can be in the least altered by the sun's rays? In my opinion, this acquired tinge is merely superficial, and he can no more transmit it to his offspring, than those savages, who besmear themselves with paint of various hues, can transmit to their children party-coloured complexions; or than the male and female Negro, painted of an European flesh colour, could beget children with European externals.

The seeds of human colour are so strongly incorporated with the stamina by the hand of nature, that I think it impossible for any external cause ever to effect a change. Male and female, of the same natural hue, will assuredly produce the same, and when of different ones, the offspring will partake in an exact degree of both. This is so fully illustrated by the various gradations of shade from white to black, which are found among the present inhabitants of the Antilles and of Spanish America, that to enter into a minute discussion of it might be deemed unnecessary.

But by way of elucidating this part of the subject, let us for a moment imagine a few European families to have formed a settlement on the southern banks of the river Senegal; their climate torrid, their soil luxuriant, and their food and manners exactly similar to those of the present inhabitants; suppose them indolently reclining within their habitations, or conversing beneath the spreading branches of their enormous calabash trees during the hottest part of the day. Suppose ten, fifteen, or twenty generations to have passed away without any intermixture with their sable neighbours, then, according to the hypothesis, this difference of climate, food, and manners, would have changed the European externals into the sable complexions and woolly hair of the native

Negroes. On the other hand, let us suppose a few Mandingo families to have been removed from the banks of the river Gambia to those of the Thames; suppose their food, their employment, their dress, &c., exactly to agree with those of their surrounding neighbours; suppose a series of unmixed generations to have taken place; and then, according to the above authorities, owing to the bleaching qualities of our temperate climate, our animal food, and our artificial manners, the African externals would gradually disappear, and the pure posterity of these Mandingoes would at length appear with the rosy countenances and flowing hair of the present English peasantry.

Such are the opinions of several eminent writers upon the above subject. But if on the eastern side of the North Atlantic, this difference of climate, food, and manners, can produce such a wonderful change in the colour of mankind, I again assert that the same causes should produce the same effects throughout the continent of America, and throughout the South Sea islands.

As yet it is but the voice of conjecture which asserts that Negroes removed to England would become white, and Englishmen removed to Guinea would become black: no one fact has ever been produced to corroborate this opinion, and therefore the best mode of reasoning upon this subject is from analogy.

Are not the copper-coloured race of the human species? Are they not born? Do they not propagate? Do they not die? And does not the great Emblem of Deity, the sun, dart his rays on all mankind without distinction? Most assuredly! Yet no degrees of heat or cold, no aliment, however various, nor manners, however dissimilar, can produce the least change in the colour of the native American, nor in the colour of the South Sea islander; nor, I firmly believe, for the reasons already advanced, in the colour of any other family of the human species.

But fearful of becoming tedious, I shall conclude with observing, that though a variety of conjectures have been formed concerning the primitive colour of mankind; yet whether Noah was white, according to Buffon, or copper-coloured, according to Clarkson, is no part of the present inquiry: some colour the Antedeluvian must have had; and the question is, if we are all his descendants, what cause or causes can be assigned for that amazing variety which is, at present, observable among the different tenants of the universe?

The seat of colour is extremely well known; but why the matter lodged in the cuticle of one human being should be white, in another black, in a third copper-coloured, &c. is the phenomenon yet to be accounted for; and while the learned authorities have in general ascribed it to climate, food, and manners, I have endeavoured to refute their observations, though without assigning any other cause for this amazing difference of mankind, than the will of that Being who rules over heaven, earth, and sea, and on whom our *mental* sight can no more steadily gaze, than our corporeal one on the glaring splendour of a torrid meridian sun.

[Rushton's note] *Buffon.

[Letter to Samuel Ryley]
(written 1814; published 1903)

Liverpool, August 12th, 1814.

Dear Ryley,

From the contents of your first letter I entertained a hope—it was indeed but a faint one—that you had viewed the situation of your old friend through the atmosphere of your own distresses, and of course I deemed him not in quite so perilous a state as you have represented. Yours of yesterday, however, has terminated the delusion. Yes, the curtain has dropped, and life's poor play is over. After an intimacy of nearly thirty years with poor Cowdroy, I think I may venture to assert that I never met with a man who had fewer asperities and more kind and benevolent affections. His nerves were not, I think, calculated for the most turbulent times, yet his love for the liberties of mankind was pure and decided. Had he possessed fewer social qualities he would probably have lived much longer. His humour, his well-told and appropriate anecdote, and his art of fascinating a company were such that it required the nerves of a stoic to resist the invitations and allurements with which he was perpetually surrounded. You may remember George Hayworth, Isaac Highfield, Tipping, Pye, &c., &c. These are all gone to the dark and narrow house, and now he who was wont to shake their sides with merriment is become like one of them, and even those who lament him must, in a few years, become what he now is. But why, friend Ryley, are you so much afraid of dying, seeing that it will come when it will come? If there be another world, let us do well here and we shall do well there, and if there be not another world, there is a vast consolation in acting our part well in this. The soundest philosophy, in my opinion, is to enjoy, but care should be taken that our enjoyment should never produce the visitations of that fiend called compunction, a fiend which destroys all pillow comfort and inflicts a sting a thousand times keener than that of the scorpion. I had condensed a few thoughts for the obituary of the *Mercury*, but Ned, going up to Casey with the intelligence, found that he had received a letter from Ben Cowdroy, and had just finished the article which you will perceive in the *Mercury*. It is rather too much amplified, but the delineation is glowing and correct.

Yours ever,

EDWARD RUSHTON.

Samuel William Ryley,
    No. 19, Charlotte Street, Manchester.

Mr Rushton's Remarks on Slavery.
(unknown date; unpublished)

[3]
[...] should ungergo, [*sic*, i.e. 'undergo'] not a nominal, but a thorough examination. This I am persuaded would produce a good effect, Merit would not shun an enquiry, ignorance indeed might [*undeciphered*, perhaps 'excuse'] it, but our bold defenders would by these means be free'd from a scourge, and, in my opinion be frequently preserv'd to their families, their friends and their Country. It is better to have no Medicine than medicine improperly apply'd, and if ever medical skill be necessary, it is surely,—to baffle diseases in ~~the juices of~~ those whose juices [?] are already in a state of contamination, owing to their long subsistence upon putrid aliment. The Seaman's food on these voyages consists chiefly of Salt Beef and Biscuit; and frequently but a short allowance of each; whatever care may be taken at home to procure these of the best quality, (which is not always the case) yet the Climate of Guinea soon converts it into a very unwholesome diet; the Beef becomes hard, dry, and strongly [*undeciphered*], and the Biscuit so perforated with Weevills, Maggots &c. that by breaking one and giving it a stroke, the inside immediately pours forth in a mixture of dust and vermin. The Slaves provisions which consists of Yams, Rice, Beans, Stock Fish &c form a less unhealthy fare and on board some Vessells the crews are indulg'd with them, but in general they are a luxury on which the poor squalid Seamen may indeed cast a ling'ring look but that is all, unless he will venture to indulge his craving appetite at the probable expense of his blood, for shou'd he be detected a severe flogging wou'd be in most instances inevitable—We next come to the want of acomodation which in a Climate so unfavourable to Europeans as that of Guinea is a matter of no small moment,—The Steerage or that apartment which in other Merchantmen is allotted to the Ships company, is in this trade appropriated to the use of the Female Slaves in all weathers, therefore the Seamen are oblig'd to remain upon deck.

[4]
In some of the Rivers, as at Bonney, where the Vessell continues at Anchor untill the purchase is compleated, A frame like that of a House is erected over her, the roof of which is coverd with a thick matting peculiar to the country. From this roof to the Gunwale, the Ship is surrounded in every direction by

a strong Nett work, and when thus finish'd, with a door or two of communi-
cation, with the Boats and the Head she has much the resemblance of a huge
Bird Cage. This is design'd, and is absolutely necessary to prevent the Slaves
from plunging into the River, which whenever the vigilince of the Centinels
can be eluded is done, and the poor wretches are instantly torn in pieces by
the voracious Sharks.—This House, as it is called which is taken down when
the Ship prepares for Sea, certainly affords a shelter while on the coast to
all on board but I am afraid its utility in this point of view, is more than
counterballanc'd by the hindrance which it gives to a free circulation of Air,
than which, in so suffocating a region nothing can be more salutary.—On
other parts of the Coast particularly to Hindward where the Vessels lye more
expos'd and are not so stationary this practice cannot be adopted, their Boats
too by which the business of Slaving is chiefly carried on, are for the most part
open.—in these the Seaman suffers not a little, in these he leaves the Ship for
weeks together;—one hour expos'd to all the violence of a Tornado, and the
next, his cloaths dried upon him by the scorching rays of a Vertical Sun.—To
the infectious dews of night he is constantly expos'd, excepting when at anchor,
he then wraps himself up in the Boats' Sails,—heaves a Sigh for his native
Country, and Sleep—the Wretches kindest friend for a time puts a period to his
sufferings.—We now come to a matter which has long calld loudly for redress.

[5]

a matter so notorious, that few will be found Shameless enough to deny it —
that is cruel usage. And here it may be ask'd, Why Seamen in this branch
of the Merchants service should be treated with more severity than the same
description of Men in any other. To this, it may be answerd, first, that the
nature of the trade has a strong tendency to blunt the feeling and render the
Human Heart callous, 2^d that a great part of this voyage is performed at a
distance from that which operates like a strong fetter upon the hands of cruelty
and oppression, namely Brittish Justice, 3dly That on board these Ships are
generally found a few Landsmen, & half, and three quarters Seamen. These
are employ'd in the lowest offices, are look'd upon with an eye of contempt,
and shoud they ever be sett about any part of a Seamans duty, which they have
not abilities to execute, derision [?] and severity are the probable consequences.
And here let me add, that the Officer who accustoms himself to what is call'd
a word and blow, finds a very easy transition from abusing one part of the
Ships company to a similar treatment of the other, particularly when by such a
conduct it is not unlikely but he establishes a reputation for smartness, vigilence
and activity, 4^{ly} When a Slave Ship is unhealthy which is not an uncommon
case—When the Smal Pox—Measles,—Scurvey, Flux &c make their dreadful
ravages, When six, eight, or ten Slaves are thrown overboard on a morning, the
Captain's agitation of mind will be easily conceiv'd, by those who consider, that
his emoluments rise in proportion to the number of Slaves which he brings to
market, and that by so many burials he loses at least, 9-12 or 15£ Sterling. When

thus he views his property daily swept away, no wonder, he becomes ~~daily~~ more & more impatient and morose. No wonder every thing goes wrong—he abuses his Docter, [?] Quarrels with his Officers, and they, irritated at being censur'd for what it is not in their power to prevent

[6]

take every opportunity to revenge themselves upon the Ships Company. Pityfull and Unmanly as such a conduct must appear, yet those who have been accustom'd to unhealthy Slave Ships will upon cool reflection readily acknowledge this picture not to be overcharg'd, and if possesst of candour will agree that in general such a situation, whether upon the Coast or in the middle passage, presents us with scarcely any thing but a scene of abuse, cruelty, and distruction. "It has grieved me (said an intelligent Sea Captain of my acquainttance who was formerly in this trade to whom I am indebted for several of the foregoing particulars.) "It has grieved me to see the treatment of Seamen on board some of these Vessels—to see a poor Sunburnt Veteran who had formerly fought the Battles of his Country, insulted and cruelly buffeted by some unthinking hot headed Officer, to see him beaten with a ropes end, or knock'd down with a billet of wood or whatever came next to hand, for the most trivial inadvertances.—Perhaps because the debilitated wretch had not sprung in a moment, (as the phrase says) or had taken up more time about some particular part of his duty, than the pamper'd, Cabin fed minion had been willing to allow. It has griev'd me when there has been no real scarcity of provisions on board, to see a Seaman swallow in a minute or two that portion of meat which had been weighd out to him as an allowance for 24 Hours,— To see a poor fellow with Tumid & ulcerated legs, whenever he wanted drink obliged to crawl to the <u>Masthead</u>, where by a small rope was suspended the Gun Barrell,—this he must bring upon deck, place in an aperture made on purpose in the Cask, suck the Water thro, and immediately return it to its former situation.—If in an unguarded moment he gave the instrument to another, a severe punishment was sure to follow.

[Letter to Thomas Walker]
(written 1806; unpublished)

Liverpool Jan.y 30 1806

My dear Sir,

About a Week ago J. Thelwall left Liverpool in order to Lecture in London where should he meet with encouragement he intends to remove his Family and cast his Sheet Anchor for Life.

To serve a Character who has been much persecuted, and who is indefatigable in his efforts to maintain a Wife and six little ones, would give me great pleasure, but Justice compels me to say, that I have never heard of any Individual whose Impediments of utterance have ever been improved, or even ameliorated by his mode of treatment, in saying this however it must not be understood that J. T. has never been successful in any of his cases, I can only say, that if [he] has been successful they have not come to my knowledge.

About three years ago, a Merchant of this Town of the name of Lyne, was under the care of J. T. for inarticulate utterance, many Lessons were given and many Guineas were pocketted [sic], and at length it was discover'd by T., that the complaint was a palsy of the Mind, and nothing beneficial could be effected. With Mr Lyne I have not the least personal Acquaintance, yet if you write to him mentioning the case minutely, and giving your reasons for the application, I have every reason to believe from his general Character, that he would favor you with his candid opinion, and thus you would form a competant [sic] idea as to the propriety of placing the son of your Friend under the tuition of J. T –. The Science of Elocution, and the cure of Impediments, are all that Thelwall has ever profess'd the Greek and Latin Classics, Mathematics &c are if I mistake not, entirely out of the question.

Report says your Friend is coming out into the Cabinet, with Windham, Grenville &c can he long agree with those high toned Gentry, those quondam Associates of Pitt, should he have a majority in the Cabinet, he may manage them, if not, they will so thwart him, and chafe him, on the great questions of Reform, Catholic emancipation, Slave Trade, &c that in a few Months, he and his Friends may probably be under the necessity of leaving the bloated Aristocracy to themselves. Remember me to Cowdroy and believe me dear Sir

Yours Affectionately

Edw Rushton

Thos Walker Esq
Longford near
Manchester

Liverpool 206
JAN 31 1806

COMMENTARY

Glossary

Rather than annotate every instance of words that were familiar to Rushton and his audience but which have slipped away from modern usage, it has seemed helpful to gloss a few of the most common in advance.

Albion] Britain.
bark] ship.
clime] region, climate.
connexions] relations, family.
craig] crag; often with this spelling in Rushton, perhaps indicating a
    dialectal pronunciation (the word is Celtic in origin).
deplore] bewail, lament.
Erin] Ireland.
Gallia] France.
lay] song, poem.
main] ocean.
mein] i.e. mien: bearing, attitude behaviour; Rushton often spells it this way.
sable] black, normally conferring a sense of value on the colour through its
    association with heraldic nobility.
strain] song.
tar] 'figurative expression for a sailor of any kind' (William Falconer,
    Universal Dictionary of the Marine, 1769), because of the tar used to
    waterproof ships' hulls.
yard] the timber pole or spar from which sails are suspended.

Commentary: Poems

An Irregular Ode

Source: Lloyd's Evening Post, 21 March 1781, over the signature '*Liverpool.*
Edward Rushton.' Not reprinted.

Variants:
57 aims] the original has 'aim'.
69 your] the original has 'you'.

Commentary: Like the rest of Rushton's early output, this poem is situated in
the latter years of the American War of Independence (1776–1783), and supports
the fading view, usually associated with the Earl of Chatham's opposition to
Lord North's victory-at-all-costs strategy, that there could still be a negotiated
settlement between Britain and the colonies which would recognise grievances
about taxation and representation, but avoid breaking up the empire. The war
would be in effect over by the end of the year. Rushton himself would soon
take a different view of Britain's role in upholding 'liberty' but the strident
tone and the theme of liberty itself is already clearly established. The doubtful
poem 'Rebellion Tottering Stands' (see Appendix I) is much more patriotically
militaristic.

Irregular] irregular in that the line lengths and spacing do not correspond
    to ordinary metrical rules. A fairly common mode in the eighteenth
    century, especially in dealing with public or national themes: compare the
    anonymous *England's Defiance. An Irregular Ode* (1779), attacking France
    and Spain for their role in the American war. Most of Rushton's later
    poems have notably strict and sometimes innovative metrical schemes.

2 green mountain] i.e. a huge wave.
3 crazy] 'broken; decrepit' (SJ).
7 instant] instantly, at once.
13 Liberty] commonly identified in British writing of the eighteenth century
    as a British virtue in contrast to continental tyranny and surveillance;

see e.g. James Thomson, *Liberty. A Poem* (1735–1736), especially part 4, and Joseph Warton, 'Ode to Liberty' in *Odes on Various Subjects* (1747). Liberty was rehoused in revolutionary France in Rushton's 'Song, Sung at the celebration of the anniversary of the French Revolution', below.

14 gripe] grasp.

15 straight] straightaway.

17 iron shores] well-defended coastlines.

19 vindicate] 'support; maintain' (SJ).

28 Slaves] not here the actual slaves of the colonies but the 'servile wretches' (40), or nations of weaker people who accept their governments' oppression.

31 Stewart] James Stuart, or James II, who vacated the throne of Britain in 1688 in the so-called 'Glorious Revolution'; the Catholic James was regarded by Whig politicians as an absolutist in the French mode and his protestant replacements, William III and Mary, were regarded as constitutional monarchs in a more modern sense.

33–36] some aspects of these lines were later incorporated in *The Dismember'd Empire*, 43–46.

35 vernal] of spring.

46 loss of sight] a poignant matter for Rushton, who went blind after contracting ophthalmia on a slaving ship in about 1776.

48 rights of man] Thomas Paine's *Rights of Man*, the famous manifesto for radical political reform, was not published until 1791, but the phrase already had a certain currency, e.g. Tobias Smollett, 'Ode to Independence', 64 (*Plays and Poems*, 1777, p. 262) associates it with the Swiss hero William Tell, and William Hayley, *Elegy on the Ancient Greek Model* (1779, p. 6, l. 50), with the controversialist Benjamin Hoadley. The *Declaration of Independence*, promulgated by the American colonists on 4 July 1776, was also a foundational statement of human rights.

49 some retir'd] presumably a reference to the Pilgrim Fathers and the establishment of early American colonies in the pursuit of liberty of religious worship and conscience, in 1620.

51–60] apparently looking for reconciliation and acceptance on Britain's part that it has to some extent provoked the secession of the colonies by ignoring the rights of the colonised in measures such as the Coercive Acts.

55 sway] control, persuasion.

60] see *The Dismember'd Empire*, 98, where a speech of this kind is given by Britannia herself.

66 conspire] agree or work together.

68 Rebellion now stalks] compare 'To the People of England', 9, and *The Dismember'd Empire*, 188, 214, 278. This again is different from the language of 'Rebellion tottering stands' (Appendix I). Rushton may be suggesting that the entry of France and Spain (the 'deadly foes' of 70)

into the war constitutes 'rebellion' in a way that resistance to British
tyranny had not, but there were also mutinies among American soldiers.

75] a return to the marine metaphor of the poem's opening.

79 Bourbon] France.

81 Northern Powers combine] Russia led an alliance of 'armed neutrality'
against Britain during the war; see *Dismember'd Empire*, 177–80.

To the People of England

Source: Morning Post and Daily Advertiser, 11 October 1782, over the signature
'Liverpool. EDWARD RUSHTON'. Not reprinted.

Commentary: The context is that of the continuing wars with Spain and France
after the loss of the American colonies. Though the poem tends more towards
warmongering than Rushton's later poems, it should be remembered that he
was genuinely patriotic, especially in defiance of the pre-revolutionary French.

3 Gallia] France declared war on Britain in July 1778 after covertly assisting
the colonists. For France, the point was to recapture some of the territory
lost in the Seven Years' War (1756–1763) and to look for territorial gains in
the West Indies.

5 Iberia … mine] Spain declared war on Britain in June 1779, with the aim
of recovering Gibraltar from a weakened Britain; its 'mines' were mainly
in its South America colonies.

6 Big with] full of.

7 Belgia] probably loosely indicating the Dutch, on whom Britain declared
war in 1780 because of their role in supplying the Americans and the
French. The modern state of Belgium was not created until 1830.

8 slaves] not actual slaves but politically subservient peoples; cf 'An Irregular
Ode', 28.

9–10] peace negotiations had been pursued alongside the military campaigns
since 1778. Although the war was effectively over in 1781, peace with
America was not officially established until the Treaty of Paris, 3
September 1783.

9 rebellion] see commentary to *Dismember'd Empire*, 188, 214, 278.

14 Pleasure's lap to die away?] the image is one of wasteful sexual
indulgence.

15–16] a reference to the fierce parliamentary debates over the means to end
the wars.

22 wont] used.

25 supine] 'careless; indolent; drowsy' (SJ).

28 corps of Volunteers] auxiliary troops rather than regular professional
soldiers, established locally in response to threats of a French or Spanish

invasion. An 'Edward Rushton' was later a lieutenant in the Royal
Manchester and Salford Light Horse Volunteers (*True Briton*, 30 June
1798), but no link to the poet is known.

30 Hibernia] Ireland. As British troops were withdrawn to fight in the wars,
   local militias, known as the Volunteers, were set up against the threat
   of invasion. These groups, mainly recruited from loyalist protestants,
   were successful in gaining some concessions from the British government
   towards local Irish powers. Rushton would later deplore the suppression of
   the more radical independence movement in Ireland in 1798.

33 frigid] unenthusiastic.

35 dastard] cowardly.

39 self-array'd] providing their own uniforms, as with their own weapons
   earlier in the line.

40 artist] artisan: all classes participate in the volunteer army.

50 meek-ey'd peace] 'meek-eyed' is an epithet often used in eighteenth-
   century poetry of abstract female virtues such as pity, charity, virtue, etc;
   the exact phrase is found in Tobias Smollett, *The Regicide* (1749, II. vii,
   p. 27).

53 Suffolk] Not Henry Howard, 12th earl of Suffolk (1739–1779), who had
   had a prominent role in Lord North's cabinet during the American war,
   as his 'sons' died in infancy and he was himself already dead. A plan
   for a county subscription to furnish a warship had been put forward by
   the inhabitants of Suffolk, however, and this is probably what Rushton
   means: see e.g. *Gazetteer*, 27 September 1782 and *Morning Chronicle*, 28
   September 1782.

54 Lowther] Sir James Lowther, baronet, later Earl of Lonsdale (1736–1802),
   politician, one of those opposing further prosecution of the war against
   America in 1781–2; see *ODNB*. He was reported as offering to fit out
   a ship of the line at his own expense to help expand Britain's naval
   capability against France; e.g. *Morning Herald*, 10 September 1782; *London
   Evening Post*, 27 September 1782; the 'patriotic plan' of '58. An anonymous
   poem celebrating Lowther's offer had already appeared in *Parker's General
   Advertiser*, 1 October 1782. Both Suffolk and Lowther reappear in *The
   Dismember'd Empire*, 324–25.

59 aweful] awe-inspiring.

60 unequal] superior.

63–68] recycled in *The Dismember'd Empire*, 327–32.

64 nerveless] weak; compare Mark Akenside, 'Hymn to the Naiads', 213
   (*Poems*, 1772, p. 357): 'To brace the nerveless Arm'.

66 Craft] 'fraud; cunning; artifice' (SJ).

70 olive wand] a sign of peace, as in e.g. Alexander Pope, 'Messiah: A Sacred
   Eclogue' (1712), 19.

72 fell] 'cruel; barbarous; inhuman' (SJ).

73 sires] forefathers.

75–76] perhaps a condensed echo of John of Gaunt's famous patriotic
  description of the 'scepter'd isle' of England, Shakespeare, *Richard II*, II. i.
  40–60.

79–80] compare *The Dismember'd Empire*, 51–58.

The Dismember'd Empire

Source: The Dismember'd Empire. A Poem (Liverpool: Printed by W. Nevett
for J. Johnson, London, No. 17, St. Paul's Church Yard, London; and J. Gore,
Liverpool, 1782). According to the *Critical Review*, it was priced at 1s 6d. It is
a well-printed quarto publication. Undated and anonymous, but firmly and
convincingly attributed by Shepherd in the 1824 *Life* and it incorporates lines
from the earlier poems. It was not reprinted, no doubt for the same reasons that
the newspaper poems were uncollected later. The preface is dated November
1782 but the poem was not reviewed until August of the following year. No
relevant newspaper advertisements before then have been located. The poem
was not collected or reprinted; the preface and first 78 lines are reprinted in
Burke, pp. 12–15.

Variant:
142] the full stop is missing from the original printing.

Commentary: Peace negotiations with America were indeed at an advanced
stage, and it was already clear that full independence was the only real option.
With France and Spain the issues were over colonial possessions and control of
trade routes. William Nevett had been active as a Liverpool printer since 1765;
John Gore, as the proprietor of commercial newspapers and trade directories
since the same period. Joseph Johnson (1738–1809) was a leading publisher of
dissenting and liberal writings; he came originally from Everton. The poem was
reviewed in *Monthly Review* 69 (August 1783), 167, which commented that its
'intrinsic merit' was enough to 'entitle it to indulgence' without consideration
of the 'circumstances under which it was composed, but that it was somewhat
pointless by this stage to hope that America would stay within the empire.
The review in the *Critical Review* 56 (September 1783), 237, likewise stated 'its
own merit co-operates so strongly with our sympathy, that we can, without
any violation of justice, assign it a favourable character'.

Title] part of the language of contemporary political debate about America:
  compare the attack on the 'host of insulting, degenerate, and time-serving
  flatterers, parasites and court sycophants, who have already fatally
  dismembered this empire', *London Courant*, 9 January 1782, and similar
  phrasing in *Morning Herald*, 20 September 1782 and 7 August 1783.

sightless existence] Rushton's loss of sight on a slaving voyage terminated his naval career; see Introduction.

boisterous element] the sea; Rushton was apprenticed to a shipping firm at the age of eleven.

blunt the finer feelings] naval characters in fiction and drama often amounted to a stereotype of bluff heartiness.

enemy to rebellion] see 188, 214, 278; 'An Irregular Ode', 68, and 'To the People of England', 9.

1 Seven times] the seven years of the American War of Independence, which began in 1775.

2 vast profound] a serious echo of the parodic image of a mental 'vast profound' in Pope, *The Dunciad* (1729), I. 112; but the phrase is found without irony in senses similar to Rushton's in Pope's translation of Homer; see *The Iliad of Homer*, 6 vols (1715–20), VIII. 162; *The Odyssey of Homer*, 5 vols (1725–26), IV. 777 and VIII. 34.

3 govern slaves] i.e. Britain was trying to turn the Americans into 'slaves' by its refusal to acknowledge their rights and grievances.

5 freedom's boasted sons] the British, who regarded 'liberty' as their birthright; see commentary to 'An Irregular Ode'.

8 three millions] Some estimates put the 1790 population of America at 3,929,214; the first British census, in 1801, recorded a British population of 16,345,646.

14 parasites] hangers-on, flatterers.

17 dastard] cowardly.

18 rude gripe] rough grasp.

28 furry tenants] wild animals of the woods.

30 front] forehead.

36 vindicate ... man] an echo of Alexander Pope, *Essay on Man* (1733–4), I. 16, 'But vindicate the ways of God to Man'.

38 Burke, p. 341, comments on the oddity of setting Liberty on the coast of Africa, where as Rushton knew, slaves were picked up by the ships (including ships from Liverpool) for transport to the West Indies; but Rushton probably intends this as an aspirational possibility, not a direct description.

39 hardy Swiss] Oliver Goldsmith expatiates on the hardiness of the Swiss in *The Traveller, or a Prospect of Society* (1764) 165–74, and Isaac Hawkins Browne uses the phrase 'hardy Swiss' in 'An Epode' (*Poems Upon Various Subjects*, 1768), 11. Rushton politicises the point that self-sufficiency means self-government; before French armies conquered its territories in 1798, Switzerland was a loose confederation of locally-governed cantons, and had no monarch. For 'disdains controul' see also *Neglected Genius*, 42.

43–46] these lines reuse material from 'An Irregular Ode', 33–36.

47 parent] Britain, the 'parent' nation of America, as in 'An Irregular Ode', 61; a conventional aspect of political debate about the relationship.

51–58] Burke, p. 341, notes that this analogy is a redirection of the simpler Lion-Lamb opposition in 'Rebellion Tottering Stands', 16–19; the Lion (a symbol of England) now meets heroic resistance. it also marks a change from the image of 'To the People of England', 79–80.

52 meagre] thin, hungry

58 crimson torrents] of the lion's blood; the phrase has a certain epic resonance, eg. Richard Glover, *Leonidas* (1737), IX. 502–3: 'With swift effusion | Gush'd a crimson torrent'.

60 great parent] possibly a distant echo of the 'magna parens' of Virgil, *Georgics*, II. 173.

63 even this rabble] this same (so-called) rabble.

65 thus] by similar resistance.

68 bearded sires] venerable forefathers; compare 'To the People of England', 73.

71 own'd] acknowledged.

75 Lack-land] soubriquet of King John (1167–1216), who reigned 1199–1216 and was the king who sealed in 1215 Magna Carta, one of the statutory guarantees of English political 'liberties' in the background of Rushton's argument here and elsewhere.

76 Charles] Charles I, king of England 1625–1649, executed by parliamentary forces at the end of the English civil war, which was fought to determine the limits of regal authority and the origin of political sovereignty.

76 William] William III, who with his wife Mary became ruler of England in the revolution of 1688–89; significant here as the absolutist James II (Charles I's younger son) had been ousted by political opposition and the arrival of William and Mary was in essence a parliamentary invitation, signalling constitutional limitations on 'divine right' theories of kingship. Compare 'An Irregular Ode', 31.

86 Bourbon] France.

92 compunctive] 'producing or tending to compunction' (*OED*), a very rare word; here, perhaps 'remorsefully'.

93–98] peace negotiations between Britain and the colonies, and discussions about concessions in parliament, had continued alongside the war since its inception, including proposals by the William Pitt, Earl of Chatham (1708–1778) and Edmund Burke (1729–1797); but Rushton refers here to official treaty negotiations taking place under a new ministry in the Autumn of 1782, towards the agreement finally signed in September 1783. See 280 below.

106 king] George III, whose personal opposition to granting concessions to the colonists exacerbated matters.

117 sincere] here probably 'pure; unmingled' (SJ).

120 Belgia] see 'To the People of England', 7, and below, 168

124 faithless Gaul] see 'To the People of England', 3. France entered the
war in alliance with the colonists in July 1778, after supplying material
assistance to the colonists.

142 county ... martial band] volunteer corps, recruited county by county,
against the threat of invasion.

147 India] the East India trade (see 215) was another major area of
competition for European powers.

149 Iberia] Spain, which entered the war in June 1779.

167 golden spear] probably an allusion to the riches of Spanish colonies in
South America; compare 'To the People of England', 5.

168 low-thoughted Holland] the Netherlands, 'low countries', or at this date
the 'United Provinces'. Britain declared war on the Dutch at the end of
1780 because of their role in protecting the shipping routes of the 'Arm'd
Neutrality' (see 179).

170 craft] 'fraud; cunning; artifice' (SJ); personified at 330 below. yellow dirt]
gold, money; the phrase recurs in the *Expostulatory Letter to Washington*.

179 Arm'd Neutrality] an association of Baltic naval powers instituted in
1780 by Catherine the Great of Russia to protect merchant fleets of those
countries, who were mostly supplying Britain's enemies.

181 low'rs] i.e. lowers, glares.

191 Trade destroy'd] it was a persistent fear that Britain's trade dominance
could not survive the secession of the colonies.

197 torrid zone] the tropics; here, the West Indies.

199 Antilles] islands of the Caribbean, such as Cuba, Jamaica, and Haiti, all
colonised by European states.

200 mantling] spreading luxuriantly.

201 cultur'd] cultivated.

208 toiling Negroes] Rushton's first mention of the slaves labouring on the
West Indian sugar plantations; the *West-Indian Eclogues* would give a less
picturesque and georgic view, though the word 'toiling' is suggestive.

229–40] this kind of thing was also predicted of Liverpool if the slave trade
were abolished.

231 domes ... distress] houses set aside for the poor and infirm.

239 moles] harbour defences.

263–64] For Rushton's own heroism in saving a ship in similar circumstances
see Introduction.

275 hundred tongues] probably recalling Pope, *Essay on Criticism* (1711), 44;
but see note to 276.

276 adamantine lungs] an echo of Pope's translation of Homer, see *The Iliad
of Homer*, II. 580–81: 'To count them all, demands a thousand Tongues, |
A Throat of Brass, and Adamantine Lungs'.

280 Shelburne ... North] William Petty, Second Earl of Shelburne
(1737–1805), one of the chief negotiators of peace with the American
colonists during the latter half of 1782; Frederick North, second Earl

of Guildford (1732–1792), prime minister during much of the war with America, who had resigned office amid much vocal criticism in March 1782.

282 Discord] recalling Pope, *Windsor-Forest* (1713), 412; Pope's lines 411–20 are probably Rushton's source for this prophetic imagery of abstract essences.

291 Seamen!] Rushton was always loyal to the conventional image of the indomitable British tar, but by this point in the war the British navy had lost its Atlantic dominance, and the plans referred to in 324–25 were insufficient to restore it.

299–300] the images are of naval warfare.

313 finny brood] flying fish; an image recycled in *West-Indian Eclogues*, II. 94–100, with a distinct shift in emphasis towards sympathy for the fish rather than the predator.

324–25 Suffolk ... Lowther] see commentary for 'To the People of England', 53–54.

328 nerveless] without strength.

West-Indian Eclogues

Source: West-Indian Eclogues. (London: Printed for W. Lowndes, Fleet-Street, and J. Philips, George-Yard, Lombard-Street. MDCCLXXXVII). A variant issue of this quarto pamphlet has the names of the publishers reversed in the imprint, presumably to give each prominence for copies sold in their own shops, but the internal texts are identical. Both issues have a list of errata on the final page, mostly matters of punctuation, silently incorporated here. The poems were not reprinted in *1806* but the first three were restored in *1824*, pp. 141–59, with notes *a*, *b*, *i*, *l*, *m*, *o*, and *q*, in some instances reduced (pp. 161–64). The fourth was probably omitted because of its frenzied and bloodthirsty character, along with 89–92 of the first. A facsimile text of the poems and notes only was published in Richardson; the first and fourth eclogues, with the prefatory material and extracts from Rushton's notes, appeared in Burke, pp. 21–28. Williamson, pp. 365–82, presents large selections.

Variants:
I. 13 heavy] heaving *1824*
26 and gave the cheering breast.] to hush him into rest; *1824*
30 the] his *1824*
57 gashes] wounds all *1824*
59 each] our *1824*
66 passionate] frantic *1824*
68 causeless] wish'd for *1824*
71 at each dext'rous lash] as they stood around *1824*

72 gash] wound *1824*
89–92] omitted *1824*

II.8 unvaried] unwearied *1824*
15 wearied] weary *1824*
40 tyrants] tyrant *1824*
48 the pale butchers] thy oppressors *1824*
75 dwell] rove *1824*
84 fled from slavery] they from slavery fly *1824*
86 cover us] cover, nor *1824*
87 the] omitted *1824*
99 a] some *1824*

III. 27 Whose] The *1824*
53 are] have *1824*
53 I mark] I've mark'd *1824*
55 and] our *1824*
62 Whilst] While *1824*
109 the big tear] then the tears *1824*
118 hoary] helpless *1824*
122 whole] vast *1824*
128 with] for *1824*

Commentary: The date of the dedication is July 1787. The earliest advertisement appears to be that giving the poems as 'Just Published', printed for the author, and sold by Philips and Lowndes, *London Chronicle*, 20 December 1787, 'wherein are contained some picturesque scenes of the manners and treatment of the Negroes in the British Colonies; with Notes explanatory and historical'; this was already quoting a positive comment from the October issue of the *English Review*; it had been reviewed also in the *General Review* for September. Lowndes advertised it further at 2s sewed, as dialogues 'between the slaves in the Island of Jamaica, with notes explanatory and illustrative', in *The World*, 14 February 1788, and again with Hugh Mulligan's poems and Rushton's *Neglected Genius*, in *The Public Advertiser*, 17 March 1788 and other papers in March. Philips put the poems among a column of slave trade publications in *Woodfall's Register*, 3 April 1788.

The 'eclogue' form was defined for the eighteenth century by Pope's four neoclassical *Pastorals* of 1709; Rushton's four poems are of a similar order of magnitude to Pope's, and set like his at various times of day, with variations on dialogue, soliloquy and natural description. After Pope exotic variants were tried, including William Collins's *Persian Eclogues* (1742); Rushton knew at least one of Thomas Chatterton's 'African Eclogues', and his Liverpool associate Hugh Mulligan produced a set of eclogues from round the globe in his 1788 volume. Rushton was also parodying the colonial georgic of James Grainger's

The Sugar-Cane (1764), set on the slave plantations of Jamaica. The colony on Jamaica received a great deal of description and publicity during the eighteenth century. Rushton may have known the naturalist Sir Hans Sloane's huge *A Voyage to the Islands Madera, Barbados, Nieves, S. Cristophers and Jamaica* [etc], 2 vols (1707), the second volume of which is a *Natural History of Jamaica*, and the first of which (pp. xlvi–lvii) contains horrific descriptions of punishments on the plantations. Other accounts of the region included Charles Leslie, *A New and Exact Account of Jamaica* (1739); Patrick Browne, *The Civil and Natural History of Jamaica* (1756); Edward Long, *The History of Jamaica*, 3 vols (1774); and the anonymous *Jamaica. A Poem, in three Parts* (1777). Increasingly Jamaica became a focus for slavery debates; shortly after Rushton came Peter Marsden, *An Account of the Island of Jamaica* (1788); and William Beckford, *Remarks upon the Situation of Negroes in Jamaica* (1788), each of which addressed conditions on the plantations, though from a different perspective. The concept of the heroic noble slave was familiar in literature from Aphra Behn's *Oroonoko* (1688) onwards, but from the 1770s poetry in particular emerged as a platform for denouncing slavery; see Richardson, a collection of (mostly) anti-slavery poems. There was a particular glut of such texts from Liverpool, by then one of the leading slave ports in Britain, in 1787–1788, with poems by William Roscoe, James Currie, Hugh Mulligan, and Peter Newby joining work by Bristol poets such as Hannah More and Ann Yearsley. It is possible that the particular atrocity of 1783, known as the Zong incident, involving a Liverpool slaving ship owned by the firm to which Rushton had been apprenticed, awakened his memories of working on slave ships as a teenager. At any rate, the high tragic language of radical resistance to oppression now takes over as Rushton's main voice. Rushton's notes are included in full here, as they were very much part of the marketing of the book, and were commented on by reviewers; they also constitute a testimony to his sense of visual pleasure from his sighted time on board ships; and in several cases, particularly in the stories of animals, fish and birds, they offer sources for the tropes of victimisation and entrapment that populate his later songs and ballads.

The poems were widely reviewed. *The General Magazine and Impartial Review*, I (September 1787), 199–200 was overpowered by the disgraceful facts revealed in the poems, which it found 'worthy of commendation, both from the motive, and from the execution'. The *English Review*, 10 (October 1787), p. 315 was likewise full of sympathy for the characters, but also drew attention to the 'natural strain of poetry, beautifully enriched with local images and allusions ... highly descriptive of the characters and sentiments of the sable race of mankind. They discover such a degree of genius as we have never before seen employed on the subject of slavery'. *The Town and Country Magazine*, 19 (Supplement, 1787), p. 587, found them 'more commendable for their design than their execution: the diction is not sufficiently elevated; yet some passages are written with spirit and feeling, and in others the scenery is bold and appropriate'. *The Monthly Review*, 77 (October 1787), pp. 283–84, found the poems 'not unpleasing' technically, but felt the horrors described must have been exaggerated, and that some discipline was necessary on the plantations because of the rebelliousness of the slaves; the slave *trade*, however, it abhorred. The notes on natural history it approved. *The Critical Review*, 64 (December 1787), pp. 434–35, felt that the 'diction is in general not sufficiently elevated, yet some passages are written with spirit and feeling, and in others the scenery is bold and appropriated'. After quibbling about some of Rushton's verbal choices, it went on:

> We applaud the author for the humanity of his design: but there is some impropriety in making the Negroes, the interlocutors in these Eclogues, chiefly employ themselves in venting imprecations, and planning revenge, against their oppressors. It is doubtless extremely natural for them to do so: but as the principal design of this performance is to excite pity for the unhappy slaves, their various calamities, not their impatience, should have been chiefly dwelt upon.

In modern times, what might be called the poetry of abolition has been the subject of intense scrutiny which has generated a very large literature. General accounts of the subject include Brycchan Carey, *British Abolitionism and the Rhetoric of Sensibility: Writing, Sentiment, and Slavery, 1760–1807* (Basingstoke: Palgrave, 2005); Marcus Wood, *Blind Memory: Visual Representations of Slavery in England and America* (London: Routledge, 2000) and *Slavery, Empathy and Pornography* (Oxford: Oxford University Press, 2002) and Debbie Lee, *Slavery and the Romantic Imagination* (Philadelphia: University of Pennsylvania Press, 2002). For Rushton's particular context and his involvement in the circle of Liverpool abolitionists, see the Introduction. Grégory Pierrot links Rushton's slave heroes with his victimised British sailors in his 'Sable Warriors and Neglected Tars: Edward Rushton's Atlantic Politics', in *Race, Romanticism, and the Atlantic*, ed. Paul Youngquist (Farnham: Ashgate, 2013), pp. 125–44. For a full analysis of the poems in their literary and political context, and survey of the critical literature on them, see Dellarosa, chapter 5.

Advertisement: resided] quite how long Rushton could be said to have 'resided' in the West Indies is open to question; he would have put in to British colony ports in Jamaica on slaving voyages and no doubt spent time ashore.

The quoted lines are from John Sheffield, Duke of Buckinghamshire, 'On Mr. Pope and his Poems', among the commendatory poems at the front of *The Works of Mr. Alexander Pope* (1717).

Dedication:] Beilby Porteus (1731–1809), Bishop of Chester at this point (from 1776–1788) and latterly Bishop of London. He came from a family of Virginia planters, and was a member of the Society for the Conversion and Religious Instruction of the Negroes in the West Indies, supporting measures to improve conditions for slaves. Rushton later identifies the 'discourse' as the seventeenth sermon of his *Sermons on Several Subjects* (1783), separately printed as *Sermon Preached before the Incorporated Society for the Propagation of the Gospel in Foreign Parts* (1783).

First Eclogue

2 Rushton's note [a]] The reptiles of Jamaica are classified in Browne, *Civil and Natural History of Jamaica* (1756), pp. 460–64.

4 Rushton's note [b]] Rushton's phrasing is similar to the account given in Charles Leslie, *A New and Exact Account of Jamaica* (1739), Letter II, pp. 21–22.

6 it's] Rushton spells the possessive this way throughout the *Eclogues*, but rarely elsewhere in the poetry.

12 sable] black, with a particular sense of heraldic richness, as in Pope, *Windsor-Forest* (1713), 407–8, envisaging a post-slavery era in which: '… the freed *Indians* in their native groves | Reap their own fruits, and woo their sable loves'. The word was often used as a polite and (at least ostensibly) value-rich way of referring to dark skin.

17 stripes] weals raised by the whip.

19 JUMBA] perhaps an echo of a slaving port of that name on the coast of Kenya.

21 YARO] perhaps an allusion to a town in what is now Burkina Faso, West Africa

22 Rushton's note [c]] Rushton's account is similar to that given by James Ramsay, *Essay on the Treatment and Conversion of African Slaves in the British Sugar Colonies* (1784), pp. 88–90.

44 liberty] this contradiction, that proponents of liberty can enslave others, is the essential point made by Rushton's prose *Expostulatory Letter to George Washington*, a decade later.

45 wing'd houses] ships.

59 Rushton's note [e]] The word 'fetish' is not in SJ. 'Fetiche' practices are described in e.g. William Snelgrave, *Some New Account of Some Parts of Guinea and the Slave Trade* (1734), though not in exactly Rushton's terms.

74 Rushton's note [f]] Sloane appears to distinguish between Eben and Ebony trees in his account of Jamaican trees, *Voyage to the Islands* (1707), II. 31–32.

92 Rushton's note [g]] This punishment is mentioned among many others in Sir Hans Sloane, *Voyage to the Islands* (1707), I. lvii, and partially confirmed by Benjamin Rush, *An Address to the Inhabitants of the British Settlements in America* (1773), p. 23.

Second Eclogue

1–18] quoted as a sample of the poem's natural history description in *Critical Review*, 64 (December 1787), p. 434, as 'entitled to praise' for its natural history qualities, but with a quibble about whether reefs are the same thing as rocky shores, 5, and whether 'reef' is merely a nautical word, inadmissible in poetry. It is not in fact in SJ, and is not common in poetry of the eighteenth century.

4 pale disease] perhaps the notorious yellow fever, spread by mosquitos, which killed many European settlers and travellers to the region; Rushton's 'Epitaph on John Taylor', who died of yellow fever, appeared in the *1824* collection. But 'pale disease' is also a very common phrase in eighteenth-century poetry; compare e.g. William Shenstone, 'An Irregular Ode, after Sickness. 1749', 105 (*Works*, 1773, I. 238).

7 spiry canes] echoing James Grainger, *The Sugar-Cane* (1764) I. 22: 'Where first the Muse beheld the spiry Cane'. 'Spiry' means pointed or tapering.

12 unnumber'd] countless.

13 Rushton's note ʰ] the Jamaican fire-fly is extensively described by Sloane in his 'Natural History of Jamaica', *A Voyage to the Islands* (1707), II. 206–7, and by Browne, *Civil and Natural History of Jamaica* (1756), pp. 431–32.

15 wearied ... return] recalling both Rushton's georgic image of the 'toiling negroes', *Dismember'd Empire*, 207–8, and 'The ploughman homeward plods his weary way', Gray, *Elegy Written in a Country Churchyard* (1751), 3.

25 Rushton's note ⁱ] Rushton refers to James Ramsay (1733–1789), an abolitionist clergyman who had served as a surgeon on slave ships and who wrote several tracts on the treatment of slaves in the 1780s, principally *An Essay on the Treatment and Conversion of African Slaves in the British Sugar Colonies* (1784). This particular story has not been located, but an instance from Tobago in 1774 is described in Thomas Clarkson, *The Substance of the Evidence...(etc.)*, (1789), p. 91, and Rushton might be recalling George Gregory, *Essays Historical and Moral* (1785), p. 310. Further contemporary allusions are in Rush, *An Address to the Inhabitants*, p. 24, and Bryan Edwards, A *Speech delivered at a Free Conference between the Honorable the Council and Assembly of Jamaica* (1789), pp. 68–69.

32 Plantains] type of banana.

54] perhaps recalling the noble suicide at the end of Thomas Gray, 'The Bard' (from *Odes by Mr Gray*, 1757).

63 life supply] compare Pope, *Essay on Man* (1733–1734), I. 3: '...life can little more supply'.

67 wain] wagon, ox-cart.

76 boiling] frothing, bubbling.

77 tyrants of the deep] dolphins and other predators. Compare Rushton's reference to this kind of natural hunting in *Dismember'd Empire*, 313, where Rushton's sympathy appeared to be with the predator.

82 Rushton's note ᵏ] Edward D'Oyley or Doyley (1617–1675) was sent to Jamaica by Cromwell to secure the island against the Spanish, and governed until 1662; Edward Trelawney (1699–1754) was governor of Jamaica 1738–1752. The agreement to which Rushton refers was made

in 1739; the mountain-dwelling escaped slaves are normally known as Maroons. Edward Long, *History of Jamaica* (1774), I. 272–83 gives some detail of D'Oyley's campaigns, as also an account of Trelawny in II. 303, 344, and a description of 'Marons', Chapter XIII section 4. Charles Leslie, *A New and Exact Account of Jamaica* (1739), 77–81, gives an account of D'Oyley which is more directly consonant with Rushton's.

89 Rushton's note ¹] A similar account, less sympathetic to the runaways, is given by Sloane, *Voyage to the Islands*, II. 298, under the heading 'The Great Black-Bird'.

94 Rushton's note ᵐ] Rushton's reference is to 'A Description of the Exocœtus Volitans, or Flying Fish', by Thomas Gordon, a paper read 4 June 1778 at the Royal Society, published in *Philosophical Transactions*, 68 (1778), pp. 791–800. 'Exocœtus volitans' is the modern scientific name for the flying fish; 'hirundo' is normally a swallow, and 'mugil alatus' a type of mullet. Sloane reports watching dolphins take flying fish, *Voyage to the Islands*, II. 343; see also Leslie, *New and Exact Account of Jamaica*, pp. 3–4, and John Atkins, *A Voyage to Guinea* (1735), pp. 33, 144. Leslie (p. 4) takes the Bonetta to be a species of Cod; Richard Brookes, *The Art of Angling* (1743), p. 165, identifies the 'Bonetto' with the Scad, or Traclurus; 'tunny' is tuna. Rushton recalls the image in 'Woman', 9.

Third Eclogue

1–30] this passage was reproduced as a 'specimen' in *Monthly Review*, 77 (October 1787), 284.

11 feather'd race] birds; a common poetic periphrasis.

13 Rushton's note ⁿ] humming-birds are described by Sloane, *Voyage to the Islands*, II. 336–39, under the species name Guainumbi, which in modern ornithology refers to a different type of bird. Browne, *Civil and Natural History of Jamaica*, pp. 475–76, describes several humming-bird species under other names. 'Trochilus' is the modern name for Jamaica's own distinctive genus of 'streamertail' hummingbirds.

16 useful Vultures] useful because they clear up carrion.

17 Pelican] normally a symbol of self-sacrifice, thanks to a long-standing myth that it fed its young with its own blood; here, and more accurately, a predator.

27 Rushton's note °] confirmed by Peter Marsden, *An Account of the Island of Jamaica* (1788), p. 22, and Peter Newby, *The Wrongs of Almoona* (1788), p. 17.

29 Tam'rind] the tamarind, a tropical tree originating in Africa but deliberately planted in the colonies.

31 QUAMINA] According to the *Sketch*, p. 474, and Shepherd, *Life*, pp. xii–xiii, Quamina was the name of an African whom Rushton taught to read and who sacrificed his own life for Rushton by giving him the cask he was using as a buoyancy aid when their boat capsized. By historical irony,

Quamina is also the name of a slave who led an unsuccessful uprising in Demerara in 1823, though he would only have been 11 at the time of Rushton's poem. Ramsay, *Essay*, (1784) p. 159, cites it as the kind of African name that slave owners would displace by a 'Christian' name.

38 yam] plant which forms edible tubers.

72 'Angola', like 'Congo', was a region of West Africa already well known to Europeans.

118 hoary] white-headed.

127 Rushton's note q] the seventeenth sermon of Beilby Porteus was collected in his *Sermons on Several Subjects* (1783), pp. 381–410.

Fourth Eclogue

5 light'ning] evidently a dramatic backdrop for Loango's passionate outburst, but Rushton's son recalled his father's vivid descriptions of tropical lightning in a letter of 1837: *Letters of a Templar*, p. 236.

10 Loango] In Rushton's day Loango was a tribal state in Africa, now part of the Republic of Congo, and was often mentioned in reporting of debates on the slave trade.

18 Rushton's note ˢ] The source for this story appears to be Charles Leslie, *A New History of Jamaica* (1740), pp. 71–73. This story is told slightly differently, but with similar sympathetic intensity, in the anonymous poem *The Wrongs of Almoona*, published at Liverpool in 1788; it is now ascribed to Peter Newby (1745–1827). Rushton's own *Briton, and Negro Slave*, in the 1806 volume, pursues the theme.

42 Rushton's note ᵗ] Rushton's derivation and description are close to the account in Leslie, *New History of Jamaica*, pp. 40–41. The etymology and history of the word are discussed in Peter Hulme, *Colonial Encounters: Europe and the Native Carribean, 1492–1797* (London: Routledge, 1986), pp. 95–101.

53 Centipedes] the poisonous giant centipede, *scolopendra gigantea*, is found in Jamaica; Peter Marsden, *An Account of the Island of Jamaica* (1788), p. 54, describes them.

64 Rushton's note ᵘ] The reference is to 'Singular Observations upon the Manchenille Apple', by John Andrew Peysonnel, read 16 November 1758; *Philosophical Transactions*, 50 (1757–8), 772–73. The modern botanical name is *Hippomane mancinella*. Its extremely poisonous qualities are described by John Luffman in *A Brief Account of the Island of Antigua* (1789), p. 71.

100 Rushton's note ˣ] Porteus, *Sermons on Several Subjects*, p. 387; Ramsay, *Essay on the Treatment and Conversion of African Slaves*, pp. 250–53. For Rushton's own 'deliverance' see commentary to III. 31 above.

109–10] Burke sees the wording here as an explicit allusion to James Grainger, *Sugar Cane* (1764), IV. 86, a warning about the tendency of the slaves to murder their owners 'fir'd with vengeance, at the midnight hour'.

The Neglected Tars of Britain

Source: London Chronicle, 9 October 1787, without ascription, giving the tune as 'The Vicar of Bray'. Reprinted with minor variants in *The County Magazine for 1786 and 1787* (Salisbury, 1788), p. 351; *The Songster's Companion* (Coventry, c. 1788), pp. 77–79; several editions of *The Musical Miscellany: or, Songster's Companion* (London and North Shields, 1789), pp. 92–94; *A Collection of the Most Favourite New Songs* (Bath, c. 1790), pp. 97–99; *The Evergreen* (Preston, 1790), pp. 86–88. By 1789 it has generally become 'The Neglected Tar'. *The New Liverpool Songster* (Liverpool, 1789), pp. 93–95, has the following note: *The following is the song sung with so much effect by Mr.* Dignum, *at the* Anacreontic Society. *It is the production of a Nautical Gentleman of this Town'.* It was perhaps collected from a newspaper; or supplied to the Liverpool publisher (T. Schofield) directly, hence the veiled ascription. (The 'Anacreontic Society' was a club for music, drinking, and singing, based in London from the mid-1780s, and several contemporary songbooks include songs from that source. 'Dignum' was Charles Dignum (c. 1765–1827), a London singer and actor, often cited in songbooks.) The song was reprinted as the first item in *The Liverpool Songster* (Liverpool: H. Hodgson, c. 1792), 'The Words by Mr. E. Rushton', pp. 1–3. A score of the song, printed as *The Neglected Tar: A Celebrated Song, adapted and sung by Mr. Dignum at the Anacreontic Society, and at the Theatre Royal Liverpool; the Words by a Gentleman of that Town*, was printed for S. A. & P. Thompson, London, about 1790; the order of printing, in relation to the dated Liverpool versions, is not clear. The song continued to feature anonymously: *The Edinburgh Musical Miscellany* (1792), pp. 257–60, presents the tune as then sung; the song is further found in *The Edinburgh Syren, or Musical Bouquet* (1792), pp. 42–45; *The Jovial Songster*, new edition (Gainsborough, 1792), pp. 17–19, as 'Song. Neglected Seaman'; *The Songster's Miscellany, or, Vocal Companion* (Kidderminster, 1792), pp. 33–35; *The Syren, or Musical Bouquet* (Edinburgh, c. 1795), pp. 38–41; *The Musical Banquet of Choice Songs* (Glasgow, 1798), pp. 41–44 (second edition, c. 1800, pp. 53–56); *The Offspring of Wit and Harmony* (Dublin, 1800), pp. 144–45; *The Jovial Sailor's Chearful Companion* (1800), pp. 5–6, and in *Pocock's Everlasting Songster* (Gravesend, 1800), pp. 87–88. Several slip song and chapbook versions of the title exist, usually without ascription: *The Neglected Tar; or, The British Seaman* (ESTC: T224857); another version, with three other ballads ('Kate and Teddy; The Maltman; Jenny Nettles'), printed at Stirling (ESTC: T222415); *The Greenwich Pensioner's Garland* (ESTC: T35877); at least four versions of *A Garland of New Songs* including two printed at Newcastle (ESTC: N30502, N30533, N30510, T40493). Another song, *The Loyalist* (ESTC: T38759), gives 'The Neglected Tar' as itself a tune title. None of these can be firmly dated. The version in *The Time-Piece*, 23 August 1797, is given as Rushton's and also follows the early text. The poem 'Neglected Tar' in *The Morning Herald*, 17

September 1807, is a heavily Americanised take on the theme. An answering song, 'The Neglected Soldier', appears with a different tune in the *Edinburgh Musical Miscellany*, vol. 2 (1793), p. 51, and a parody, *The Neglected Fair*, in *The Hampshire Syren* (Southampton, 1794), p. 113.

Rushton and M'Creery noted the presence of single-sheet printings by including a picture of one in the engraving at the head of *Will Clewline* (1801). Rushton's poem appeared with substantial alterations in *1806*, pp. 23–27, and *1824*, pp. 126–29. Prompted by *1806*, James Plumptre reprinted it in his *Collection of Songs, Moral, Sentimental, Instructive, and Amusing* (1806), pp. 242–45. Leigh Hunt printed the whole song in his extended article on 'Distressed Seamen', *The Examiner*, 11, 18 and 25 January 1818. The chorus (later version) was subsequently printed in an advertisement for Egerton Smith's *Desultory Suggestions for Preservation from Shipwreck* (1825); see *The Liverpool Mercury*, 20 May 1825 and *The Kaleidoscope*, 21 June 1825; and also in an advertisement for *Hints on the Impressment of Seamen*, *Morning Chronicle*, 19 March 1827. *The Cornwall Royal Gazette*, 31 March 1848, printed the poem (early version) 'for the consideration of those who would now destroy the navigation Laws'. Part of the chorus was quoted in reports on the Belfast Sailors Home, *Belfast News-Letter*, 10 February 1854 (and again, 6 December 1856). The *Hampshire Advertiser and Salisbury Guardian*, 6 October 1855, in a report on naval matters, recalls that after the peace of 1815 the streets of Britain were filled with disabled mariners singing the chorus of the song (early version). It was reproduced under an elaborate engraving of a disabled Trafalgar veteran in *The Book of British Song Illustrated by Several Distinguished Artists* (otherwise known as *How's Illustrated Book of British Song*), volume II (c. 1846). This was a high-quality volume, issued in sixpenny numbers, with the 'Vicar of Bray' tune 'rendered more flowing and graceful' by being arranged in triple time. The song was included in *Sea Songs and Ballads. By Dibdin and Others* (1863), pp. 258–60, and in Harland and Wilkinson (1875), pp. 523–35. The *Ipswich Journal*, 9 Feb 1884, has a report of 'Missions to Seamen' in which the chorus is once again quoted, though ascribed to Dibdin.

Variants:

In *1806* and *1824* the order of the third and fourth stanzas is reversed and the chorus is placed at the end.

1–7] *1806*, *1824* read:
> To ocean's sons I lift the strain,
>   A race renown'd in story;
> A race whose wrongs are Britain's stain,
>   Whose deeds are Britain's glory.
> By them when courts have banished peace,
>   Your sea-girt land's protected,
> But when war's horrid thunderings cease,

11] *1806, 1824* substitute:
    And if pure justice urge the war,
17 white-topp'd] foam-capt *1806, 1824*
19–20] *1806, 1824* substitute:
    The seaman feels, yet nobly braves,
      The storm's terrific howling.
21 When] Now *1806, 1824*
22] Behold him at his station, *1806, 1824*
24] And moves all animation. *1806, 1824*
25–28] *1806, 1824* substitute:
    The battle roars, the ship's a wreck,
      He smiles amid the danger,
    And tho' his messmates strew the deck,
      To fear his soul's a stranger.
33 Britain's] that loved *1806, 1824*
34 plenty still is] joys are ever *1806, 1824*
35 They call the watch] The watch is call'd *1806, 1824*
46 then] thus *1806, 1824*
49–51] *1806, 1824* substitute:
    He asks a birth with downcast eye,
      His prayers are disregarded,
    Refus'd—ah hear the veteran sigh,
53] *1806, 1824* substitute:
    Much to these fearless souls you owe,
54] In peace would you neglect them? *1824*
55 Britain's sons] patriot souls *1806, 1824*
56 Protect them and] Admire, protect, *1806*; Admire, preserve, protect *1824*
57–60] *1806, 1824* substitute:
    And oh! reflect, if war again
      Should menace your undoing,
    Reflect, who then would sweep the main,
      And shield your realm from ruin.

Commentary: Britain was at war for perhaps the majority of the eighteenth century and would continue to rely heavily on its naval resources through the Napoleonic wars; Rushton was hardly alone in drawing attention to the plight of wounded servicemen. The poem is an early instance of Rushton's heartily patriotic sense of British naval hardiness, expressed in populist lyric, ready for singing in pubs, music halls, and on ships, garnering for itself a rich and varied textual life quite beyond his control, and certainly in contexts unsuited to his political point. *The Critical Review*, writing on the 1806 volume (April 1806, p. 439), declared that Rushton 'has the praise of having written the popular and pathetic ballad of the 'Neglected Tar'. Bannister, in *Worthies of the Working Classes*, (1854) p. 9, says that it was recalled affectionately by Liverpudlians in the 1804s when the Sailors' Home was founded. In reprinting it, *How's Illustrated Book of British Song* (c. 1850) declared 'our readers will agree with us in thinking [the song] is one of the finest sea-songs in our language, containing sentiments which ought ever to be cherished by the people of England'.

8 bulwarks] defences.
21 sulphurous] because gunpowder has sulphur in it; but there is perhaps also a suggestion of the fires of hell.
31 supine] hanging down, lifelessly.
39 hoary] white.
41–42 these lines, with the phrase 'pure justice' from the variant in line 11, were singled out in the *Monthly Review* account of the 1806 volume (May 1806), as instances of 'a few of those more prominent defects which attracted our attention'.
49 *var.* birth] – i.e. berth, shelter or employment.

Neglected Genius

Source: *Neglected Genius: Or, Tributary Stanzas to the Memory of the Unfortunate Chatterton* (Printed for J. Philips, George Yard, London. 1787). Advertised with *West-Indian Eclogues* at 1s sewed, *Public Advertiser*, 17 March 1788; *Morning Herald*, 21 March; *The World*, 24 and 25 March 1788; advertised by Lowndes, *Whitehall Evening Post*, 12 July 1788, at 2s. The price was given as 1s 6d in the *General Magazine* review, below.

  1806 reprinted the poem in a shortened and rearranged form as *To the Memory of the Unfortunate Chatterton*, pp. 152–63, the final poem in the volume; similarly in *1824*, pp. 45–53.

Variants:
1806 and *1824* cut the prose Preface and the epigraph and retained only notes *a*, *h*, *k* and *l*, renumbered *a-d*. There were several cuts and rearrangements within the verses themselves, *1824* following the *1806* arrangement, as follows.

1–24] retained in *1806/1824*
25–36] positioned as the fourth stanza in *1806/1824*
37–72] omitted in *1806/1824*
73–84] positioned as the third stanza in *1806/1824*
85–132] omitted in *1806/1824*
133–240] retained in *1806/1824*

Introduction:
Testimony] emended from '*Tistimony*'.
7 touch] paint *1806, 1824*

8 make] bid *1806, 1824*

18 seeming] solemn *1806, 1824*

23 alas! did all thy Pow'rs] to thee did poesy *1806, 1824*

29 Gods!] heavens! *1806, 1824*

32 Uncolleg'd] Untutor'd *1806, 1824*

33–36] replaced in *1806, 1824* with:

> Should pour in these enlighten'd days,
> On Britain's ear, such matchless lays,
> Yet find on British ground neglect and woe,
> And envy's cankering sting, when in the grave below!

73–75] replaced in *1806, 1824* with:

> Ah penury! thou chilling sprite,
> Thou pale depresser of the mind,
> That with a cloud opaque as night,

77 little boots the Poet's] what avails the minstrel's *1806, 1824*

81–82] replaced in *1806, 1824*, with:

> When on thy sterile common thrown,
> The strongest powers must pine unknown;

136 'lures] lur'st *1806, 1824*

153–54] replaced in *1806, 1824* with:

> Wreaths of dark foxglove, hemlock green,
> And poppy round his brows were seen,

160 Shade] form *1806, 1824*

185–89] replaced in *1806, 1824* with

> Gaze on his corse, ye gloomy train,
> Whom fortune tries to bless—in vain.
> Gaze on his corse, ye foodless crowd,
> And you whom torturing pangs have bow'd;
> Gaze too ye ardent sons of song,

196 And] While *1806, 1824*

206] replaced in *1806, 1824* with

> Whilst thou wert listening to the shade,

210 dank] dark *1806, 1824*

222 has] hast *1806, 1824*.

223 clay cold] earthy *1806, 1824*

224] replaced in *1806, 1824* with

> Scarce known amidst th' unhonoured dead,

227 will] shall *1806, 1824*

228–29] *1806, 1824* insert the following new stanza between these lines:

> For thee, Compassion oft shall plead,
> Her tenderest plaints for thee shall flow,
> Her hand shall brush away each weed,
> Which envy o'er thy turf may throw;
> And kindly soft that hand shall bring,

> For thee each blighted flower of spring,
> The violet, scenting nature's breath,
> Then, from her storms receiving death,
> The lowly primrose born to blow,
> Then 'whelm'd beneath the drifted snow,
> And oft with these, and tufts of wither'd bloom,
> Compassion dewy-eyed, shall deck thy early tomb.

Commentary: Thomas Chatterton (1752–1770) was a young Bristol poet who came to London to seek a living as a writer for magazines and died after an overdose which was treated at the time as deliberate but is thought by some modern scholars to have been accidental; see *ODNB*. Chatterton had created a large body of pseudo-medieval poetry in the person of a monk, Thomas Rowley, and when this was published in 1777 it caused a frenzy of scholarly debate about its authenticity. By 1783 it was largely accepted that Chatterton had created the poems, at which point the myth of the youthful genius destroyed by the indifference of society began to emerge. Rushton's poem was a contribution to what was eventually a somewhat distended category of elegiac tributes to Chatterton, which also included an important poem by Samuel Taylor Coleridge (1772–1834), 'A Monody on the Death of Chatterton', of which some seven versions survive, and which in its various forms shows how strongly Coleridge was impressed with Rushton's poem; see Paul Magnuson, 'Coleridge's Discursive "Monody on the Death of Chatterton", *Romanticism on the Net*, 17 (February 2000). Nick Groom's edited collection, *Thomas Chatterton and Romantic Culture* (Basingstoke: Macmillan; New York: St Martin's Press, 1999), includes John Goodridge's catalogue of these creative responses (pp. 262–92): 'Rowley's Ghost: A Checklist of Creative Works Inspired by Thomas Chatterton's Life and Writings'. More recently Daniel Cook takes up Rushton's title in his study of the relevant reception history, *Thomas Chatterton and Neglected Genius, 1760–1830* (Basingstoke: Palgrave Macmillan, 2013). Rushton's poem was reviewed by the *Monthly Review*, 78 (May 1788), 440–41, which summarizes approvingly Rushton's enthusiastic praise of Chatterton's genius, but alludes drily to his accusations against those who deprecate Chatterton's moral character: 'Mr. Walpole is found among the delinquents'. It then refers readers seeking 'a specimen of our author's poetical talents' to their earlier review of *West-Indian Eclogues*. The *General Magazine and Impartial Review* 2 (June 1788), 308–9, agrees that Chatterton should have been rewarded, and is more openly critical of Walpole's behaviour. It goes on: 'With respect to the composition before us, we have only to lament its brevity; and our poetical readers will be glad to learn, that these "Tributary Stanzas" are not unworthy of the subject they are intended to commemorate'. The *Critical Review* (April 1806, p. 439), writing on the *1806* collection, felt the revised poem was 'among the worst' in the volume.

Title] the complaint that talent is neglected by those who have power to
support it was common in eighteenth-century poetry, but Rushton is probably
remembering Alexander Pope, *Epistle to Dr Arbuthnot* (1735), 256–58:
> ... For they left me Gay;
> Left me to see neglected genius bloom,
> Neglected die, and tell it on his tomb:

Introduction] Most of the people mentioned here, together with quotations and
statements, are further identified in Rushton's notes at the end of the poem
and in editorial commentary. It will be convenient, however, to identify the
following here:

CROFT: Herbert Croft (1751–1816), afterwards fifth Baronet Croft, lawyer
and writer, whose *Love and Madness: A Story Too True* (1780) was one of
Rushton's main sources of information on Chatterton.

HAYLEY: William Hayley (1745–1820) depicted Chatterton's demise in *An
Essay on Epic Poetry in Five Epistles* (1782), pp. 81–82, Epistle VI, 207–48,
and 333–42.

KNOX: Vicesimus Knox (1752–1821), author of an expanding series of *Essays
Moral and Literary*, including one (no. 144) on the Rowley poems, from
which Rushton quotes at the end of his Introduction: ninth edition, 3 vols
(1787), III. 205–11.

TYRWHITT: Thomas Tyrwhitt (1730–1786), editor of *Poems, Supposed
to have been Written at Bristol, by Thomas Rowley, and Others, in the
Fifteenth Century* (1777), the first scholarly publication of the disputed
texts; Tyrwhitt subsequently published evidence that the poems were by
Chatterton.

LAMBERT: John Lambert (dates unknown), the Bristol attorney to whom
Chatterton was articled; the details here are from Croft, *Love and
Madness*, (1780) p. 146.

Epigraph] from *The Odyssey of Homer*, XXII. 450, in the translation published
(1725–1726) as the work of Alexander Pope; this book of the translation was
actually drafted by Elijah Fenton.

2 satst brooding] an echo of Milton, *Paradise Lost* (1667/1674), I. 20–22,
where the Holy Spirit 'sat'st brooding on the vast abyss' as part of the
original creation.

9 HOMER's glowing Strain] Chatterton did not write any Homeric epics, but
as Burke suggests, Rushton is probably alluding to Homer's status as the
fount of Western poetry; the essay on Homer with which Pope prefaced
his translation of the *Iliad* in 1715 laid down a fundamental appreciation
of Homer's poetic fire, sublimity, and genius.

11–12] recalling Milton, *Paradise Lost*, I. 13–16, where Milton speaks of his
> ... adventurous song

That with no middle flight intends to soar
... while it pursues
Things unattempted yet in prose or rhyme.

13 Church Yards] aligning Chatterton's romantic medievalism with the churchyard Gothic of poets such as Thomas Parnell (1679–1718), Robert Blair (1699–1746), and Thomas Gray (1716–1771).

16 Fairies] while officially scorned by rationalist eighteenth-century writers, there was a certain admiration for what Addison describes, following Dryden, as 'the fairy way of writing' in *Spectator* no. 419 (1 July 1712), and the latter half of the eighteenth century certainly saw a growth in interest in folk tales of the supernatural.

18 seeming] possibly because the 'Lyre' only 'seemed' to be 'Gothic' (medieval); the later change to 'solemn' simplifies the sense, however.

19 Rushton's note a] Rushton's source for this story was Croft, *Love and Madness* (1780), p. 146. For Chatterton's mother and sister, see *ODNB*.

21–22 HASTINGS ... BIRTHA ... BALDWIN] Chatterton wrote two parts of a poem called 'Battle of Hastings'; Birtha was the heroine of his tragedy 'Ælla'; his narrative poem *The Execution of Sir Charles Bawdin* (1772) appeared in Tyrwhitt's 1777 edition as 'The Bristowe Tragedie'.

23–24] reviewing the *1806* text, the *Monthly Review* 50 (May 1806), p. 96, disapproved of the rhyming of 'produce' with 'abuse' and the ambient phrasing.

32 uncolleg'd] not educated at university; apparently a word of Rushton's own invention.

34 Bard ... men of rhimes] recalling Pope's ironic description of the hack poet as 'the man of rhyme', *Epistle to Dr Arbuthnot*, 13, and aligning Chatterton with the true poet or 'Bard', in the propehtic and proto-romantic spirit of Thomas Gray's poem, *The Bard* (1757).

39 learned skill] referring to scholars such as Thomas Tyrwhitt, Thomas Warton, and Edmond Malone, Jeremiah Milles and Jacob Bryant, who took part in the so-called 'Rowley controversy' concerning the authenticity of the poems in the period 1777–1783 and regarded here as merely pedantic and unpoetic (see 44, 112, 226).

42 disdains controul] aligning Chatterton's genius with all opposition to powerful oppression; cf *The Dismember'd Empire*, 39.

48 ENGLAND's shame and boast] compare Pope, *An Essay on Criticism* (1711), 696, on Erasmus: 'The glory of the Priesthood, and the shame!'.

49–84] these lines were cut in *1806*, presumably because Rushton had by then accepted that Walpole was less to blame than he originally thought.

53 WALPOLE] Horace Walpole (1717–1797), son of Britain's first prime minister Sir Robert Walpole, writer, architect of the gothic revival house Strawberry Hill, and a leading antiquarian, to whom Chatterton sent some material in March 1769. After initial enthusiasm the spurious nature of the documents was pointed out to him and he wrote to Chatterton

advising him to stick to his profession as a legal clerk. Controversy
about Walpole's role erupted after Chatterton's death when the preface
to *Miscellanies in Prose and Verse; by Thomas Chatterton* (1778), xviii–xix,
pointedly referred to this supposed neglect, though without naming him.
Walpole responded in *A Letter to the Editor of the Miscellanies of Thomas
Chatterton* (1779), and modern scholarship has tended to view Walpole's
communications to Chatterton as mildly patronising rather than culpable.
Lines 53–72 were quoted in the review of the poem in the *General
Magazine*.

56 Rushton's note *b*] Walpole's innovative 'gothic' novel, *The Castle of
Otranto*, appeared late in 1764 in the guise of a translation from a late
medieval source; Walpole's authorship was indeed revealed in a second
edition, 1765. Rushton's point had already been made in Croft's *Love and
Madness* (1780), p. 136. Chatterton himself is supposed to have demanded
'Who wrote Otranto?' in some lines, 'Walpole! I thought not I should
ever see', but the authenticity of this poem is itself uncertain. Chatterton's
prose story 'Memoirs of a Sad Dog' satirises 'Baron Otranto'.

60 all Forgeries are ally'd] referring to the section of Walpole's *Letter to the
Editor* (1779), p. 24 which declares 'all of the house of forgery are relations'
and suggesting that Chatterton might have graduated from innocent
literary forgeries to criminal ones, as quoted in Rushton's Introduction.

61 antique Cloak] the pseudo-medieval diction and phrasing that Chatterton
had constructed.

70 Bays] the laurel wreath of classical literary achievement.

71 Rushton's note *c*] Walpole repeats Chatterton's accusation and uses the
italicised phrase during his account of the affair in *A Letter to the Editor*,
p. 37.

73 Penury] this image of poetry struggling with economic dependence and
failure probably owes something to Samuel Johnson, *London: a Poem,
in Imitation of the third Satire of Juvenal* (1738), 177: 'Slow rises Worth, by
Poverty deprest', and his well-known views on the uselessness of patrons.

83–84] Compare Pope's *Essay on Criticism* (1711), 420–25:

> What woeful stuff this madrigal would be,
> In some starv'd hackney sonneteer, or me?
> But let a Lord once own the happy lines,
> How the wit brightens! how the style refines!
> Before his sacred name flies ev'ry fault,
> And each exalted stanza teems with thought!

85 BRISTOL patrons] in particular George Catcott and William Barrett, local
antiquaries to whom Chatterton originally brought his productions.

88 Rushton's note *d*] Thomas Warton (1728–1790), *History of English Poetry*,
3 vols (1771–1781), gives a brief outline of Chatterton's catastrophic
career at II. 141–42, and then discusses the poems themselves. He calls
Chatterton a 'prodigy of genius' at p. 157. In the 'Emendations and

Additions' to the volume (unpaginated; keyed to p. 164) Warton expanded on Chatterton's supposedly lamentable moral character, including the charge of being 'unprincipled', which he repeated in *An Enquiry into the Authenticity of the Poems attributed to Thomas Rowley* (1782), p. 86. Much of the material presented in the *Miscellanies* was from the non-Rowleian side of Chatterton's output, which contained youthful and worldly satire of a kind that gave some handle to adverse moral judgments.

100 Rushton's note *e*] Jeremiah Milles (1714–1784), Dean of Exeter and president of the Society of Antiquaries, produced in 1782 an edition of *Poems, Supposed to have been Written at Bristol, in the Fifteenth Century, by Thomas Rowley, by Thomas Rowley, Priest &c.*, in which he argued for the real existence of Thomas Rowley and against the authorship of Chatterton, partly on linguistic grounds (the 'Diction obsolete' of 101) and partly on the grounds that Chatterton's moral character was too poor to have produced poetry of such beauty and imagination. Rushton's quotation is from p. 364 of Milles's edition.

105 sacerdotal] priestly.

108 Dulness] low-grade literary culture, most memorably explored in Pope's *The Dunciad* (1728/1729 and 1743).

110] Chatterton was born in 1752.

111 Charity] Chatterton was a pupil at Colston's School, the 'Bluecoat' or Charity school in Bristol.

117 Rushton's note *f*] actually line 583, p. 267 of the second edition of Tyrwhitt's 1777 text.

120] i.e., once the quality of the poems was acknowledged, Chatterton would have acknowledged his authorship.

129 Sexton] Chatterton's father, also Thomas Chatterton (1713–1752), was actually a writing master at St Mary Redcliffe Pile Street School, Bristol, though he was interested in the tradition that members of the Chatterton family had held the post of sexton at the church.

130 Rushton's note *g*] The letter from which Rushton quotes appears in Croft, *Love and Madness* (1780), p. 174.

134 Ignis Fatuus] will of the wisp, a type of low flame seen over marshes and bogs and perhaps caused by emissions of methane. Compare Rochester, *Satyr [Against Reason and Mankind]* (1680), 12: 'Reason, an *Ignis fatuus*, in the *Mind*'.

135 Syren] siren, in classical mythology a sea nymph who lured sailors to destruction by singing; thus, a delusive, seducing figure.

144 pois'nous Phial] it was widely assumed by Chatterton's contemporaries that he had committed suicide, using arsenic; some modern scholars surmise that his overdose was accidental or unintentional; see *ODNB*.

147 Rushton's note *h*] This story was told in Croft, *Love and Madness*, (1780) pp. 194–95.

152 fell SUICIDE] Depictions of Chatterton's deathbed include a picture by

John Flaxman, 'Chatterton receiving a bowl of poison from Despair', dated c. 1775–1780, which bears a certain resemblance to Rushton's scene; see Goodridge, 'Rowley's Ghost'.

156 front] forehead.

159 wily Tongue] this passage resembles the seduction of Eve by the serpent/ Satan in Milton, *Paradise Lost*, IX. 494–678.

162 Orb] the planet Earth.

168 Phoebus] Apollo, god of the sun (hence perhaps 'glowing') and of poetry, amongst other things.

180 tore ... Lay] according to early reports, the floor of the room where Chatterton died was littered with torn manuscripts; see e.g. Croft, *Love and Madness* (1780), pp. 197–98.

190 Rushton's note *i*] Rushton quotes from Croft, *Love and Madness* (1780), p. 196.

203 wond'rous Boy] a pre-echo of Wordsworth's 'marvellous Boy' description of Chatterton, 'Resolution and Independence', 43, one of many 'Romantic' appreciations of Chatterton's promising youthfulness.

207 Rushton's note *k*] Thomas Fry (1718–1772), president of St John's from 1757 until his death; Fry was himself from Bristol, and had a major hand in extracting materials from Chatterton's Bristol patrons.

209 parish shell] the cheap shroud of a pauper burial, rather than a wooden coffin.

218 Rushton's note *l*] See 'An Excelente Balade of Charitie', l.24 (Tyrwhitt's 1777 edition, p. 205). 'Glebe' is normally land tied to a church benefice. Chatterton was buried in an unmarked grave, as Rushton indicates; the site was subsequently cleared for development, and all the burials removed.

221 RADCLIFF] the area around St Mary Redcliffe, south of the centre of Bristol, where Chatterton was born and grew up, and about which he wrote in various pieces.

226 knaw'd] i.e. gnawed, the reading of *1806* (though *1824* has the 'k' spelling).

229] Chatterton now becomes the ghost of the landscape previously haunted by his inspirations, in the second stanza of the poem.

233 SAVAGE] Richard Savage (c. 1698–1743), supposedly the illegitimate offspring of Earl Rivers and the Countess of Macclesfield, poet and friend of Alexander Pope and Samuel Johnson. Always impecunious and quarrelsome, he died in a Bristol debtor's prison.

235 OTWAY] Thomas Otway (1652–1685), poet and dramatist, who died in poverty in London. There was no special Bristol connection.

Poor Ben

Source: *The Liverpool and Lancashire Weekly Herald*, 27 March 1790, in the section 'PARNASSIAN BUDGET'. Reprinted with an additional stanza in *1806*, pp. 117–20, but not in *1824*. The original heading reads:

> To the *PRINTER OF THE WEEKLY HERALD.*
>
>   SIR,
>   THE the [*sic*] readiness with which you inserted my former little Piece,
>   has induced me to send you another. Z. Z.

Variants:
1806 supplies an additional stanza between the present lines 6 and 7, copied here in the revised format of the later version.

> The softest rosy tints that grace,
>   The dying dolphin's side, are weak,
> Compar'd with those I wont to trace,
>   On Mary's lip, on Mary's cheek;
> Her face and person were indeed most rare,
> But oh! she was as false as she was fair.

4 which] that *1806*
5 fairer wench] lovelier girl *1806*
13 blast] winds *1806*
20 British warriors oft hath] many a British tar has *1806*
21 But] And *1806*

Commentary: The identity of 'my former little Piece' is untraced, as this is the only issue of the newspaper, in which Rushton at one point held an editorial share, known to survive (Liverpool Record Office, 072 HER).

1 mess-mate] companion on board ship.
5 wench] a fairly 'low' term even in the 1790s, hence the *1806* variant.
20 sultry line] the equator.
25 Jamaica] British colonial territory, scene of the *West-Indian Eclogues*.
37 can] bottle, i.e. alcohol.
38 grog] a drink based on rum, supposedly named after the 'grogram' cloak worn by Admiral Vernon, who introduced the drink (as a diluted ration) in 1740.
39 yellow fever] the illness was borne by mosquitoes, not contaminated liquid (Rushton may be implying that the alcohol weakened Ben's resistance to infection).
41 Spring-Path] Rushton's note is confirmed by Thomas Clarkson, *The Substance of the Evidence of Sundry Persons on the Slave Trade* (1789),

p. 92, which describes Spring Path as 'the cemetery of the negroes'. In *The Interesting Narrative of the Life of Olaudah Equiano* (1789), II. 101, Equiano says that Spring Path was where African slaves were brought on Sundays to dance according to inherited tribal African practices. Equiano, a former slave himself, also discusses tribal funerals at this point.

43] compare *West-Indian Eclogues*, I. 2 and commentary, and II. 9.

45 tamarind] compare *West-Indian Eclogues*, III. 29 and commentary.

Additional stanza:
the surprising and beautiful coloration of a dying dolphin is described in William Falconer, *The Shipwreck* (1762), I. 247–77.

A SONG, Sung at the celebration of the anniversary of The French Revolution, at Liverpool, July 14, 1791.

Source: New-York Journal, 21 September 1791, in 'Poet's Corner', p. 4; according to p. 2 it was sung at one of at least two meetings in Liverpool held on 14 July 1791 to commemorate the revolution. It was probably reported in a Liverpool newspaper, not otherwise traced. The author's name was not given. Printed as having been sung (and printed) at Belfast celebrations, in *Walker's Hibernian Magazine* (July 1792), pp. 78–79. An altered version of the poem was reprinted in *Liberty Scraps* (1794), pp. 3–4, as 'Song In Commemoration of the French Revolution. 1791.', also anonymously (see Appendix I). The poem was not however included in *1806*. Its authorship was discussed in the *Belfast Monthly Magazine*, VIII.45 (April 1812), 249, and approvingly asserted to be Rushton's. Reprinted as Rushton's in *1824*, 102–4, under the *Liberty Scraps* title, and thence in Burke, pp. 36–37. The *Walker's Hibernian Magazine* text, *Liberty Scraps* text, and subsequent texts divide the poem into 8-line stanzas.

Variants:
4 that] *New-York Journal*; when *1824*
19 crouch'd] *Walker's Hibernian Magazine, Liberty Scraps, 1824*; *New-York Journal* reads 'couch'd'
31 craig] rock *Walker's Hibernian Magazine*
31 midst the] *New-York Journal, Walker's Hibernian Magazine, Liberty Scraps*; among *1824*
39 radiance] *Walker's Hibernian Magazine, Liberty Scraps, 1824*; *New-York Journal* reads 'radience'

Walker's Hibernian Magazine reverses the order of 9–16 and 17–24. *Liberty Scraps* and *1824* cut *New York Journal*'s lines 17–24, inserting between 8 and 9 the following stanza, which recycles material from the present 21–24:

Gainst a movement so vast, tho' the privileg'd train,

> With all their proud minions inveigh,
> Yet high-minded France eyes the crew with disdain,
>   And the rubbish of time sweeps away;
> And hark her strong voice bids the nations arise,
>   And enjoy what the Deity gave;
> To be free is a duty man owes the All-wise,
>   And he sins who is tamely a slave.

In *1824*, 'eyes the crew' becomes 'views the scene'.

Commentary: Many poets greeted the French revolution of 1789 with enthusiasm, at least initially; William Blake's prophetic poem *The French Revolution* was published in 1791, though Rushton would almost certainly not have known of it. There was, however, evidently considerable support for the revolution in many urban centres, some, like Liverpool, holding anniversary meetings to celebrate it. Lines 33–40 were quoted with high approval for Rushton's 'lofty independence', in the *Belfast Monthly Magazine*, XII.69 (April 1814), 341, as appropriate to the crisis of the fall of Napoleon.

1 vile shackles] perhaps recalling Smollett, 'Ode to Independence', 84, *Plays and Poems* (1777), p. 264: 'And forge vile shackles for the free-born mind'.

3 sway] power.

5 assemble] the Riot Act of 1714 had stipulated forceful measures against any groups of more than twelve people 'unlawfully, riotously, and tumultuously assembled', and these and other provisions, known as 'gagging acts', were used by authorities to subdue popular protest in the revolutionary era; Rushton's use of the word 'assemble' is pointed.

11 lordling] 'a diminutive lord' (SJ): Rushton's contemptuous term for an aristocrat.

13 learning's bright rays] the Enlightenment, sometimes credited with fomenting rational protest against the ancien regime throughout Europe.

14 Columbia] poetical name for the Americas, after the European discoverer Christopher Columbus; the 'strong tempest' is the war of Independence, 1775–1783, discussed in very different terms in Rushton's earliest poems.

25–32] Liberty's residence in post-revolutionary France contrasts with her arrival in England, in the earlier 'Irregular Ode'.

29 man's rights] Thomas Paine's cornerstone radical tract *Rights of Man* appeared in 1791, but the phrase was already familiar from debate about American independence.

31 crag] France is now the rock that Britain once was: compare *Dismember'd Empire*, 133, 269.

33 electrical force] lightning.

36 Iberian] Spanish.

38–40] the 'hurl'd/world' rhyme is perhaps recalled from Alexander Pope, *An Essay on Man* (1734–1735), I. 85–86.

The Fire of Liberty

Source: Manchester Herald, 28 July 1792, without ascription. Printed anonymously as the lead song in *A Choice Collection of Civic Songs* (1795). Reprinted in America in *The Time-Piece*, 27 December 1797. as 'By E. Rushton'. Not in *1806*, but subsequently much remodelled as 'The Fire of English Liberty', in *1824* (below, pp. 166–67), so the ascription is secure. Reprinted from *Manchester Herald* in Michael Scrivener (ed.), *Poetry and Reform: Periodical Verse from the English Democratic Press 1792–1824* (Detroit: Wayne State University Press, 1992), pp. 52–53, without awareness of authorship.

Variants:
7 moulder'd] smoulder'd *Time-Piece*, and in the remodelled 'Fire of English Liberty'.
8 Scarce] supplied from *Civic Songs*; *Manchester Herald* has 'Scare'.
19] comma supplied from *Civic Songs*.

Commentary: A version of the myth, powerful among radical libertarians, of Anglo-Saxon freedom curtailed by the 'Norman Yoke' imposed by a foreign elite, and an extended celebration of the 'Glorious Revolution' of 1688 which limited royal prerogative and gave some colour to the political theory that sovereignty derived from the people rather than from God. Rushton would have absorbed something of the anti-Norman tradition from Pope's *Windsor-Forest* (1713). William Roscoe had recited a 'Secular Song, on the Revolution of 1688', during anniversary celebrations; *Poetical Works of William Roscoe* (1853), pp. 73–74.

1 sea-encircled] in patriotic verse, the island status of Britain always signals its natural superiority.
2 Norman Conqu'ror] William of Normandy 1027–1087, who claimed the throne of Britain after the Battle of Hastings, 1066.
3] a curfew was imposed by the Normans, requiring the conquered English to put out fires after a bell was rung; this was taken as a repressive measure designed to prevent seditious meetings, in something of the manner of Pitt's government's attempts to suppress opposition in the 1790s.
8 John] King John (c. 1167?–1216), who signed, under pressure from his nobles, the Magna Carta at Runnymede (10–12); the document guaranteed certain civil, legal and political liberties and which therefore stood as the fundamental principle of representation for the people and limitation on the power of kings for radical thinkers.
16–17] Charles I (1600–1649), executed by the parliamentary forces at the conclusion of the English Civil War and thus a model for the downfall of absolutist monarchs.

19 William] William of Orange (1650–1702) who with his wife Mary
occupied the throne of England in 1689 following the 'Glorious
Revolution' of 1688.
20 bigot] James II (1633–1701), a Catholic, who abandoned the throne under
political pressure in 1688.

Human Debasement

Source: Human Debasement. A Fragment. [1793]. A four-page leaflet dated at
the end 'Harrogate, Sepr. 15th 1793', but lacking any other form of identification
or date. Reprinted in *A Tribute to Liberty* (1793), pp. 85–88; *To the Public, alias
the "Swinish Multitude"* (1794), pp. 7–8; *Cabinet of Curiosities* (1795), pp. 113–16;
Fragments on the Origin of Kings, and Human Debasement (c. 1795); *A Tribute to
the Swinish Multitude* (New York, 1795), pp. 87–90, at which point it becomes
associated with 'the celebrated R. Thompson'. Not otherwise associated with
Rushton until *1824*, pp. 137–40, where it is called 'Superstition', but accepted
here on that authority. Reprinted in *Sketches of Obscure Poets, With Specimens of
their Writings* (1833), pp. 67–71, the 'specimen' forming evidence for the 'sketch'
(pp. 46–66), otherwise much derived from Shepherd's 1824 *Life*. The poem also
appeared as 'A Fragment on Human Debasement' in *The Glasgow Herald*, 5
November 1856, ascribed to the Oriental scholar Sir William Jones (1746–1794).
Printed as Rushton's in *The New Oxford Book of Eighteenth-Century Verse*, ed.
Roger Lonsdale (Oxford: Oxford University Press, 2009), pp. 792–94.

Variants:
3] *1824* substitutes: And still should be, the light of nature shews
21 right] rights *1824*
27 spirit] sprite *1824*
40 that] which *1824*
41 heart] hearts *1824*
50 fount?] adopted from *1824*; 'font.' in *Human Debasement*.
53 like] as *1824*
62 corroding] eroding *1824*
75 ears] eyes *1824*
80 dark-brow'd] adopted from *1824*; 'dark-brown'd' in *Human Debasement*.

Commentary: if this is Rushton's it is his only work in blank verse, apart from
the 'Parody of a Passage in Measure for Measure', below, and 'Briton, and Negro
Slave'. It is consistent with his political thought and with his contributions to
'Jacobin' discourse in the 1790s. See Dellarosa, chapter 4.

2] a tenet of Whig political theory, by which sovereignty is derived from the
will of the people (see also 40–42); Rushton's phrasing distantly recalls

the travesty of that theory put forward ironically, in the mouth of the villainous Whig leader, by John Dryden in *Absalom and Achitophel* (1681), 409–10: 'If not, the people have a right supreme | To make their kings; for kings are made for them'.

3] a defective line, perhaps prompting editorial filling-out.

4 slaves] as often in Rushton, subjects who do not resist their own oppression.

7 great first cause] i.e. God as the Creator. Rushton's references to God are generally oblique and more Unitarian than Anglican in flavour. See also 62. Rushton's intellectual circle was Quaker-Unitarian, and his early biographer, Shepherd, was a Unitarian minister at Gateacre, but there is little in Rushton's work that ties him to a specific form of faith.

12 tithe] tenth; more normally used of the 'tenth' which was supposedly due as a sort of local payment to a Church of England parish priest.

17 sophies] the Sophi was 'the emperor of Persia' (SJ); here, another dispensable despot.

32 seven hundred millions] the population of the world at the time of Rushton's death was probably in the region of 1000 million.

51 radiant orb] the sun, always Rushton's image of God and of Liberty.

56 tint] skin colour.

56 swart] 'black; darkly brown; tawny' (SJ).

61 felon] convicted criminal.

78 demi-god] 'partaking of divine nature; half a god' (SJ).

81 opiates] sedatives derived from opium, a drug of wide use, medicinal and otherwise, in Rushton's period.

Seamen's Nursery

Source: Liberty Scraps (1794), pp. 10–11. Reprinted *1806*, pp. 107–10, under the title 'The Seaman's Nursery'. Not in *1824*.

Variants:
14 Nancy] Nanny *1806*
25 Jem] James *1806*
32 ff] *1806* inserts an extra stanza:
Now o'er his grave, with breezy motion,
    The drooping wild-cane sighs,
And from the ever-beating ocean
    Hoarse gloomy murmurs rise.
Swift thro' the weeds and flowers that cover
    His turf, the lizards play,
While o'er the spot dark vultures hover,
    And eye the earth for prey.
36] punctuation from *1806*.

Commentary: a radical version of the marine ballad, first found in a pamphlet which must have had a strong Liverpool connection (see Appendix I).

2 Afric's trade] the triangular trade between Britain, the African coast, and the West-Indian plantations, into which Rushton had himself, like the Jem of the poem, been tempted by promotion.

10 store] gain, prizes.

21 smokes] Alexander Falconbridge, *An Account of the Slave Trade on the Coast of Africa* (1788), p. 51, refers to 'the smokes' as a name local to Guinea for 'a noxious vapour, arising from the swamps about the latter end of autumn', often producing a fever. Mosquitoes were a more likely cause of Jem's death.

26 half-mast ensign] i.e the ship's flag is at half-mast, signifying a death on board.

Stanzas on the Anniversary of the American Revolution

Source: Liberty Scraps (1794), pp. 12–13. This poem was hugely popular in American newspapers, and was reprinted under a variety of titles, usually with the omission of 25–32, and often anonymously (though sometimes with 'written by an Englishman' in the headline), sometimes citing *Liberty Scraps* as the source: *The Independent Gazetteer*, 11 July 1795; *The Rising Sun*, 3 November 1795; *The Columbian Centinel*, 14 October 1795; *Time Piece*, 3 July 1797; *The Bee*, 13 November 1799; *Constitutional Telegraph*, 20 November 1799 (and 9 July 1800); *Rhode-Island Republication*, 26 December 1801 (the only complete version in the American papers, 'by Edward Rushton, of Liverpool'); *Political Calendar*, 12 July 1804; *Democrat*, 14 July 1804; *The Farmer's Register*, 11 August 1807; *North Star*, 29 August 1807; *Republican Star*, 8 September 1807; *New-York Weekly Museum*, 30 July 1810; *Essex Register*, 6 July 1814; *Ohio Register*, 23 July 1814; *Eastport Centinel*, 1 January 1820; *Westchester Herald*, 20 June 1820. The version in *New-York Weekly Museum*, evidently reprinting from another newspaper, alludes to Rushton's blindness, and says that the poem had been copied by Rushton's daughter for a friend recently arrived; the version in *Westchester Herald* specifically highlights the anti-slavery aspect. Rushton printed it in *1806*, pp. 69–71, and it was reprinted in *1824*, pp. 38–40, under the title 'American Independency'. It also appeared in *Songs, Odes, and Other Poems on National Subjects* (1842), pp. 23–24, with a note by Rushton's erstwhile radical friend John Binns.

Variants:
2] nerved your gigantic domain *1806, 1824*
4] gave the vast world a new reign *1806, 1824*

7 the wide world] ancient realms *1806, 1824*
8] Tho' coerc'd, was resolved to be *1806, 1824*
9 worthies] warriors *1806, 1824*
11 deeds] worth *1806, 1824*
13 daring exploits] sufferings and deeds *1806, 1824*
14–16] *1806, 1824* substitute:
    Go forth on the wings of the wind,
  And as man, prostrate man, your high destiny reads,
    May he learn his own chains to unbind.
18 gratitude] energy *1806, 1824*
21 transport] rapture *1806*
22 takes root in] illumines *1806, 1824*
24 plunderers] spoilers *1806, 1824*
25–32] omitted in *1806* and *1824*, as well as in most of the American printings.
35 plains] groves *1806, 1824*
36 your] their *1806, 1824*

Commentary: Rushton's song echoes his celebration of the French revolution, and marks a complete turn from the anxieties of *The Dismember'd Empire*; it also marks a shift of attention towards the issue of slavery in America. As with France, America was hailed by some poets as having inaugurated an era of freedom; William Blake's illuminated book *America. A Prophecy*, was published in 1793. The *Anti-Jacobin Review* 23 (March 1806), 336, objected to the poem as a defence of rebellion.

title] the anniversary was celebrated on 4 July; see note to 6.
1 Columbia] poetical name for America, after the explorer Christopher Columbus
6 congress ... decree] the Declaration of Independence, 4 July 1776, the foundation of the independent American constitution.
15 Ambition] compare *The Dismember'd Empire*, 47.
    trench] entrench, encroach.
17 glebe] land; see *Neglected Genius*, 218.
19 Warren ... Montgomery] early American casualties: Joseph Warren (1741–1775), doctor and soldier, killed at Breed's Hill; Richard Montgomery (1738–1775) solider who defected to the Americans, killed leading an attack on Quebec.
20 Washington] George Washington (1732–1799), leader of the American forces and first president of the independent United States of America; see also final note below.
30 tythe-men and tax-men] British taxation of the colonies had been one of the major grievances which led to the Declaration of Independence.
34] as with his interpretation of British atrocities in Ireland, in later work,

Rushton views the vulnerability of women to rape as a symbol of political oppression.

37–48] this is essentially the point of Rushton's *Expostulatory Letter to George Washington*, on the title page of which Rushton quotes 37–40 of this poem.

The Tender's Hold

Source: Liberty Scraps (1794), pp. 13–15, without ascription; also in *Choice Collection of Civic Songs* (1795), p. 38, a collection which reprinted Rushton's 'Fire of Liberty' as well as Roscoe's *Day-Star of Liberty* and other pieces from *Liberty Scraps*. First ascribed to Rushton in *The Time-Piece*, 30 August 1797, which links it, plausibly, with *The Neglected Tar*; then in *The Suffolk Gazette*, 15 December 1810 and *The Shamrock*, 20 June 1812, as 'The British Tender's Hold. By Edward Rushton'; also in *New Hampshire Patriot and State Gazette*, 25 December 1810, and *Alexandria Herald*, 20 December 1811. It was included anonymously in *The Columbian Songster* (New York, 1797), pp. 175–77. Two undatable broadside printings exist: ESTC T196934 (a shorter version which identifies the tune as 'The Hardy Tar') and N37895 (in the National Archives, presumably because it was originally deemed seditious). This is one of the more convincing ascriptions from American newspapers, even though Rushton did not reprint the poem himself, perhaps preferring 'Will Clewline', with which it has obvious links, along with 'The Neglected Tar'. The use of 'connexion' and 'noxious' is characteristic of Rushton, as is the picture of the family, with the idealised 'Kate' and prattling youngsters.

Commentary: For the use of impressment to boost naval crews, see commentary to 'Will Clewline'.

3 Tender] see 'Will Clewline', 33.

9 pensioned] living off a state salary; aimed at politicians.

20 slavery] a pointed reminder of recent debates about conditions on slave ships.

32 reformation] reform of the political system.

37 Russia's bloody jade] Catherine the Great (1729–1796), Empress of Russia from 1766.

56 workhouse] the major source of social welfare in Rushton's time, feared as punitive and humiliating. A new one had been built in Liverpool in 1772; Henry Smithers, *Liverpool, its Commerce, Statues, and Institutions* (1825), p. 296.

59 prate] talk boringly.

Blue Eyed Mary

Source: Songs. Elegiac. Sea. (Manchester, Printed by G[eorge] Nicholson ... Sold by T. Knott ... and Champante & Whitrow, ... London. 1796), pp. 11–12. This was a chapbook of anonymous songs, with no evidence that Rushton (who is not named as the author) authorised the publication; the poem was probably copied from a newspaper now untraced. Nicholson reprinted the pamphlet in duodecimo at Ludlow in 1799, with the poem again on pp. 11–12, differently set, and again at Ludlow in a further undated issue. In 1799 Rushton published it himself on a single sheet bearing the imprint '*Published by* E. Rushton, *Liverpool, August,* 1799, *and sold by* S. W. Fores, *No.* 50, *Piccadilly, London.*' (ESTC: t213439). Another issue with the imprint 'J. McCreery, printer, 1799', is textually identical but bears a melodramatic engraving of Mary on her deathbed at the head (ESTC: T1613; the engraving is signed by Matthew Houghton). The song also appears in *The Jovial Songster, or Musical Miscellany* (c. 1800), pp. 29–30; *The Myrtle and Vine; or, Complete Vocal Library* (c. 1800); and *The Songster's Companion* (c. 1800); in these three anthologies it is assigned to the tune 'High-Mettled Racer', presumably that attached to the song, about a spent racehorse, which was next to *Blue-Ey'd Mary* in its first publication. Reprinted *1806*, pp. 65–67, and *1824*, pp. 111–13. It featured in American newspapers, without ascription: *The Political Repository*, 10 November 1801; *The Hampshire Federalist*, 18 March 1807; *The Washingtonian*, 2 October 1810 ('from a London paper'); *The Merrimack Intelligencer*, 6 October 1810; and *The Farmer's Register*, 10 May 1814 ('a picture from the hand of a master, correct, natural, and affecting'). It was listed among *Riley's Flute Melodies* (*New-York Daily Advertiser*, 28 November 1817) and was widely sung at concerts (e.g. *Baltimore Patriot*, 31 December 1821). 'Blue Eyed Mary' was later the name of a schooner. Several later printings of the poem with other ballads exist (e.g. *Captain Mulligan*, Boston 1835). Small provincial collections such as *Six Favourite Songs* (c. 1840) and *Four Excellent New Songs* (c. 1820) include it. *Blue Eyed Mary, or, the Lily of the Village* appears to have been acted in London in 1835. J. Birt of Seven Dials, London, printed *Blue Eyed Mary or, the Victim of Seduction*, with a woodcut, in about 1840, with another poem, *The Better Land*.

Variants:
4 monarch] hermit *1806, 1824*
25 next] now *1806, 1824*
33–34] Rushton's 1799 broadside text, *1806*, and *1824* substitute:
    Whilst thus the barb'd arrow sinks deep in her soul,
    She flies for relief to that traitor the bowl,

Commentary: a full melodramatic expression of an anxiety about female sexuality that surfaces in a number of Rushton poems, in a narrative based on the standard *Harlot's Progress* of the eighteenth century, established by the sequence of six engravings of that title by William Hogarth (1732). The role of the squire, culpable but untouched by justice, indicates however a continuing theme of aristocratic oppression and abuse of power. One of Rushton's radical associates, John Thelwall (1764–1834), wrote a much longer poem on this theme: see his 'The Seducer: or, Damon and Amanda' (in *Poems on Various Subjects*, 1787). The *Anti-Jacobin Review*, 23 (March 1806), thought the poem 'one of the best' in the volume, and identified it as a 'parody' of the 'well-known song of the Race-Horse', presumably 'High-Mettled Racer'.

1 cottage] traditional rural setting of innocence into the romantic era; Wordsworth's well-known 'Lucy' poems, where the innocent maiden is confined to her cottage setting, date from exactly the same period as Rushton's poem.
14 Hoyle] Edmond Hoyle, 1672–1769, author of a hugely popular series of books on card games, starting with *A Short Treatise on the Game of Whist* (1742).
19 character] character reference, a document used in the hiring of servants.
20 skill at her needle] i.e. the ability to work as a seamstress, a traditional means of support for a working-class woman.
24 on the town] i.e. as a prostitute.
32 impure] harlot. As a noun, 'impure' was relatively recent (*OED*'s first citation is 1784).
34 *variant* bowl] drinking.
36 disease] syphilis.

Elegy [*To the Memory of Robert Burns*]

Source: apparently first printed in *Liverpool Phenix*, and then reprinted in the undated *Liverpool Testimonials to the Departed Genius of Robert Burns, the Scottish Bard*, Printed and Sold by Merritt and Wright, Castle Street, Liverpool, pp. 16–19, the final poem in the sequence of four and the copytext here. It is printed over the initials 'E. W.', but this is corrected to 'Edward Rushton' in MS in the British Library and Liverpool SCA copies. Reprinted as Rushton's in *Fugitive Pieces: A Collection of Original Poems, the Greater Part by the Most Eminent Writers of the Present Age* (1797), pp. 99–103, under the title 'Stanzas to the Memory of Robert Burns'; and in the American paper *The Time-Piece*, 10 November 1797. In *1806*, pp. 78–82, as 'To the Memory of Robert Burns'; in *1824*, pp. 1–7; and in Burke, pp. 32–35. The poem was reprinted complete in the *Critical Review*'s account of the *1806* volume as the best piece in the collection: the verses 'are uniformly good, and are worthy of their subject'.

Variants:

1–6 omitted *1806, 1824*

3 stowre] the reading of *Fugitive Pieces*; *Liverpool Testimonials* has 'flower', an obvious mistake

31 glen] glens *Fugitive Pieces, 1806, 1824*

32 untutor'd] uncultur'd *1806, 1824*

34 sonsy] dulcet *1806, 1824*

39 learning] fortune *1806*

41 proud turrets] *Fugitive Pieces* and *1806, 1824*; *Liverpool Testimonials* has 'loud torrets'

54 bloated] haughty *1824*

55 dulcet] witching *1806, 1824*

70 terror] tremor *Fugitive Pieces, 1806, 1824*

79 While] When *1824*

83 clearly] cheerly *1806, 1824*

85 ah!] oh! *Fugitive Pieces, 1806, 1824*

87 wing] Bard *1824*

88 loftier] higher *1806, 1824*

92 Columbus's] Columbia's *1806, 1824*

97 earthy] earthly *Fugitive Pieces*; earthy *1806, 1824*

99 her] its *1824*

Commentary: To Rushton, Robert Burns (1759–1796), the Ayrshire poet who had come to prominence in 1786 with *Poems, Chiefly in the Scottish Dialect*, was another version of Chatterton (see *Neglected Genius*): a natural poet, without financial resources, culpably neglected by the powerful, dying young. Rushton's account was based on very limited information. The other poems in *Liverpool Testimonials* are by W.R. (William Roscoe), G.P. (George Perry, author of 'The Prophecy of Commerce' which opens William Enfield's *Essay Towards the History of Leverpool*, 1773), and I.B. (identified in Liverpool SCA copy as Jno Bree; not further identified). The volume opens with a list of subscribers to a fund in support of Burns's family. Currie contributed 10 guineas, and William Roscoe and William Rathbone both 5; Rushton is not named among the contributors. The volume must be earlier than 1800, as Burns died in 1796, and one would expect the subscription to be fairly early. This elegy, like Roscoe's, inhabits the form of Burns's poem 'To a Mountain Daisy', from which it quotes pointedly; like Roscoe's, it is politically radical. Wordsworth's poem 'At the Grave of Burns' also equates Burns with the frail flower of his own poem, and Carol McGuirk, *Robert Burns and the Sentimental Era* (Athens, GA: University of Georgia Press, 1985) suggests that Burns framed himself in elegiac terms in his own late work. For Romantic-period poetic autopsies of Burns, see Nicholas Roe, 'Authenticating Robert Burns', in Robert Crawford (ed.) *Robert Burns and Cultural Authority* (Edinburgh: Edinburgh University Press, 1997), pp. 159–79. Rushton, by now running a bookselling and publishing business in Paradise

Street, Liverpool, was later one of the agents for James Currie's monumental and controversial edition, printed by M'Creery, of *The Works of Robert Burns*, 4 vols (1800). Currie told a correspondent that both Roscoe and Rushton attacked 'the ingratitude of Burns's countrymen too violently'; in his edition (I. 339–55), he included a new set of 'Tributary Verses' by Roscoe. See *Memoir of the Life, Writings and Correspondence of James Currie MD*, ed. William Wallace Currie, 2 vols (1831), I. 268.

3–6 stern ... gem] quotation from Burns, 'To a Mountain Daisy'; 'stowre' is dust, earth.

quips and cranks] apparently from Milton, *L'Allegro* (1645), 27: 'Quips and Cranks, and wanton wiles'. A 'crank' is a verbal trick or humorous turn of speech.

19 spark o' nature's fire] quoting Burns, 'Epistle to J. L*****K, An Old Scotch Bard', 73.

21 admire] wonder

23–24 lyre ... ecstasy] an echo of Gray, *Elegy in a Country Churchyard* (1751), 64: 'wak'd to extasy the living lyre'. Burns fulfils, albeit partially, the curtailed prophecy of the peasant poets Gray imagines in the graveyard at Stoke Poges.

33 rude hind] uneducated peasant.

34 sonsy] not in SJ; a classic Burns word, meaning lucky, auspicious.

37 Anon] soon.

43 what avail'd] perhaps recalling Pope, *Windsor-Forest* (1713), 145: 'Ah! what avail his glossy, varying dyes...'.

45 infant brood] Burns left several children; *Liverpool Testimonials* was partly a charitable venture to raise funds to support his family. But Rushton always focused on the domestic circle as the source of virtue and happiness.

55 bloated train] rich people who do not use their position to support the disadvantaged.

59 opulent disdain] apparently echoed in William Hamilton Drummond's poem 'The Signs of Genius', an elegy on Burns published in *The Man of Age*, second edition (1798), 60.

61 Dumfries] where Burns lived and worked as an exciseman, and where he died. Burns attacked the failure of patrons himself, e.g. 'To William Simson, Ochiltree', 19–24.

64 this side Tweed] on this side of the Scottish border. The Tweed flows into the sea at the border town of Berwick.

65 poor bards] perhaps an allusion to Chatterton, or to Rushton himself.

68 slaves] i.e. time-serving or subservient lackeys.

75 sly, slow] perhaps echoing Pope's *Essay on Man* (1733–1734), IV. 216: 'All sly, slow things'.

80 storm-cock] the missel thrush, or sometimes the fieldfare, reputed to sing

in bad weather; see John Aikin, *An Essay on the Application of Natural History to Poetry* (1777), p. 121, and Beilby and Bewick, p. 96.

81 Æolian lyre] an instrument, named after the Greek god of the wind, which makes sounds from air passing over strings. It was thus a symbol in the Romantic period for poetic inspiration; Samuel Taylor Coleridge's poem 'The Eolian Lyre' dates from 1796.

84 routh of rhymes] Burns, 'Scotch Drink', 123, 'rowth o' rhyme'. 'Rowth' means 'abundance'.

86 pile] building.

87 some wing] Burke suggests Rushton might conceivably be thinking of Robert Bloomfield's success with his *Farmer's Boy* (1800) but the appearance of the poem in *Fugitive Pieces* (1797) indicates that this cannot be right and that Burke is also right to suggest the poem must date from nearer Burns's death; the reference is not specific to any single poet.

91–92 Ganges ... Columbus' waters] indicating the Indian subcontinent and North America, regions to which some Scots ('Scotia's sons', 93) have emigrated.

96 witching] bewitching.

101 mountain daisy] making explicit the underlying tribute to Burn's poem, 'To a Mountain Daisy On Turning One Down with the Plough April 1786'.

110 sea-beat] beaten by the sea.

112 elate] enraptured, inspired.

Sonnet [*The Swallow*]

Source: Fugitive Pieces (Edinburgh, 1797), p. 103, as by the same author as the elegy on Burns, which gives Rushton's authorship; presumably printed earlier, perhaps in *Liverpool Phenix*, though no earlier printing has been traced, except possibly the verbally identical text (unascribed) in the *Moral and Political Magazine*, the publicity organ of the radical London Corresponding Society, 2 (1797), 48. Reprinted as '*By Mr. Rushton, of Liverpool*' in the American newspapers *The Time Piece*, 25 September 1797; *The Medley*, 20 October 1797; and *New-York Gazette*, 2 October 1797. *Poulson's American Daily Advertiser*, 19 April 1803, printed it as 'Helpless Swallow', by Roscoe, and at least six other American papers to 1813 followed suit in that ascription. Reprinted in *1806*, p. 83, as 'The Swallow', and *1824*, p. 21. It was further reprinted in *The Kaleidoscope*, 22 November 1825, 162, as it 'feelingly and beautifully depicted the power of sympathy for the suffering child of genius'; in *The Preston Chronicle*, 13 October 1832, with some approving commentary on Rushton and his son; and (with slightly less of a puff) in *The Leicester Chronicle*, 26 January 1833. It was also quoted approvingly in an article on social issues in *The Liverpool Mercury*, 28 August 1846. The generally hostile review in *The British Critic* 28

(November 1806), 561–62, reprinted is as an acceptable specimen. Reprinted in Burke, p. 35, and in Scrivener, *Poetry and Reform*, p. 130. The final (originally blank) leaf of the University of Liverpool Special Collections and Archives copy of *Liverpool Testimonials to the Departed Genius of Robert Burns* has a MS text of the poem, following Rushton's 'Elegy' on Burns, without ascription, in an early nineteenth-century hand. See http://www.liv.ac.uk/library/sca/images/litmssburns1.jpg. The left hand edge has been trimmed in the binding. This is a fair copy, not a working manuscript, and has no doubt been copied into the volume to 'complete' it, from an early printed text.

Variants:
In *1806* and *1824* the indentation is the other way round until the final couplet and there is no gap between the stanzas.

4 twitt'rer] flutterer *1806, 1824*
12 the full stop is supplied from the text in the *Moral and Political Magazine*; *Fugitive Pieces* has a comma

Commentary: Rushton's swallow is emblematic rather than ornithologically accurate (though the same might be said of Keats's nightingale or Shelley's skylark). Rushton has distilled the essence of his longer Burns elegy to the compact form of a sonnet, a new formal direction for him. Given his recommendation of patronage here, it is of interest to recall that Shepherd (pp. xxi, xxvii) insists that Rushton himself refused offers of financial assistance from people such as William Rathbone and William Roscoe.

1 turfy] grassy.
6 caterer] breadwinner.
10 wight] archaic poetical term for 'person'.
14] an Alexandrine, or twelve-syllable verse.

The Remedy [The Leviathan]

Source: The Time-Piece, 9 June 1797, no doubt from another newspaper, not found. It appears under a general heading, 'Poetical Communications' as the second of a pair of sonnets, the first being 'Hibernia', beginning 'Hast thou e'er seen the dull ey'd Turtle laid', in which Ireland is compared to the hunted turtle; this poem is then offered as 'the remedy'. The pair were also printed in the *Independent Chronicle*, 23 August 1807. Neither paper ventured an ascription. Rushton printed this poem on its own, slightly altered and under the title 'The Leviathan', in *1806*, p. 147, and in *1824*, p. 54; there is no mention of the other poem. It was printed from the *1806* text in the *Liverpool Mercury* of 8 January 1819; it was then sent in again as 'applicable to the present time' by 'an admirer of the poet, patriot, and philanthropist', to the same newspaper, which printed it under the heading 'A Nation Rising'; and the same paper printed it a third time on 13 February 1855, in the hope that 'public men' would find it relevant to 'the present state of affairs'.

Variants:
In *1806* all lines but the final two are offset, with even-numbered lines slightly more offset than the odd-numbered.

2 seas] ice *1806, 1824*
8 death and terror] devastation *1806, 1824*
10 his] the *1806, 1824*
14 kings ... proud] splendor, wealth, and power, in one sad *1806, 1824*

Commentary: The Leviathan is a biblical sea creature, later casually identified in European literature with the whale. While whaling was never a major part of Liverpool's industry, Rushton could certainly have encountered whaling ships in the port: there were twenty or so operating from Liverpool in 1788. Thomas Hobbes's book *Leviathan*, which describes the structure of political society, was published in 1651 and Rushton loosely picks up the idea of the political mass as a unitary 'body'. The idea is that once the people recognise their oppression they will rise up and smash the state. The changes Rushton made for *1806* to the last line of the poem render it much less specifically revolutionary and it is taken out of the Irish context altogether. For Rushton's views on British activity in Ireland, see commentary to 'Mary le More'.

14] an Alexandrine, or 14-syllable line, often used by Rushton to conclude a sonnet.

Song [*Mary le More*]

Source: The first dated text found is *Carey's United States' Recorder*, 9 August 1798, where it is assigned a tune, 'Oh! the moment was sad', from George Colman's *The Surrender of Calais* (1791). It was reprinted in several other American papers, none giving an ascription: *The Time Piece*, 18 August 1798, introduced it thus: '*The heart that the following Lines will not melt into sympathy must be harder than adamant. They exhibit a picture but too true, as every village in Ireland can bear testimony. ... it would give us much pleasure if we could add, that to the beauties of delicate poesy, which they possess in a very eminent degree, they united its fictions also.*' It appeared also in *Weekly Museum*, 18 August 1798, with the first half of that introduction; *Centinel of Freedom*, 21 August 1798; *Alexandria Times*, 21 August 1798; *Independent Chronicle*, 3 September 1798; *Minerva*, 20 September 1798; *The Companion*, 29 September 1798; *Carolina*

Gazette, 15 May 1800; *Carlisle Gazette*, 23 July 1800; *Federal Galaxy*, 3 Jan 1803 (a partial reprint); *New-Jersey Journal*, 10 April 1804; *Farmer's Cabinet*, 25 February 1806 (partial), naming the tune as 'Exile of Erin'; *Newburyport Herald*, 4 March 1806; *Essex Register*, 9 November 1808. These versions are all close to the earliest printing, as is the version in *Petersburg Daily Courier*, 7 February 1815, though by then Rushton's revised text was available from *1806*. *The Shamrock*, 14 December 1811, denounced Rushton's *1806* version as a mutilation and literary fraud, and presented its own 'correct copy'.

The poem has not been traced in British newspapers. It appeared in the Dublin peridical *The Olio, or, Anything-arian Miscellany*, III (2 April 1800), 24, without ascription. Evidently many broadside versions were produced in Britain. One, printed by W. Armstrong in Banastre Street, Liverpool, is in the New York Public Library (ESTC: N473389). This may derive from an authorial source, given the Liverpool connection, but is undated, as is another slip song version, illustrated with a woodcut of a coffin at its head, in the National Archives, HO 42/26/213–214B (the slip song itself and the accompanying letter). Several clearly nineteenth century versions can be viewed at http://ballads.bodleian.ox.ac.uk/. The poem thus had a vigorous independent life in broadsides, chapbooks, and similar popular collections, often in provincial towns; versions are recorded at Strabane (n.d.); Stirling (1808); Edinburgh (c. 1820); York (c. 1830). It was included in collections such as *Cupid Wounded or the Mischievous Bee* (1830), *The Frisky Songster* (Stirling, 1813), *Five Excellent Songs* (Edinburgh, c. 1825), and *The Pocket Encyclopaedia of Scottish, English and Irish Songs* (Glasgow, 1816), II. 211–12. It is also in several song books, usually with the tune 'Erin Go Bragh' (otherwise 'Savourna Delish' or 'The Exile of Erin'; e.g. *The Universal Songster* (London, 1826), III. 185.Tracing an exact bibliography is almost impossible because poems called 'Mary le More' and listed as such in catalogues often turn out to be 'The Maniac', the second instalment of Rushton's sequence about the ill-fated Irish heroine. The situation is further complicated by versions rewritten as 'Ellen O'More' and ascribed to the Irish poet George Nugent Reynolds (1771–1802), apparently by confusion with his sentimenal lyric *Kathleen O'More*. John Daly Burk, *History of the Late War in Ireland* (Philadelphia, 1799), pp. 105–9, prints a partial 'Ellen' version with the dubious claim that it was actually sung at the battle of Vinegar Hill in 1798. The poem was, however, reprinted by Rushton in a revised version in *1806*, pp. 52–55; it is in *1824*, pp. 8–10. Reprinted in *Letters of a Templar*, pp. 147–49, with discussions of the authorship reprinted from the *Liverpool Journal* (1844) and *The Nation*, 17 January 1846. See also *Kaleidoscope*, 24 May 1825, for Irish appropriation of an unnamed song by Rushton, perhaps this one, and *Liverpool Mercury*, 4 May 1832. Reprinted as Rushton's in *Literary Remains of the United Irishmen of 1798*, ed. R. R. Madden (Dublin, 1887), pp. 29–30, with discussion at pp. 351–53; and in Burke, pp. 30–32. See further Dellarosa, chapter 3.

Variants:
Only variants between the first located datable text and *1806/1824* are recorded here.

1 soldiers of Britain] cold-hearted strangers *1806, 1824*
3 the] yon *1806, 1824*
11 The fierce soldiers] Th' assailants soon *1806, 1824*
12 yet] and *1806, 1824*
19 relate] describe *1806, 1824*
20 That blasted] Who blasted *1806*; Which blasted *1824*
22 his life's blood] the life's stream *1806, 1824*
25 infernal] inhuman *1806, 1824*
36 And by force they deflower'd the poor] And ruin'd by force the sweet
    1806, 1824
37 wide] wild *1806, 1824*
38 soldiers of Britain] cold-hearted strangers *1806, 1824*
40 fall] flow *1806, 1824*
45–48] *1806, 1824* substitute:

> And while your blue eyes are with pity o'erflowing,
> Or with strong indignation your white bosoms glowing,
> Oh! reflect that the tree of delight may yet grow in,
>   The soil where now wanders poor Mary le More.

Commentary: The rising of the 'United Irishmen' against British rule in Ireland took place between May and October 1798 and the struggle was marked by particularly brutal military atrocities. The speed with which Rushton's poem reached America suggests he was quick off the mark in producing a protest poem. The Nottingham version was sent to the (third) Duke of Portland (1738–1809), a leading Whig politician, then Home Secretary (later Prime Minister), presumably on the grounds that it was seditious. The letter, from George Cartwright, is dated from Nottingham on 1 January 1799: 'The enclosed was given to me, this morning, by a person who informed me, that several of them had lately been privately distributed in this town'. The *1806* version is less obviously seditious, since it removes direct references to British soldiers; Rushton also takes out 'the Union', which in 1798 meant the United Irishmen, but from 1802 onwards denoted the union of parliaments which abolished the Irish house of commons and brought in direct rule from Westminster. *The Monthly Review* (50: May 1806, p. 96), commenting on this poem and its two sequel poems 'The Maniac' and 'Mary's Death', declared 'The tale is deeply pathetic: but we cannot forbear from expressing our regret that the author should dwell, with so much gloomy complacency, on the remembrance of events which must to every mind be painful, and can only tend to rekindle the dying embers of animosity and discontent'. Rushton would return, however, to the theme in 'Jemmy Armstrong'. Apart from its continuing life as a song, the story seems to have hit the stage (Sadler's Wells, 28 August 1838) in James P. Hart's *Mary le More; Or the Irish Maniac. An Original Domestic Drama, in Three Acts* (1838). The poem is discussed in its Irish context, though without awareness of its English authorship, in Mary Helen Thomas, 'Liberty, Hibernia, and Mary le More: United Irish Images of Women', in *The Women of 1798*, eds. Dáire Keogh and Nicholas Furling (Dublin: Four Courts Press, 1998), pp. 9–25. The Irish nationalist Daniel O'Connell (1775–1847) is recorded as declaring *Mary le More* 'the finest ballad ever written on the wrongs of Ireland'; he was apparently accused of treason for merely quoting it (*Letters of a Templar*, pp. 147, 149). See further Dellarosa, chapter 3.

7 Freedom's firm sons] the United Irishmen.
15 Munster] the south-west province of Ireland.
25 banditti] outlaws, brigands; often used in a gothic or European context.
27 friends of the castle] i.e. Dublin Castle, the seat of British power in Ireland.

Written for the Anniversary of the Liverpool Marine Society

Source: single-sheet broadside of this title, over an imprint which is cropped on the only known copy, at the National Library of Scotland (ESTC: T179582) but which can be reconstructed as reading 'Published by Ed. Rushton, Liverpool'. The date is given as '1799?' in ESTC; this is supported by the poem's appearance in an American newspaper, *The Weekly Museum*, 2 August 1800, with the statement 'Published September 1799'. It comments further 'The following beautiful production has been in our possession some weeks'. It was further reprinted in *The United States Oracle*, 7 May 1803, and *The Providence Phoenix*, 3 September 1806; *Gleanings*, pp. 15–16; the last is the only American printing to give Rushton's identity. Reprinted *1806*, pp. 71–73, and *1824*, pp. 89–91, with the insertion of the word 'Lines' at the start of the title.

Variants:
24 will] may *1824*

Commentary: Articles of Agreement for the foundation of the Liverpool Marine Society were drawn up and printed on 13 February 1789. According to Rushton's *Few Plain Facts*, below, the plan started at a convivial society of which he was a member. At least one charity sermon on its behalf is known from 1791, and its work was reported in newspapers, e.g. *The Observer*, Sunday 6 January 1799. The same newspaper, Sunday 12 January 1800, reported an anniversary dinner on 'Tuesday', which would have been 7 January. A song of the same type as Rushton's, by 'Mr Harpley', for a later meeting, was printed in *The Lancaster Gazette*, 14 January 1804. The society was evidently, like Rushton's original idea for the Blind School, a sort of benefit club for social support in the absence of adequate social welfare programmes, and it was again close to Rushton's own interests. The song was no doubt a fundraising effort, part of a celebration dinner. See also Rushton's similar poem for the Lancaster Marine Society, below. Ann Yearsley's poem 'To the Bristol Marine Society', on similar themes, was published in her *Poems on Various Subjects* (1787). The second stanza of Rushton's poem was quoted as an epigraph to a 'Biographical Sketch of Madame Roland' in the *Belfast Monthly Magazine*, IV.20 (March 1810), 194. See also Smithers, *Liverpool*, pp. 304–5.

2 terraqueous] 'composed of land and water' (SJ).

6 canvass] sail.

8 masts by the board] over the side of the ship.

13 meridian] 'the line drawn from north to south, which the sun crosses at noon' (SJ).

20 tackle] equipment.

29–30] an unusually political point for this type of poem.

33 prattling throng] orphaned children of a seafarer.

37] 'God tempers the wind ... to the shorn lamb', Laurence Sterne, *A Sentimental Journey through France and Italy*, 2 vols (1768), II. 175–76, apparently translating a French proverb.

38] see Proverbs 6:6 and 30:25.

Song [From *Hymns &c. for the Blind*]

Source: HYMNS, &c. FOR THE BLIND, AT THE SCHOOL OF INDUSTRY, Liverpool. J. M'CREERY, PRINTER. This single-sheet publication of six lyric poems was evidently produced either for use in the Liverpool School for the Instruction of the Indigent Blind, founded in 1791, in the manner of the later volume, *A Selection of Psalms, Hymns, Anthems &c. Sung at the School for the Blind, Liverpool* (1819), or for sale to aid the institution. It survives in a single copy in the National Library of Scotland. All six poems are anonymous. The first, 'The Comforts of Religion' is by Anne Steele (1717–1778), from her *Poems on Subjects Chiefly Devotional*, 3 vols (Bristol 1780), II. 35–36. The third, 'The German Hymn' is drawn from stanzas in John Cennick, *Sacred Hymns for the Children of God* (1742), pp. 66–68; the fourth, at the head of the second column, 'The dying Christian to his soul', is by Alexander Pope (1688–1744). The sixth 'Song.' ('Hark! Sisters hark! that bursting sigh') was by the Rev. John Smyth of Liverpool, according to *The Eighth Report of the Society for Bettering the Condition and Increasing the Comforts of the Poor* (1799), p. 82, where it is reprinted; see also Henry Lilley Smith, *Observations on the Prevailing Practice of supplying Medical Assistance to the Poor* (1819), p. 22. Smyth was minister of St. Anne's, Liverpool and one of the early members of the group which met to plan the institution, and therefore known to Rushton (Royden 1991, p. 33).

Against the word 'SONG.', the title of the second poem in the first column, there is a pencilled annotation of unknown date, 'by Edwd Rushton', which is the source of the attribution. Rushton does not mention the poem in his prose accounts of his role in the founding of the institution, and the poem was not reprinted in Rushton's later acknowledged editions. There is no date on the sheet and catalogue records merely give '1800? as a rough guess. The School itself dates from January 1791; M'Creery, the printer of the sheet, began printing independently in Liverpool in 1792, though the datable printing that he did for Rushton appears later, between 1799 and 1801, as does his work for the Blind School itself. Whatever the date of Rushton's composition (if his), the printing itself probably dates from about 1799. A poem by William Smyth, another of the so-called 'Roscoe circle' of Liverpool liberals, called 'For the Blind Asylum, Liverpool', appeared in Smyth's *English Lyricks*, printed by M'Creery in 1797. A different Rushton, Thomas, of Blacklow Brow, Huyton, Liverpool, sent William Roscoe a 'feeble attempt' at an 'Inscription for the Asylum for the Blind' (14 lines, beginning 'Stranger, within these walls you'll find') on 8 August 1800 (Liverpool Record Office, 920 ROS/4259) and it is possible that he was somehow involved; but the connection with M'Creery makes Edward Rushton's authorship reasonably likely.

Commentary: Rushton had become almost totally blind as a teenager after an outbreak of ophthalmia on his ship (see Introduction). The story of his involvement in the founding of what is now the Royal School for the Blind, Liverpool (where, in its more recent Wavertree incarnation, Rushton's portrait still hangs) is well told in Mike Royden's study (see Introduction, note 32), though Royden does not seem to have seen this broadside. Rushton fell out with the clergyman, Henry Dannett, who ran the fundraising campaign for the school over the issue of the credit due for the original idea (see his prose account, 'A Few Plain Facts', below). If the poem is Rushton's, and its emphasis on the difficulty of being blind and the usefulness of practical help (compared with the Christian resignation of most of the other poems on the sheet) certainly makes it likely, it would constitute Rushton's earliest contribution to philanthropic or charity-focused poetry. It offers a pre-echo of his own later poems, such as 'Stanzas on Blindness'. The scripting of hymns of gratitude for (particularly) children to sing in charitable institutions was a common eighteenth-century practice and will also remind some readers of William Blake's 'Holy Thursday' poems in *Songs of Innocence and of Experience* (1789–1794). Rushton will have known nothing of Blake, but will have been familiar with the models that Blake was to some extent parodying, such as the hymns of Isaac Watts. Edward Larrissy's study, *The Blind and Blindness in Literature of the Romantic Period* (Edinburgh: Edinburgh University Press, 2007), provides context but does not mention Rushton.

3 mantled] covered, disguised.

5 tho' fortune be join'd] even for wealthy people.

9–16] it is typical of the conventional gendering of Rushton's time, and of his own recurrent imagery, to adopt a crushed flower as the motif of the girls and women, and a storm-tossed boat as the emblem of the boys and men.

The Maniac

Source: The Monthly Magazine, 8.53 (January 1800), 986, without ascription. Reprinted in the Dublin periodical *The Olio, or, Anything-arian Miscellany*, II (29 March 1800), 16. The poem may have appeared earlier in a newspaper which has not been located; 'Mary le More' was clearly available in 1798 and it is likely this sequel followed it fairly quickly. Like 'Mary le More', it appeared in several American newspapers, without ascription but often on the assumption that it directly described actual historical atrocities: *Farmer's Weekly Museum*, 15 September 1800; *Mercantile Advertiser*, 22 September 1800; *Salem Gazette*, 30 September 1800; *Constitutional Telegraph*, 1 October 1800; *The Hive*, 13 September 1803 ('supposed to be written by Mrs. Robinson', i.e. Mary Robinson, c. 1758–1800, an ascription often repeated thereafter, presumably by confusion with her own poem of the same title); *The Democrat*, 31 March 1804; *The American Citizen*, 7 April 1804; *Republican Watch-Tower*, 11 April 1804; *New-Jersey Journal*, 17 April 1804; *American Mercury*, 19 April 1804; *Vermont Gazette*, 19 May 1806. In *The Providence Phoenix*, 11 January 1806, the version was 'Ellen o'Moore'. In Britain it appeared as 'The Maniac' in the *Poetical Register*, 4 (1806), 338–40, and in Rushton's own *1806* volume, where it was on pp. 56–59; it was in *1824* at pp. 11–13. It appeared under the title 'Mary le More, or the Irish Maniac' in an 8-page chapbook, *Come Under my Plaidy*, printed by C. Randall at Stirling around 1800, but impossible to date with any accuracy, and in *The English Musical Repository*, new edition (London: B. Crosby, 1808), pp. 153–56, to the tune of 'Savourna Delish'. *The Shamrock* (Glasgow, 1830), pp. 22–27, has the poem sung to the tune 'The Exile of Erin', identified with 'Savourna Delish'. Thereafter it was often printed, sometimes under the name of 'Mary le More', in broadside form; it is recorded in versions printed in the 1810s at London by J. Pitts; at Limerick, by Stephen B. Goggin, c. 1825; at Falkirk, with some Burns poems, by R. Taylor, c. 1825; at Hull, by J. Ferraby, between 1803 and 1838; at London, with an illustration, by J. Catnach, c. 1840 (under the title 'Mary le Moor'); at Preston, by J. Harkness, c. 1850; at Durham, c. 1850; Cork, c. 1860. A version printed by Robert McIntosh of King Street, Calton, Glasgow, in 1849, is available on the website of the National Library of Scotland, and several can be viewed online at the Bodleian's ballad collection, http://ballads.bodleian.ox.ac.uk/. Like 'Mary le More', the poem has been otherwise attributed to the Irish writer George Nugent Reynolds (1770–1802) and also to the Scottish poet Thomas Campbell (1777–1844); see e.g. *Paddy's Resource*, second edition (Dublin, n.d., probably 1803), pp. 3–5. It was printed, as Rushton's, under the title 'Mary le More', in *Literary Remains of the United Irishmen of 1798*, ed. R. R. Madden (Dublin, 1887), pp. 1–7, with extensive commentary on the authorship question.

Variants:
2 While] When *1824*
4 wild] mild *1806*; wild *1824*
9 blasts] blast *1806, 1824*
13 While] Whilst *1824*
20 the] his *1806, 1824*
21 they've laid] they have laid *1806, 1824*
29 Britons] strangers *1806, 1824*
37 lies] is *1806, 1824*
41 raved the poor] raved the moor *1806*; raved the poor *1824*

Commentary: as the second in the sequence of 'Mary le More' poems, this shares the iconography of the raped women as the representative of a distressed Ireland. The pathetic madwoman on the moors, however, is also well known from other poems of the period, such as Wordsworth's 'The Thorn', in *Lyrical Ballads* (1798). See the discussion in Dellarosa, chapter 3.

6 crowflowers] a type of buttercup. The association of crowflowers with daisies cements Rushton's obvious allusion to Shakespeare's *Hamlet*; Ophelia, driven mad by the death of her father, makes a garland 'Of crow-flowers, nettles, daises, and long purples' (IV. vii. 137–40) before drowning.
24 blue wave of Erin] very similar phrasing is found in James Macpherson's 'Ossianic' epic poem, *Temora* (1763), book 1.
25 furze] a flowering bush of wild places, sometimes known as gorse.
26] compare 'On the Death of Hugh Mulligan', 2.
31 sea mew] seagull.
36 screech owls and ravens] birds of ill omen, warning of vengeance against the soldiers; compare 'The Throstle', 79–80.

Lucy's Ghost

Source: Lucy's Ghost. A Marine Ballad. By Edward Rushton. Liverpool, Printed by J. M'Creery, Houghton-Street. 1800. One copy of this 8-page pamphlet (ESTC t170921) is known to survive, at the National Library of Scotland. Reprinted in *1806*, pp. 46–51, and *1824*, pp. 55–59, under the title 'Lucy'.

Variants:

17–81] The lines of Lucy's speech are marked by quotation marks in *1806*, *1824*

22 falshoods] falsehood *1806, 1824*

28] note omitted *1806, 1824*

35 soothe] *1806, 1824*; the 1800 reading is 'sooth'.

36 Yet] Grief's *1806, 1824*

38 what a scene] what a sight *1806, 1824*

86 by] with *1806, 1824*

Commentary: the phrase 'marine ballad' is apparently Rushton's own, but he was drawing on a very long tradition of sea songs and literary ballads about Britain's seafaring life, such as Richard Glover's *Admiral Hosier's Ghost* (c. 1740), and the songs of Charles Dibdin (1768–1833). There was an especially strong tradition of such songs in Liverpool in the 1790s; some publishers, such as Stephen Summersides, appear to have issued little else. Ghosts and betrayed lovers populate the ballad tradition from the renaissance onwards, though John Donne's 'The Apparition' offers a more literary example of the scenario. The gothic ballad of the 1790s had begun to be influenced also by Germanic traditions; for the poem in this context see Dellarosa, chapter 2. Mary Robinson's sonnet sequence *Sappho and Phaon* (1796) ends with the prospect of the abandoned woman plunging from a precipice into the sea.

1 abaft] 'from the forepart of the ship, towards the stern' (SJ); 'abaft the beam' is behind the line that runs through the middle of the ship from side to side.

3 reefs] part of the sail designed to facilitate reduction of the amount of sail exposed to the wind.

4 weather shrouds] ropes holding the mast tight on the 'weather' or 'windward' side of the ship.

5 middle watch] normally from midnight to 4 a.m.

11 welkin] sky; 'out of use, except in poetry' (SJ).

13 winding-sheet] the shroud in which a corpse is wrapped for burial.

16 mate] naval officer subordinate to the master of a ship; Rushton was second mate on the ship on which he caught the disease which blinded him.

21 shade] ghost.

28 Anana] the Latin botanical name for pineapple, Ananas.

48 rude] uncivilised.

61 where sea-fowls lodge] i.e. on cliff-faces.

66] perhaps recalling the song, 'Full fathom five', from Shakespeare, *The Tempest*,

I. ii. 462.

82 The disappearance of the ghost at break of day is reminiscent of the departure of Hamlet's father's ghost in Shakespeare, *Hamlet*, I. v.

Sonnet by a Poor Man. On the Approach of the Gout.

Source: Portsmouth Telegraph, 16 March 1801, without ascription. This is the earliest version located, though it seems an unlikely place for its actual first appearance, and therefore probably comes before 'Will Clewline'. In Britain, it also appeared in *The Poetical Register* (1802), p. 340. It was published in America in the *Salem Gazette*, 16 June 1801; *Weekly Museum*, 23 February 1805; and *Windham Herald*, 3 September 1812, without ascription. Reprinted in *1806*, p. 14, under the title 'On the Approach of the Gout'; *1824*, p. 24. Also in *Salem Gazette*, 17 May 1825, as '*By Edward Rushton, of Liverpool, a poet, blind and poverty stricken*', and Burke, p. 30.

Variants:
1 thy] the *1806, 1824*
10 rack] fill *1806, 1824*
12 blunt] bear *1806, 1824*

Commentary: gout is a painful form of joint inflammation caused by crystallisation of excess uric acid from the bloodstream. It was usually thought to affect older, male, affluent patients with a high alcohol intake and was the subject of a huge number of treatises, treatments and satiric pictures in the eighteenth century. It had also been the subject of a number of poems, such as Isaac Hawkins Browne's 'On a Fit of the Gout. An Ode' (*Poems upon various Subjects*, 1768), and Gilbert West's 'Triumph of the Gout' (*Odes of Pindar*, 1753). The *Poetical Works* of Samuel Bishop (1796) contain a number of poems about gout. Thomas Tickell's *A Poem in Praise of the Horn-Book* (1728) was supposedly written 'under a fit of the gout'. Light in tone as it is, this remains a poem of opposition, ironically against the 'aristocratic' illness. Rushton returned to the subject in 'To the Gout', also in *1806*. His death was ascribed to the toxic effects of a gout remedy, 'Eau Medicinale'; *Life*, pp. xxv–xxvi.

2 Turkey carpet] one of the oldest and most expensive types of carpet available in Britain, hence a sign of wealth.
3 board] table.
8] Rushton had kept a tavern in earlier life, but is clearly here signalling that he does not drink alcohol; consumption of alcohol was associated with gout in eighteenth-century medicine (see 'To the Gout').
14] an Alexandrine.

Will Clewline

Source: Will Clewline. By Edward Rushton. Published by Edward Rushton, Liverpool, March 1801. J. M'Creery, printer. Single-sheet broadside with text in two columns and a dramatic illustration at the top, including the detail of a scroll bearing the title of 'The Neglected Tar'; unusually careful work for a printed ballad, part of M'Creery's aspirational campaign for fine Liverpool printing, as evinced in his own poem *The Press* (1803). A coloured version of this engraving (only) is at the National Maritime Museum, Greenwich. The poem appeared, usually with Rushton's name, sometimes under the title 'The Press Gang', in several American newspapers: *The Salem Impartial Register,* 8 October 1801; *The Columbian Courier,* 16 October 1801; *The Weekly Museum,* 21 November 1801; *Western Constellation,* 23 November 1801; *The Herald of Liberty,* 23 November 1801. *The Bee,* 25 November 1801, prints it with a highly approbatory summary of Rushton's poetic career and political views, which latter it proceeded to amplify in an attack on British policy; it associates the poem with 'the well-known melancholy air of *The Galley-Slave'.* It was printed without ascription in John Aikin's *Monthly Magazine* 15 (June 1803), 432, and in *Walker's Hibernian Magazine* (June 1803), 368. Further American instances are in *The Statesman,* 8 December 1808; *American Patriot,* 20 December 1808; *The Essex Register,* 23 September 1809; *The Native American,* 23 January 1813; and *The Yankee,* 29 January 1813, with a long paragraph of commentary on Rushton's work. All of these texts appear to stem from the first broadside copy, rather than the version in *1806,* pp. 10–13. Also in *1824,* pp. 114–16, and in Harland and Wilkinson (1875), pp. 517–19. The 1801 version was reprinted in facsimile by The Castlelaw Press, West Linton, Peeblesshire in a limited edition of 250 copies, 1970.

Variants:
3 those] the *1806, 1824*
17 in] on *1806, 1824*
22 Their] The *1806, 1824*
23 each accent, each glance is desire] delight fills the breast of the sire *1806, 1824*
28 ruffians] hirelings *1806, 1824*
34 the] your *1806, 1824*
56 Let those sufferings and wrongs] O let the foul stain *1806, 1824*

Commentary: impressment, or the policy of crewing ships by forcing those known to have served on ships into the navy during wartime, was a standard British practice, exacerbated at the time Rushton wrote the poem by the pressure to expand the navy during the wars with France. It was also hugely unpopular and controversial, and the subject of much legal as well as lyric complaint; a poem ascribed to John Gay, 'Black-Ey'd Susan', is an early eighteenth-century instance of sentimental attention to the domestic ruptures caused by the practice; Robert Anderson, 'Song XLIV. The Press-Gang', in *Poems on Various Subjects* (1798), is an example from Rushton's own time. See generally Daniel Ennis, *Enter the Press-Gang: Naval Impressment in Eighteenth-Century British Literature* (Newark, NJ: University of Delaware Press, 2002), and for Rushton's poems and the sometimes violent Liverpool context, Dellarosa, chapter 2. 'The Tender's Hold', ascribed to Rushton, is on a similar theme, and the press gang is part of the mental scenery of 'The Return'. Rushton's editorship of the *Liverpool Herald* had been terminated after he refused to withdraw an article against 'an act of atrocity, perpetrated in the port of Liverpool, by a Press Gang' written 'in the language of just indignation'. The Lieutenant in charge of the gang attempted to bully Rushton into a retraction, without success, but his partner, apparently Hugh Mulligan, was sufficiently alarmed for Rushton to relinquish his share in the paper (Shepherd, *Life*, xvi-xvii).

Title] a clewline is a 'tackle connecting the clew of a sail to the upper yard or the mast' (*OED*). A 'captain Clewline' appears in Tobias Smollett's *Lancelot Greaves* (1762), and a sailor called 'Tom Clewline' appears in a song in the collection *The Skylark* (1800), p. 96. An advertisement in *The Morning Chronicle*, 4 May 1810, and *The Morning Post*, 7 May 1810, suggests that 'Will Clewline' may have become a stage or musical character.

1 Jamaica's hot clime] the setting of the *West-Indian Eclogues*, and hence the sugar cargo of line 2; the 'pestilent dews' recall II. 4–5 of that poem. The first line was quoted by Rushton's son, in a letter of 10 March 1832, while he was considering the possibility of an appointment as Attorney General to Jamaica; W. L. Rushton, *Letters of a Templar*, p. 112.

3 boatings] 'the action of loading something on to a boat in preparation for transportation' (*OED*), a no doubt 'perilous' procedure in Rushton's time; he himself nearly drowned when a small boat capsized during his career at sea; see Shepherd, *Life*, xii–xiii.

11–14] the domestic scene is reminiscent of Gray, *Elegy Written in a Country Church-Yard* (1751), 23–24.

15 cocoa-nuts] see *West-Indian Eclogues*, II. 75.

15 tamarind] a fruit-bearing tree, sometimes called the Indian date, native to Africa but widely cultivated in tropical regions.

17–24] the alterations soften the sexual element.

20 younglings] youngsters.

33 tender] William Falconer, himself a poet-sailor, identifies the tender as a small vessel in the King's service used 'to receive volunteers and impressed men, and to carry them to a distant place' in *An Universal Dictionary of*

the Marine (1769), 'Tender'. More generally, it is 'a small ship attending on a larger' (SJ).

39 cat hauling] the 'cat' is the arrangement of tackle which draws up the anchor: Will is hearing the boat move off.

41 Plymouth] one of the main British naval dockyards.

41–42] an insistence on paradox typical of Rushton's political stance; Clewline is treated like a slave by the proponents of national liberty. 'Is to combat', i.e. is made to fight.

48 parish ... relief] the so-called Poor Laws required parishes to provide basic assistance to those born there, if without other means of subsistence. The irony here is that family fails to assist the orphaned children and only the meagre and often harsh conditions of parish relief (often based on the workhouse model, see commentary to 'The Tender's Hold', 56) offer any practical help. Compare Rushton's 'The Neglected Tars of Britain'.

51 bulwarks] defensive fortification; metaphorically, the naval defence of the land during the naval wars.

52 human rights] in the tradition of the American Declaration of Independence, 1776, and Thomas Paine's *Vindication of the Rights of Man* (1791).

53 felons] convicted criminals, who might be 'transported' to the colonies by ship.

53 sons of the main] sailors.

Ode. Sung at St. John's Chapel, Lancaster...

Source: Lancaster Gazetteer, Saturday 24 October 1801, p. 4. Not reprinted or collected. The account on p. 3 of the paper gives the authorship: 'Tuesday last, being the anniversary of the Lancaster Marine Society, a very respectable number of its members went in procession to St. John's chapel, in this town, where, after the service of the day was read, an ode (written for the Society by Mr. Rushton, of Liverpool, *and for which see our last page*), was sang by the charity boys...'. There seems no reason to doubt this ascription; the poem is in Rushton's manner and was probably omitted from the *1806* and *1824* collections because of its similarity to the Liverpool version. It was reprinted as Rushton's, and as not previously published, in Harland and Wilkinson, pp. 527–28, among the 'sea songs'.

Commentary: The Lancaster Marine Society appears to have been constituted on lines similar to those of the Liverpool society. 'Waller' was probably Bryan Waller (1765–1842), whose book *Poems on Several Occasions* was published at Lancaster, as well as London and Cambridge; it contains several Lancastrian allusions, and the dedication is signed from Lancaster. 'Langshaw' was John Langshaw (1763–1832); see ODNB.

21 Lune] The River Lune, which gives Lancaster its name.

23 dearest connexions] the family, illustrated in the next stanza; compare Rushton's use of the phrase 'nearest connexions' in his 'Song' for the Blind School, 4.

30 Sensibility's tear] Sensibility was a late eighteenth-century cultural phenomenon based on human sympathy and dramatically open expression of emotion, particularly through weeping; it was parodied in Jane Austen's *Sense and Sensibility* (1811). 'The Tear of Sensibility' was a well-known song, used as the tune for William Roscoe's celebratory *Song. Sung by Mr. Dignum*, to commemorate the revolution of 1688 (1792).

33 petrel] the storm petrel was associated with tempests from early times.

37] in the tropics.

41–48. The 'Chorus' adds a specifically religious aspect absent from Rushton's poem.

43–44] 'There's a special providence in the fall of a sparrow'; Shakespeare, *Hamlet*, V. ii. 220.

Ode, To France

Source: *Morning Chronicle*, 24 August 1802, over the signature 'Liverpool. Edward Rushton'. According to the Spenserians website, it was also printed in *The Star* of 25 August 1802. In America, it was printed in the *Alexandria Expositor* of 29 November 1802, the *Commercial Register* of 10 December 1802 and the *Salem Register* of 30 December 1802, in each case over Rushton's name but giving the source as the *Manchester Gazette*. As this was edited by Rushton's friend William Cowdroy, it is a very plausible source, but a relevant issue has not been found. The *Monthly Repository of Theology and General Literature*, 9 (June 1814), 362–63 printed the poem with headnote: 'We copy the following verses from the Cambridge Intelligencer, a newspaper published by Mr. B. Flower, during the war of the French Revolution, but which has been so long discontinued that the extract will be new to most of our readers'. Benjamin Flower (1755–1829) was a Unitarian and radical writer, and the *Monthly Repository*, also a Unitarian organ, was in a position to be accurate about the story, but it has not been possible to verify a date of publication in *The Cambridge Intelligencer*. Reprinted as 'To France', *1806*, 32–37, *1824*, 25–30, and in *British War Poetry in the Age of Romanticism: 1793–1815*, ed. Betty Bennett (New York and London: Garland, 1976), pp. 276–78.

Variants:

2 in] of *1806, 1824*

10 Bonaparte] proud Napoleon *1806, 1824*

21–22] *1806* and *1824* substitute:

    When vaunting freemen join'd th' array,

And gloomy squadrons prowl'd for prey,

24 a watry] an oozy *1806, 1824*
45 But] And *1806, 1824*
51 thine] thy *1806, 1824*
58 Despot's] miscreant's *1806, 1824*
66 weak, the timid] weak and timid *1806, 1824*
76 sweep this impious scourge] brush th' audacious wretch *1806*; sweep the audacious wretch *1824*

Commentary: Napoleon Bonaparte (1769–1821), a commander of the French army in the European wars following the French Revolution of 1789, had in effect seized control of government in 1799, by taking the title of First Consul; he was crowned Emperor in 1804, after the first publication of this poem, but earlier admirers of his military prowess had already begun to voice opposition to his apparently megalomaniac pursuit of power. Rushton's poem is unusual in seeing France as the brave land of liberty, during a war which was still very much in progress, despite the peace of Amiens, signed 25 March 1802. See Dellarosa, chapter 7.

1–2] Compare Rushton's 1791 'Song' commemorating the French Revolution, above pp. 76–77.
4 Augean] cleaning out the Augean stables was one of the twelve labours of Hercules in Greek mythology.
19 smoking] steaming.
21] France declared war on Britain in 1793, already being at war with Spain, Portugal, and many other *ancien regime* states of Europe.
28 elate] raised high.
30 submissive act] i.e. of surrender, which would have rescued them from drowning but made them prisoners of war.
33 Matron] mother.
42 huge Brute] a 'war elephant' used in conflicts on the Indian subcontinent.
55] Louis XVI had been executed in January 1793.
69 upheld ... breath] maintained in power by the army.
70 mine] primitive land mines were already in use in Europe and America during the eighteenth century; Rushton's point is the fragility of Napoleon's apparently secure grasp on power.
71 Meteor] i.e. a shooting star, destined to burn out quickly.
75 Bayonet's sway] martial power.
78 adore] worship slavishly.
80] alluding to the pole star used by mariners in navigation.

Stanzas on Blindness

Source: Merrimack Magazine, 21 December 1805. This printed the poem at the request of 'Lysander', who had seen it in *'a Liverpool paper of March last'* and was struck by its *'elegance and taste'* and *'philanthropy'*. The Liverpool paper has not been identified. The poem was in *1806*, pp. 15–17, under the title 'Blindness', and in *1824*, pp. 22–23. After the *1806* publication it was printed in sundry American newspapers: *Enquirer*, 11 August 1807; *Suffolk Gazette*, 31 August 1807; *Miller's Weekly Messenger*, 1 October 1808 (as a specimen of the work of 'the blind bookseller of Liverpool'); *Democratic Press*, 12 December 1810; *The Gleaner*, 1 February 1811; *The Courier*, 20 February 1811; *Essex Register*, 4 December 1825; *Salem Gazette*, 6 December 1825; *New-Hampshire Gazette*, 17 January 1826. It was the first poem in *Gleanings*, pp. 5–6. In Britain it was one of the poems featured in *The Annual Review and History of Literature* 5 (1806), 523, and it appeared without ascription in *La Belle Assemblée*, April 1807, 208–9. The poem was quoted in full in James Wilson's *Life of Thomas Blacklock* (1838), pp. 150–57, and in an article on 'Blind Poets' in *Chambers's Journal*, 465 (26 December 1840), p. 389. The opening was quoted in an article on 'Blind Authors' in *The St. James's Magazine* 17 (August 1866), 111–28. A version of the poem was quoted entire in Thomas Lund's sermon for the Liverpool School for the Blind, *Blindness: Or, Some Thoughts for Sighted People* (Liverpool, 1887), pp. 8–9. Rushton's was a case in point for the chaplain, who also appended a biographical memoir drawn from Shepherd. Partially reproduced in Hugh Gawthrop, *Fraser's Guide to Liverpool and Birkenhead* (London: c. 1855), pp. 289–90.

Variants:
7 mid] 'midst *1806, 1824*
9 can] shall *1806, 1824*
17 If] When *1806, 1824*
28 that] the *1806, 1824*

Commentary: For Rushton's blindness, see commentary on the *Song* from *Hymns, &c.* above. Blind poets had always enjoyed a kind of epic status, because of the legendary blindness of Homer and the documented blindness of Milton, who wrote several poems about it. In the eighteenth century much was made of the Scottish poet Thomas Blacklock (1721–1791), blind from birth. There were contemporary poems by William Wordsworth such as 'The Blind Highland Boy' and Anna Seward's 'Blindness', the latter written for an artist who had lost his sight (*Poetical Works*, 1810), but it is not known if Rushton was aware of these. Rushton does not claim status from his condition, nor make it a personal case; he requests sympathy for all blind people from those who are in a position to help. Rushton would shortly experience some return of sight; see his poem to Benjamin Gibson, below.

11 Sire] father. The domestic scene is reminiscent of that in 'Will Clewline'.
19 red-breast] robin; see 'To a Redbreast'.
26 countless thousands] that is, plenty of money. The idea chimes with the
  'Song' from *Hymns &c. for the Blind*.

To a Redbreast in November, Written near one of the Docks of Liverpool

Source: 1806, pp. 1–6; reprinted in *1824*, pp. 62–66, and Burke, pp. 28–30.

Variants:
55 tempest] tempests *1824*
68 The] That *1824*

Commentary: the folklore of the robin, or redbreast, is very ancient; see Cocker and Mabey, pp. 335–39, and Beilby and Bewick's contemporary *History of British Birds* (1797), which contains the ornithology of the bird as then known. The robin was a favourite character in late eighteenth-century children's literature, e.g. Sarah Trimmer, *History of the Red-Breast Family* (1793). The rhyme 'The North Wind doth Blow', which also features a robin in winter, was known from the seventeenth century, as was the tale of Cock Robin. The robin is less usually celebrated for its song than the other birds Rushton cites, but that is part of the point. He may have known Robert Anderson's sonnet 'To a Redbreast' (*Poems on Various Subjects*, 1798), or some of John Langhorne's poems such as 'Monody, Sung by a Redbreast' or 'To a Favourite Redbreast' (the latter is particularly consonant with Rushton's address). Roscoe contrasts the hum of the town with the song of the robin in his poem *Mount Pleasant* (1777), p. 31. Rushton mentions the robin in other poems, such as 'Stanzas on Blindness'. The wider point of the poem is to attack the inhumanity of Liverpool's trading practices and to offer sympathetic help for the avian poet-figure against a cruel world. It also offers a poignant picture of the confusing sound-world of Liverpool for a blind person in 1806, especially at 44–50. Dellarosa, chapter 1, reads the poem as a riposte to the celebrations of commerce in the work of other Liverpool poets of the time.

1–4] alluding to the ancient tale, known in ballads form from the late
  sixteenth century, of the Babes in the Wood, and the robins who cover
  the lost (dead, in the early stories) children with leaves.
6 sequester'd] separated, private.
13 Throstle] song thrush.
14 nervous] strong; vigorous (SJ).
15 briery bower] bower formed from briars.
20 Chaunt'st] chantest, i.e. sings.

28 half nutrition] half the normal diet.
31–34 notes] punning on the idea of a note of exchange or bank note; compare 'The Throstle', 74.
32 cent. per cent.] recalling Pope's attack on the dominance of money motives in *Epistle to Bathurst*, 372: 'one abundant show'r of *Cent. per Cent*'.
35 Ruddock] one of the earliest English names for the Robin.
47 windlass-song] a sea shanty sung to keep the action of winding the windlass (used on a ship to weigh anchor) in fixed rhythm.
67 craw] 'the crop or first stomach of birds' (SJ).
71 brood] his children, of whom there were at least three.
77 doublet] waistcoat.

Solicitude

Source: 1806, pp. 7–9; reprinted in *1824*, pp. 105–6.

Commentary: there is perhaps some reminiscence, in the use of a repeated name as lyric refrain, of William Cowper's poem 'To Mary', or of Burns's 'John Anderson my Jo', but those are both poems about ageing; Rushton's is on one of his major themes, sexual anxiety.

13 beaux] suitors.
17 gorgeous] 'glittering in various colours; showy' (SJ).

Toussaint to his Troops

Source: 1806, pp. 18–22; reprinted in *1824*, pp. 94–97, and in Williamson, pp. 413–16.

Variants:
The question marks in 10, 14, and 60 are supplied from the *1824* text, as is the spelling of 'whirlwind', 53. *1824* alters 'slave!' to 'slave?', line 38, probably in error.

Commentary: Toussaint Louverture (1743–1803) was a freed slave who became the leader of the slave rebellion on the French colony of Saint Domingue. After much switching of allegiances across the Spanish/French border on the island, the French under Napoleon sent forces to recapture power in late 1801; Toussaint was captured in 1802 and deported to France, where he died in April 1803, though the revolution continued, producing the state of Haiti in 1804. The rebellion and its implications were urgently discussed, in the context of the slave economy, the abolition movement, the threat of violence, and rivalry with France; William Roscoe had written a pamphlet about it in 1792, and an anonymous *Ode: the Insurrection of the Slaves at St Domingo* appeared in the same year. To many liberal commentators, Toussaint seemed to embody the prophetic 'Black Spartacus' predicted by the Abbé Raynal in his huge *Histoire Philosophique de Politique du Commerce et des Etablissements des Européens dans les Deux Indes* (1770), a book much quoted in Hugh Mulligan's book of *Poems, Chiefly on Slavery and Oppression* (1788), which itself includes portrayal of a slave rebellion. For a reconstruction of the events, see Robin Blackburn, *The Overthrow of Colonial Slavery, 1776–1848* (London-New York: Verso, 1998), pp. 161–264; for debate in England see David Geggus, 'British Opinion and the Emergence of Haiti,' in James Walvin, ed., *Slavery and British Society, 1776–1846* (Baton Rouge: Louisiana State University Press, 1982), pp. 123–49; for extracts from the literary material, Williamson 383–420; for a sophisticated analysis of Rushton's poem in terms of the politics of mimicry, see Dellarosa, chapter 6. A number of poets addressed consolatory or celebratory poems to Toussaint himself, in what has been seen as a Romantic mythologisation which potentially dissolved Toussaint's historically specific moment (see Marcus Wood, *Slavery, Empathy and Pornography* (Oxford: Oxford University Press, 2002), p. 234). William Wordsworth's sonnet to Toussaint was published in *The Morning Post*, 2 February 1803, and focused on the imaginative power of the imprisoned Toussaint; even though Toussaint was dead by the time Rushton's poem was published, Rushton presents him as a charismatic and inspiring leader, at the high moment of the live struggle. For Rushton, Toussaint had achieved something of what the rebellious slaves in *West-Indian Eclogues* desired, and was thus a hero. The French, meanwhile, had betrayed their own libertarian revolution of 1789 by succumbing to Napoleon and now by attempting to suppress rebellion. The reviewer in *Monthly Review*, 50 (May 1806), p. 95, commented that Rushton's poem was 'bold and spirited: but it is too long for us to insert, and too compact to be dismembered'.

4 dress] tend.
11–20] Dellarosa, chapter 6, suggests that this stanza echoes the opening lines of Hannah More's *Slavery, A Poem* (1788) in its political invocation of the sun as the figure of Liberty for all.
15 sable warriors] a phrase used by William Mickle, *The Lusiad* (1776), I. 605, to indicate Moorish fighters and by William Broome, 'A Poem on the Seat of War in Flanders' (in *Poems on Several Occasions*, 1739), 209, to indicate an Indian army; more often it signifies a knight wearing black, or Edward the 'Black Prince'. Rushton adapts a heroic martial tradition to include a black resistance army.
28 liberty or death] a slogan more normally associated with the American War of Independence, but it had also been used by the rebellious slaves themselves.
29 usurpation] i.e. Napoleon's seizing of power; see 59, and 'Ode. To France', 65.
35–36] compare Rushton's presentation of sexual violence by white owners ('pallid brood') against female slaves in *West-Indian Eclogues*, IV.

41 tiny race] children. Once again Rushton sees the domestic family as the foundation of all virtue.

43 tamarind] compare *West-Indian Eclogues*, III. 29 and commentary.

55–56] The British, having sent tens of thousands of men to the island in an effort to recapture territory from the French, had withdrawn from their stations in 1798, following heavy losses, and a negotiated treaty.

59 Buonaparte] Napoleon, by this time Emperor of France; compare the 'Ode. To France', above.

67 sharks] compare *West-Indian Eclogues*, III. 63.

68 vultures] compare *West-Indian Eclogues*, III. 16 and commentary.

On the Death of Hugh Mulligan

Source: 1806, pp. 28–30; reprinted in *1824*, pp. 30–32. Printed in America in *Massachusetts Spy* 4 October 1815; *The Shamrock*, 7 October 1815; and the *New-York Weekly Museum*, 11 November 1815.

Commentary: Hugh Mulligan was an Irish writer, copperplate engrave and painter, who came to Liverpool in the 1780s. His book *Poems Chiefly on Slavery and Oppression, with Notes and Illustrations*, was published in 1788 and contained (pp. 38–43) a long 'Epistle to Mr. E— R—.', clearly Rushton, addressed familiarly as 'Ned'. William Roscoe paid him a gentle tribute as a 'kind of Mentor in my youthful years' (Henry Roscoe, *The Life of William Roscoe*, 2 vols (1833), I. 10) and M'Creery featured him as a radical hero in *The Press* (1803), p. 28. The date and place of his death are not certainly known (he married a Sarah Grainger on 15 November 1767 and had several children, but IGI records no death record); but M'Creery appears to lament him as already dead by 1803. In Rushton's elegy, Mulligan appears as Chatterton and Burns had done, a bard of nature and wildness, like a song-bird or shy flower, overlooked if not trampled on by the powerful. The second stanza was quoted in the 'Biographical Sketch of Edward Rushton', *Belfast Magazine*, December 1814, p. 478, as applicable to Rushton's own situation and character. The third stanza was reproduced in the *Monthly Review*'s account of the *1806* volume (50: May 1806, p. 95), with the words 'The reader of sensibility will thank us for inserting the following Stanza'.

2 carols] songs. Compare 'The Maniac', 26.

19–20] Compare Gray, *Elegy Written in a Country Church-Yard* (1751), 55–56: 'full many a flower is born to blush unseen, | And waste its sweetness on the desert air', and Wordsworth, 'She dwelt among the untrodden ways', 5: 'A violet by a mossy stone, | Half hidden from the eye!'.

27 comforting rays] the text in the *New-York Weekly Museum* identifies these as 'The notice of Dr. Corry, and W. Roscoe, Esq.', i.e. John Currie

and William Roscoe, two of the main patrons of the radical circle in Liverpool. Franca Dellarosa points out to me that there was actually a John Corry, an Irish journalist involved in Thomas Troughton's *History of Liverpool* (1810), but the reference here is probably to Currie.
39 meet] appropriate.

To a Bald-Headed Poetical Friend

Source: 1806, p. 31; reprinted in *1824*, p. 92. The whole poem was reprinted, on the score of 'whimsicality', in the *Anti-Jacobin Review*, 23 (March 1806), 336.

Commentary: Baldness is a theme of ancient fables, such as those by Phaedrus, translated into verse by poets including William Somervile and Christopher Smart in the eighteenth century, but it is not itself a common theme of poetry. The friend in question is probably John M'Creery, the Liverpool printer and poet whose *The Press. A Poem* appeared in 1803.

The Ardent Lover

Source: 1806, pp. 38–40 (listed as 'The Lover' on the contents page); reprinted in *1824*, pp. 107–8. Reprinted in Harland and Wilkinson (1875), pp. 339–41.

Variants:
The question mark in 16 is supplied from *1824*.

Commentary:
10 mandate] command.
11 Helen] of Troy.
12 dowdy] 'an awkward, ill-dressed, inelegant woman' (SJ).
14 towering dreams] of a socially-advantageous marriage for his daughter, analogous to the scheming mother's plans in the previous line.
16 sublim'd] uplifted.
21 mantling] blushing, suffused with excitement and colour.
24 strains] strives to win.
24 all nerve] completely 'nerved' or set on the task.
26 pleader] advocate.
31 sacred shrine] church altar, in a marriage service.

The Lass of Liverpool

Source: 1806, pp. 41–43; reprinted in *1824*, pp. 109–10. A piano score for the song, composed by Maththew King (1773–1823), appeared in *La Belle Assemblée*, I. 5 (June 1806), 283–87. Collected in Harland and Wilkinson 1875, pp. 525–26; partly reprinted in Hugh Gawthrop, *Fraser's Guide to Liverpool and Birkenhead* (London, c. 1855), pp. 291–92; reprinted in Joan Pomfret, ed., *Lancashire Evergreens* (Nelson: H. Garrard, 1969), pp. 136–37.

Commentary: one reviewer of the *1806* volume (*Monthly Review*, 50, May 1806, p. 96) commented:'The first two stanzas … present a variety of rich and lively images'.

1 cocoas] see *West-Indian Eclogues* II. 75 and III. 38.
3 Mulatto] a contemporary category designating a person of mixed race.
9 conch] see *West-Indian Eclogues*, III. 27 and commentary.
15 pettrel] i.e. petrel, a family of seabirds; occasionally seen in the Mersey
    estuary. See Cocker and Mabey (2005), pp. 11–27.
21 noxious] because of tropical diseases.

Woman

Source: 1806, pp. 42–43; reprinted in *1824*, pp. 60–61.

Commentary: Rushton revisits some of his exotic imagery to explore further the theme of the vulnerable woman.

1 warbler] i.e. small bird of the type taken by peregrines and other birds of
    prey.
2 north] i.e. north wind.
9 dolphin … prey] see *West-Indian Eclogues*, II. 94–98, and commentary.
23 rattle-snake] used as an image of a male seducer in Samuel Richardson,
    Clarissa (1748), vol. 3, letter XX, a modernisation of the serpent that
    seduces Eve in the Garden of Eden. Rattlesnakes occur throughout the
    Americas, and do prey on small birds.
23 fell] destructive.

Mary's Death

Source: 1806, pp. 60–63; reprinted in *1824*, pp. 14–16.

Variants:
3 'Mong] Thro' *1824*

Commentary: the poem shares the tradition of the pathetic and sentimental madwoman already explored in the two first 'Mary le More' poems.

4 chaunting] chanting.

5 straw shed] perhaps recalling the 'straw-built shed' of Gray's *Elegy Written in a Country Church-Yard* (1751), 18

21 day star] i.e. the sun, normally associated with equality and liberty, as in Roscoe's ballad 'The Day-Star of Liberty'.

44 mantles] spreads over.

45 spoiler] despoiler.

45] in some ways Rushton's intent was clearly to provide a sort of singable folk-tale to be adopted by Irish resistance movements, and this appears to have happened in the case of the two first poems of the set.

The Halcyon

Source: 1806, p. 64; not reprinted in *1824*.

Commentary:

HALCYON] Kingfisher, a bird with much folklore attached to it from ancient times, most notably the idea that it presaged 'halcyon days' or good weather. See Cocker and Mabey (2005), pp. 300–1. Poems had been written about the Halcyon by William Shenstone (1714–1763) and William Hayley (1745–1820); Rushton's kingfisher is rather a predator than a thing of beauty, however.

3 finny train] fish: a common poetic periphrasis in the eighteenth century.

7 lynx-like beam] the eyesight of the lynx was proverbial, but Rushton may be remembering in particular Pope, *Essay on Man*, I. 204, 'the lynx's beam'. See also the *Expostulatory Letter to Washington*.

12] an Alexandrine or extended, 12-syllable line.

The Shrike

Source: 1806, p. 74; not reprinted in *1824*.

Commentary: a variant on 'The Halcyon', except that birds of the shrike family are 'dingy' (2) or dull in colour; its feeding habits, however, earned it the name of 'butcher bird' and it is its predatory habits that Rushton finds emblematic. Beilby and Bewick, pp. 56–61, call it 'the boldest and most sanguinary of the rapacious tribe' and mention the tradition that it can imitate the calls of other birds for hunting purposes. It is much less commonly invoked in poetry than the kingfisher or halcyon. See also Cocker and Mabey (2005), pp. 396–97.

3 throstle] song thrush; see Rushton's poem of the name, below.

6 brake] thicket.

14 reputation dies!] recalling Pope, *Rape of the Lock* (1714), III. 16: 'At ev'ry word a reputation dies'.

Briton, and Negro Slave

Source: 1806, pp. 84–88; not reprinted in *1824.*

Commentary: Rushton omitted the *West-Indian Eclogues* from *1806,* but this poem, in dramatizing a passive woman as the sexualised object of contention between oppressor and oppressed condenses much of those four poems, especially the last. As in the *Eclogues,* the slave speaks in high heroic language, not some version of 'slave' language. *The British Critic* 28 (Nov 1806), 561–62 agreed with Rushton's opposition to slave trade but objected to his characterisation of the West-Indian Planter as 'Briton'.

11 Obi] obeah, a form of folk magic practised in the West Indies, apparently based on Igbo rituals brought by enslaved Africans; compare James Grainger's scornful account, *The Sugar Cane* (1764), IV. 379–405.
18 gibbetted alive] compare *West-Indian Eclogues,* II. 25 and commentary.
21 Egbo] Igbo, one of the main West African peoples targeted by slave traders in the eighteenth century.
29 Shark] compare *West-Indian Eclogues,* III. 63.
44 musquito] the mosquito, the main vector of fever in the tropics.
50 sweets] delights, pleasures.
52 rolling ... eyes] compare 'Toussaint to his Troops', 61.
58 humours] moods, alluding to the renaissance medical theory of the 'humours' of the blood.

Absence

Source: 1806, pp. 89–91; reprinted in *1824,* pp. 130–31. Collected in the section of sea songs in Harland and Wilkinson, pp. 522–23.

Variant:
28 all her sex] all the world *1824*

Commentary:
10 brayls] brails; nautical term for ropes used in the furling of sails. Falconer, *Universal Dictionary of the Marine* (1769), has a full explanation of the term.
21 Pettrels] petrel, a type of seabird; compare 'Lass of Liverpool', 15.
23 Ebon] ebony, a highly-valued black wood.

On the Death of a Much Loved Relative

Source: 1806, pp. 92–96; reprinted in *1824*, pp. 41–44. The poem appeared complete in a sympathetic review of the *1806* volume in the *Annual Review and History of Literature* 5 (1806), 523–25. It appears with Rushton's name in the *Salem Gazette*, 20 April 1808, and in the *Merrimack Intelligencer*, 25 May 1811; *Gleanings*, pp. 12–14.

Commentary: the name of Rushton's sister is not known. According to Rushton's son (*Sketch*, p. 475) and Shepherd (*Life*, p. xiv), Rushton's father set him and one of his sisters up in a tavern after they were expelled from the house; this may be the same sister. In his *The Press, A Poem. Part the Second* (1827), John M'Creery inserted among the 'Miscellaneous Poems' the consolatory verses 'To my Friend, Mr. Edward Rushton, of Liverpool, on the Death of his Sister' (pp. 55–57).

25 sea-boy] Rushton's naval career began at the age of 11.

30] According to Shepherd, p. xiv, Rushton's father took him to London, 'in order to obtain the advice of the most skilful surgical practitioners on his deplorable case. Among others he consulted the celebrated Baron Wenzel, oculist to the King: but neither the Baron, nor any of his brethren of the profession, could render him the least service'. However, he was operated on with more success in 1807 by Benjamin Gibson; see his poem to Gibson, below.

35] according to Shepherd, p. xv, Rushton defended his sister against their stepmother, prompting their expulsion from their father's house: 'an interference on his part to prevent the ill treatment of one of his sisters, so strongly excited the indignation of his father, that, helpless as he was, he banished him from his house, and doomed him to subsist as he could, on the miserable allowance of four shillings a week'.

44 hectic] a type of long-term wasting fever, generally ending in consumptive collapse.

50 pledges] i.e. her children, 'pledges' of her domestic affections.

58 beamless] sightless.

Entreaty

Source: 1806, pp. 97–99; reprinted in *1824*, pp. 132–33.

Variant:
12] the semi-colon is supplied from *1824*; *1806* has a full stop.

Commentary: another poem on the theme of sexual rivalry, with the honest sailor played off against effeminate but wealthier suitors.

9 sparks] fops, overdressed and idle young men.
10 humming-birds] compare *West-Indian Eclogues*, III. 13, IV. 44 and commentary.

A Caution to my friend J. M.

Source: 1806, p. 100; not reprinted in *1824*.

Commentary: similar in theme to 'To a Bald-Headed Poetical Friend'. 'J. M.' here is John M'Creery, the radical printer of Liverpool, who had worked on many of Rushton's poems and whose own poem, *The Press*, which first appeared in 1803, is luxuriant enough of phrase perhaps to prompt this caution. See Introduction.

3 doublet] waistcoat.
3 Nightingale] see commentary to 'The Complaint', 21–22. The nightingale is an undistinguished grey-brown in appearance.
4 Lark] see commentary to 'The Complaint', 17.
6 cocoa] the cocoa bean has a thick rough pod round it.
7 anana] pineapple; compare *Lucy's Ghost* (which M'Creery printed), 29.
7 Pomona] Roman goddess of fruit.
8 stuff] material.
10 deep] dark.

The Throstle

Source: 1806, pp. 101–6; not reprinted in *1824*.

Commentary:
Throstle] song thrush; for the associated behaviour and folklore, see Cocker and Mabey (2005), pp. 355–59, and for contemporary description of its song and nesting habits, Beilby and Bewick, pp. 100–1.
2 dizen'd] to dizen is 'to dress; to deck; to rig out. A low word' (SJ).
4 Gripus] conventional name for a miser, e.g. Pope, *Essay on Man* (1733–1734), IV. 270
16 trills] fast series of alternating notes.

The Complaint

Source: 1806, pp. 111–13; reprinted in *1824*, pp. 134–36.

Commentary:
1] the bullfinch does in fact have a natural song, though not a particularly memorable one, but Rushton refers to the fact that the bird was often

trapped and trained as a singing bird; see Cocker and Mabey, pp. 456–57, and Beilby and Bewick, pp. 138–39.

5] the *Monthly Review* 50 (May 1806), p. 96, objected to line 5, as a defect, paraphrasing 'had formed an attachment'. *1824* dropped the first comma, but left the phrase as it was.

15 cordials] medicines for the heart.

17 Lark] the skylark, subject of many eighteenth-century and romantic-era poems, because of its high song.

19 Robin] see Rushton's 'To a Redbreast', above.

21–22] the nightingale, 'most musical, most melancholy' (Milton, *Il Penseroso* (1645, 62), bird, about whom romantic poets such as Coleridge and Keats wrote with particular intensity, is not found north of a line between the Humber and the Severn; see Beilby and Bewick, pp. 199–202, for a contemporary view and Cocker and Mabey, pp. 340–42 for modern review.

26 disgusting] distasteful.

30 urchin] hedgehog, which hunts by night.

31 harass'd] by hunting. Hares are not actually nocturnal.

38 sue] plead.

39 swain] antiquated poetic term for lover, especially in pastoral verse.

The Pier

Source: 1806, pp. 114–16; not reprinted in *1824*.

Commentary: a relatively straightforward example of Rushton's marine or pierhead songs, a sort of happy-ending 'Will Clewline'.

22 gasket] originally a rope or strip of cloth for securing a furled sail to a yard; Ben is tying off his last sail.

Mary

Source: 1806, pp. 121–27; not reprinted in *1824*.

Commentary: essentially an echo poem to *Lucy's Ghost*, with the gender roles reversed, and a variant on the 'Poor Ben' narrative.

18 tamarind] see *West-Indian Eclogues*, III. 29 and commentary.

31 palsied thing] a decrepit old husband.

56 imprest] pressed on, with a kiss.

66 maniac wildness] compare Rushton's 'The Maniac'.

73 ensign] flag.

93 pompous] highly ceremonial.

The Origin of Turtle and Punch

Source: 1806, pp. 128–31; not reprinted in *1824*.

Commentary: 'Turtle' was a luxury dish, often served with punch at formal dinners and in inns, with the two regarded as natural partners. Despite having run a pub, Rushton presents himself as avoiding alcohol in other poems (e.g. 'Sonnet … On the Approach of the Gout'). This is also one of his few ventures in classical mythology. The song pattern (and the setting) is like that of 'To Anacreon in Heaven', a song from the mid-1780s, the tune of which was used in a number of pro-liberty ballads of the 1790s.

1 ambrosia] the food of the gods in Greek mythology.
3 Bacchus] Greek god of wine and conviviality.
4 yon rolling orb] the earth.
11 termagant] scolding.
11 Juno] wife of Jupiter, the Roman version of Zeus, the ruler of the gods.
14 Neptune] Roman god of the ocean.
16 Venus] Roman goddess of love.
16 Pallas] Athena, Greek goddess of wisdom and technology.
19 God of the strings] Apollo, Greek god of music, pictured with a lyre or harp.
21 Momus] Greek god of mockery and imitation.
22 Hermes] Greek god of messengers.
26–27] the turtle supposedly represents a fusion of three types of animal.
29 hoar] hoary, aged.
35 viands] provisions, food.
37 quoth old thunder] said Jupiter/Zeus, as god of Thunder.

Parody of a Passage in Measure for Measure

Source: 1806, p. 132; not reprinted in *1824*.

Commentary: The speech this blank-verse sonnet parodies is spoken by Claudio in Shakespeare, *Measure for Measure*, III. i. 129ff.

4 mummy] an embalmed corpse.
12 stone] kidney stone or stone in the bladder, in the eighteenth century treated by surgery with no anaesthetic.
13 amputated limb] a task which commonly fell to surgeons on navy ships during the Napoleonic wars.
13 gout] see Rushton's poems 'Sonnet … On the approach of the Gout' and 'To the Gout'.

The Farewell

Source: 1806, pp. 133–36; reprinted *1824*, pp. 117–19; in the section of sea songs in Harland and Wilkinson, pp. 520–21; and in Joan Pomfret, ed., *Lancashire Evergreens* (Nelson: H. Garrard, 1969), pp. 137–38.

Variants:
In *1824*, the speeches are marked by quotation marks.

Commentary: the first of a pair of marine ballads, in the tradition of John Gay's 'Black-Eyed Susan'.

1] the highest sails are fully extended to the ends of the yardarms.
2 windlass] a winding device for the hauling of anchor or pulling of cables, often worked with a rhythmic song to keep time.
7 Mary's imagination could easily have been fuelled by the reports of naval campaigns during the wars with Napoleon: Nelson's death at the Battle of Trafalgar, 1805, had been very extensively reported.
13 handspike] a lever used on ships to maneouvre heavy items such as cannon.
17 blocks] the pullies used in manipulating and controlling ropes and rigging; see Falconer's *Universal Dictionary of the Marine* (1769), article 'Block'.
20 sea-boy] once Rushton's own role; see 'On the Death of a Much Loved Relative', 25
40 abaft] towards the rear of a ship or boat.
51 cat … hawling] see 'Will Clewline', 39, and commentary.
54 skiff] a light boat used for transport between a ship and a port.

The Return

Source: 1806, pp. 137–41; reprinted in *1824*, pp. 120–22.

Commentary: an answer to 'The Farewell', as well as a more optimistic take on the 'Will Clewline' idea, though the sailor's dread of the 'press' (43) and the secret routes taken to get safely home (55) are still emphasised.

1 Cambrian] Welsh.
11 cankering] inwardly gnawing.
15 pursy] 'short-breathed and fat' (SJ).
15 pomp] ceremony, grandeur.
21 sable point] dark headland.
29 sea-mew] gull.

38 gibe] ribbing, teasing.
39 port] bearing.
43 press] impressment, or the press-gang, as in 'Will Clewline'.
44 ought] aught, i.e. anything.

To the Gout

Source: 1806, p. 141; reprinted in *1824*, p. 93.

Commentary: see the earlier poem, 'Sonnet ... On the Approach of the Gout', and commentary.

11] Erasmus Darwin's *Zoonomia; or, the Laws of Organic Life* (1794) has much to say about gout, e.g. at I. 246–47; Darwin firmly associates the illness with the consumption of alcohol.
14 pure element] water.

On the Death of Miss E. Fletcher

Source: 1806, pp. 142–43; not reprinted in *1824*.

Commentary:
The identity of the nineteen-year-old Miss E. Fletcher has not been established.

1 king of terrors] conventional name for Death.
8 temperance] self-control, rather than avoidance of alcohol specifically.
8 dart] arrow, as wielded by Death in the last stanza.
17 unerring] Rushton appears to have forgotten that he has used this adjective at 11 already.

The Chase

Source: 1806, pp. 144–46; not reprinted in *1824*.

Commentary: the poem is similar in theme and vocabulary to Robert Anderson's 'Hark Away', in *Poems on Various Subjects* (1798). Anthony Pasquin, 'A Hunting Song' (from his *Poems*, 1789), also offers a model.

1 clown] 'a coarse, ill-bred man' (SJ), used here to signal someone of low status, compared to the aristocratic 'his ... grace'.
2 brocade] type of lace adornment on cloth, here signifying wealth.
3 hobbies] hobby-horses, particular passions.
4 hark away] a hunting call.

doubles] doubles back, like a pursued animal.

Mock patriots] politicians who claim extravagant love of country but are really interested in career advancement.

Fancy] imagination.

grin … grimace] smile falsely at such mean affectation.

son of Neptune] sailor (Neptune being the Roman god of the ocean).

dun horse] a pun; a dun horse is of a dark colour, but Rushton means that the tradesman must employ a 'dun' or bailiff to recover his money.

The Winter's Passage

Source: 1806, pp. 148–51; reprinted in *1824*, pp. 123–25, as 'The Winter Passage'. It was also quoted complete in the review of the *1806* volume in the *Annual Review and History of Literature* 5 (1806), p. 525.

Commentary:

1 noxious] diseased.

4 sea-beat] beaten by the sea, a common eighteenth-century locution.

5 list] listen.

7 convivial bowls] social drinking.

9 Hibernia] Ireland; a ship returning to Liverpool from America across the Atlantic would see Ireland before Britain.

27 pumps] bilge pumps, hand-operated in Rushton's time.

30 seaboy] Rushton's own first naval role. The sea-boy often features as a focus of pathos in the poems of Mary Robinson.

34 putrid] rotten (after a long voyage).

44 plenteous boards] tables with plenty of food.

53 divers] a family of seabirds often visible around the coast; probably Rushton intends the black-throated diver.

54 snow-clad land] Wales, as in 'The Return'.

Stanzas on the Recovery of Sight…

Source: The Belfast Monthly Magazine II.8 (March 1809), 205. Reprinted in *The Athenaeum*, V.29 (May 1809), 433–35, as STANZAS TO MR. BENJAMIN GIBSON, SURGEON, MANCHESTER, and in *1824*, pp. 84–88, under the title, LINES ADDRESSED TO BENJAMIN GIBSON, OCULIST, OF MANCHESTER, By whose consummate skill the Author was again ushered to the light, after almost total blindness for 33 years, in the year 1807.' In the later versions every second line is slightly indented. It featured in *The Otsego Herald*, 1 December 1810, as reprinted from *The Albany Register*, as a sample of Rushton's work within a larger article on him, and was included in *Gleanings*, pp. 6–9.

Variants:
7 talent] talents *Athenaeum, 1824*
10 famed solution] far-famed science *1824*
20 my ear] the ear *Athenaeum, 1824*
40 Compar'd to] Compared with *Athenaeum, 1824*
74 our young ones] my children *1824*
76 that] which *1824*

Commentary: eye treatments as successful as this were fairly rare in Rushton's time, though one was credibly reported in *The Tatler*, 13–16 August 1709, and many miraculous cures were less credibly reported by practitioners such as John Taylor (1703–1772), who claimed to have cured the composer Georg Handel's blindness. Rushton consulted Benjamin Gibson (1774–1812), an oculist and literary man (he was vice-president of the Literary and Philosophical Society of Manchester), in 1805. Gibson later gave a detailed description of Rushton's condition and the treatment which restored him some sight in *Practical Observations on the Formation of an artificial Pupil, in several deranged States of the Eye* (1811), pp. 75–82, under the heading '*Central Opacity of the Cornea, and total Opacity of the Crystalline Lens, or its Capsule; with or without Adhesions of the Iris to the Cornea*'. Rushton described how much he could see, after the operation, in a letter published posthumously in the *Belfast Monthly Magazine*: see below. Shepherd, *Life*, p. xxiv, says: 'His sight, indeed, was somewhat misty; but it was so far restored, that he could accurately distinguish colours, and the lineaments of the human countenance. He could even discern and discriminate distant objects. He could walk the streets without a guide; and, by the aid of a glass, could read tolerably sized print.' The success of the operation was celebrated in at least three poems: see Appendix II. Gibson died in 1812, prompting *Elegiac Stanzas to the Memory of Benjamin Gibson, Esq.*, in the *Monthly Magazine or British Register*, 33 (June 1812), 452, with words of commendation which do not quite explicitly ascribe the elegy to Rushton (see Appendix I).

1 orbs] eyes.
3 far-off regions] The *Sketch*, p. 475, and Shepherd, *Life*, p. xiv, describe
 Rushton's blindness as caused by Ophthalmia, contracted during an
 outbreak among the slaves on Rushton's ship, near Domenica.
9–11] Shepherd, p. xv, says that Rushton's father took him to many oculists,
 both in Liverpool and London, with no success..
14] these 'ills' are described in Rushton's poem 'Blindness' and in the 'Song'
 for the Liverpool Blind School ascribed to him, above.
17] Rushton went blind at the age of about 18.
69–70] i.e. Rushton can now read independently; see the extracts from his
 letters, below.
81–88] Rushton imagines a situation of this kind in 'The Return'. The

final idea bears some resemblance to the conclusion of Pope's 'Eloisa to Abelard' (1717).

Lines, to the Memory of William Cowdroy

Source: Liverpool Mercury, 9 September 1814. The poem also appeared in the *Lancaster Gazetteer* of 10 September 1814 over the date *'August* 19, 1814' and with the heading: *'FOR THE LANCASTER GAZETTE.* The following Lines to the Memory of Mr. W. COWDROY, late proprietor of the Manchester Gazette, are from the pen of E. Rushton, of Liverpool, a gentleman who was intimately connected with the deceased in bonds of the purest friendship, for upwards of twenty years'. It is possible the poem was earlier published in Cowdroy's own newspaper, but this has not been confirmed. The poem was reprinted in *1824*, pp. 81–83, under the title LINES to the memory of william cowdroy, with every second line slightly indented, and without the date and the subscription 'A Friend'. Reprinted in Richard Wright Procter, *Literary Reminiscences and Gleanings* (Manchester, 1860), pp. 145–46, and in *Letters of a Templar*, pp. 4–5.

Variants:
13 eloquent] bright beaming *Lancaster Gazette*
20 those] these *1824*
28 Freedom's] nature's *1824*
31 corrodes] erodes *Lancaster Gazette*
38 diffuser] dispenser *1824*
40 descended to] gone down to the *Lancaster Gazette*

Commentary: William Cowdroy (1752–1814) was a writer and publisher who had been apprenticed to a Chester printer, John Monk, from 1764 to 1777. After editing the *Chester Chronicle*, and working as a playwright and actor in Chester, he moved to Salford in 1794 and ran the radical *Manchester Gazette* from November 1795, along lines to which Rushton was politically sympathetic. He died on 10 August 1814 and as Rushton himself died on 22 November of the same year, this must be one of the last poems published in Rushton's lifetime. Rushton's letter on the subject is dated 12 August 1814, but was not published until 1903 (below). An obituary of Cowdroy, very similar in character to Rushton's poem, was reprinted from the *Liverpool Mercury* of 12 August 1814 in *Letters of a Templar*, pp. 3–4.

3 perilous rites] presumably, drinking sessions.
6 please and illume] the standard classical requirement of literature, following the Roman poet Horace, to be 'utile et dulce', 'useful and pleasing'.
   fiat] command; 'Nature's dread fiat' is death.

9 There are] there are those.

11 night's 'witching hours] an echo of 'tis now the very witching hour of night', Shakespeare, *Hamlet*, III. ii. 380.

23 PLUMS] eighteenth-century slang term for £100,000.

35 day-star] the sun, associated with the cause of Liberty.

The Fire of English Liberty

Source: Liverpool Mercury, 25 October 1816, as 'By the late Mr. Edward Rushton'. It was reported as having been recited at the second anniversary of the Liverpool Independent Debating Society, of which Rushton had been a member; *Liverpool Mercury*, 7 April 1815. Reprinted in *1824*, pp. 17–20, and in *The Leicester Chronicle*, 15 October 1836. A shorter version of this poem is given above, as 'The Fire of Liberty'.

Variants:

24 shew'd] glow'd *1824*

43 that] this *1824*

50 good] bliss *1824*

Commentary:

2 Norman conqueror] William I (reigned 1066–1087). Rushton would have known accounts of Norman oppressions through Pope's *Windsor-Forest* (1713), though the rest of his poem is at variance with Pope's devotion to the Stuarts and antogonism to post-1688 Protestant kings.

3 curfew] see 'The Fire of Liberty', 3.

4 Saxon hind] peasant of the defeated Saxon people.

14 John] King John (reigned 1199–1216), who signed the Magna Carta in 1215, guaranteeing certain political and civil liberties, which then became part of the mythology of British liberty.

17 Runnymede] site of the signing of Magna Carta.

22 Hampden] John Hampden (1595–1643), whose opposition to Charles I over the issue of ship money was one of the proximate causes of the Civil War which resulted in the execution of the King.

23 Charles] Charles I, reigned from 1625, executed in 1649.

25 Belgic William] William of Orange, who with his wife Mary was invited to accept the crown of England when Charles's son James II (the 'Stuart' of 26) fled to France in 1688.

37 reprobated] i.e. accused by the state of fomenting sedition.

[*Lines addressed to Robt. Southey, Esq.*]

Source: Liverpool Mercury, 4 April 1817, in the 'Original' section, under the heading '*BY THE LATE EDWARD RUSHTON*'. In the same paper, 25 April 1817, appeared an advertisement for the publication that day of '*Lines Addressed to Robt. Southey, Esq. Poet Laureat, on the Publication of his Carmen Triumphale. By the late Edward Rushton*. Printed and sold by E. Smith & Co. Price Two-Pence'. Presumably this was a broadside, like some of Rushton's earlier poems, but no copy has been found. The poem was also printed under an abbreviated title in the *Monthly Repository of Theology and General Literature* 12 (April 1817), 243, and in William Hone's *Reformist Register* I. 20 (7 June 1817). *The Richmond Enquirer*, 19 August 1817, carried the poem, with a note cited below, citing the *Philadephia Democratic Press* as a source. Reprinted in *1824*, pp. 33–37, under a slightly modified title, with a larger indent and the second to last line of each stanza moved to the margin, matching the last line.

Variants:
title] LINES ADDRESSED TO ROBERT SOUTHEY, ON READING HIS "CARMEN
    TRIUMPHALE." *1824*
26 his prey] its prey *1824*
34 men?] the question mark, missing in the copytext, is adopted from *1824*.
44 message] charter *1824*

Commentary: Robert Southey (1774–1843) was a poet associated with what we would now think of as mainstream Romanticism, that is the Lake School of Wordsworth and Coleridge. He had written in 1794 a highly radical, agit-prop drama, *Wat Tyler*, and was associated with many social-reformist causes, including abolition (the *Slave Trade Sonnets*). In February 1808 he visited Liverpool and met Rushton; his signed copy of Rushton's 1806 volume is British Library 1465.c.26, dated 'Liverpool. Friday 19 February. 1808' in a different hand. On 29 March 1808 Southey wrote to Rushton, apparently to forward him some information about the cost of getting vignettes engraved. The letter (which is among the Rathbone papers in the University of Liverpool Library, Special Collections and Archives, RP XXI.9.3.1) concludes (omitting deletions):

> If choice or chance should at any time lead you to our Land of Lakes, I hope you will remember that there is a man living beside Derwentwater who loves poetry & liberty as righteously as you do, & who will be right glad to bid you welcome there.

However, European events were already leading Southey towards more conservative views, and he was appointed Poet Laureate in 1813, an apparent rejection of the radical cause which earned him much public scorn, including the ironic reprinting of *Wat Tyler*. His *Carmen Triumphale for the Commencement of the year 1814* (1814) was a dutifully patriotic celebration of British military success. In reprinting Rushton's poem, which must be one of his latest, Hone's *Reformist Register* recorded Southey's visit in terms which suggest the contents of his letter had become public:

> Mr. RUSHTON, of LIVERPOOL, a patriot, a poet, and an excellent man, of whom, when he died, Mr. ROSCOE said, he was "the last of the Romans," was visited a *few* years ago by Mr. SOUTHEY. That gentleman was then neither Poet-Laureate, nor pensioner. Genius is not confined to aristocracy—RUSHTON was a bookseller, and SOUTHEY took his leave of RUSHTON, who, like MILTON, was blind, across the shop counter, in these words, "If you come to the Lakes, and visit *me*, you will find a man as fond of poetry and *LIBERTY* as yourself." They squeezed each other's hands, and parted. Rushton lived to recover his eye-sight, to see SOUTHEY Poet-Laureate, to read his *Carmen Triumphale*, and to write the following 𝔓𝔬𝔢𝔪...

In its reprint of the poem, the *Richmond Enquirer* made it a kind of political epitaph for Rushton himself:

> *EDWARD RUSHTON is no more! One of the purest and most eloquent advocates of Freedom, one of the kindest, best of men has sunk into the silent grave. I knew him well, I admired his talents, I reverenced his principles, did homage to his virtues, and with feelings of deep regret I learned that he had been consigned to "the house appointed for all living." The following is one of Rushton's last essays in defence of sound principles. It is every way worthy of him and of the cause. Our readers will bear in mind, that Southey was once an able advocate of liberty; he is now Poet Laureat, he is a pensioner of the Crown, and after the battle of Waterloo wrote the impious Ode, the principles of which Mr. Rushton has represented in the following poem.*

See further Dellarosa, chapter 4.

8] the traditional image of the poet as inspired bard, in the manner of Thomas Gray's *The Bard* (1757).

10] As the *Reformist Register* notes with disgust, the quoted line is 'the burden of Mr. SOUTHEY's first effort as Poet Laureate'.

11 boyish brood] Southey and his wife had six daughters and two sons.

46 combin'd] possibly an ironic hit at the 'Combination Acts' of 1799, a legislative measure designed to suppress workers' 'combinations' or unions, widely regarded as subversive during the wars with France.

48 nurse's dreams] superstitious fears and fantasies.

53 immortal stroke] probably the French revolution of 1789, celebrated by Rushton in a number of poems; less likely, the execution of Louis XVI in 1793.

60 resistless] irresistible.

62 partition'd Poland] see Rushton's poem 'To the Memory of Bartholomew Tilski', below.

69 groves of pikes] pikes, essentially a pointed blade on a pole, designed

for thrusting, were used as a mass infantry weapon in European warfare up to about 1700, and thereafter sporadically as a makeshift weapon of popular uprisings, including in Poland in 1794 and Ireland in 1798.

75] i.e. as Southey was widely alleged to have done.

77] as happened to, for example, Rushton's associate John Thelwall, and others such as William Hone, and Thomas Holcroft, under revisions to the definition of seditious libel introduced under William Pitt's government in the 1790s in order to stifle dissent.

The Exile's Lament

Source: 1824, pp. 67–71.

Commentary: like 'Jemmy Armstrong', this late poem belongs in the context of the United Irishmen uprisings of the late 1790s, which also lie behind Rushton's 'Mary le More' triptych. Thomas Campbell's 'Exile of Erin' and George Nugent Reynolds's 'Exiled Irishman's Lamentation', are among many poems providing models.

9 Ross] Rushton probably intends New Ross, County Wexford, site of a battle in the 1798 uprising.

10 Gorey] a town in County Wexford, where some of the fighting in the 1798 uprising took place.

12 hoary] white-haired, hence venerable.

13 stay] prop, support.

30 girt] surrounded.

31 foreign shore] Rushton supplies a number of details (see e.g. 66–67) suggesting that the exile is taking place in a much warmer climate, or possibly among several warmer regions, but nothing that locates any specific region. Many fugitives and other emigrants from Britain went to America, which may be in Rushton's mind here.

45–48] the duty of self-determination, even if it involves 'rebellion' against authority, had been endorsed by Rushton in the *West-Indian Eclogues* and in many other subsequent poems.

51 bland] mild.

57 Zephyrs] poetic name for the West wind, traditionally gentle.

58 Flora ne'er reposes] Flora is the goddess of flowers; her not resting suggests the climate is perpetually springlike.

61 genial] cheerful.

79 grand stroke] Rushton is thinking of an event such as the French Revolution, so much celebrated in his other poems.

The Coromantees

Source: 1824, pp. 72–76. Reprinted in Williamson, 199–202.

Commentary: 'Coromantees' is a name, corrupted from the West African coastal town of Kormantse in modern Ghana, given to slaves taken from that region, often to Jamaica, where they developed a reputation for hard work, but also for resistance and rebellion; see e.g. 'Africanus', *Remarks on the Slave Trade* (1788), pp. 51, 67. Hence their fierce fighting capability in Rushton's poem, and the fears of the master of the ship. As Williamson notes, the event depicted would date from before the abolition of the slave trade in 1807, though the poem itself was written later. There would be no need to suppose a single factual basis for what is essentially an exemplary narrative: there is a long tradition, from Aphra Behn's *Oroonoko* (1688) if no earlier, of the faithless European betraying the heroic African. However, Rushton's friend Shepherd told a similar story of a Liverpool slave ship under attack from a French privateer in 1794, during a speech to the Concentric Society in Liverpool, reported in the *Belfast Monthly Magazine*, 11.65 (December 1813), 484–89, at p. 487. This was no doubt the speech that Rushton advertised as available from his shop in the *Liverpool Mercury*, 21 January 1814. See Dellarosa, chapter 4.

1 Barbadoes] Barbados had been colonised by the British since 1627; by 1660 it had been largely converted to sugar plantations, worked by slaves.

3] i.e. a ship bringing new slaves from Africa.

5 quarter] 'that part of a ship's side which lies towards the stern'; Falconer, *Universal Dictionary of the Marine*, (1769) s.v. 'Quarter'.

6 tri-colour'd flag] of France.

7 nine-pounders] cannon.

13–15] these creatures are all earlier described by Rushton in *West-Indian Eclogues*.

37] compare 'Toussaint to his Troops', 61.

61] the Bull Shark is found in freshwater rivers, including the Congo.

66 bashaw] 'a title of honour and command among the Turks' (SJ); used ironically here to mock the renewed self-confidence of the whites on the ship.

73 lordling] Compare 'Song, Sung at the celebration of the anniversary of the French Revolution', 11.

78 oculist] no doubt inspired by Rushton's productive treatment by the oculist Benjamin Gibson.

An Epitaph on John Taylor...

Source: 1824, p. 77. *The New York Times* of 5 January 1896 prints a version of
the poem, with a tentative ascription to Roscoe, as having been inscribed on
Taylor's grave. The stone is reported as neglected and mutilated. The epitaph
is said to be widely published, and widely admired, but the only printed
source cited is Benson J. Lossing, *Vassar College and Its Founder* (New York,
1867), where Matthew Vassar, founder of Vassar College, is recorded as having
particular admiration for the final line. It is reprinted, from the *1824* text with
due ascription to Rushton, in *Records of Christ Church*, ed. Helen Wilkinson
Reynolds (1911), p. 242.

Commentary: according to the same newspaper report, Taylor's tombstone is
'in front of Christ Church on Academy Street, Poughkeepsie, New York' and
bears the following confirmatory details:

> In this spot
> was interred
> John Taylor
> Attorney at Law
> the eldest son
> of Doctor John Taylor
> of Bolton le Moors, England,
> who died of the yellow fever
> Sept. 11th, 1805.
> Aged 36 years.

The particular connection with Rushton is not known, though the political
sympathy is obvious; Taylor's father is supposed to have been an associate
of Roscoe. In *Records of Christ Church*, Reynolds gives further details of the
location of the stone, which had been brought from the original grave in New
York to the 'English Burying Ground at Poughkeepsie' by Taylor's relatives.
Yellow fever is mentioned in several of Rushton's poems, though normally in
connection with tropical regions.

6] John Hampden (1595–1643), John Milton (1608–1674) and John Bradshaw
   (1602–1659) were all heroes on the parliamentary side of the English Civil
   War because of their opposition to the autocracy of Charles I. Hampden
   and Milton were mentioned together in Thomas Gray's *Elegy Written in a
   Country Church-Yard* (1751), though less sympathetically than in Rushton's
   poem.
14 slave] as often, Rushton uses the literal word 'slave' to indicate a
   metaphorical state of willing submission to an oppressive political state.

To the Memory of Bartholomew Tilski

Source: 1824, pp. 78–80.

Commentary: Poland was partitioned for a third time in 1795, effectively ending its status as an independent nation and leaving it divided between Austrian, Russian and Prussian overlordship. The third partition was drawn up after an unsuccessful nationalist rising led by Andrzei Tadeusz Kosciuszko (1746–1817), a figure celebrated in a number of romantic-era poems, e.g. Henry Cary, *Ode to General Kosciusko* (1797), and John Keats, 'To Kosciusko' (*Poems,* 1817). William Smyth, another poet in the 'Roscoe circle', wrote a poem about Kosciuszko in his *English Lyricks* (1797, p. 41). British awareness of the situation was generally high; see Dellarosa, chapter 4. After the failure of the 1794–5 uprising, there were several further nationalist rebellions, of the kind Rushton refers to here; Poland did not become a full nation state again until after the First World War, and was not free from Russian influence until the fall of the Berlin Wall. Rushton refers to the Polish situation in his '[Lines Addressed to Robt. Southey]', 62. Nobody else appears to have written a poem about Tilski, or indeed anything at all: I have been unable to find any reference to this particular event in standard histories of Poland.

13 awful] awe-inspiring.
14 melting] with pity. In poetry 'melting maid' normally signals amorous warmth.
17 vampires] bloodsuckers. The vampire as a figure was yet to feature prominently in popular horror literature of Britain, but had appeared in Robert Southey's epic poem *Thalaba the Destroyer* (1797).
34 Bartle] i.e. Bartholomew.
37 Dwina] the main river of modern Poland is the Vistula; the Western Dvina, as it is now known, enters the Baltic in the Gulf of Riga, in modern Latvia.

Jemmy Armstrong

Source: 1824, pp. 98–101.

Commentary: an expression of Rushton's ongoing concern with the situation in Ireland, in the same period as the 'Mary le More' triptych; mentioned by Rushton's son as a recent poem in the *Biographical Sketch,* p. 477. Charles Hamilton Teeling, *Sequel to Personal Narrative of the "Irish Rebellion" of 1798* (1832), pp. 44–45, records the Armstrong story as an actual truth, 'so affectingly recorded in the simple and beautiful lays of my late valued friend—the friend of the human race—Edward Rushton of Liverpool'. Teeling sets the event in Lisburn, but it remains unconfirmed in modern accounts. The materials collected in *Literary Remains of the United Irishmen of 1798*, ed. R. R. Madden (1887), include a number of similar narratives of rebels refusing the offer of pardon in exchange for information, such as 'Death Before Dishonour; or, The Four Irish Soldiers', pp. 177–79, and it seems likely that Rushton exemplified an attitude in the poem rather than recording an actual event; see also Dellarosa, chapter 3.

9 wrongs of the female] Rushton probably intends this to refer to rape, used
  as weapon of oppression, as in 'Mary le More'.
11 fire-brand] i.e. the kind of cottage-burning also narrated in 'Mary le
  More'.
12 castle] Dublin castle, the seat of British government in Ireland.
17–18] for similar views see 'Toussaint to his Troops'.
21 union] the United Irishmen movement associated with Wolfe Tone
  (1763–1798)
26 state culprit] Armstrong is deemed to be a traitor by the state.

Commentary: Prose

Expostulatory Letter to George Washington

Source: Expostulatory Letter to George Washington, of Mount Vernon, in Virginia, on his continuing to be a Proprietor of Slaves. By Edward Rushton. Liverpool Printed, 1797.

This is a 24-page duodecimo pamphlet, perhaps printed by M'Creery. A 16-page octavo version was printed in Lexington, Kentucky, in 1797, by the abolitionist John Bradford (1749–1830) (ESTC: W5158). A New York broadside (ESTC: W17382), originally thought to date from 1797 but now redated to the 1830s, also exists. It was also prominently reprinted in *The Time-Piece*, 26 May 1797. The text was quoted and discussed in the *Belfast Monthly Magazine*, I.2 (October 1808), pp. 90–91, by 'N. K.', in an article entitled 'Strictures against the Character of General Washington'. It was more fully reprinted in the same magazine, VIII.45 (April 1812), pp. 266–71, and in *1824*, pp. 165–80. A later American text was printed by William Lloyd Garrison at Boston in 1831, as part of his campaign to free American slaves; and by the same publisher in *The Abolitionist* (Boston, 1833), pp. 11–14 and *The Liberator*, 12 January 1833. It also appeared on the front page of the New York paper *The Colored American*, 18 November 1837.

Variants:
children that] children who *1824*
inferior order of being] inferior order of beings *1824*

Commentary: George Washington (1732–1799), the hero and first president of the newly-independent America, indeed had slaves on his estate at Mount Vernon, Virginia; for discussions of Washington's position in respect of his slaves and the partial solutions reached at his death, see Henry Wiencek, *An Imperfect God: George Washington, His Slaves, and the Creation of America* (New York: Farrar, Straus and Giroux, 2003), and Philip D. Morgan, '"To Get Quit of Negroes": George Washington and Slavery', *Journal of American Studies*, 32. 3 (2005), pp. 403–29.

The pamphlet appears to have been conveyed to Washington on 21 October

1796 by the agency of Ralph Eddowes, an emigré Liverpool Unitarian (see Dellarosa, chapter 7, for a full discussion). Rushton was far from the only writer to hold that the American ideal of liberty was incompatible with the keeping of slaves; Samuel Johnson's anti-colonist pamphlet, *Taxation no Tyranny* (1775), p. 89, had sneered 'how is it that we hear the loudest yelps for liberty among the drivers of negroes?'. Rushton had already made the point in his poem on the American revolution, and he would make it again in his letter to the radical political theorist Thomas Paine, below. Rushton's pamphlet was tartly reviewed by the Tory journal the *British Critic*, 11 (1798), 216. The printing of the *Letter* in *The Time-Piece* prompted a poem of appalled protest from 'Matilda' in the same paper, 29 May; as Dellarosa shows (chapter 7) 'Matilda' was Hannah Lawrence Schieffelin, wife of a New York merchant. She was answered in the same paper, by 'Caroline', 23 June 1797; a hostile account was given in the *Minerva and Mercantile Evening Advertiser*, 9 June 1797, with a short prose rejoinder in *The Herald*, 10 June 1797. *The Time Piece* of 12 June 1797 further defended Rushton's views against attack. As the publication history shows, it remained a powerful document in the struggle for abolition in America, though William Cobbett took issue with Rushton's stance in *Cobbett's Weekly Register*, 26 June 1830. A sketch of 'Liverpool Fifty Years Ago' by Richard Davis Webb, published in *The Liberty Bell* (Boston, 1849), contains a tribute to Rushton based on the effects of the *Letter*.

Epigraph] Adapted from Rushton's 'Stanzas on the Anniversary of the American Revolution', 37–40.

Where there is yet shame ... virtue] Samuel Johnson, *A Journey to the Western Islands of Scotland* (1775), p. 10.

private citizen ... unambitious] on the classic Roman model of Cincinnatus, 519–430 BC, who took command of Rome during an invasion and relinquished the status of dictator immediately the threat was defeated, returning to his farm. Cincinatti is named after him, partly as an honour to Washington. 'Ambition' had been a key enemy in Rushton's poems of the American War of Independence.

Arthur Young] Young (1741–1820), a voluminous writer on agriculture and economics, and a vehement opponent of the 'enlightenment' effects of the French Revolution, e.g. *The Example of France a Warning to Britain* (1793). The exact quotation has not been traced.

Hurricanes] see *West-Indian Eclogues*, IV. 42.

Potowmack] the Potomac, river flowing into Chesapeake Bay on the Atlantic coast of America; Mount Vernon lies on its northern bank.

torpedo] in Rushton's day, a fish which gave an electric shock when touched.

Jefferson] Thomas Jefferson (1743–1826), one of the authors of the American Declaration of Independence, and president of the United States of America, 1801–1809, during which time he drafted the law banning importation of slaves into America, answering Britain's Abolition of the

Slave Trade. The quotation can be found more fully in his *Notes on the State of Virginia* (1794), p. 201. 'Crawford' is Adair Crawford (1748–1795), author of *Experiments and Observations on Animal Heat* (1787).

sable race] for this term see commentary to *West-Indian Eclogues*, I. 12.

lynx's eye ... noon-tide bats] poignant once more, given Rushton's own physical blindness; the 'noon-tide bats' appear to be his own invention, though the lynx's eye is proverbial; compare 'The Halcyon', 7.

"born in a land of liberty"] as Rushton's note indicates, the words are from Washington's response to the French Ambassador's speech; widely reported, e.g. in *A Prospect from the Congress-Gallery, during the Session, begun December 7, 1795* (1796), pp. 60–62.

quakers] as in Britain, Quakers were among the most prominent abolitionists in America; Pennsylvania, founded by the Quaker William Penn, had passed a law manumitting the future children of slaves in 1780, and other states in the North passed similar laws.

cow-skin] i.e. a whip; compare *West-Indian Eclogues*, I. 28.

"Then what is man ...] William Cowper, *The Task* (1785), II. 26–28.

"ages to come...] from the same speech as "born in a land of liberty", above.

yellow dirt] gold, money; compare *The Dismember'd Empire*, 170.

[*Letter to Thomas Paine*]

Source: *Belfast Monthly Magazine*, 3:17 (December 1809), pp. 417–18. Identified by 'K' (John Hancock, one of the editors), as the work of Rushton in the obituary in the same magazine, December 1814, p. 478n, which quotes from the text, and also by the running title on p. 417 of the present issue: '*E. Rushton's Letter to T. Paine, on the Slave-trade*', and in the Index to volume 3. Reprinted as Rushton's in *Gleanings*, pp. 9–12; in *The Liberty Bell* (Boston, 1849), pp. 155–60; and *The Liberator*, 23 February 1849.

Commentary: Thomas Paine (1737–1809) had written *Common Sense* (1776) in defence of the separatist American colonies and *Rights of Man* (1791) in defence of the French revolution. It is not entirely clear whether he was the author of the abolitionist tract, *African Slavery in America* (1775) sometimes attributed to him. See James W. Lynch, 'The Limits of Revolutionary Radicalism: Thomas Paine and Slavery', *The Pennsylvania Magazine of History and Biography*, 123.3 (July 1999), pp. 177–99, and Dellarosa, chapter 7.

Osnaburgh Frock] a kind of rough linen outergarment, named after a town in Germany, the common dress of Jamaican slaves, according to John Stewart, *An Account of Jamaica* (1808), p. 232.

"tyranny and martyrdom...] from Paine, *The American Crisis* (1796), p. 13.

Jefferson] see commentary to *Expostulatory Letter to George Washington*,
above.

Horne Tooke] John Horne Tooke (1736–1812), radical politician, tried for and
acquitted of high treason during the height of Pitt's repression in 1794.

Cobbett] William Cobbett (1763–1835), a vociferous campaigner for political
reform; brought Thomas Paine's remains back to Britain in 1819, and,
according to W. L. Rushton's *Letters of a Templar* (1903), pp. 60–61, gave
Rushton's son Edward a fragment of Paine's gravestone. Cobbett had
voiced objections to the elder Rushton's pamphlet against Washington, and
nick-named the son, also a prominent reformer, 'Roaring Rushton', during a
long series of political stand-offs; see also *Letters of a Templar*, p. 57.

[*Monthly Retrospect of Politics*]

Source: The Belfast Monthly Magazine, V.25 (August 1810), pp. 150–51. Identified
as Rushton's work in the *Biographical Sketch* of Rushton, in the same magazine,
December 1814, p. 478n.

Commentary:
Cobbett] See commentary to the [Letter to Thomas Paine], above. Cobbett
had been sentenced to two years' imprisonment in 1810 after publishing an
article critical of the flogging of some militiamen engaged in a protest at Ely.
ideal picture] imaginary scene.

[*Extracts from Letters*]

Source: Biographical Sketch of Edward Rushton, in *Belfast Monthly Magazine*,
XIII.77 (December 1814), 474–85, the section following the sketch proper, by
Rushton's son Edward, with further comments from 'K', the co-editor John
Hancock, including this selection of private letters, introduced with the words:
The mind of a virtuous ingenuous man may be best known by his
writings, and familiar letters written in the freedom of friendship, are
peculiarly illustrative of the mental temperament. The writer of these
pages is happy to have it in his power, to communicate some extracts
from letters with which Edward Rushton occasionally favoured him,
which shew the man ...
The selection begins with Rushton's comments on 'public' matters, then turns
to 'the domestic scene, the true place for the display of all the milder virtues'.

Commentary:
Orange faction] i.e. the supporters of Protestant ascendancy in Ireland,
which had since 1802 been governed directly from Westminster.
outrages] including, according to his son, being shot at; see Introduction.

Roscoe] William Roscoe was elected, somewhat surprisingly, as one of the
Liverpool members, in the election of November 1806; Rushton voted for
him. There were many songs and ballads amongst the public propaganda,
but nothing suggesting Rushton's involvement in the campaign. The
figure on election spending is taken from *A Compendious and Impartial
Account of the Election at Liverpool … November 1806.* (1806), p. x, and
confirmed in Wilson (2008), pp. 141–42. See also *An Impartial Collection
of the Addresses, songs, squibs, etc. that were published at Liverpool, during
the election of members of Parliament, in November, 1806. …* (1806).
Rushton did not apparently vote in the 1807 election which unseated
Roscoe (*The Poll for the Election of members of Parliament, for the Borough
& Corporation of Liverpool … May 1807* (1807). Roscoe's son Edward was
among the proponents of parliamentary reform, to remove the 'borough
mongers', which resulted in the Reform Bill of 1832; much of *Letters of a
Templar* is concerned with his activities in that respect.
soap-lees] the dregs formed in the making of soap, sometimes used as a
medicine in the eighteenth century, but also regarded as a smelly nuisance.
most wretched state] because of the collapse in trade caused by the war with
the French.
Maelstrom] the Moskstraumen or tidal whirlpool among the Lofoten Islands
of Norway, but figuratively, any whirlpool.
answer every demand] pay every debt and financial commitment.
stuff … dreams] from Prospero's speech, Shakespeare, *The Tempest*,
IV. i. 156–57.
The —] Rushton probably wrote something like 'The Ministry'.
breech itself] put on breeches as a sign of maturity, as a male child would do
at a certain point in his upbringing, in Rushton's time.
such a —] presumably some insulting term for the government.
Gibson] Benjamin Gibson, oculist, of Manchester, to whom Rushton
addressed a poem of thanks, above. Three of the poems listed in
Appendix II celebrate the partial return of Rushton's sight.
marriage of my daughter] *The Athenaeum*, I.6 (June 1807), 655, reported
the marriage of 'Mr. Richard Preston, liquor merchant, to Miss Isabella
Rushton, eldest daughter of Mr. Edward Rushton, of Paradise Street'; also
announced in the *Lancaster Gazette*, 23 May 1807, giving the name as
Richard Prescott.
wife … daughter] The death of Mrs Rushton was reported in the *Monthly
Magazine or British Register*, 31.210 (March 1811), 187, and that of Ann
in the same magazine, 31.214 (July 1811), 587, giving her age as 19. Ann's
death was also announced in the *Lancaster Gazette*, 1 June 1811. A visit
to their gravestone in St. James's Cemetery is recorded with a transcript
in Richard Wright Procter, *Literary Reminiscences and Gleanings* (1860),
p. 142; the dates given there are 31 January 1811 for Isabella (then aged 56)
and 25 May 1811 for Ann (aged twenty).

the Lord giveth] from the Book of Job, I.21.

every evil is necessary] the argument that since God is all-wise and good,
   every bad thing that happens must serve a higher purpose, espoused by e.g.
   Soame Jenyns, *A Free Enquiry into the Nature and Origin of Evil* (1757).

whatever is, is right] from Alexander Pope, *Essay on Man* (1733–1734), I. 294.

greatest misery] more or less Rushton's own words in the letter of 11
   September 1806.

A Few Plain Facts Relative
to the Origin of the Liverpool Institute for the Blind

Source: Liverpool Mercury, 12 and 19 December 1817, with the split occurring
just before Christie's letter is quoted. Rushton's 'first letter' is reprinted in
Royden, p. 262.

Commentary: Royden, pp. 26–41, discusses the rival claims of Dannett, Christie
and Rushton, quoting liberally from this text and from archive material; the early
documents are partially reprinted among the appendices. Apparently Rushton
drew up this account in 1804, having heard that Dannett was claiming more
than his due. Rushton's son later sent the material to the *Liverpool Mercury*, which
published his covering letter on 31 October 1817, though the material itself did
not appear until December. The writing has many aspects in common with the
'Song' for the Blind School and his 'Stanzas on Blindness'. Rushton seems to have
had little to do with the Blind School after its foundation, though one Thomas
Rushton forwarded Roscoe a verse inscription for the doorway on 8 August 1800
(Liverpool Record Office, 920 ROS/4259).

Marine Society] see Rushton's poem 'Written for the Anniversary of the
   Liverpool Marine Society'.

"Our doubts are traitors ...] Shakespeare, *Measure for Measure*, I. iv.77–78.

Lowe] Robert Lowe, according to Royden, pp. 32, 39.

Dannett] The Reverend Henry Dannett, Anglican clergyman, chaplain of St.
   John's Church, Liverpool, and author of an abolitionist tract, *A Particular
   Examination of Mr. Harris's Scriptural Researches on the Licitness of the
   Slave Trade* (1788).

Christie] John Christie, d. 1811.

gratuitous] free.

Alanson] Edward Alanson (1747–1823), surgeon to the Liverpool
   Dispensary and author of *Practical Observations on Amputation, and the
   After-treatment* (1779); see *ODNB*.

Gore] John Gore (1738–1803), printer and bookseller, proprietor of the
   newspaper then known as *Gore's General Liverpool Advertiser* as well as of
   the most notable trade *Directory* of Liverpool in the period.

Billinge] Thomas Billinge, Liverpool printer and bookseller, proprietor of the *Liverpool Advertiser and Marine Intelligencer.*

Roscoe] William Roscoe (1753–1831), Liverpool scholar, radical and philanthropist; see Introduction, and *ODNB.*

Smyth] The Rev. John Smyth; see commentary to the 'Song'. [From *Hymns &c. for the Blind*].

Carson] Richard Carson, according to Royden, pp. 33, 39.

Sutton] not identified.

An Attempt to Prove Prove that Climate, Food, and Manners, are not the Causes of the Dissimilarity of Colour in the Human Species.

Source: 1824, pp. 181–212.

Commentary: Shepherd (p. xviii) suggests this essay was read to an early meeting of the Literary and Philosophical Society; more probably, it was read posthumously in tribute, as indicated by the *List of Communications Laid Before the Literary & Philosophical Society of Liverpool, Since its Institution in 1812, to the end of Session Tenth, 1821* (Liverpool, 1822), p. 12, whch lists 'On the Colour of the Skin of the Negro', an 'unpublished essay' by Rushton, as having been read on 7 April 1815.

"When a rich man speaketh..."] Ecclesiasticus, 13.23; but see also commentary to *Neglected Genius*, 83–84.

leviathan] see commentary on Rushton's poem 'The Remedy' ['The Leviathan'] above.

sable] black; widely used in Rushton's poems as a poetic indicator of value.

Benin] country in West Africa, in the slave trade region.

Calabar] city in what is now Nigeria, West Africa.

Negroland] term widely used in Rushton's period to denote African territories; a map of *Negroland and Guinea, with the European Settlements* was published by Hermann Moll in 1736.

Barbary] North Africa, home to the Berber peoples (now known as the Maghreb).

Moors] term denoting North African Muslim peoples, particularly from Morocco.

Buffon] Georges-Luis Leclerc, Comte de Buffon (1707–1788), naturalist, whose *Natural History of Animals, Vegetables, and Minerals*, 6 volumes (1775–1776) is the main focus of Rushton's counter-argument; see Buffon's chapter 'Of the Varieties in the Human Species', I. 171–292.

Clarkson] The abolitionist, Thomas Clarkson (1760–1846), who called on Rushton in 1787, discussed colour as a racial marker in *An Essay on the*

Slavery and Commerce of the Human Species, Particularly the African (1786), part III, chapter VIII, pp. 178–216.

Ramsey] The Rev. James Ramsay, whose *An Essay on the Treatment and Conversion of African Slaves in the British Sugar Colonies* (1784) Rushton cites in *West-Indian Eclogues*; Ramsay discusses influences on skin colour in Chapter IV, 'Natural Capacity of African Slaves Vindicated'.

Jamaica] see Commentary to *West-Indian Eclogues*.

Antilles] the group of islands between the Caribbean and Florida, most of which were run as European colonial slave plantations in the eighteenth century.

Senegal] river of West Africa forming the border between the modern countries of Senegal and Mauritania.

Nile] African river which discharges into the Mediterranean at Cairo. The Nile and the Senegal do not share a source.

patriarchal] after the manner of the biblical patriarchs, i.e. living by nomadic farming.

Tongataboo] Tongatapu, the main island of the Tonga group in the south Pacific; it had been visited by Captain James Cook on his first major expedition, 1772–1775.

extensive view of mankind] recalling the opening of Samuel Johnson, *The Vanity of Human Wishes* (1749): 'Let Observation with extensive view, | Survey Mankind, from *China* to *Peru*'.

Framer of the Universe] Rushton tends to avoid using the word 'God' and instead uses abstractions such as these, in a fashion which indicates Unitarian sympathies.

Cape of Good Hope] conventionally thought of as the southernmost tip of the African continent.

St. Lawrence] river flowing from Lake Ontario to the Atlantic, marking the border between modern Canada and the United States of America.

Kamschatka] a peninsula at the eastern extremity of Russia.

Nootka Sound] between Nootka Island and Vancouver Island in modern British Columbia.

Labrador] north-eastern region of modern Canada.

Brazil … Mozambique … Angola] modern Mozambique is slightly south of Angola, on the African continent, and both are south of Brazil.

Mississippi] river running more or less south into the Gulf of Mexico, forming a natural border between several states of the United States.

Chili] i.e. Chile, on the west side of the South American continent.

Magellanic coast] on either side of the Straits of Magellan, at the southern end of the South American landmass.

Terra del Fuego] the southernmost region of South America.

Caribbs] i.e. Caribs, the indigenous peoples of the northern coasts of the South American continent, after whom the Caribbean is named.

Aborigines] indigenous peoples, not specifically Australian.

naturalist] Buffon, as Rushton notes.

Quito] capital city of modern Ecuador.

Andes] the chain of mountains running down the western side of South America.

New Zealanders] New Zealand had been known to Europeans since the seventeenth century, but it became much better known in Britain after Captain Cook's visit of 1769.

Friendly, Society and Sandwich islands] groups of islands in the Pacific; the 'Friendly' islands are now known as Tonga; the Society Islands are now part of French Polynesia; the Sandwich Islands are part of the Hawaii group.

Pennant] Thomas Pennant (1726–1798), travel writer and natural historian.

Barrington] Daines Barrington (c. 1727–1800), jurist who had written about the potential for travelling to the North Pole, among other natural history topics.

Forster] either Johann Reinhold Forster (1729–1798), or Georg Forster (1754–1794), both of whom had published accounts of circumnavigations, the latter with Cook. The former taught at the Warrington Academy for dissenters.

Otaheite] the name by which modern Tahiti, visited by Cook in 1769, was then known.

sophistry] artificial reasoning.

Darien] area of the Panamanian isthmus, scene of a disastrous attempt to establish a Scottish colony in the 1690s.

New Holland] colonial-era name for the continent of Australia.

New South Wales] the first British colony in Australia, from 1788.

Adventure Bay] area of the island of Tasmania, named after one of Cook's ships in 1773.

Endeavour River] river of northern Queensland, Australia, named after Cook's own ship, in 1770.

Van Dieman's Land] modern Tasmania.

Cook] James Cook (1728–1779), the most famous of the explorers sent out from Britain to map lesser known areas of the ocean; his three main voyages were extensively covered in the travel literature of the late eighteenth century.

Adanson] Michel Adanson (1727–1826), *A Voyage to Senegal, the Isle of Goree, and the River Gambia* (1759), p. 67.

St. Vincent] a volcanic island in the Caribbean.

Plantain] see *West-Indian Eclogues*, II. 32.

Kangaroo] 'discovered' (for Europeans) by Sir Joseph Banks (1743–1820), naturalist on Cook's first major voyage, in 1770.

yeddoes] perhaps the eddoe, an Asian root vegetable introduced into the West Indies in the colonial era; it does not seem to be associated with South Sea islands, however.

finny tribe] i.e. fish; compare 'The Halcyon', 3.
lympit, welk] limpet, whelk.
Owhyhee] Hawaii.
Gambia] one of the main rivers running through Senegal.
Mandingo] West African ethnic group.
Are not the copper-coloured race...] the series of rhetorical questions is
    reminiscent of Shylock's defence of the humanity of Jews in Shakespeare's
    The Merchant of Venice, III. i.

[*Letter to Samuel Ryley*]

Source: Letters of a Templar, ed. W. L. Rushton (1903), pp. 2–3.

Commentary: For Samuel William Ryley (1759–1837), an actor and playwright
who had worked in both Liverpool and Manchester, see *ODNB*. Ryley was
president of the Liverpool Forum, with which Rushton was involved, and
Rushton was an agent for Ryley's memoirs, *The Itinerant* (advertisement in
Liverpool Mercury, 26 July 1811, and 11 March 1814). For William Cowdroy
(1752–1814), see Rushton's poem in his memory, above, and *ODNB*; the
obituary mentioned here appeared in the *Liverpool Mercury*, 12 August 1814,
following Cowdroy's death on the 10th. 'Ned' is Rushton's son, also Edward
(1795–1851), a notable reformer, barrister, and magistrate. 'Casey' delivered a
eulogy on Rushton after his death, at the meeting of the Concentric Society of
which he was a member, also reprinted in *Letters of a Templar*, pp. 6–7; 'Ben
Cowdroy' is one of William Cowdroy's four sons.

life's poor play] echoing Shakespeare, *Macbeth*, V. v. 24: 'Life's ... a poor
    player', probably via Pope, *Essay on Man* (1733–1734), II. 282.

Mr Rushtons Remarks on Slavery

Source: Liverpool Record Office 920 ROS/4260, 'Mr Rushtons Remarks on
Slavery'. Two leaves, four pages of text numbered 3–6, though 3 is on the back
of 6, and clearly lacking a first leaf and probably further leaves. Apparently
never published.

Commentary: The document appears to have been written in some haste, with
insertions, deletions, and some unorthodox spelling, uncorrected here, and
some words not easy to decipher. There is no date, no indication of who took
the notes (assuming this is from before the partial restoration of Rushton's
sight) and no indication of why the document is among Roscoe's papers. In
one possible scenario it dates from early in the abolitionist campaign, as part of
the gathering of evidence done in the later 1780s by Roscoe and London-based

abolitionists such as Thomas Clarkson; in his *Essay on the Impolicy of the African Slave Trade* (1788), *The Substance of the Evidence of Sundry Persons on the Slave-Trade, Collected in the Course of a Tour made in the Autumn of the Year 1788* (1789) and *An Essay on the Comparative Efficiency of Regulation or Abolition, as applied to the Slave Trade* (1789), Clarkson quotes a number of accounts of conditions (for seamen as well as for slaves), of a similar import. But the handwriting could be later and it might date from Roscoe's brief career as MP (1806–1807), during which the bill to abolish the slave trade was finally passed. It is possible that the missing sheet dealt more with slavery, as the cover note suggests; the surviving portion is more to do with the condition of the mariners, in tune with Rushton's concerns for the welfare of the British 'tar' in much of the poetry. It was politically a strong point for abolitionists such as Clarkson and Wilberforce that the slave trade was not providing employment for British seamen so much as putting them in danger.

Salt Beef] beef cured with salt to preserve it.

Biscuit] ship-biscuit, sea-bread, or hard-tack, a term for the flour-based cracker baked hard for preservation which formed the basis of rations on long voyages; notoriously prone to infestation.

Guinea] country in West Africa, one of the principle areas from which slaves were collected.

Stock Fish] unsalted, air-dried fish, usually cod.

Steerage] 'an apartment without the great *cabin* of a ship, from which it is separated by a thin partition … In merchant-ships it is generally the habitation of the inferior officers and ship's crew'; Falconer, *Universal Dictionary of the Marine* (1759), s.v. 'Steerage'.

cast a ling'ring look] alluding to Thomas Gray, *Elegy Written in a Country Churchyard* (1751), 88: 'Nor cast one longing lingering look behind'.

Bonney] the Bonny River, which flows into the Gulf of Guinea through modern Nigeria, one of the chief areas of the slave market.

Gunwale] the rim or top of the outer edge of a ship's hull.

Head] the figurehead at the front of a ship, as illustrated in plate IV of Falconer, *Universal Dictionary of the Marine* (1759); sometimes indicating the whole of the front end of a ship.

Sharks] mentioned by Rushton in a number of poems: *West-Indian Eclogues*, III.63; 'Will Clewline', 4; 'Toussaint to his Troops', 67; see also the mock 'Petition' from the 'Sharks of Africa', Appendix I.

Scurvey] scurvy was a potentially fatal illness caused by vitamin C deficiency, common on long voyages with poor nutrition; already identified as treatable with citrus fruit by James Lind in *A Treatise of the Scurvy*, (1753), but Royal Navy ships in the latter half of the eighteenth century persisted in experimenting with doses of malt, sauerkraut and other preparations as an anti-scorbutic, with generally poor success.

Flux] dysentery.

billet] stick or small log.
Masthead] the top of the mast, sometimes used as a destination for
   punishment.

[*Letter to Thomas Walker*]

Source: British Library Add. MS 88955, ff. 351–52; transcription by Franca
Dellarosa.

Commentary: Thomas Walker (1749–1817) was a Manchester-based radical and
abolitionist, who collected much correspondence, now in the British Library.

Thelwall] John Thelwall (1764–1834), a leading radical lecturer and the
   intellectual figurehead of the London Corresponding Society from 1792;
   he was arrested and charged with treason in 1794, and even after acquittal
   was harassed and spied upon by government agents, causing him to
   withdraw towards a literary career and the work on elocution and speech
   alluded to here. He later returned to political journalism. He had set up
   in in Liverpool in 1805. See Appendix II for his poem about Rushton.
Lyne] not traced.
friend] not identified.
Windham] William Windham (1750–1810).
Grenville] William Wyndham Grenville (1759–1834), just about to become
   Prime Minister when Rushton wrote this letter.
Pitt] William Pitt 'the younger' (1759–1806), the Prime Minister, and
   architect of what Rushton regarded as a repressive surveillance state, who
   had just died (23 January).
Cowdroy] William Cowdroy, editor of the *Manchester Gazette*; see Rushton's
   Lines to his memory.

Appendix I

Other poems possibly by Rushton

(1780–1781) ['Rebellion Tottering Stands']. A 44-line poem, beginning with those words, printed by Burke, pp. 11–12, from a clipping from an unknown newspaper kept by the Tarleton family, annotated in pencil 'Edward Rushton'. The poem is headed 'To the Printer: Sir, should the following have merit enough to entitle it to a place in your paper, the insertion will obliged [sic] your humble servant, E. R.'. Burke's reference is 'Tarleton papers, Liverpool Central Library, H920/TAR 27/[19]', but this class mark does not correspond to the current organisation of the papers and the archivists in Liverpool Record Office have not been able to trace the cutting. The poem itself has not been otherwise located among the surviving runs of local newspapers. News of the Catawba Falls victory (August 1780), which it celebrates, was published in e.g. the *General Evening Post*, 10 October 1780, and the poem was very likely written and published shortly afterwards, certainly before it became obvious that Britain would lose the war, which ended at Yorktown a year later. It was not reprinted or collected in Rushton's lifetime. The militaristic patriotism of the poem is greatly at odds with Rushton's later views; he later celebrated the result of the American War of Independence (1775–1783) as a triumph for liberty. It is possible that this (which would be his earliest known poem) emerged from some more youthful sense of patriotic fervour, or at least the desire to get into print; and an 'Edward Rushton, Mariner' does appear to have voted for Tarleton (Sir Banastre Tarleton, 1754–1833, politician and soldier, son of John Tarleton, 1719–1773, of Aigburth, Liverpool, a merchant and shipowner trading in sugar and slaves) at the election of 1790, though he was exactly the kind of swaggerer Rushton was already denouncing by then. Without having access to the source document, however, it has seemed safest to leave the poem as doubtful.

(1792) 'Ode. To Liberty', beginning 'THY real friends, O Liberty!'
Printed in W. Belcher, *An Appendix to the Account of the Birmingham Riots* (1792), p. 93, without ascription, among a number of anonymous poems (one of them by

William Roscoe) which had appeared in newspapers following the destruction of Joseph Priestley's laboratory and house in July 1791, during riots connived at by the authorities. A slightly different version appeared in the *American Apollo*, 27 March 1794, as 'From a London paper', under the title *LINES. Written Immediately after the Birmingham Riots*, but again without ascription; and in *Time-Piece*, 11 September 1797, as 'Lines on the Riots in Birmingham', '*By* E. Rushton, *of Liverpool*', apparently the sole ascription to Rushton. As the piece was not elsewhere considered as Rushton's, and as he makes no other reference to Birmingham or to Priestley, it is regarded as doubtful. Shepherd's *Epistle to Edward Rushton* of 1792 (see Appendix II), comments on the events.

(1794) Poems from *Liberty Scraps*.
This sixteen-page pamphlet of radical verse appeared with no marks of identification of any kind beyond the imprint 'Printed in the Year 1794'. It was noticed in America: *The Rising Sun*, 3 November 1795, reprinted a letter from Amicus which reported the pamphlet as published in England and recently imported. None of the poems contains any indication of authorship, but three of them were later printed, in revised versions, by Rushton himself as his own work. The 8-line epigraph on the title page is from Shepherd's *Epistle* to him (see Appendix II), and another of the poems makes reference to the Liverpool Infirmary and a local clergyman, so there is clearly some connection with Rushton's circle. Some of the poems were ascribed to Rushton in American, but not British, newspapers; this in itself is not completely reliable, as there was a certain amount of confusion between Rushton and Roscoe, and Shepherd's work also turned up in similar contexts. Leaving out work known to be Rushton's, the contents are:

pp. 2–3. 'Verses Addressed to Englishmen', beginning 'When, exulting, we tell how our fathers of yore'; found earlier in Thomas Spence's *One Pennyworth of Pig's Meat, or Lessons for the Swinish Multitude* (1793), pp. 180–82, under the title 'English Injustice to the French'; in *Dunlap and Claypoole's American Daily Advertiser*, 27 December 1793, as received from England; and *Newport Mercury*, 27 April 1794, as from an Irish paper. Not apparently ascribed to Rushton.

pp. 5–6. 'Lines Occasioned by a Passage in a Sermon Preached for the Benefit of the Liverpool Infirmary, in July, 1791', beginning 'When Brownlow from the pulpit strove'. Not located elsewhere; no ascription to Rushton.

pp. 6–7 'To the English Friends of French Freedom', beginning 'Again O ye spirits who feel for mankind'. Found earlier in *The Manchester Herald*, 7 July 1792, and later in *Choice Collection of Civic Songs* (Sheffield 1795), p. 4, without ascription.

pp. 7–8. 'To the Right Honourable the Lords Spiritual and Temporal' [a pro-slavery mock-petition from the 'Sharks of Africa']. Found earlier in *The Bee: or, Literary Weekly Intelligencer*, 10 (11 July 1792), 34–36; reprinted in *Dunlop's American Advertiser*, 20 September 1792; also *United States Chronicle*,

28 November 1792, 'from a late London paper', and *The Philadelphia Gazette*, 14 July 1794, as having come in a recent dispatch from England, probably *Liberty Scraps* itself; also in *The Diary or Loudon's Register*, 9 September 1797, and *The Friend*, 10 January 1807, with a note of historical explanation. None of these has any ascription. Rushton does mention sharks eating escaped slaves in the 'Mr Rushton's Remarks on Slavery'.

pp. 8–9. 'Song Written for the 14th July 1793', beginning 'Ever dear be the day, ever sacred the deed'. Reprinted (giving the year as '1794') in *The Time-Piece*, 14 July 1797, ascribed to Rushton. It is not an implausible ascription (see Dellarosa, chapter 7); but there is no particular reason beyond the paper's own claim to confirm the attribution.

pp. 11–12. 'For the Fast in 1794', beginning 'Is this the far-fam'd spot of earth'. Reprinted in the *New-Jersey Journal*, 14 December 1796, 'from a late London paper', as the work of 'Mrs. Barbauld' (i.e. Anna Letitia Barbauld, 1743–1825), and in *The Temple of Reason*, 11 November 1801, without ascription. Ascribed to Rushton in *The Time-Piece*, 9 May 1798. Again, a not implausible ascription, without much distinctive to cement it.

pp. 13–15. 'The Tender's Hold'. This has seemed the most likely ascription, and I have accepted it into the main text.

pp. 15–16 'A Political Creed', in prose, beginning 'I believe that God is the impartial father of the whole human race'. Not identified anywhere else, with or without ascription.

p. 16 'On the Flannel Waistcoat Subscription', beginning 'When Britons fought in freedom's glorious cause'. Not located elsewhere; the flannel waistcoat subscription, for the British Army serving in Flanders, was widely reported, e.g. in *The Sun*, 9, 11 and 16 November 1793; *The World*, 13 November and 20 December 1793; *Morning Post*, 19 and 22 September 1794; *True Briton*, 26 November 1794.

(1797) 'Lines composed for the 10th August 1796', beginning 'Tho' we praise the proud day which beheld mighty France'. Printed in *The Time Piece*, 11 August 1797, ascribed to Rushton. Not found elsewhere. A plausible ascription, but the poem contains nothing distinctive enough to be certain.

(c. 1799). *Hymns &c. for the Blind* (see 'Song'. *From Hymns &c. for the Blind*). The broadsheet contains six poems, four of which are identified as the work of other authors in the notes to the 'Song' included here, which is ascribed to Rushton. A further poem, another 'Song' ('Ere yet you leave our calm retreat'), remains of undetermined authorship; the text has not been traced anywhere else. The pencil annotation in the left-hand column has a mark after it which might conceivably indicate that the Rushton attribution is intended to apply this poem also. This second 'Song' is once more written from the point of view of the blind child, presenting much the same argument as the poem clearly ascribed to him. The insistence on human economic aid (as opposed to acceptance of divine will) is similar in each poem, and consonant with what is known of Rushton's original involvement in the plan (see 'A Few Plain Facts...'). It is possible that he wrote both, or, indeed, neither. Without more definite evidence it has seemed safer to print the one with a clear note of ascription.

(1801) 'O'er the vine-cover'd hills and gay regions of France'; ascribed to Rushton by *The Bee*, 25 November 1801, reprinting 'Will Clewline'. The poem is by Roscoe, and generally known as 'The Day-Star of Liberty'; it had been in circulation since the early 1790s and was printed in radical collections such as *Penny-worth of Pig's Meat* (1793) and *Choice Collection of Civic Songs* (Sheffield 1795); printed as Roscoe's in the *Time Piece*, 19 July 1797, and included in his *Poetical Works* (1853), p. 76.

(1812) 'Elegiac Stanzas to the Memory of Benjamin Gibson, Esq.'; printed in the *Monthly Magazine or British Register* 33 (June 1812), 452, with words of commendation: 'Rushton, of Liverpool, with whose poems the readers of the Monthly Magazine are doubtless acquainted, received very considerable restoration of sight from an operation which Mr. Gibson performed on him'. The magazine does not quite ascribe the poem (which is dated 19 April 1812) to Rushton. The poem itself states 'Long, long, shall Rushton venerate thy name, | And in harmonious accents speak thy praise; | Whilst in his bosom gratitude's pure flame | Spreads and grows brighter with his length of days'. This does not appear sufficient to claim the poem as Rushton's; he was by no means shy of identifying himself as an author, and his own poem of gratitude to Gibson had already been openly published.

(1815) 'Napoleon's Farewell', beginning 'Farewell to the land, where the gleam of my glory'. Printed in an article on 'Napoleonana' in the *Liverpool Mercury*, 4 August 1815, as from *The Examiner*. The *Liverpool Mercury* made no claim for Rushton's authorship and the note it reprints from the *Examiner* suggests the author was known to the London rather than the Liverpool periodical. Reprinted in the *Albany Register*, 3 October 1815; *The Reporter*, 11 October 1815; the *Alexandria Herald*, 13 October 1815, and *The Union*, 20 October 1815, all without ascription. The *Commercial Advertiser* of 6 October 1815 printed the poem with a paragraph attributing it to Rushton on the grounds of its pathos and Rushton's skill in that mode, though no doubt the source in the *Liverpool Mercury* suggested the attribution, which was repeated in the *Albany Register*, 11 October 1815; the *New-Jersey Journal*, 17 October 1815; *American Beacon*, 18 October 1815; and *Green-Mountain Farmer*, 3 June 1816. Never a likely ascription, given Rushton's antipathy to Napoleon; the poem is in fact by George Gordon, Lord Byron (1788–1824).

Appendix II

Poems to and about Rushton

1. Hugh Mulligan, 'Epistle to Mr. E— R—', in *Poems Chiefly on Slavery and Oppression, with Notes and Illustrations* (1788), pp. 38–43.

2. William Shepherd, *An Epistle to Edward Rushton; Who, like Milton, Deprived of the Blessing of Sight, like him, is favoured with the Visits of the Muse, and, like him, Glows with an ardent Love of Liberty* (1792). Though not in ESTC, copies of a printed version of this, dated 1792, are in the Liverpool Athenaeum and Liverpool Record Office, and in the Shepherd archive, volume IX, Manchester College, Oxford. This is the anonymous item listed under 1792 in Thomas Dawson, 'The Pamphlet Literature of Liverpool', *Transactions of the Historic Society of Lancashire and Cheshire* (1864), p. 80, as *An Epistle to Edward Rushton*. *Liberty Scraps* (1794) quotes eight lines of it as a title-page epigraph. The whole poem was reprinted in Rushton's *Poems and Other Writings* (1824), Appendix, pp. 1–7. Sometimes wrongly ascribed to Roscoe.

3. 'Matilda', 'The Vindication. To Edward Rushton', in *The Time-Piece*, 29 May 1797. See *Expostulatory Letter to George Washington* (1797), commentary.

4. John M'Creery, *The Press. A Poem* (1803), p. 28: a sequence of lines identifying Rushton among the worthies of Liverpool.

5. James Gilland, 'On Reading the Poems of Edward Rushton, of Liverpool'. Dated November 1806, and published 'some years ago in the Belfast Commercial Chronicle', according to the *Belfast Monthly Magazine*, XII.71 (June 1814), 471, which reprinted the encomium on 'that intrepid and unbending patriot'. Also printed in the *Liverpool Mercury*, 16 December 1814.

6. J[ohn] M['Creery], 'To my dear Friend Edward Rushton, of Liverpool, on the Recovery of his Sight, by the skilful Operation of Mr. Gibson, of

Manchester'; in *The Athenaeum*, II. 7 (July 1807), 49. Dated from 12, Hatfield-street, Blackfriars, 10ᵗʰ June, 1807, where M'Creery had moved.

7. John Thelwall, 'Ode to Edward Rushton of Liverpool, on his Restoration to Sight, after a Blindness of upwards of Thirty Years, by a Series of Operations performed by Mr. Gibson, of Manchester'; in *Monthly Magazine* 24 (August 1807), 49; reprinted in the *Poetical Register*, 8 (Jan 1814), 510–12.

8. Mary Leadbeater, 'To Edward Rushton, of Liverpool: on the Recovery of his Sight'; in her *Poems* (1808), pp. 395–96.

9. J[ohn] M['Creery], 'To the Memory of the much Lamented and Respected Edward Rushton', in *Liverpool Mercury*, 16 December 1814.

10. Thomas Noble, 'Rushton'; reported as having been read out at the Independent Debating Society, *Liverpool Mercury*, 7 April 1815; printed in Noble's *Poems* (1821), pp. 191–92; partially reprinted in the *Black Dwarf*, 17 October 1821, p. 545; and again, in full, along with what Shepherd calls an 'animated Apostrophe' in prose, in Rushton's *Poems, and Other Writings* (1824), Appendix, pp. 8–10.

11. John M'Creery, *The Press, A Poem. Part the Second* (1827), p. 48; lines on Rushton among a list of the Liverpool heroes now dead, and a note, p. 75, on Rushton's 'inflexible independence'.

12. John M'Creery, 'To my Friend, Mr. Edward Rushton, of Liverpool, on the Death of his Sister'; in *The Press, A Poem. Part the Second* (1827), pp. 55–57.

Bibliography

Eighteenth-century printed items do not map straightforwardly onto modern bibliographic conventions. Titles are often very long, and have in the list that follows sometimes been truncated. Information given in imprints does not readily correspond with the conventional publication details required in modern references; sometimes only a printer's name is given (though the printer may the 'publisher' in the legal sense); sometimes a 'trade publisher' or subsidiary agent is given; sometimes only a retail agent ('sold by') is given; sometimes several agents in different places are listed; or any combination of these. The information can be deliberately false, or there can be no information at all, especially in the case of pirated or potentially seditious printing. Many items were in effect self-published ('printed for the author'). Details given for early printed books in the following list are therefore only simplified versions of imprint details where these are given, sometimes with additional information or conjecture about place or date of publication supplied from other sources; it is hoped this will be sufficient to identify a particular edition of any item referred to in the text.

(a) Manuscript materials

British Library Add. MS 88955, ff. 351–52: Edward Rushton to Thomas Walker, 30 January 1806

Liverpool Record Office, 920 ROS/2874: Thomas Parkes to William Roscoe, 18 November 1809

Liverpool Record Office, 920 ROS/3765: Robert Roscoe to William Roscoe, 24 November 1814

Liverpool Record Office, 920 ROS/4016: William Stanley Roscoe to William Roscoe, 1 September 1797

Liverpool Record Office, 920 ROS/4259: Thomas Rushton to Roscoe, 8 August 1800

Liverpool Record Office 920 ROS/4260: 'Mr Rushton's Remarks on Slavery'

University of Liverpool Library, Special Collections and Archives, Rathbone Papers, RPII. 4. 16, p. 57: Rathbone's Scrapbook 1790–1808

University of Liverpool Library, Special Collections and Archives, Rathbone Papers, RP XXI.9.3.1, Robert Southey to Edward Rushton, 29 March 1808

University of Liverpool Library, Special Collections and Archives,
Y78.3.747(1), printed copy of *Liverpool Testimonials to the Genius of the
Departed Burns* (Liverpool, c. 1796), with MS addition of 'The Swallow'

(b) Separately-printed items by Edward Rushton
The Dismember'd Empire. A Poem (Liverpool: W. Nevett for J. Johnson,
London; and J. Gore, Liverpool, 1782)
West-Indian Eclogues (London: W. Lowndes, and J. Philips, 1787)
*Neglected Genius: Or, Tributary Stanzas to the Memory of the Unfortunate
Chatterton* (London: J. Philips, 1787)
*The Neglected Tar: A Celebrated Song, adapted and sung by Mr. Dignum at
the Anacreontic Society, and at the Theatre Royal Liverpool; the Words by a
Gentleman of that Town* (London: S. A. & P. Thompson, c. 1790)
The Neglected Tar; or, The British Seaman (no place, no publisher's name,
c. 1790)
The Neglected Tar; to which are added, Kate and Teddy [etc...] (Stirling: no
publisher's name, c. 1790)
Human Debasement. A Fragment (Harrogate: no publisher's name, 1793)
*Expostulatory Letter to George Washington, of Mount Vernon, in Virginia, on his
continuing to be a Proprietor of Slaves* (Liverpool: no publisher's name, 1797)
Written for the Anniversary of the Liverpool Marine Society (Liverpool: Ed.
Rushton, c. 1799)
Blue Eyed Mary (Liverpool: E. Rushton; London: S. W. Fores, 1799)
Blue Eyed Mary (Liverpool: J. McCreery, printer, 1799)
Blue Eyed Mary or, the Victim of Seduction (London: J. Birt, c. 1840)
Lucy's Ghost. A Marine Ballad (Liverpool: J. M'Creery, 1800)
Will Clewline (Liverpool: Edward Rushton, 1801) [reprinted in a limited
edition facsimile, West Linton, Peeblesshire: The Castlelaw Press, 1970]
Mary le More (Liverpool: Printed by W. Armstrong, c. 1798)
Mary Le More ([Newcastle?], c. 1798)
Poems, By Edward Rushton (London: J. M'Creery for T. Ostell, 1806)
*Poems and other Writings by the late Edward Rushton; to which is added, A
Sketch of the Life of the Author, by the Rev. William Shepherd* (London:
Effingham Wilson, 1824)

(c) Other early printed works
Adanson, Michel, *A Voyage to Senegal, the Isle of Goree, and the River
Gambia* (London: J. Nourse and W. Johnston, 1759)
Aikin, John, *An Essay on the Application of Natural History to Poetry*
(Warrington and London: W. Eyres and J. Johnson, 1777)
Akenside, Mark, *The Poems of Mark Akenside, M.D.* (London: W. Bowyer,
J. Nichols, J. Dodsley, 1772)
Alanson, Edward, *Practical Observations on Amputation, and the
After-Treatment* (London: J. F. and C. Rivington, 1779)

Anderson, Robert, *Poems on Various Subjects* (Carlisle: J. Mitchell for the author; London: W. Clarke, 1798)

Atkins, John, *A Voyage to Guinea, Brasil, and the West-Indies* (London: Caesar Ward and Richard Chandler, 1735)

Bannister, Saxe, *The Worthies of the Working Classes and their Friends* (London: T. C. Newby, 1854)

Beckford, William, *Remarks upon the Situation of Negroes in Jamaica* (London: T. and J. Egerton, 1788)

Beilby, Ralph, and Thomas Bewick, *History of British Birds*, volume I, *Land Birds* (Newcastle: Beilby & Bewick; London: G. G. and J. Robinson, 1797)

Belcher, W., *An Appendix to the Account of the Birmingham Riots* ([Birmingham]: no publisher's name, 1792)

Binns, John, *Recollections of the Life of John Binns* (Philadelphia: for the author, 1854)

Bishop, Samuel, *The Poetical Works of the Rev. Samuel Bishop, A.M.* (London: Cadell and Davies and others, 1796)

Bloomfield, Robert, *The Farmer's Boy; a Rural Poem* (London: Vernor and Hood, 1800)

The Book of British Song Illustrated by Several Distinguished Artists, vol. II [*How's Illustrated Book of British Song*] (London: Jeremiah How, c. 1850)

Brooke, Richard, *Liverpool as it was During the last Quarter of the Eighteenth Century, 1775 to 1800* (Liverpool: J. Mawdesley and Son; London: John Russell Smith, 1853)

Brookes, Richard, *The Art of Angling* (London: J. Watts, 1743)

Broome, William, *Poems on Several Occasions* (London: Henry Lintot, 1739)

Browne, Isaac Hawkins, *Poems Upon Various Subjects, Latin and English* (London: J. Nourse and C. Marsh, 1768)

Browne, Patrick, *The Civil and Natural History of Jamaica* (London: for the author, 1756)

Buffon, Georges Louis Leclerc, Comte de, *The Natural History of Animals, Vegetables, and Minerals*, 6 vols (London: T. Bell, 1775–1776)

Burke, John, *History of the Late War in Ireland* (Philadelphia: Francis and Robert Bailey, 1799)

Burns, Robert, *Poems, Chiefly in the Scottish Dialect* (Kilmarnock: John Wilson, 1786)

Burns, Robert, *The Works of Robert Burns*, edited by James Currie, 4 vols (Liverpool: J. M'Creery; London: T. Cadell and W. Davies, and others, 1800)

Cabinet of Curiosities (London: no publisher's name, 1795)

Campbell, Thomas, *The Complete Poetical Works of Thomas Campbell*, ed. J. Logie Robertson (London: Oxford University Press, 1907).

Captain Mulligan (Boston: L. Deeming, c. 1835)

Cary, Henry Francis, *Ode to General Kosciusko* (London: T. Cadell and W. Davies, 1797)

Cennick, John, *Sacred Hymns for the Children of God* (London: John Lewis for the author, 1742)

Chatterton, Thomas, *Miscellanies in Prose and Verse* (London: Fielding and Walker, 1778)

A Choice Collection of Civic Songs ('London' [Sheffield]: no publisher's name [John Crome], 1795)

Clarkson, Thomas, *An Essay on the Slavery and Commerce of the Human Species, Particularly the African* (London: J. Phillips and T. Cadell, 1786)

——, *An Essay on the Impolicy of the African Slave Trade* (London: James Phillips, 1788)

——, *The Substance of the Evidence of Sundry Persons on the Slave-Trade, Collected in the Course of a Tour made in the Autumn of the Year 1788* (London: James Phillips, 1789)

——, *An Essay on the Comparative Efficiency of Regulation or Abolition, as applied to the Slave Trade* (London: James Phillips, 1789)

——, *The History of the Rise, Progress and Accomplishment of the Abolition of the African Slave-Trade by the British Parliament*, 2 vols (London: Longman, Hurst, Rees and Orme, 1808)

A Collection of the Most Favourite New Songs (Bath: W. Gye, c. 1790)

Collins, William, *Persian Eclogues* (London: J. Roberts, 1742)

Colman, George, *The Surrender of Calais* (London: T. Cadell, 1791)

The Columbian Songster, or, Jovial Companion (New York: Greenleaf's Press, 1797)

Come Under my Plaidy (Stirling: C. Randall, c. 1800)

A Compendious and Impartial Account of the Election at Liverpool ... November 1806. (Liverpool: Wright and Cruikshank, 1806)

Cowper, William, *The Task, a Poem, in Six Books* (London: J. Johnson, 1785)

——, *Poems, by William Cowper, of the Inner Temple, Esq.* (London: J. Johnson, 1782)

Crawford, Adair, *Experiments and Observations on Animal Heat* (Philadelphia: Thomas Dobson, 1787)

Croft, Herbert, *Love and Madness: A Story Too True* (London: G. Kearsley, 1780)

Cupid Wounded: or, the Mischievous Bee (London: J. Pitts, c. 1820)

Currie, William Wallace, *Memoir of the Life, Writings, and Correspondence of James Currie, M.D.*, 2 vols (London: Longman, Rees, Orme, Brown and Green, 1831)

Dannett, Henry, *A Particular Examination of Mr. Harris's Scriptural Researches on the Licitness of the Slave Trade* (London: J. Philips and T. Payne, 1788)

Darwin, Erasmus, *Zoonomia; or, the Laws of Organic Life*, 2 vols (London: J. Johnson, 1794)

Dawson, Thomas, 'The Pamphlet Literature of Liverpool', *Transactions of the Historic Society of Lancashire and Cheshire*, 16 (1864) 73–138.

Drummond, William Hamilton, *The Man of Age*, second edition (Glasgow: no publisher's name, 1798)

Dryden, John, *Absalom and Achitophel* (London: Jacob Tonson, 1681)

The Edinburgh Musical Miscellany (Edinburgh: W. Gordon, T. Brown and others, 1792)

The Edinburgh Musical Miscellany, vol. 2 (Edinburgh: John Elder, T. Brown and others, 1793)

The Edinburgh Syren; or, Musical Bouquet (Edinburgh: Thomas Brown, 1792)

Edwards, Bryan, A *Speech delivered at a Free Conference between the Honourable the Council and Assembly of Jamaica* (Kingston, Jamaica: Alexander Aikman, 1789)

The Eighth Report of the Society for Bettering the Condition and Increasing the Comforts of the Poor (Dublin: W. Watson and Son, 1799)

Enfield, William, An *Essay Towards the History of Leverpool* (Warrington: no publisher's name, 1773)

England's Defiance. An Irregular Ode (London: T. Payne and Son, 1779)

The English Musical Repository, new edition (London: B. Crosby, 1808)

The Evergreen; Or, the Songster's Pocket-Companion (Preston: E. Sergent, 1790)

Falconbridge, Alexander, *An Account of the Slave Trade on the Coast of Africa* (London: James Phillips, 1788)

Falconer, William, *An Universal Dictionary of the Marine* (London: T. Cadell, 1769).

——, *The Shipwreck* (London: A. Millar, 1762)

Five Excellent Songs (Edinburgh: J. Morren, c. 1825)

Fragments on the Origin of Kings, and Human Debasement (no place or name; c. 1795)

The Frisky Songster (Stirling: M. Randall, 1813)

Four Excellent New Songs (Whitehaven: T. Wilson, c. 1820)

Fugitive Pieces: A Collection of Original Poems, the Greater Part by the Most Eminent Writers of the Present Age (Edinburgh: J. Johnstone, 1797)

Gawthrop, Hugh, *Fraser's Guide to Liverpool and Birkenhead* (London: Kent; Liverpool: Fraser, c. 1855)

Gibson, Benjamin, *Practical Observations on the Formation of an artificial Pupil, in several deranged States of the Eye* (Warrington: J. Haddock; London: Cadell and Davies, 1811)

Gleanings: Consisting of Extracts from the Writings of Edward Rushton, (The Blind Poet of Liverpool,) and various other Authors (Nantucket: R. and G. S. Wood, 1829)

Glover, Richard, *Leonidas* (London: R. Dodsley, 1737)

——, *Admiral Hosier's Ghost* (London: Webb, 1740)

Goldsmith, Oliver, *The Traveller, or a Prospect of Society* (London: J. Newbery, 1764)

Gordon, Thomas, 'A Description of the Exocœtus Volitans, or Flying Fish', *Philosophical Transactions*, 68 (1778), 791–800

Gore's Liverpool Directory, for the Year 1774 (Liverpool: J. Gore, 1774)

Gore's Liverpool Directory, Containing an Alphabetical List of the Merchants, Tradesmen, and Principal Inhabitants of the Town of Liverpool (Liverpool: J. Gore, 1781)

Gore's Liverpool Directory, or, Alphabetical List of the Merchants, Tradesmen, and Principal Inhabitants, of the Town of Liverpool (Liverpool: no publisher's name, 1796)

Grainger, James, *The Sugar-Cane: a Poem* (London: R. and J. Dodsley, 1764)

Gray, Thomas, *Elegy Written in a Country Church Yard* (London: R. Dodsley, 1751)

——, *Odes by Mr Gray* ([London]: R. and J. Dodsley, 1757)

The Greenwich Pensioner's Garland ([Newcastle]: no publisher's name, c. 1792)

Gregory, George, *Essays Historical and Moral* (London: J. Johnson, 1785)

The Hampshire Syren (Southampton: T. Skelton, 1794)

Harland, John, ed., *Ballads & Songs of Lancashire, Ancient and Modern*, second edition, corrected, revised and enlarged, by T. T. Wilkinson (London: Routledge, 1875)

Hart, James, P., *Mary le More; Or the Irish Maniac. An Original Domestic Drama, in Three Acts* (London: J. Pattie, c. 1838)

Hayley, William, *An Elegy on the Ancient Greek Model* (Cambridge: Francis Hodson; London: T. Payne, 1779)

——, *An Essay on Epic Poetry* (London: J. Dodsley, 1782)

Hoyle, Edmond, *A Short Treatise on the Game of Whist* (London: John Watts for the author, 1742)

HYMNS, &c. for the Blind, at the School of Industry, Liverpool ([Liverpool]: J. M'Creery, c. 1799)

Jamaica, a Poem, in three Parts (London: William Nicoll, 1777)

Jenyns, Soame, *A Free Inquiry into the Nature and Origin of Evil* (London: R. and J. Dodsley, 1757)

An Impartial Collection of the Addresses, Songs, Squibs, etc. that were published at Liverpool, during the election of members of Parliament, in November, 1806. ... ('Dublin' [Liverpool?]: no publisher's name, c. 1806)

Jefferson, Thomas, *Notes on the State of Virginia* (Philadelphia: Matthew Carey, 1794)

Johnson, Samuel, *London: a Poem, in Imitation of the third Satire of Juvenal* (London: R. Dodsley, 1738)

——, *The Vanity of Human Wishes* (London: R. Dodsley, 1749)

——, *A Dictionary of the English Language*, 2 vols (London: W. Strahan, J. and P. Knapton, and others, 1755)

——, *Taxation no Tyranny* (London: T. Cadell, 1775)

——, *A Journey to the Western Islands of Scotland* (London: W. Strahan and T. Cadell, 1775)

The Jovial Sailor's Chearful Companion (London: A. Cleugh, 1800)

The Jovial Songster, or Sailor's Delight (Gainsborough: J. M. Mozeley and Co., 1792)

The Jovial Songster, or the Musical Miscellany (London: West and Hughes, [1800])

Knox, Vicesimus, *Essays Moral and Literary*, ninth edition, 3 vols (London: Charles Dilly, 1787)

Langhorne, John, *The Poetical Works of John Langhorne*, 2 vols (London: T. Becket and P. A. De Hondt, 1766)

Leadbeater, Mary, *Poems* (Dublin: Martin Keane; London: Longman, Hurst, Rees and Orme, 1808)

Leslie, Charles, *A New and Exact Account of Jamaica* (Edinburgh: R. Fleming for A. Kincaid, 1739)

——, *A New History of Jamaica* (London: J. Hodges, 1740)

Liberty Scraps ('Printed in the Year, 1794')

Lind, James, *A Treatise of the Scurvy* (Edinburgh: Sands, Murray and Cochran; London: A Millar, 1753)

A List of Communications Laid Before the Literary & Philosophical Society of Liverpool, Since its Institution in 1812, to the end of Session Tenth, 1821 (Liverpool: Harris, 1821)

The Liverpool Songster, second edition (Liverpool: H. Hodgson, c. 1792)

Liverpool Testimonials, to the Departed Genius of Robert Burns, the Scottish Bard (Liverpool: Merritt and Wright, c. 1796)

Long, Edward, *The History of Jamaica*, 3 vols (London: T. Lowndes, 1774)

Lossing, Benson J. *Vassar College and Its Founder* (New York: C. A. Alvord, 1867)

Luffman, John, *A Brief Account of the Island of Antigua* (London: T. Cadell, 1789)

Lund, Thomas, *Blindness: Or, Some Thoughts for Sighted People* (Liverpool: A. Holden, 1887)

Madden, R. R., ed., *Literary Remains of the United Irishmen of 1798* (Dublin: J. Duffy, 1887)

Macpherson, James, *Temora* (London: T. Becket and P. A. De Hondt, 1763)

Marsden, Peter, *An Account of the Island of Jamaica* (Newcastle: for the author, 1788)

M'Creery, John, *The Press: A Poem* (Liverpool: J. M'Creery, 1803)

——, *The Press, A Poem. Part the Second* (London: J. M'Creery, T. Cadell, and others, 1827)

——, *The Press: A Poem, in Two Parts*, second edition (London: William Pickering, 1828)

Mickle, William, *The Lusiad; or, The Discovery of India* (Oxford: Jackson and Lister, 1777)

Milles, Jeremiah, ed., *Poems, Supposed to have been Written at Bristol, in the Fifteenth Century, by Thomas Rowley, Priest, &c.* (London: T. Payne, and Son, 1782)

Mulligan, Hugh, *Poems Chiefly on Slavery and Oppression, with Notes and Illustrations* (London: W. Lowndes, 1788)

The Musical Banquet of Choice Songs (Glasgow: A. MacGoun, 1798)

The Musical Miscellany: or, Songster's Companion (North Shields: W. Thompson; London: W. Lane, 1789)

The Myrtle and Vine; or, Complete Vocal Library (London: West and Hughes, c. 1800)

The New Liverpool Songster; or, Musical Companion (Liverpool: T. Schofield, 1789)

[Newby, Peter], *The Wrongs of Almoona, or the African's Revenge* (Liverpool: H. Hodgson; London: W. Lowndes and T. Booker,1788)

Noble, Thomas, *Poems* (Liverpool: Smith and Melling, for the author, 1821)

The Offspring of Wit and Harmony (Dublin: T. Henshall, 1800)

Paddy's Resource, or the Harp of Erin, Tuned to Freedom (Dublin: no publisher's name, no date, c. 1803)

Paine, Thomas, *The American Crisis* (Philadelphia: Styner and Cist, 1776–1777)

——, *Common Sense* (Philadelphia: John Carter, 1776)

——, *Rights of Man* (London: J. S. Jordan, 1791)

Pasquin, Anthony, *Poems* (London: J. Strahan, 1789)

Peysonnel, John Andrew, 'Singular Observations upon the Manchenille Apple', *Philosophical Transactions*, 50 (1757–1758), 772–73.

Plumptre, James, *A Collection of Songs, Moral, Sentimental, Instructive, and Amusing* (London: F. C. and J. Rivington, 1806)

The Pocket Encyclopaedia of Scottish, English and Irish Songs, 2 vols (Glasgow: no publisher's name, 1816)

Pocock's Everlasting Songster (Gravesend: R. Pocock, 1800)

The Poetical Register, and Repository for Fugitive Poetry for 1801 (London: F. and C. Rivington, 1802)

The Poll for the Election of Members of Parliament, for the Borough & Corporation of Liverpool ... May 1807 (Liverpool: J. Gore, 1807)

Pope, Alexander, *An Essay on Criticism* (London: W. Lewis, 1711)

——, *Windsor-Forest* (London: Bernard Lintott, 1713)

——, *The Rape of the Lock* (London: Bernard Lintott, 1714)

——, *The Works of Mr. Alexander Pope* (London: W. Bowyer for Bernard Lintott, 1717)

——, *The Iliad of Homer, translated by Mr. Pope*, 6 vols (London: W. Bowyer, for Bernard Lintott, 1715–1720)

——, *The Odyssey of Homer*, 5 vols (London: Bernard Lintott, 1725–1726)

——, *The Dunciad. With Notes Variorum, and the Prologomena of Scriblerus* (London: Lawton Gilliver, 1729)

——, *An Essay on Man* (London: John Wright for Lawton Gilliver, 1733–1734)

——, *An Epistle from Mr. Pope, to Dr Arbuthnot* (London: John Wright for Lawton Gilliver, 1735)

——, *The Works of Mr. Alexander Pope. Volume II* (London: John Wright for Lawton Gilliver, 1735)

Porteus, Beilby, *A Sermon Preached before the Incorporated Society for the Propagation of the Gospel in Foreign Parts* (London: T. Harrison and S. Brooke, 1783)

Procter, Richard Wright, *Literary Reminiscences and Gleanings* (Manchester: T. Dinham; London: Simpkin, Marshall and Co., 1860)

A Prospect from the Congress-Gallery, during the Session, begun December 7, 1795 (Philadelphia: Thomas Bradford, 1796)

Ramsay, James, *An Essay on the Treatment and Conversion of African Slaves in the British Sugar Colonies* (London: James Phillips, 1784)

Raynal, Abbé, *A Philosophical and Political History of the Settlements and Trade of the Europeans in the East and West Indies. Translated from the French by J. Justamond, M. A.*, 4 vols (London: T. Cadell, 1776)

Remarks on the Slave Trade, and the Slavery of the Negroes (London: J. Phillips, 1788)

Richardson, Samuel, *Clarissa*, 7 vols (London: S. Richardson, 1748)

Robinson, Mary, *Sappho and Phaon* (London: S. Gosnell for the author, 1796)

Roscoe, Henry, *The Life of William Roscoe*, 2 vols (London: T. Cadell, 1833)

Roscoe, William, *Mount Pleasant: a Descriptive Poem* (Warrington: W. Eyres; London: J. Johnson, 1777)

——, *A New Song. Sung by Mr. Dignum* (London: R. Dawes, 1792)

——, *The Poetical Works of William Roscoe* (Liverpool: Henry Young, 1853)

Rush, Benjamin, *An Address to the Inhabitants of the British Settlements in America, upon Slave-Keeping* (Philadelphia: John Dunlap, 1773)

Rushton, Edward, *Lament for Caubul* (London: no publisher's name, 1845).

Rushton, William Lowes, ed., *Letters of a Templar, 1820–50* (London: Simpkin, Marshall &Co.; Liverpool: Ed. Howell, 1903)

Rushton, Edward (Jr.), 'Biographical Sketch of Edward Rushton, Written by his Son', *Belfast Monthly Magazine* 13.77 (December 1814): 474–78

Ryley, Samuel, *The Itinerant, or, Memoirs of an Actor*, 3 vols (London: Taylor and Hessey, 1808)

Sea Songs and Ballads. By Dibdin and Others (London: Bell and Daldy, 1863)

A Selection of Psalms, Hymns, Anthems &c. Sung at the School for the Blind, Liverpool (1819)

Seward, Anna, *The Poetical Works of Anna Seward* (Edinburgh: J. Ballantyne and Co., 1810)

The Shamrock: a Collection of Irish Songs (Glasgow: no publisher's name, 1830)

Shenstone, William, *The Works, in Verse and Prose, of William Shenstone, Esq.*, 4th edition, 2 vols (London: J. Dodsley, 1773)

Six Favourite Songs. The Sailor's Epitaph [...] (Glasgow: no publisher's name, c. 1840)

Sketches of Obscure Poets, With Specimens of their Writings (London: Cochrane and M'Crone, 1833)

The Skylark (London: Vernor and Hood, 1800)

Sloane, Sir Hans, *A Voyage to the Islands Madera, Barbados, Nieves, S. Cristophers and Jamaica*, 2 vols (London: for the author, 1707)

Smith, Egerton, *Desultory Suggestions for Preservation from Shipwreck* (Liverpool: Rushton and Melling, 1825)

Smith, Henry Lilley, *Observations on the Prevailing Practice of Supplying Medical Assistance to the Poor* (London: Philanthropic Society, 1819)

Smithers, Henry, *Liverpool, its Commerce, Statues, and Institutions* (Liverpool: T. Kaye, 1825)

Smollett, Tobias, *The Regicide* (London: J. Osborn and A. Millar, 1749)

——, *Lancelot Greaves* (London: J. Coote, 1762)

——, *Plays and Poems* (London: T. Evans and R. Baldwin, 1777)

Smyth, William, *English Lyricks* (Liverpool: J. M'Creery; London: Cadell and Davies, 1797)

Snelgrave, William, *A New Account of Some Parts of Guinea, and the Slave Trade* (London: James, John and Paul Knapton, 1734)

Songs. Elegiac. Sea. (Manchester: G. Nicholson, 1796)

Songs. Elegiac. Sea. (Ludlow: G. Nicholson, 1799)

Songs, Odes, and Other Poems on National Subjects (Philadelphia: W. McCarty, 1842)

The Songster's Companion, second edition (Coventry: M. Luckman, c. 1788)

The Songster's Companion, third edition (Coventry: M. Luckman, c. 1800)

The Songster's Miscellany, or, Vocal Companion (Kidderminster: G. Gower, 1792)

Southey, Robert, *Carmen Triumphale for the Commencement of the year 1814* (London: Longman, Hurst, Rees, Orme and Brown, 1814)

Spence, Thomas, *One Pennyworth of Pig's Meat; or, Lessons for the Swinish Multitude* (London: T. Spence, 1793)

Steele, Anne, *Poems on Subjects Chiefly Devotional*, 3 vols (Bristol: T. Pine; London: T. Cadell and others, 1780)

Sterne, Laurence, *A Sentimental Journey through France and Italy*, 2 vols (London: T. Becket and P. A. De Hondt, 1768)

Stewart, John, *An Account of Jamaica, and its Inhabitants* (London: Longman, Hurst, Rees and Orme, 1808)

The Syren or Musical Bouquet (Edinburgh: Elder and Brown, c. 1795)

Teeling, Charles Hamilton, *Sequel to Personal Narrative of the "Irish Rebellion" of 1798* (Belfast: John Hodgson, 1832)

Thelwall, John, *Poems on Various Subjects*, 2 vols (London: for the author, 1787)

——, *Poems Chiefly Written in Retirement* (Hereford: W. H. Parker, 1801)

Thomson, James, *Liberty. A Poem* (London: A. Millar, 1735–1736)

Thompson, R., *To the Public, alias the "Swinish Multitude"* (London: Daniel Isaac Eaton, 1794)

Tickell, Thomas, *A Poem in Praise of the Horn-Book* (Dublin: J. Gowan, 1728)

A Tribute to Liberty; or, a New Collection of Patriotic Songs; entirely original (London: R. Thompson, 1793)

A Tribute to the Swinish Multitude (New York: Samuel Loudon and Son, 1795)

Trimmer, Sarah, *History of the Red-Breast Family* (London: Darton and Harvey, 1793)

Troughton, Thomas, The *History of Liverpool down to the Present Time* (Liverpool: William Robinson, 1810)

Tyrwhitt, Thomas, ed., *Poems, Supposed to have been Written at Bristol, by Thomas Rowley, and Others, in the Fifteenth Century* (London: T. Payne and Son, 1777)

The Universal Songster, 2 vols (London: no publisher's name, c. 1826)

Waller, Bryan, *Poems on Several Occasions* (London: E. Hodson, 1796)

Walpole, Horace, *A Letter to the Editor of the Miscellanies of Thomas Chatterton* (Strawberry-Hill: T. Kirgate, 1779)

Warton, Joseph, *Odes on Various Subjects* (London: R. Dodsley, 1747)

Warton, Thomas, The *History of English Poetry, from the Close of the Eleventh to the Commencement of the Eighteenth Century*, 3 vols (London: J. Dodsley and others, 1774–1781)

——, *An Enquiry into the Authenticity of the Poems attributed to Thomas Rowley* (London: J. Dodsley, 1782)

West, Gilbert, O*des of Pindar, with several other Pieces in Prose and Verse, Translated from the Greek*, 2 vols (London: R. Dodsley, 1753)

Williams, William Henry, *Observations Proving that Dr. Wilson's Tincture for the Cure of Gout and Rheumatism is Similar in its Nature and Effects to that Deleterious Preparation, the Eau Medicinale* (London: Callow, 1818)

Wilson, James, *Biography of the Blind: or the Lives of such as have distinguished themselves as Poets, Artists, Philosophers, &c*, 4th edition (Birmingham: J. W. Showell, 1838)

Yearsley, Ann, *Poems on Various Subjects* (London: for the author, and G. G. J. and J. Robinson, 1787)

Young, Arthur, *The Example of France, a Warning to Britain* (London: W. Richardson, 1793)

(d) Modern printed sources

Anstey, Roger, and P. E. H. Hair, eds, *Liverpool, The African Slave Trade, and Abolition* ([Liverpool]: Historic Society of Lancashire and Cheshire, 1976)

Barker, J. R., 'John McCreery: a radical printer, 1768–1832', *The Library*, 5th ser., 16 (1961), 81–103

Belchem, John, ed., *Liverpool 800: Culture, Character and History* (Liverpool: Liverpool University Press, 2006)

Bennett, Betty, ed., *British War Poetry in the Age of Romanticism: 1793–1815* (New York and London: Garland, 1976)

Blackburn, Robin, *The Overthrow of Colonial Slavery, 1776–1848* (London: Verso, 1998)

Burke, Tim, "'Humanity is now the pop'lar cry'": laboring-class writers and the Liverpool slave trade, 1787–1789', *Eighteenth Century*, 42:3 (2001), 245–63.

Burke, Tim, ed., *Eighteenth-Century English Labouring-Class Poets 1700–1800*, Volume 3, *1780–1800*, (London: Pickering and Chatto, 2003)

Carey, Brycchan, *British Abolitionism and the Rhetoric of Sensibility: Writing, Sentiment, and Slavery, 1760–1807* (Basingstoke: Palgrave, 2005)

Cocker, Mark, and Richard Mabey, *Birds Britannica* (London: Chatto and Windus, 2005)

Cook, Daniel, *Thomas Chatterton and Neglected Genius, 1760–1830* (Basingstoke: Palgrave Macmillan, 2013)

Dellarosa, Franca, *Talking Revolution: Edward Rushton's Rebellious Poetics, 1782–1814* (Liverpool: Liverpool University Press, 2014)

Ennis, Daniel, *Enter the Press-Gang: Naval Impressment in Eighteenth-Century British Literature* (Newark, NJ: University of Delaware Press, 2002)

Geggus, David, 'British Opinion and the Emergence of Haiti,' in James Walvin, ed., *Slavery and British Society, 1776–1846* (Baton Rouge: Louisiana State University Press, 1982), pp. 123–49

Goodridge, John, 'Rowley's Ghost: A Checklist of Creative Works Inspired by Thomas Chatterton's Life and Writings', in *Thomas Chatterton and Romantic Culture*, ed. Nick Groom (Basingstoke: Macmillan 1999), pp. 262–92

Hulme, Peter, *Colonial Encounters: Europe and the Native Carribean, 1492–1797* (London: Routledge, 1986)

Hunter, Bill, *Forgotten Hero: The Life and Times of Edward Rushton, Liverpool's Blind Poet, Revolutionary Republican & Anti-Slavery Fighter* (Liverpool: Living History Library, 2002)

Isaac, Peter, *John M'Creery: A Revised Checklist of His Printing* (Wylam: Allenholme Press, 1999)

Johnston, Kenneth, *Unusual Suspects: Pitt's Reign of Alarm and the Lost Generation of the 1790s* (Oxford: Oxford University Press, 2013)

Larrissy, Edward, *The Blind and Blindness in Literature of the Romantic Period* (Edinburgh: Edinburgh University Press, 2007)

Lee, Debbie, *Slavery and the Romantic Imagination* (Philadelphia: University of Pennsylvania Press, 2002)

Lonsdale, Roger, ed., *The New Oxford Book of Eighteenth-Century Verse* (Oxford: Oxford University Press, 2009)

Magnuson, Paul, 'Coleridge's Discursive "Monody on the Death of Chatterton", *Romanticism on the Net*, 17 (February 2000), http://www.erudit.org/revue/ron/2000/v/n17/005900ar.html.

McGuirk, Carol, *Robert Burns and the Sentimental Era* (Athens, GA: University of Georgia Press, 1985)

Milton, John, *John Milton: The Major Works*, ed. Stephen Orgel and Jonathan Goldberg (Oxford: Oxford University Press, 2008)

Morgan, Philip D., '"To Get Quit of Negroes": George Washington and Slavery', *Journal of American Studies*, 32. 3 (2005), 403–29

Oxford Dictionary of National Biography, ed. H. C. G. Matthew and Brian Harrison (Oxford: Oxford University Press, 2004)

Perkin, Michael, *The Book Trade in Liverpool to 1805* (Liverpool: Liverpool Bibliographical Society, 1981)

Pierrot, Grégory, 'Sable Warriors and Neglected Tars: Edward Rushton's Atlantic Politics', in *Race, Romanticism, and the Atlantic*, ed. Paul Youngquist (Farnham: Ashgate, 2013), pp. 125–44

Pomfret, Joan, ed., *Lancashire Evergreens: A Hundred Favourite Old Poems* (Nelson: H. Garrard, 1969)

Pope, Alexander, *The Twickenham Edition of the Poems of Alexander Pope*, general editors John Butt and Maynard Mack, 11 vols (London: Methuen; New Haven, CT: Yale University Press, 1938–1968)

Reynolds, Helen Wilkinson, ed., *The Records of Christ Church, Poughkeepsie, New York: A Study of Origins and Developments* (Poughkeepsie, NY: no publisher's name, 1911)

Richardson, Alan, ed., *Slavery, Abolition, and Emancipation: Writings in the British Romantic Period*, Volume 4, *Literary Forms: Verse* (Brookfield, VT: Pickering and Chatto, 1999)

Richardson, David, Suzanne Schwarz and Anthony Tibbles, eds., *Liverpool and Transatlantic Slavery*, (Liverpool: Liverpool University Press, 2007)

Roe, Nicholas, 'Authenticating Robert Burns', in Robert Crawford (ed.) *Robert Burns and Cultural Authority* (Edinburgh: Edinburgh University Press, 1997), pp. 159–79

Rose, R. B., 'The Jacobins of Liverpool', *Liverpool Bulletin: Libraries, Museums and Arts Committee*, 9 (1960–61), 37–49

Royden, Mike, *Pioneers and Perseverance: A History of the Royal School for the Blind, Liverpool, 1791–1991* (Liverpool: Countryvise Ltd, 1991)

Scrivener, Michael, ed., *Poetry and Reform: Periodical Verse from the English Democratic Press 1792–1824* (Detroit: Wayne State University Press, 1992)

Shakespeare, William, *The Complete Works of Shakespeare*, ed. David Bevington, seventh edition (London: Longman, 2012)

Sutton, Ian, 'The extended Roscoe Circle: art, medicine and the cultural politics of alienation in Liverpool, 1762–1836', *British Journal for Eighteenth Century Studies*, 30 (2007), 439–58

Thomas, Mary Gladys, *Edward Rushton* (London: National Institute for the Blind, 1949)

Thomas, Mary Helen, 'Liberty, Hibernia, and Mary le More: United Irish Images of Women', in *The Women of 1798*, eds. Dáire Keogh and Nicholas Furling (Dublin: Four Courts Press, 1998), pp. 9–25

Whittingham-Jones, Barabara, 'Liverpool Political clubs, 1812–1830', *Transactions of the Historical Society of Lancashire and Cheshire*, III (1959), 117–38

Wiencek, Henry, *An Imperfect God: George Washington, His Slaves, and the Creation of America* (New York: Farrar, Straus and Giroux, 2003)

Williamson, Karina, ed., *Contrary Voices: Representations of West Indian Slavery, 1657–1834* (Kingston, Jamaica: University of West Indies Press, 2008)

Wilson, Arline, *William Roscoe: Commerce and Culture* (Liverpool: Liverpool University Press, 2008)

Wood, Marcus, *Blind Memory: Visual Representations of Slavery in England and America* (London: Routledge, 2000)

——, *Slavery, Empathy and Pornography* (Oxford: Oxford University Press, 2002)

——, (ed.) *The Poetry of Slavery: An Anglo-American Anthology 1764–1865* (Oxford: Oxford University Press, 2003)

Wright, Jonathan Jeffrey, *The 'Natural Leaders' and their World: Politics, Culture and Society in Belfast, c.1801–1832* (Liverpool: Liverpool University Press, 2012)

Index

abolition movement 4–5, 235, 236, 238, 239, 301, 309–12, 314, 318–19
  see also slaves and slavery
Adanson, Michel, explorer (1727–1826) 317
Addison, Joseph, writer (1672–1719) 2, 248
Africa 315–19
Aikin, Arthur, editor (1773–1854) 12
Aikin, John, editor (1747–1822) 12, 13, 265, 277
Akenside, Mark, poet (1721–1770) 228
Alanson, Edward, physician (1747–1823) 314
America, 6, 8, 17, 254, 258–60, 265, 279, 303, 315–18
  American War of Independence 3, 8, 10, 225–27, 229–33, 258–60, 285, 309–11, 321
Anderson, Robert, poet (1770–1833) 278, 283, 296
Anson, Commodore George, admiral (1697–1762) 1
Atkins, John, naval surgeon (1685–1757) 239
Austen, Jane, novelist (1775–1817) 280

Banks, Sir Joseph, naturalist (1743–1820) 317
Barbauld, Anna Letitia, writer (1743–1825) 12, 323
Barrett, William, local historian (1733–1789) 249

Barrington, Daines, naturalist (c. 1727–1800) 317
Beckford, William, writer on Jamaica (d. 1799) 235
Behn, Aphra, writer (c. 1640–1689) 235, 304
Belfast Monthly Magazine 13, 14, 15, 17, 23n23, 253–54, 309, 311, 312
Billinge, Thomas, newspaper proprietor (active 1782–1800) 315
Binns, John, radical writer (1772–1860) 9, 23n19, 258
Bishop, Samuel, poet (1731–1795) 276
Blacklock, Thomas, poet (1721–1791) 17, 282
Blair, Robert, poet (1699–1746) 248
Blake, William, poet (1757–1827) 17, 254, 259, 272
Bloomfield, Robert, poet (1766–1823) 265
Bonaparte, Napoleon, military commander (1769–1821) 243, 281, 284–86, 294, 295, 324
Bradford, John, abolitionist (1749–1830) 309
Bradshaw, John, republican (1602–1659) 305
Bristol 4, 5, 235, 246, 249, 250, 251, 271
British Empire 3, 225–27, 231, 259, 286
Brookes, Richard, writer on fishing (active 1721–1763) 239

Broome, William, poet (1689–1745) 285

Browne, Isaac Hawkins, poet (1706–1760) 276

Browne, Patrick, historian (c. 1720–1790) 235, 237, 238, 239

Bryant, Jacob, scholar (1715–1804) 248

Buffon, Georges-Luis Leclerc, Comte de, naturalist (1707–1788) 315–16

Burke, Edmund, writer and politician (1729–1797) 231

Burns, Robert, poet (1759–1796) 8, 9, 262–66, 284, 287

Byron, George Gordon, Lord, poet (1788–1824) 16, 324

Campbell, Thomas, poet (1777–1844) 19, 274, 303

Cary, Henry, poet (1772–1844) 306

Cennick, John, poet (1718–1755) 271

Charles I, King (1600–1649) 231, 255, 300

Chatterton, Thomas, poet (1752–1770) 5, 234, 244–51, 263, 264, 287

Christie, John, musician (d. 1811), 314

Clarkson, Thomas, abolitionist (1760–1846) 4–5, 22n8, 238, 252, 315, 318–19

Cobbett, William, political reformer (1763–1835) 310, 312

Coleridge, Samuel Taylor, poet (1772–1834) 5, 246, 265, 293, 301

Collins, William, poet (1721–1759) 234

Cook, Captain James, explorer (1728–1779) 316–17

Cowdroy, William, editor (1752–1814) 5, 14, 17, 280, 299–300, 318, 320

Cowper, William, poet (1731–1800) 1, 2, 17, 284, 311

Crawford, Adair, scientist (1748–1795) 311

Croft, Herbert, writer and lawyer (1751–1816) 247, 248, 249, 250, 251

Currie, James, physician and abolitionist (1756–1806) 4, 6, 9, 22n9, 235, 263–64, 286

Dannett, Henry, clergyman (dates unknown, active 1788–1804) 272, 314

Darwin, Erasmus, poet (1731–1802) 296

Dibdin, Charles, songwriter (1745–1814) 5, 17, 242, 275

Dignum, Charles, singer (c. 1765–1827) 241

D'Oyley, Edward, soldier (1617–1675) 238–39

Dryden, John, poet (1631–1700) 248, 257

Edwards, Bryan, historian (1743–1800) 238

Enfield, William, historian (1741–1797) 263

Equiano, Olaudah, freed slave and writer (c. 1745–1797) 253

Falconbridge, Alexander, writer on slavery (d. 1792) 258

Falconer, William, mariner and poet (1732–1770) 253, 278, 290, 295, 304

Fenton, Elijah, poet (1683–1730) 247

Flaxman, John, artist (1755–1826) 251

Flower, Benjamin, radical publisher (1755–1829) 280

France, 226–27, 228, 231, 232, 243, 259, 277, 281–82, 284–86, 294, 295, 302, 313

French Revolution 6, 8, 253–54, 259, 281, 302, 303, 310

Fry, Thomas, president of St. John's College, Oxford (1718–1772) 251

Gay, John, poet (1685–1732) 5, 278, 295

Gibson, Benjamin, eye-surgeon (1774–1812) 13, 291, 298–99, 304, 313, 324, 325

Gilland, James, poet (dates unknown) 13

Glorious Revolution 255–56

Glover, Richard, poet (1712–1785) 275

Goldsmith, Oliver, writer (c. 1728–1774) 230

Gore, John, Liverpool publisher (1738–1803) 229, 314

Grainger, James, poet (c. 1721–1766) 235, 238, 240, 290

Gray, Thomas, poet (1716–1771), 2, 6, 17, 238, 264, 278, 286, 288, 302, 305

Gregory, George, writer (1754–1808) 238

Grenville, William Wyndham, politician (1759–1834) 320

Haiti 284–86

Hall, Thomas, poet (dates unknown) 8

Hampden, John, opponent of Charles I (1595–1643) 300, 305

Hancock, John, editor (1762–1823) 13, 14, 15, 311, 312

Haughton, Moses, artist (1773–1849) 2, 261

Hayley, William, writer (1745–1820) 226, 247, 289

Hobbes, Thomas, political theorist (1588–1679) 267

Hogarth, William, artist (1697–1764) 262

Holcroft, Thomas, radical writer (1745–1809) 303

Homer, epic poet 230, 247

Hone, William, radical publisher (1780–1842) 303

Hoyle, Edmond, writer on card games (1672–1769) 262

Hunt, Leigh, journalist (1784–1859) 242

India 232, 265, 281, 285

Ireland 8, 10, 13, 228, 259, 266, 267–70, 274, 289, 297, 303, 306–7, 312

James II, King (1633–1701) 226, 231, 256, 300

Jefferson, Thomas, US president (1743–1826) 310, 312

Jenyns, Soame, philosopher (1704–1787) 314

John, King (c. 1167–1216) 231, 255, 300

Johnson, Joseph, publisher (1738–1809) 229

Johnson, Samuel, writer (1709–1784) 2, 249, 251, 310, 316

Jones, Sir William, oriental scholar (1746–1794) 256

Keats, John, poet (1795–1821) 16, 266, 293, 306

Knox, Vicesimus, essayist (1730–1786) 247

Kosciuszko, Andrzej Tadeusz, Polish nationalist (1746–1817) 306

Lambert, John, attorney (dates unknown) 247

Lancaster Marine Society 271, 279

Langhorne, John, poet (1735–1779) 283

Langshaw, John, organist (1763–1832) 279

Leadbeater, Mary, poet (1758–1826) 13, 326

Leslie, Charles, historian (dates unknown) 237, 239, 240

Liberty Scraps 6–7, 253, 322–23

Liverpool Blind School, see Royal School for the Blind, Liverpool

Liverpool, 1, 4, 6, 9, 19, 232, 260, 267, 270–71, 275, 283
  Liverpool, politics and political groups 6, 7, 13, 14, 15, 17, 23n13, 24n26, 254, 258, 313, 318, 319, 321; Literary and Philosophical Society 14, 16, 315; Concentric Society 14, 304; Independent Debating Society 14, 300, 326.
London Corresponding Society, 23n19, 265, 320
Long, Edward, historian (1735–1813) 235, 239
Louis XVI, King (1754–1793) 281, 302
Louverture, Toussaint, Haitian leader (1743–1803) 284–86
Lowther, Sir James, baronet (1736–1802) 228, 233

Macpherson, James, poet (1736–1796) 274
Magna Carta 231, 255, 300
Malone, Edmond, scholar (1741–1812) 248
Marsden, Peter, historian (dates unknown) 235, 239
Marvell, Andrew, poet and politician (1621–1678) 7
M'Creery, John, printer and poet (1768–1832) 8, 9, 13, 20, 23n18, 242, 261, 264, 271, 272, 277, 278, 287, 288, 292, 325–27
Mickle, William, poet (1735–1788) 285
Milles, Jeremiah, clergyman (1714–1784) 248, 250
Milton, John, poet and republican (1608–1674) 2, 247, 251, 264, 293, 302, 305, 325
Montgomery, Richard, soldier (1738–1775) 259
More, Hannah, writer (1745–1833) 235, 285

Mulligan, Hugh, poet and engraver (dates unknown, active 1788–1800) 4, 7, 10, 234, 235, 278, 285, 286–87, 325

Napoleon, see Bonaparte
Nevett, William, Liverpool printer (dates unknown, active 1765–1794) 229
Newby, Peter, poet (dates unknown) 4, 235, 239, 240
North, Lord Frederick, politician (1732–1792) 225, 232–33
Noble, Thomas, journalist and poet (dates unknown, active 1808–1821) 14, 16, 326

O'Connell, Daniel, Irish nationalist (1775–1847) 270
Otway, Thomas, poet (1652–1685) 251

Paine, Thomas, radical activist (1737–1809) 15, 279, 311–12
Parnell, Thomas, poet (1679–1718) 248
Pasquin, Anthony, writer (1761–1818) 296
Pennant, Thomas, naturalist (1726–1798) 317
Perry, George, poet (dates unknown) 263
Petty, William Shelburne, Earl of, politician (1737–1805) 232
Peysonnel, John Andrew, scientist (dates unknown) 240
Pitt, William, Earl of Chatham, politician (1708–1778) 3, 225, 231
Pitt, William, 'the Younger', politician (1759–1806) 255, 303, 320
Poland, 306
Pope, Alexander, poet (1688–1744) 2, 5, 17, 228, 230, 232, 233, 236, 247, 248, 249, 250, 251, 254, 255, 264, 271, 284, 289, 292, 299, 300, 314

Porteus, Beilby, bishop (1731–1809)
236–37, 239, 240
Priestley, Joseph, scientist (1733–1804)
322

Quakers 4, 6, 311
Quamina, African sailor (dates
unknown) 2, 239–40

Rain or Rains, Isabella, Rushton's
wife (c. 1756–1811) 3, 8, 14, 22n6,
313
Ramsay, James, abolitionist
(1733–1789) 237, 238, 239, 315–16
Rathbone, William, merchant
(1757–1809) 4, 6, 7, 13, 16, 263,
266
Reynolds, George Nugent, poet
(1771–1802) 268, 273, 303
Richardson, Samuel, novelist
(1689–1761) 288
Robinson, Mary, poet (c. 1758–1800)
273, 275, 297
Roscoe, William, poet and politician
(1753–1831), and 'Roscoe Circle' 4,
6, 7, 8, 13, 22n9, 23n21, 255, 263,
264, 265, 266, 275, 280, 283, 284,
287, 288, 289, 302, 305, 313, 315,
318–19, 322, 324
Royal School for the Blind,
Liverpool, 2, 15, 17, 19, 270–72,
282, 314–15
Rushton, Edward, the poet (1756–1814)
biography:
education and marine career 1–2,
232, 239–40, 241–44, 257–58,
260, 270–71, 277–79, 291, 295,
297
blindness and recovery of sight
2, 11, 12, 13, 15, 271–73, 291,
297–99, 302, 314–15, 325–26
tavern keeper 3, 276, 294
family 2, 3, 14, 18, 22n6, 291, 313,
326

illness and death 14–15, 24n29,
276, 296, 326
edits newspaper 7, 252, 278
bookshop and publishing business
7–8, 13, 14, 23n22, 261, 263,
270, 277, 301, 302, 304
abolitionist views 2, 4, 5, 8, 9,
15, 16, 17, 19, 22n4, 233–40,
284–86, 290, 304, 309–12,
318–20, 321–24
radical politics 5, 6, 7, 8, 13, 14,
19, 253–57, 258–60, 266–70,
273–74, 280–81, 288–89, 301–3,
306–7, 312–14
writings by and ascribed to Rushton:
numbers in bold indicate the
pagination of the texts in this
volume.
1806 volume 5, 9–11, 20, 23n21
1824 volume 5, 15–17, 23n21
Absence 134, 290
Ardent Lover, The 125, 287
Attempt to Prove that Climate,
Food, and Manners, are not
the Causes of the Dissimilarity
of Colour in the Human
Species, An 16, 205–15, 315–18
Blue Eyed Mary 9, 89–90, 261–62
Briton, And Negro Slave 9, 16,
132–33, 240, 290
Caution to my Friend J. M., A
138, 292
Chase, The 158, 296–97
Complaint, The 11, 142–43,
292–93
Coromantees, The 16, 174–76, 304
Dismember'd Empire, The 3,
33–40, 226, 227, 228, 229–33,
238, 248, 254, 259, 311
Entreaty 137, 291
Elegy. [To the Memory of Robert
Burns] 8, 11, 91–94, 262–65
Epitaph on John Taylor, An 16,
20, 177, 238, 305

writings by and ascribed to Rushton:
continued
Exile's Lament, The 171–73, 303
Expostulatory Letter to George
    Washington 8, 16, 185–90, 232,
    260, 289, 309–11, 312, 325
[Extracts from Letters] 196–99,
    298, 312–14
Farewell, The 152–53, 295
Few Plain Facts Relative to
    the Origin of the Liverpool
    Institute for the Blind, A 6, 15,
    200–4, 272, 314–15, 324
Fire of English Liberty, The 13, 16,
    166–67, 300
Fire of Liberty, The 6, 78–79,
    255–56, 300
Halcyon, The 130, 289, 311, 317
Human Debasement 80–82,
    256–57
Irregular Ode, An 3, 27–29,
    225–27, 230, 231, 254
Jemmy Armstrong 13, 180–81, 303,
    306–7
Lass of Liverpool, The 126,
    287–88, 290
[Letter to Samuel Ryley] 216, 299,
    318
[Letter to Thomas Paine] 191–93,
    310, 311–12
[Letter to Thomas Walker]
    220–21, 320
Lines, To the Memory of William
    Cowdroy, Proprietor of the
    Manchester Gazette 14, 164–65,
    299–300
[Lines Addressed to Robt.
    Southey, Esq.] 13, 15, 168–70,
    301–3, 306
Lucy's Ghost 9, 104–6, 274–75,
    292, 293
Maniac, The 102–3, 273–75, 286,
    293
Mary 146–48, 293

Mary le More, see 'Song. [Mary
    le More]'
Mary's Death 128–29, 288–89
[Monthly Retrospect of Politics]
    194–95, 312
Mr. Rushton's Remarks on Slavery
    5, 217–19, 318–20
Neglected Genius 5, 11, 20, 21,
    64–73, 234, 244–51, 259, 263,
    315
Neglected Tars of Britain, The 4,
    11, 62–63, 241–44, 260, 277,
    279
Ode. Sung at St. John's Chapel,
    Lancaster, on Tuesday last,
    being the Anniversary of the
    Lancaster Marine Society
    110–11, 271, 279–80
Ode, To France 112–14, 280–81,
    286
On the Death of a Much Loved
    Relative 3, 12, 135–36, 291, 295
On the Death of Miss E. Fletcher
    157–58, 296
On the Death of Hugh Mulligan
    10, 11, 122–23, 274, 286–87
Origin of Turtle and Punch, The
    149–50, 294
Parody of a Passage in Measure
    for Measure 151, 294
Pier, The 144–45, 293
Poor Ben 7, 74–75, 252–53, 293
[Rebellion Tottering Stands]
    225–26, 231, 321
Remedy, The [The Leviathan] 96,
    266–67, 315
Return, The 154–55, 278, 295–96,
    298
Seamen's Nursery 83–84, 257–58
Shrike, The 16, 131, 289
Solicitude 119, 284
Song [From *Hymns, &c. for the
    Blind*] 9, 101, 271–73, 280, 282,
    283, 299, 314, 323–24

Song [Mary le More] 8, 10, 20,
  97–98, 267–70, 303, 306–7
Song, Sung at the celebration of
  the anniversary of The French
  Revolution, at Liverpool, July
  14, 1791, A **76–77**, 253–54, 281,
  304
Sonnet by a Poor Man. On the
  Approach of the Gout **107**, 276,
  294
Sonnet. [The Swallow] 10, **95**,
  265–66
Stanzas on Blindness 12, 20, **115**,
  272, 282–83, 299
Stanzas on the Anniversary of the
  American Revolution **85–86**,
  258–60, 310
Stanzas on the Recovery of Sight;
  addressed to Mr. B. Gibson,
  Surgeon of Manchester 13,
  161–63, 282, 291, 297–99, 304,
  313, 324
Tender's Hold, The **87–88**, 260,
  278, 279
Throstle, The 16, **139–41**, 274, 284,
  289, 292
Winter's Passage, The 12, **159–60**,
  297
To a Bald-Headed Poetical Friend
  124, 287, 292
To a Redbreast in November,
  Written near one of the Docks
  of Liverpool **116–18**, 283–84,
  293
To the Gout **156**, 276, 294, 296
To the Memory of Bartholomew
  Tilski **178–79**, 302, 306
To the People of England 3,
  30–32, 226, 227–29, 230, 231,
  232
Toussaint to his Troops 9, 11,
  120–21, 284–86, 290, 304, 307
West-Indian Eclogues 4, 5, 9, 16,
  21, 23n21, **42–61**, 232, 233–40,

246, 253, 278, 285, 286, 288,
  290, 291, 293, 303, 304, 310, 311,
  316, 319
Will Clewline 9, **108–9**, 242, 260,
  276, 277–79, 283, 293, 295, 296,
  319, 324
Woman **127**, 239, 288
Written for the Anniversary of
  the Liverpool Marine Society
  99–100, 270–71, 279, 314
Rushton, Edward, son of Rushton
  the poet (1795–1857) 2–3, 13, 14, 15,
  16, 17, 239, 265, 278, 286, 291, 298,
  306, 312, 313, 318
Rushton, Thomas, father of the poet
  (dates unknown) 1–2, 21n3, 22n5,
  291, 299
Russia 227, 232, 260, 306
Ryley, Samuel William, actor and
  playwright (1759–1837) 216, 318

Savage, Richard, poet (c. 1698–1743)
  251
Seward, Anna, poet (1742–1809) 282
Shakespeare, William, playwright
  (1564–1616) 2, 229, 274, 275, 280,
  294, 300, 313, 314, 318
Sheffield, John, Duke of
  Buckinghamshire, poet
  (1647–1721) 236
Shelley, Percy Bysshe, poet
  (1792–1822) 16, 266
Shenstone, William, poet (1714–1763)
  238, 289
Shepherd, William (1768–1847),
  Unitarian minister and poet 6, 7,
  16, 17, 304, 322, 325
  Life of Rushton 1, 2, 5, 7, 9, 15–17,
  256, 257, 266, 278, 282, 291, 299
slaves and slavery, 1–2, 4, 6, 8, 9,
  233–40, 258, 259, 260, 284–86,
  290, 298, 300, 304–5, 309–12,
  318–20
  see also abolition movement

Sloane, Sir Hans, naturalist (1660–1753) 235, 237, 238, 239

Smith, Egerton, newspaper proprietor (1774–1831) 14, 15, 242

Smollett, Tobias, writer (1721–1771) 226, 228, 254, 278

Smyth, John, clergyman (dates unknown) 271, 315

Smyth, William, poet and historian (1765–1849) 6, 272, 306

Snelgrave, William, historian (d. 1763) 237

South America 315–18

Southey, Robert, poet (1774–1843) 13, 15, 17, 301–3, 306

Spain 226, 227, 229, 232, 254, 281

Steele, Anne, poet (1717–1778) 271

Steele, Richard, writer (1672–1729) 2

Sterne, Laurence, writer (1713–1768) 271

Suffolk 228, 233

Switzerland 230

Tarleton, Sir Banastre, soldier and politician (1754–1833) 321

Taylor, John, oculist (1703–1772) 298

Taylor, John, attorney (1769–1805) 305

Thelwall, John, poet and radical (1764–1834) 13, 23n22, 262, 303, 320, 326

Thomson, James, poet (1700–1748) 226

Tickell, Thomas, poet (1685–1740) 276

Tone, Wolfe, Irish nationalist (1763–1798) 307

Tooke, Horne, radical politician (1736–1812) 312

Trelawny, Edward, colonial governor (1699–1754) 238–39

Trimmer, Sarah, writer (1741–1810) 283

Tyrwhitt, Thomas, scholar (1730–1786) 247, 248, 250, 251

Unitarians 4, 6, 14, 280, 310

Vassar, Matthew, merchant and college founder (1792–1868) 305

Walker, Thomas, abolitionist (1749–1817) 320

Waller, Bryan, poet (1765–1842) 279

Walpole, Horace, writer and politician (1717–1797) 246, 248, 249

Warren, Joseph, soldier (1741–1775) 259

Warton, Joseph, poet and critic (1722–1800) 226

Warton, Thomas, scholar (1728–1790) 248–50

Washington, George, US president (1732–1799) 8, 259, 309–11

West, Gilbert, poet (1703–1756) 276

West Indies 232, 233–40, 252, 278, 290, 304, 316

Wilberforce, William, abolitionist campaigner (1759–1833) 4, 319

William III, King (1650–1702), and Mary, Queen (1662–1694) 226, 231, 256, 300

William, of Normandy, King (1027–1087) 255, 300

Wordsworth, William, poet (1770–1850) 17, 19, 251, 262, 263, 274, 282, 285, 286, 301

Wright, John, Unitarian minister (dates unknown) 14, 15

Yearsley, Ann, poet (1753–1806) 235, 271

Young, Arthur, writer on agriculture (1741–1820) 310